Collins
Children's
World Atlas

Collins
Children's
World Atlas

Contents

Collins
An imprint of HarperCollins Publishers, Westerhill Road, Bishopbriggs, Glasgow, G64 2QT
© HarperCollins Publishers 2013
Maps © Collins Bartholomew Ltd 2013

First published 2013
ISBN 978-0-00-751426-7
Imp 001

Printed and bound in Hong Kong
Design ©HarperCollins Publishers

British Library Cataloguing in Publication Data. A catalogue record for this book is available from the British Library.

visit our websites at: www.collins.co.uk   www.collinseducation.com   www.collinsbartholomew.com

Dates in this publication are based on the Christian Era and the designations BC and AD are used throughout. These designations are directly interchangeable with those referring to the Common Era, BCE and CE respectively.

Dynamic World

200 million years ago

Our planet is 4,000 million years old and is always changing. About 250 million years ago all landmasses drifted together to form one giant continent called Pangaea. This started to break up again around 200 million years ago. Today our world map is still gradually changing. Continental drift never stops. Whole continents drift like vast icebergs over the earth's surface.

150 million years ago

100 million years ago

50 million years ago

Structure of the Earth

Crust 6–50 km

Upper Mantle (soft) 370 km

Transitional Zone 600 km

Lower mantle (hard) 1,700 km

Outer Core (liquid) 2,100 km

Inner Core (solid) 1,350 km

The earth is made up of three main layers. The outer layer, known as the crust, ranges in thickness from a few kilometres under the oceans to almost 50 km under mountain ranges. The middle layer, known as the mantle, makes up 82 per cent of the earth's volume. At the centre (core) of the earth, temperatures reach 4,300 °C.

Tectonic Plate Boundaries

The earth's crust is broken into huge plates which fit together like parts of a giant jigsaw. These float on the semi-molten rock below. The boundaries of the plates are marked by lines of vocanoes and earthquake activity.

=== Divergent boundary - mid ocean ridge
▲▲▲ Convergent boundary
— Conservative boundary
→ Direction of movement

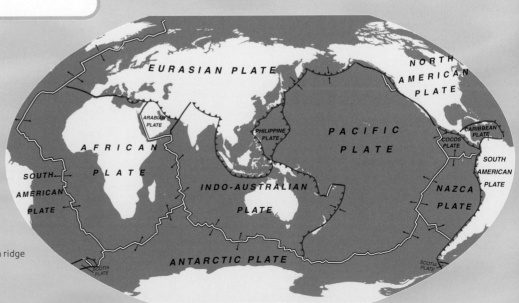

EURASIAN PLATE

NORTH AMERICAN PLATE

ARABIAN PLATE

PHILIPPINE PLATE

PACIFIC PLATE

CARIBBEAN PLATE

COCOS PLATE

AFRICAN PLATE

SOUTH AMERICAN PLATE

SOUTH AMERICAN PLATE

INDO-AUSTRALIAN PLATE

NAZCA PLATE

ANTARCTIC PLATE

SCOTIA PLATE

SCOTIA PLATE

Volcanoes

Volcanoes differ in shape and formation, and in the way they erupt. Fissure volcanoes, such as Laki in Iceland, erupt along cracks in the crust and their lava flows to the sides, producing a long, low mound. Stromboli an Italian vocano is a scoria cone and the eruption type is called Strombolian after it. These eruptions are frequent and involve many small explosions. The lava is thrown upwards and falls back to build the cone.

Vulcanian eruptions explode with no release of magma, shattering the overlying solidified lava and hurling it high into the air, mixed with ash and gas. Mt Fuji is a strato-volcano, built up from layers of solidified lava alternating with layers of ash and loose rock. Shield volcanoes are broad cones with gently sloping sides. They are made from very liquid lava and their eruptions produce spectacular fire fountains. Many Hawaiian volcanoes are of this type.

Eruption ▲

Stromboli is constantly active with minor eruptions

Earthquakes

● Deadly earthquake, significant loss of life

● Earthquakes, magnitude over 7.5

• Earthquakes, magnitude over 5.5

Plate Structure: Asia to South America

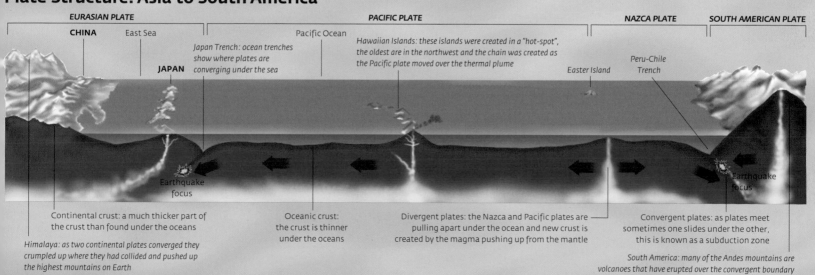

EURASIAN PLATE · **PACIFIC PLATE** · **NAZCA PLATE** · **SOUTH AMERICAN PLATE**

CHINA — East Sea — **JAPAN** — Japan Trench: ocean trenches show where plates are converging under the sea — Pacific Ocean — Hawaiian Islands: these islands were created in a "hot-spot", the oldest are in the northwest and the chain was created as the Pacific plate moved over the thermal plume — Easter Island — Peru-Chile Trench

Earthquake focus

Continental crust: a much thicker part of the crust than found under the oceans

Himalaya: as two continental plates converged they crumpled up where they had collided and pushed up the highest mountains on Earth

Oceanic crust: the crust is thinner under the oceans

Divergent plates: the Nazca and Pacific plates are pulling apart under the ocean and new crust is created by the magma pushing up from the mantle

Convergent plates: as plates meet sometimes one slides under the other, this is known as a subduction zone

Earthquake focus

South America: many of the Andes mountains are volcanoes that have erupted over the convergent boundary

World Countries

The number of independent countries is fast approaching 200. In 2011 South Sudan became an independent state and the world's newest country. Vatican City (0.5 sq km), is the smallest, the Russian Federation the largest at 17 million sq km.

Caribbean Countries

Abbreviations

AL.	ALBANIA
B.H.	BOSNIA AND HERZEGOVINA
CZ.R.	CZECH REPUBLIC
K.	KOSOVO
L.	LUXEMBOURG
M.	MACEDONIA (F.Y.R.O.M.)
MO.	MONTENEGRO
NETH.	NETHERLANDS
R.F.	RUSSIAN FEDERATION
SL.	SLOVENIA
SLA.	SLOVAKIA
SW.	SWITZERLAND

European Countries

World Relief and Landforms

The World –
Top to Bottom

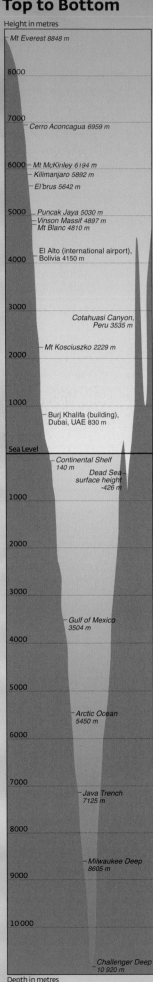

Height in metres

- Mt Everest 8848 m
- 8000
- 7000
- Cerro Aconcagua 6959 m
- 6000 — Mt McKinley 6194 m
  - Kilimanjaro 5892 m
  - El'brus 5642 m
- 5000 — Puncak Jaya 5030 m
  - Vinson Massif 4897 m
  - Mt Blanc 4810 m
- 4000 — El Alto (international airport), Bolivia 4150 m
- 3000
  - Cotahuasi Canyon, Peru 3535 m
- 2000 — Mt Kosciuszko 2229 m
- 1000
  - Burj Khalifa (building), Dubai, UAE 830 m

Sea Level
- Continental Shelf 140 m
  - Dead Sea surface height −426 m
- 1000
- 2000
- 3000
  - Gulf of Mexico 3504 m
- 4000
- 5000 — Arctic Ocean 5450 m
- 6000
- 7000 — Java Trench 7125 m
- 8000
  - Milwaukee Deep 8605 m
- 9000
- 10 000
  - Challenger Deep 10 920 m

Depth in metres

Longest River

Statistics

OCEANS	Deepest point metres	LONGEST RIVERS	km	LARGEST LAKES
Pacific Ocean	10 920	Nile, Africa	6695	Caspian Sea, Asia/Europe
Atlantic Ocean	8605	Amazon, South America	6516	Lake Superior, North America
Indian Ocean	7125	Chang Jiang, Asia	6380	Lake Victoria, Africa
Arctic Ocean	5450	Mississippi-Missouri, North America	5969	Lake Huron, North America
		Ob'-Irtysh, Asia	5568	Lake Michigan, North America
		Yenisey-Angara-Selenga, Asia	5550	Lake Tanganyika, Africa
		Huang He, Asia	5464	Great Bear Lake, North Amer
		Congo, Africa	4667	Lake Baikal, Asia
		Río de la Plata-Paraná, South America	4500	Lake Nyasa, Africa
		Irtysh, Asia	4440	Great Slave Lake, North Amer

ARCTIC OCEAN

New Siberia
Islands

Novaya
Zemlya

Central

Verkhoyanskiy Khrebet

Bering
Sea

Yenisey

Siberian
Plateau

Siberia

Lena

Aleutian Is

West
Siberian
Plain

A S I A

Kamchatka Pen.

Ural Mountains

Ob'

Irtysh

Lake
Baikal

Amur

Dnieper

Volga

Aral
Sea

Altai Mountains

Gobi

Manchurian
Plain

Hokkaidō

El'brus
5642

Caspian Sea

Lake
Balkhash

Tien Shan

Huang He

Honshū

Black Sea

Turan
Lowland

Kunlun Shan

Qilian Shan

Euphrates

Zagros Mts

Plateau of Tibet

Chang Jiang

PACIFIC

Sea

Libyan
Desert

Arabian

Indus

Himalaya

Mt Everest ▲ 8848

Ganges

Ryukyu Is

Nile

Peninsula

Deccan

OCEAN

Rub'al Khali

Bay
of
Bengal

Mekong

South
China
Sea

Challenger
Deep
10 920 ▽

Marshall
Islands

Blue Nile

Ethiopian
Highlands

Sri
Lanka

Philippines

Caroline Islands

White Nile

Maldives

Peninsular
Malaysia

Great Rift Valley

Lake
Victoria

Borneo

Celebes

Puncak Jaya
5030 ▲ New
Guinea

5892 Kilimanjaro

Sumatra

Solomon Is

Lake
Tanganyika

Seychelles

Greater Sunda Islands

Java

Lake
Nyasa

I N D I A N

Java
Trench ▽
7125

O C E A N I A

Zambezi

Madagascar

Mauritius

Fiji

Réunion

O C E A N

Australia

Great
Victoria
Desert

Darling

Great Dividing Range

Murray

Tasmania

New Zealand

North
Island

South
Island

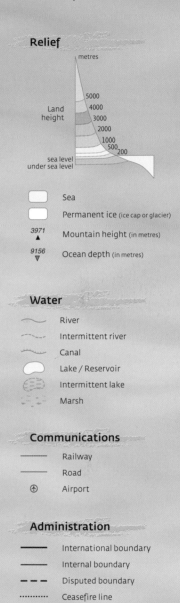

Relief

metres

Land
height

5000
4000
3000
2000
1000
500
200

sea level
under sea level

☐ Sea

☐ Permanent ice (ice cap or glacier)

▲ 3971 Mountain height (in metres)

▽ 9156 Ocean depth (in metres)

Water

〜 River

〜 Intermittent river

〜 Canal

Lake / Reservoir

Intermittent lake

Marsh

Communications

Railway

Road

⊕ Airport

Administration

International boundary

Internal boundary

--- Disputed boundary

·········· Ceasefire line

Settlement

National capital	Population classification
■ PARIS	Over 10 000 000
▣ ATHENS	1 000 000 – 10 000 000
☐ SKOPJE	500 000 – 1 000 000
☐ NICOSIA	100 000 – 500 000
☐ LUXEMBOURG	Under 100 000

Other city or town	Population classification
● İstanbul	Over 10 000 000
◓ İzmir	1 000 000 – 10 000 000
○ Antalya	500 000 – 1 000 000
○ Split	100 000 – 500 000
○ Dubrovnik	Under 100 000

● Antarctic research station

Highest Mountain

	LARGEST ISLANDS	sq km	HIGHEST MOUNTAINS	sq km
sq km				
000	Greenland, North America	2 175 600	Mt Everest, Asia	8848
100	New Guinea, Oceania	808 510	Cerro Aconcagua, South America	6959
870	Borneo, Asia	745 561	Mt McKinley, North America	6194
600	Madagascar, Africa	587 040	Kilimanjaro, Africa	5892
800	Baffin Island, North America	507 451	El'brus, Europe	5642
600	Sumatra, Asia	473 606	Puncak Jaya, Oceania	5030
328	Honshu, Asia	227 414		
500	Great Britain, Europe	218 476		
500	Victoria Island, North America	217 291		
568	Ellesmere Island, North America	196 236		

1

North America

ARCTIC OCEAN

ALASKA U.S.A.

GREENLAND (Denmark)

Arctic Circle

Baffin Bay

Anchorage

Great Bear Lake

Great Slave Lake

Hudson Bay

Nuuk (Godthåb)

Iqaluit

C A N A D A

St John's

Edmonton

Calgary

Vancouver

Seattle

Winnipeg

Lake Superior

Lake Huron

Quebec

Montreal

Ottawa

Halifax

Portland

Minneapolis

Lake Michigan

Toronto

Lake Ontario

Boston

PACIFIC OCEAN

Chicago

Detroit

Lake Erie

New York

ATLANTIC OCEAN

San Francisco

Sacramento

Salt Lake City

Denver

Kansas City

St Louis

Pittsburgh

Washington D.C.

UNITED STATES

Los Angeles

San Diego

OF AMERICA

Phoenix

Atlanta

Bermuda (UK)

El Paso

Dallas

Tropic of Cancer

Houston

New Orleans

THE BAHAMAS

Miami

Nassau

Gulf of Mexico

Monterrey

Havana

CUBA

DOMINICAN REPUBLIC

ANTIGUA AND BARBUDA

MEXICO

HAITI

PUERTO RICO (USA)

DOMINICA

ST LUCIA

Guadalajara

Mexico City

Puebla

JAMAICA

Kingston

Caribbean Sea

BARBADOS

GRENADA

BELIZE

GUATEMALA

HONDURAS

Guatemala City

EL SALVADOR

NICARAGUA

Panama City

Managua

PANAMA

COSTA RICA

0   500   1000   1500   2000 km

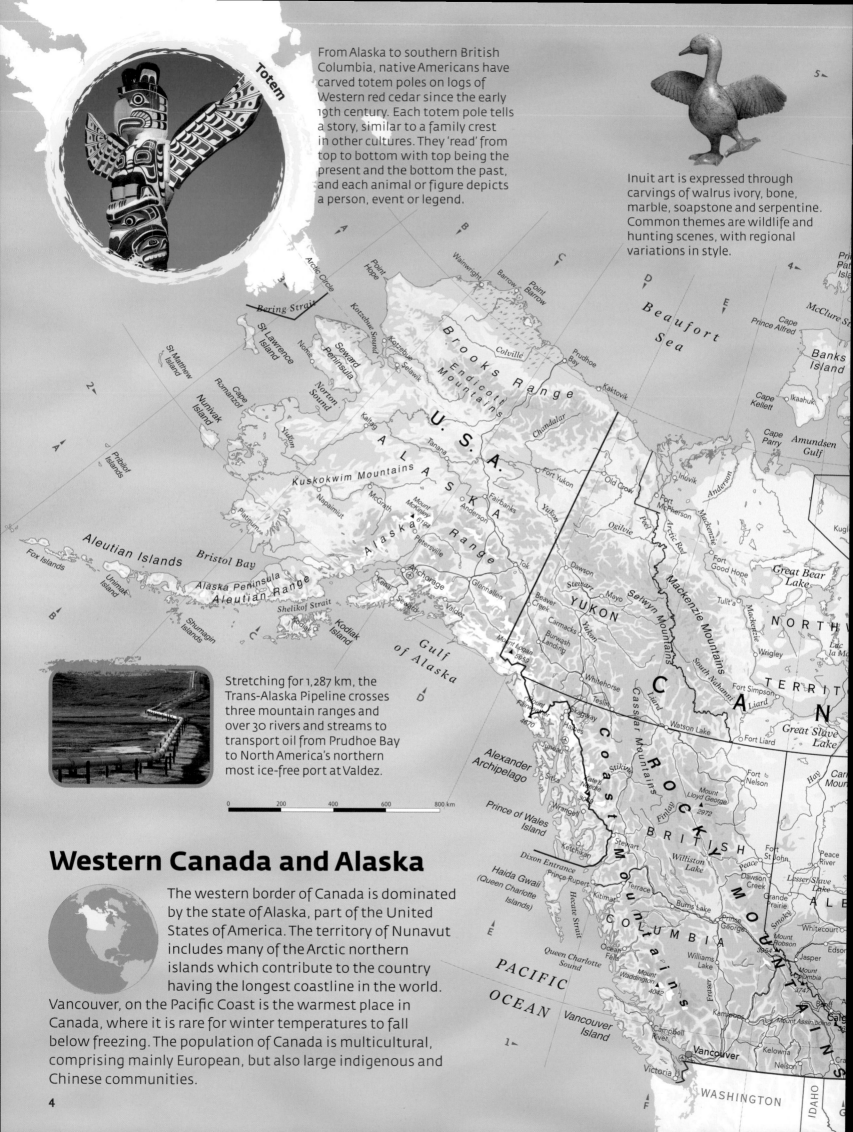

Totem

From Alaska to southern British Columbia, native Americans have carved totem poles on logs of Western red cedar since the early 19th century. Each totem pole tells a story, similar to a family crest in other cultures. They 'read' from top to bottom with top being the present and the bottom the past, and each animal or figure depicts a person, event or legend.

Inuit art is expressed through carvings of walrus ivory, bone, marble, soapstone and serpentine. Common themes are wildlife and hunting scenes, with regional variations in style.

Stretching for 1,287 km, the Trans-Alaska Pipeline crosses three mountain ranges and over 30 rivers and streams to transport oil from Prudhoe Bay to North America's northern most ice-free port at Valdez.

0   200   400   600   800 km

Western Canada and Alaska

The western border of Canada is dominated by the state of Alaska, part of the United States of America. The territory of Nunavut includes many of the Arctic northern islands which contribute to the country having the longest coastline in the world. Vancouver, on the Pacific Coast is the warmest place in Canada, where it is rare for winter temperatures to fall below freezing. The population of Canada is multicultural, comprising mainly European, but also large indigenous and Chinese communities.

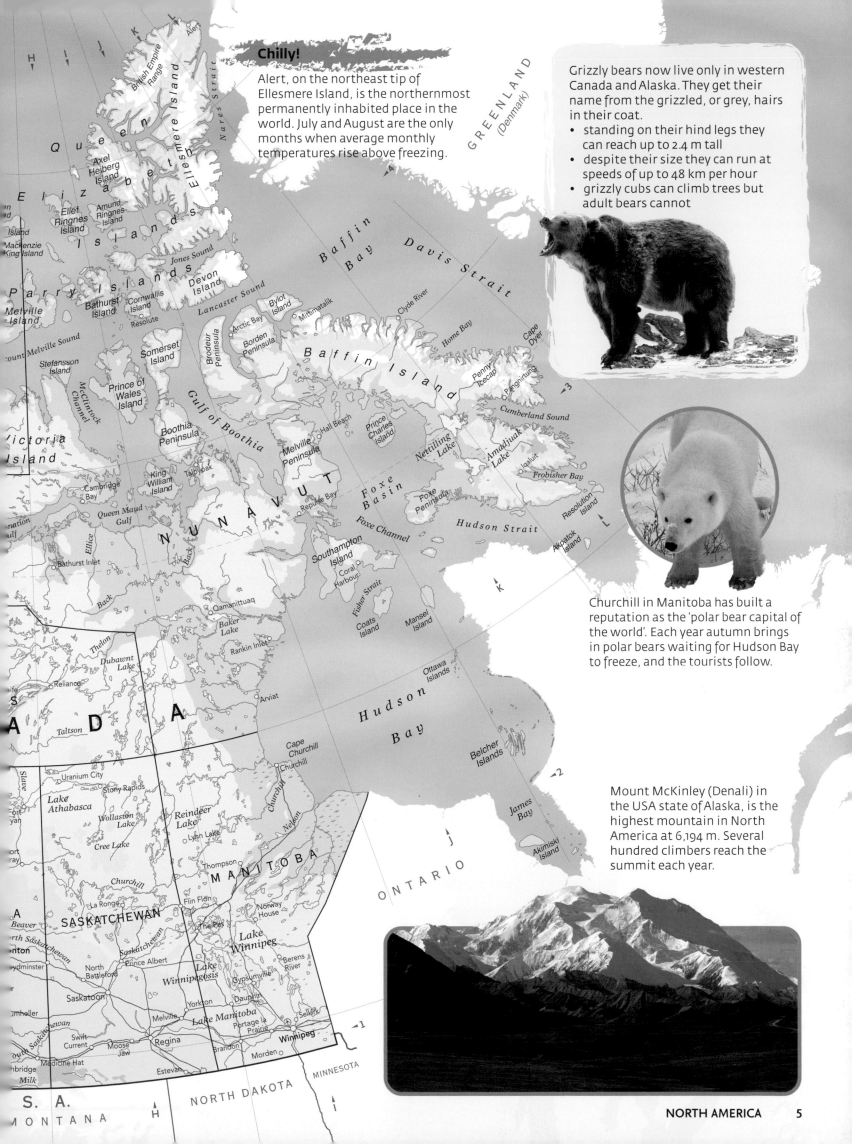

Chilly!

Alert, on the northeast tip of Ellesmere Island, is the northernmost permanently inhabited place in the world. July and August are the only months when average monthly temperatures rise above freezing.

Grizzly bears now live only in western Canada and Alaska. They get their name from the grizzled, or grey, hairs in their coat.
- standing on their hind legs they can reach up to 2.4 m tall
- despite their size they can run at speeds of up to 48 km per hour
- grizzly cubs can climb trees but adult bears cannot

Churchill in Manitoba has built a reputation as the 'polar bear capital of the world'. Each year autumn brings in polar bears waiting for Hudson Bay to freeze, and the tourists follow.

Mount McKinley (Denali) in the USA state of Alaska, is the highest mountain in North America at 6,194 m. Several hundred climbers reach the summit each year.

Eastern Canada

Eastern Canada and particularly the area around the Great Lakes is where the majority of the Canadian population live, mainly in urban areas. The Great Lakes themselves, which are shared with the United States, contain a fifth of the world's fresh water. The northern parts of Canada have a polar and sub-polar climate, compared to a continental climate in the rest of the country. Canada's fishing community is dominant on the east coast of Nova Scotia, New Brunswick and Newfoundland. The territory of Quebec is largely French speaking, and the issue of separatism is ongoing. The national capital, Ottawa, is in Ontario, on the border with Quebec.

Québec produces about three-quarters of the world's maple syrup. It is tapped from maple trees, concentrated and poured on pancakes for a sweet and distinctive flavour.

Joseph Armand-Bombardier, from Québec, is credited as one of the main players in the invention of the snowmobile. He experimented with motorising a sled with a Ford Model T motor in 1922, when he was just 15 years old. In 1960 he invented an open cockpit snowmobile for one or two people, which he called a skidoo.

Shared between Canada and the USA, Lake Superior is the largest lake in the world by surface area – although not by depth or volume of water.

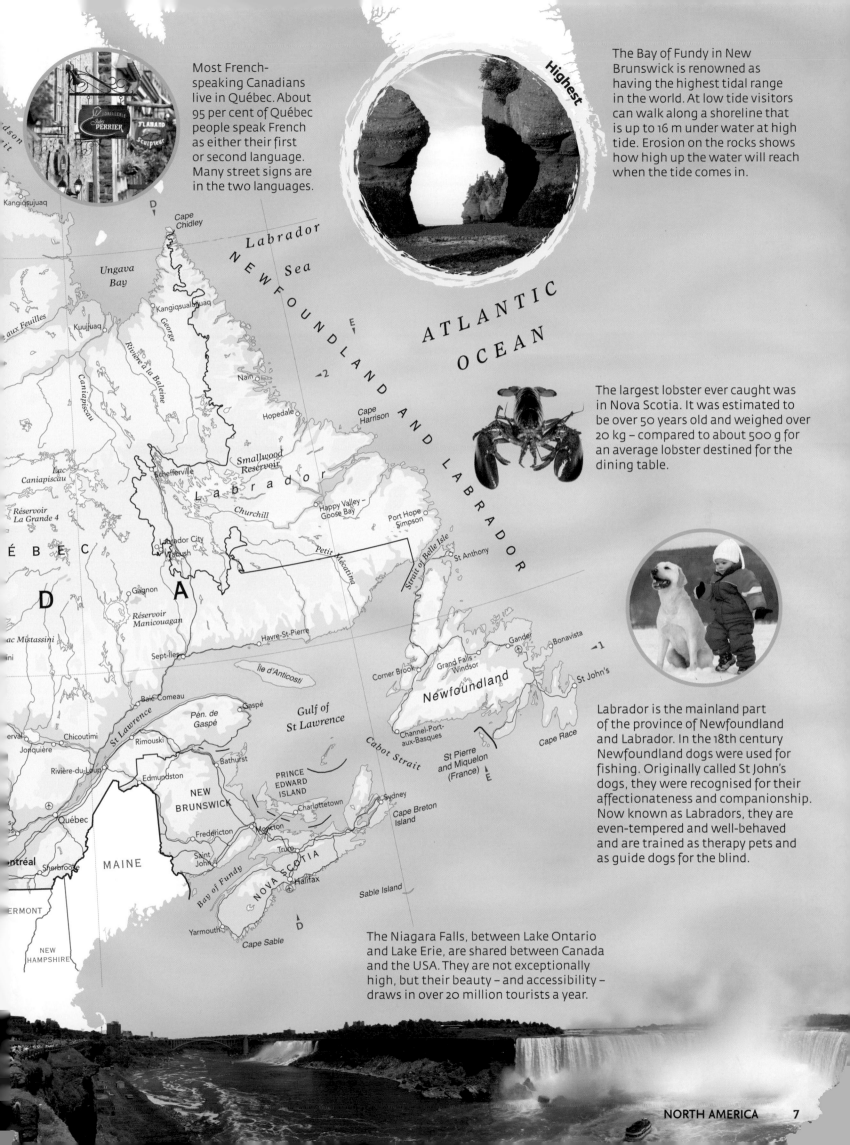

Most French-speaking Canadians live in Québec. About 95 per cent of Québec people speak French as either their first or second language. Many street signs are in the two languages.

Highest

The Bay of Fundy in New Brunswick is renowned as having the highest tidal range in the world. At low tide visitors can walk along a shoreline that is up to 16 m under water at high tide. Erosion on the rocks shows how high up the water will reach when the tide comes in.

The largest lobster ever caught was in Nova Scotia. It was estimated to be over 50 years old and weighed over 20 kg – compared to about 500 g for an average lobster destined for the dining table.

Labrador is the mainland part of the province of Newfoundland and Labrador. In the 18th century Newfoundland dogs were used for fishing. Originally called St John's dogs, they were recognised for their affectionateness and companionship. Now known as Labradors, they are even-tempered and well-behaved and are trained as therapy pets and as guide dogs for the blind.

The Niagara Falls, between Lake Ontario and Lake Erie, are shared between Canada and the USA. They are not exceptionally high, but their beauty – and accessibility – draws in over 20 million tourists a year.

Kangiqsujuaq

Ungava Bay

aux Feuilles

Kuujjuaq

Kangiqsualujjuaq

George

Rivière à la Baleine

Caniapiscau

Lac Caniapiscau

Réservoir La Grande 4

ÉBEC

D A

Lac Mistassini

Gagnon

Réservoir Manicouagan

Sept-Îles

Baie-Comeau

Pén. de Gaspé

Gaspé

St Lawrence

Chicoutimi

Jonquière

Rimouski

Rivière-du-Loup

Québec

Sherbrooke

Montréal

Edmundston

NEW BRUNSWICK

Fredericton

Saint John

MAINE

VERMONT

NEW HAMPSHIRE

Cape Chidley

Labrador Sea

NEWFOUNDLAND AND LABRADOR

Nain

Hopedale

Cape Harrison

Smallwood Reservoir

Labrador

Schefferville

Churchill

Happy Valley – Goose Bay

Labrador City
Wabush

Petit Mécatina

Port Hope Simpson

Strait of Belle Isle

St Anthony

ATLANTIC OCEAN

Gander

Bonavista

Corner Brook

Grand Falls – Windsor

St John's

Newfoundland

Cape Race

Havre-St-Pierre

Île d'Anticosti

Gulf of St Lawrence

Channel-Port-aux-Basques

Cabot Strait

St Pierre and Miquelon (France)

PRINCE EDWARD ISLAND

Charlottetown

Bathurst

Sydney

Cape Breton Island

Moncton

Truro

Saint John

Bay of Fundy

NOVA SCOTIA

Halifax

Sable Island

Yarmouth

Cape Sable

USA: West

Lying to the west of the Rocky Mountains, the western states of the USA comprise of extensive plains and plateaus, separated by multiple mountain ranges. Two of the most famous physical features of the area are Death Valley in California and the Grand Canyon in Arizona, which is over 1.6km deep in places. Many of the Spanish place names on the west coast, such as Los Angeles and San Francisco, date from early colonial Spanish rule. The Spanish language is still widely spoken today. California is the most highly populated state of the USA, with 35 million people.

The 'ice pop' or 'popsicle' iced lolly was accidentally invented by Frank Epperson on a cold San Francisco night in 1905 when he was only 11 years old. He left a glass of homemade soda outside overnight, temperatures plummeted, and in the morning he found it frozen with its stirring stick ready embedded as a handle.

A sacred bird to some North American cultures, the Bald eagle is also the national bird of the USA. Its image is found on the backs of coins, on most official seals of the USA government and on the presidential flag. With its head of white feathers it is not actually bald – its name is derived from an old term meaning 'white-headed'.

CANADA

BRITISH COLUMBIA

ALBERTA

SASKATCHEWAN

NORTH DAKOTA

SOUTH DAKOTA

WASHINGTON

OREGON

IDAHO

MONTANA

WYOMING

ROCKY M

Vancouver Island

Cape Flattery
Port Angeles
Mount Olympus 2428
Bellingham
Mount Baker 3285
Glacier Peak 3213
Everett
Seattle
Tacoma
Olympia
Chehalis
Astoria
Tillamook
Newport
Cape Blanco

Lake Chelan
Okanogan
Franklin D. Roosevelt Lake
Columbia
Spokane
Ellensburg
Yakima
Ritzville
Bonners Ferry
Sandpoint
St Joe
Mount Rainier 4392
Mount St Helens 2550
Vancouver
Portland
Oregon City
Salem
Albany
Eugene
Roseburg
Grants Pass
Medford
Upper Klamath Lake
Klamath Falls
The Dalles
Mount Hood 3427
Madras
Bend
Burns
Harney Basin
Steens Mt.
Snake
Columbia
Pendleton
La Grande
Walla Walla
Moscow
Lewiston
Grangeville
Baker
Eagle Cap 2925
Blue Mountains
Jordan Valley
Payette
Boise
Mountain Home
Snake
Columbia Plateau
Salmon River Mountains
Salmon
Challis
Arco
Idaho Falls
Pocatello
Bitterroot Range
Mount McGuire 3073
Libby
Thompson Falls
Flathead Lake
McDonald Peak 2993
Missoula
Deer Lodge
Butte
Dillon
Lewis Range
Mount Cleveland 3184
Shelby
Conrad
Great Falls
Townsend
Madison
Missouri
Bear Paw Mountain 2116
Havre
Malta
Glasgow
Sidney
Missouri
Glendive
Miles City
Forsyth
Hardin
Billings
Livingston
Granite Peak 3901
Bighorn
Yellowstone
Sheridan
Cloud Peak 4013
Buffalo
Bighorn Mountains
Worland
Thermopolis
Gillette
Newcastle
Douglas
Cheyenne
Casper
Pinedale
Gannett Peak 4202
Grand Teton 4190
Yellowstone Lake
Twin

0   100   200   300   400 km

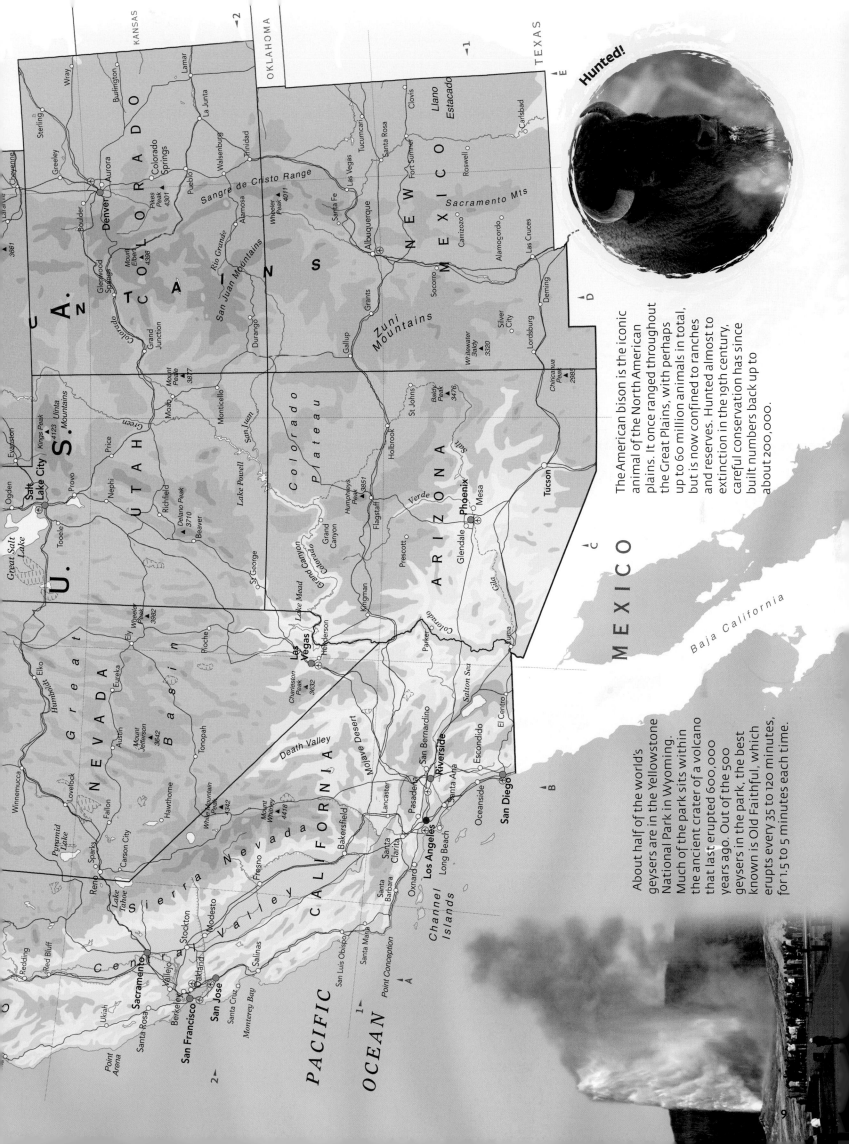

Hunted!

The American bison is the iconic animal of the North American plains. It once ranged throughout the Great Plains, with perhaps up to 60 million animals in total, but is now confined to ranches and reserves. Hunted almost to extinction in the 19th century, careful conservation has since built numbers back up to about 200,000.

About half of the world's geysers are in the Yellowstone National Park in Wyoming. Much of the park sits within the ancient crater of a volcano that last erupted 600,000 years ago. Out of the 500 geysers in the park, the best known is Old Faithful, which erupts every 35 to 120 minutes, for 1.5 to 5 minutes each time.

KANSAS

OKLAHOMA

TEXAS

2

1

E

D

C

B

A

1

2

COLORADO

Cheyenne

Laramie

3661

Sterling

Wray

Burlington

Greeley

Boulder

Lamar

La Junta

Denver

Aurora

Colorado Springs

Pikes Peak 4301

Pueblo

Walsenburg

Trinidad

Sangre de Cristo Range

Wheeler Peak 4011

Alamosa

Santa Fe

Las Vegas

Tucumcari

Santa Rosa

Clovis

Llano Estacado

Carlsbad

Roswell

Fort Sumner

Albuquerque

NEW MEXICO

Socorro

Grants

Sacramento Mts

Canizozo

Alamocordo

Las Cruces

Deming

Silver City

Lordsburg

Whitewater Baldy 3320

Chiricahua Peak 2985

Zuni Mountains

Gallup

St Johns

Baldy Peak 3476

Holbrook

Humphreys Peak 3851

Flagstaff

Prescott

Grand Canyon

Kingman

Verde

Salt

Phoenix

Mesa

Glendale

ARIZONA

Gila

Colorado

Parker

Yuma

Tucson

Salton Sea

El Centro

Escondido

Oceanside

San Diego

Santa Ana

Long Beach

Los Angeles

Pasadena

Oxnard

San Bernardino

Riverside

Lancaster

Santa Clarita

Santa Barbara

Santa Maria

San Luis Obispo

Channel Islands

Point Conception

Mojave Desert

Bakersfield

Mount Whitney 4418

Death Valley

White Mountain Peak 4342

Fresno

Salinas

Santa Cruz

San Jose

Oakland

Berkeley

San Francisco

Vallejo

Stockton

Modesto

Sacramento

Central Valley

Sierra Nevada

C A L I F O R N I A

Monterey Bay

Point Arena

Santa Rosa

Ukiah

Red Bluff

Redding

Lake Tahoe

Carson City

Sparks

Reno

Pyramid Lake

Winnemucca

Lovelock

Fallon

Hawthorne

Tonopah

Mount Jefferson 3642

Austin

Eureka

Elko

Humboldt

NEVADA

Great Basin

Ely

Wheeler Peak 3982

Pioche

Charleston Peak 3632

Las Vegas

Henderson

Lake Mead

Grand Canyon

St George

Lake Powell

Colorado

Richfield

Delano Peak 3710

Beaver

Nephi

Provo

Price

Moab

Mount Peale 3877

Monticello

San Juan

Durango

San Juan Mountains

Rio Grande

Mount Elbert 4398

Colorado

Glenwood Springs

Grand Junction

Green

Kings Peak 4123

Uinta Mountains

Salt Lake City

Ogden

Evanston

Tooele

UTAH

Great Salt Lake

U. S. A.

R O C K Y   M O U N T A I N S

G R E A T   P L A I N S

Santa Fe

MEXICO

Baja California

PACIFIC OCEAN

9

USA: Southwest

The southwest is characterised by the contrast between the high plateaus and Rocky Mountains to the west, and the flatlands and river networks of these southern states. Texas, known as the Lone Star State, due to its former independence, is the country's biggest producer of oil. The region has been heavily influenced by its long border with Mexico, leading to a large mix of cultures. New Orleans, built on the sediment brought down to the delta by the Mississippi river, suffered severe flooding and destruction after hurricane Katrina in 2005.

A symbol of the 'wild west', the Texas longhorn steer has horns that can extend 2.1 m from tip to tip. It was bred from cattle imported by early colonists to produce a tough, drought-resistant breed that is valued for its lean meat.

The fierce-looking Texas horned lizard is regarded as sacred by some native American peoples. Native to Lousiana and Arkansas, it lives in areas with little vegetation on a diet made up of 70 per cent harvester ants. Its numerous horns are made of bone and are part of its skull.

Since the establishment of NASA's centre for the development and operation of manned space flight in the 1960s, Houston, Texas has become 'Space city'.

The discovery of oil in Texas in the early 20th century helped turn the state from rural to heavily industrialized. Houston developed as one of the world's main areas for oil refining and petrochemical plants

Dixieland jazz was developed in New Orleans in the early 20th century as one of the earliest styles of jazz music. It usually includes trumpet, trombone, clarinet and a rhythm section.

COLORADO

K A

NEW MEXICO

U.

T E

MEXICO

Boise City
Guymon
Perryton
Woodward
Alva
Stratford
Dalhart
Canadian
Dumas
Canadian
Elk City
Clinton
Amarillo
O
Canyon
Hereford
Prairie Dog Town Fork
Hobart
Altus
Lawton
Muleshoe
Plainview
Childress
Vernon
Paducah
Llano Estacado
Littlefield
Wichita Falls
Levelland
Lubbock
Seymour
Brazos
Brownfield
Post
Gr
Mineral
Seminole
Lamesa
Snyder
Abilene
Stephenv
Andrews
Big Spring
Sweetwater
El Paso
Guadalupe Peak ▲ 2667
Midland
Odessa
Coleman
Ballinger
Brownwood
Pecos
San Angelo
Colorado
Big Lake
Van Horn
Brady
Mount Livermore ▲ 2554
Fort Stockton
Pecos
Edwards
Rio Grande (Rio Bravo del Norte)
Alpine
Sonora
Junction
Marfa
Plateau
Fredericksburg
Sanderson
Kerrville
Presidio
Amistad Reservoir
San Antonio
Emory Peak ▲ 2389
Del Rio
Hondo
Uvalde
Eagle Pass
Pleasanton
Crystal City
Carrizo Springs
Nueces
Laredo
MEXICO
Zapata
Falcon Lake
Rio Grande City

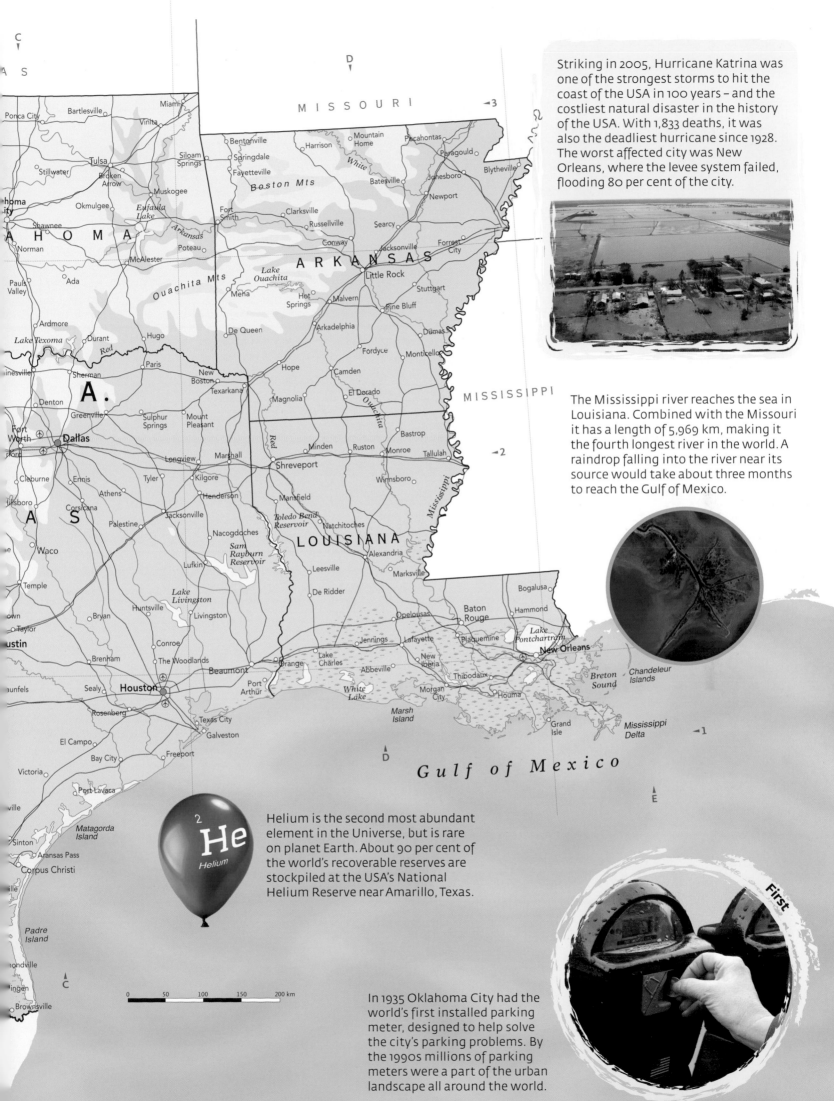

Striking in 2005, Hurricane Katrina was one of the strongest storms to hit the coast of the USA in 100 years – and the costliest natural disaster in the history of the USA. With 1,833 deaths, it was also the deadliest hurricane since 1928. The worst affected city was New Orleans, where the levee system failed, flooding 80 per cent of the city.

The Mississippi river reaches the sea in Louisiana. Combined with the Missouri it has a length of 5,969 km, making it the fourth longest river in the world. A raindrop falling into the river near its source would take about three months to reach the Gulf of Mexico.

Helium is the second most abundant element in the Universe, but is rare on planet Earth. About 90 per cent of the world's recoverable reserves are stockpiled at the USA's National Helium Reserve near Amarillo, Texas.

In 1935 Oklahoma City had the world's first installed parking meter, designed to help solve the city's parking problems. By the 1990s millions of parking meters were a part of the urban landscape all around the world.

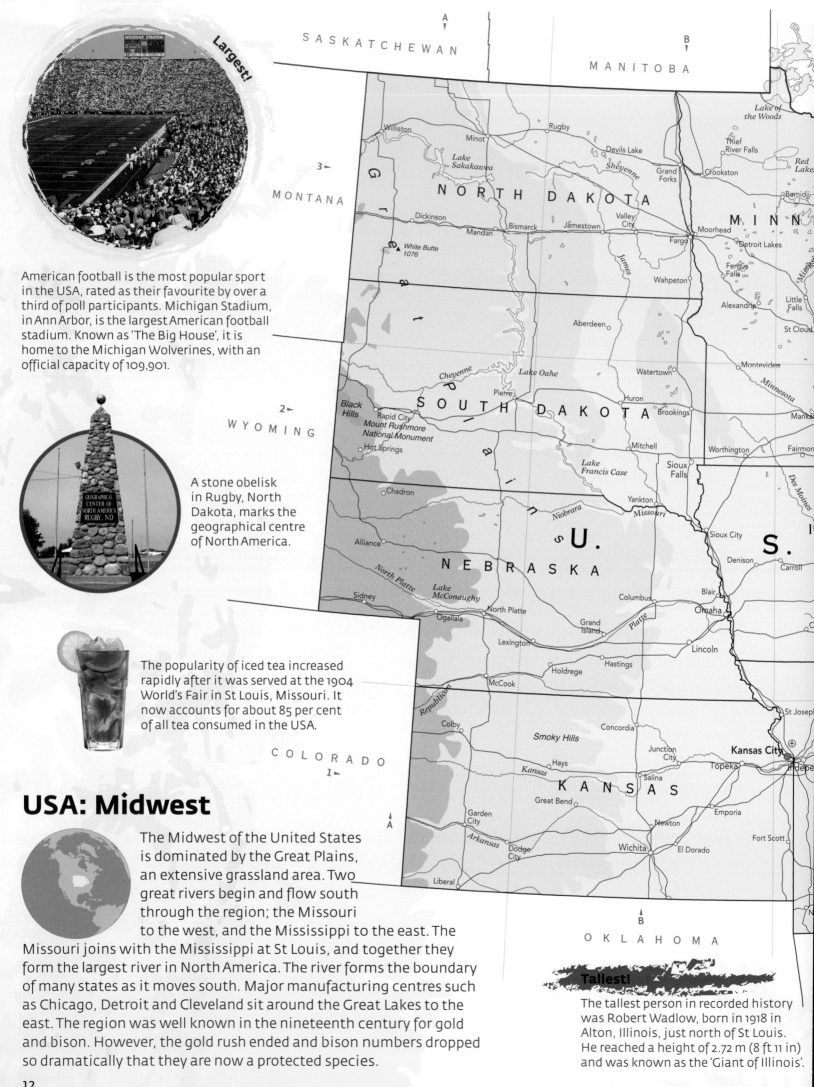

American football is the most popular sport in the USA, rated as their favourite by over a third of poll participants. Michigan Stadium, in Ann Arbor, is the largest American football stadium. Known as 'The Big House', it is home to the Michigan Wolverines, with an official capacity of 109,901.

A stone obelisk in Rugby, North Dakota, marks the geographical centre of North America.

The popularity of iced tea increased rapidly after it was served at the 1904 World's Fair in St Louis, Missouri. It now accounts for about 85 per cent of all tea consumed in the USA.

USA: Midwest

The Midwest of the United States is dominated by the Great Plains, an extensive grassland area. Two great rivers begin and flow south through the region; the Missouri to the west, and the Mississippi to the east. The Missouri joins with the Mississippi at St Louis, and together they form the largest river in North America. The river forms the boundary of many states as it moves south. Major manufacturing centres such as Chicago, Detroit and Cleveland sit around the Great Lakes to the east. The region was well known in the nineteenth century for gold and bison. However, the gold rush ended and bison numbers dropped so dramatically that they are now a protected species.

Tallest!

The tallest person in recorded history was Robert Wadlow, born in 1918 in Alton, Illinois, just north of St Louis. He reached a height of 2.72 m (8 ft 11 in) and was known as the 'Giant of Illinois'.

George Nissen, a 16 year-old school gymnast from Iowa, invented the trampoline in the 1930s. It is now an Olympic sport and a family favourite in gardens all around the world.

Twister!

'Tornado Alley' is the part of Midwest USA most prone to dangerous twisters. The country's most destructive tornado on record tore through Missouri, southern Illinois and Indiana in 1925. In just 3.5 hours it flattened 15,000 homes, uprooted trees, overturned cars and killed nearly 700 people. In 1939 the film *Wizard of Oz* also made sure that Kansas was firmly in the public eye as a tornado-prone area.

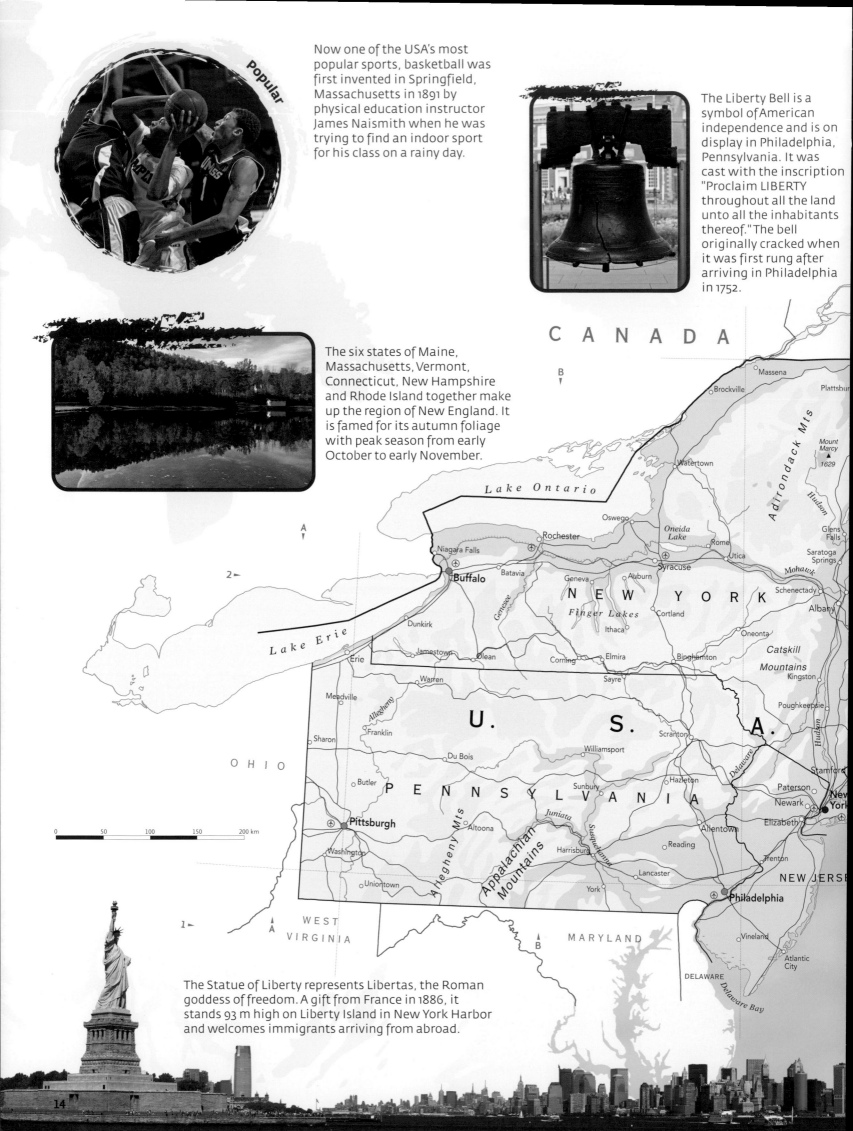

Now one of the USA's most popular sports, basketball was first invented in Springfield, Massachusetts in 1891 by physical education instructor James Naismith when he was trying to find an indoor sport for his class on a rainy day.

Popular

The Liberty Bell is a symbol of American independence and is on display in Philadelphia, Pennsylvania. It was cast with the inscription "Proclaim LIBERTY throughout all the land unto all the inhabitants thereof." The bell originally cracked when it was first rung after arriving in Philadelphia in 1752.

The six states of Maine, Massachusetts, Vermont, Connecticut, New Hampshire and Rhode Island together make up the region of New England. It is famed for its autumn foliage with peak season from early October to early November.

The Statue of Liberty represents Libertas, the Roman goddess of freedom. A gift from France in 1886, it stands 93 m high on Liberty Island in New York Harbor and welcomes immigrants arriving from abroad.

CANADA

U. S. A.

Lake Ontario

Lake Erie

OHIO

PENNSYLVANIA

NEW YORK

Finger Lakes

Catskill Mountains

Adirondack Mts

WEST VIRGINIA

MARYLAND

NEW JERSEY

DELAWARE

Massena
Brockville
Plattsburg
Watertown
Mount Marcy 1629
Oswego
Oneida Lake
Glens Falls
Rochester
Rome
Utica
Saratoga Springs
Niagara Falls
Batavia
Geneva
Auburn
Syracuse
Schenectady
Buffalo
Cortland
Albany
Dunkirk
Ithaca
Oneonta
Erie
Jamestown
Olean
Corning
Elmira
Binghamton
Kingston
Warren
Sayre
Poughkeepsie
Meadville
Williamsport
Scranton
Stamford
Sharon
Franklin
Du Bois
Hazleton
Paterson
Newark
New York
Butler
Sunbury
Elizabeth
Pittsburgh
Altoona
Juniata
Reading
Washington
Harrisburg
Trenton
Uniontown
Lancaster
York
Philadelphia
Vineland
Atlantic City

Niagara Falls
Allegheny
Allegheny Mts
Appalachian Mountains
Susquehanna
Genesee
Mohawk
Hudson
Delaware
Delaware Bay

0   50   100   150   200 km

14

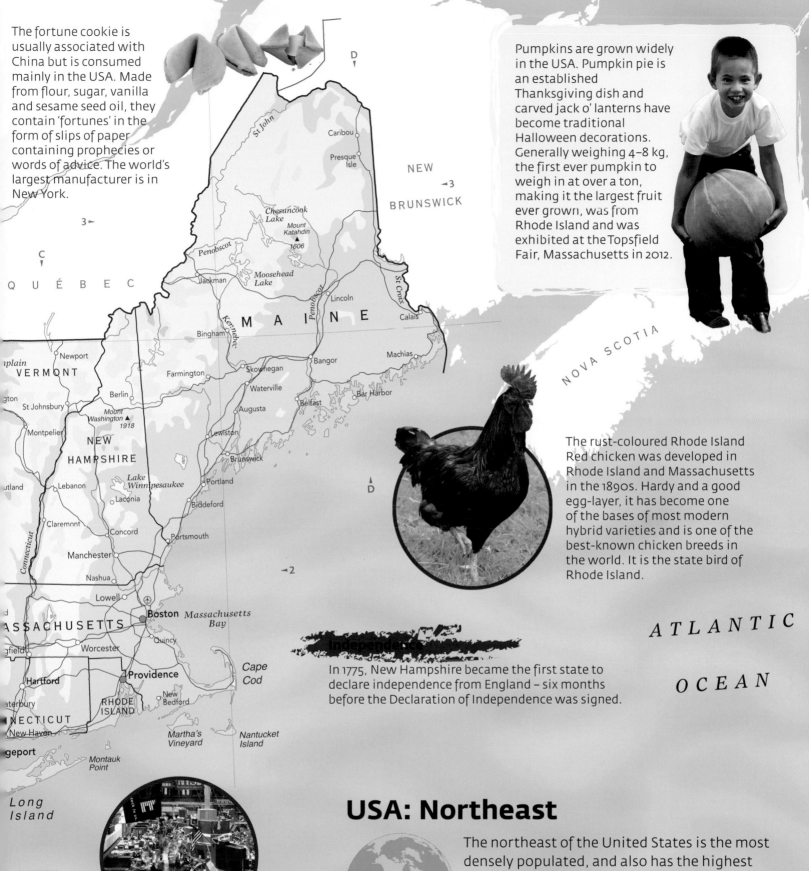

The fortune cookie is usually associated with China but is consumed mainly in the USA. Made from flour, sugar, vanilla and sesame seed oil, they contain 'fortunes' in the form of slips of paper containing prophecies or words of advice. The world's largest manufacturer is in New York.

Pumpkins are grown widely in the USA. Pumpkin pie is an established Thanksgiving dish and carved jack o' lanterns have become traditional Halloween decorations. Generally weighing 4–8 kg, the first ever pumpkin to weigh in at over a ton, making it the largest fruit ever grown, was from Rhode Island and was exhibited at the Topsfield Fair, Massachusetts in 2012.

The rust-coloured Rhode Island Red chicken was developed in Rhode Island and Massachusetts in the 1890s. Hardy and a good egg-layer, it has become one of the bases of most modern hybrid varieties and is one of the best-known chicken breeds in the world. It is the state bird of Rhode Island.

Independence Day

In 1775, New Hampshire became the first state to declare independence from England – six months before the Declaration of Independence was signed.

New York is the USA's largest city, and the financial capital of the world. The New York Stock Exchange at 11, Wall Street has made the name Wall Street synonymous with USA financial markets.

USA: Northeast

The northeast of the United States is the most densely populated, and also has the highest density of individual states. It is entirely bordered by Canada to the north. The smallest state is Rhode Island, on the Atlantic Coast, while the city of New York is the biggest city in the United States. New York City is particularly famous for its architectural features, including the Statue of Liberty. The entire region has about 16 per cent of the total population of the United States, in less than 2 per cent of the land area. The most famous natural feature of the region is Niagara Falls (see page 7), which lies on the USA/Canada border. The waterfalls are a major tourist attraction, and the combined falls have the highest flow rate of any waterfall in the world.

USA: South

The Southern USA usually refers to states in the southeast of the country. The Mississippi flows south at the western edge of the region, whilst the centre and east are dominated by the Appalachian Mountains. These formed a barrier to early pioneer east-west travellers and run through many of the region's states. The low-lying south of the region is often affected by storms and hurricanes which originate in the Atlantic Ocean. Florida is one of the world's major holiday destinations, possessing major cities and wildlife-rich wetlands, known as the Everglades.

The Wright Flyer was the world's first successful powered aircraft and in 1903, Kitty Hawk, North Carolina, was the suitably isolated spot for the Wright Brothers to try it out. With limited resources Orville and Wilbur Wright had shown great ingenuity in their design. The first flight lasted 12 seconds and covered a distance of 36.5 metres.

The Pentagon is the headquarters of the United States Department of Defense, located in Arlington, Virginia, near Washington D.C. It is the world's largest office building by floor area. It has five sides, five floors above ground, and five ring corridors per floor. Altogether over 30,000 people work in the building.

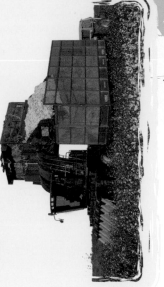

Long, hot summers and rich soils make the southern USA ideal for growing cotton. African-American slaves hand-picking cotton on large plantations produced three-quarters of the world's cotton in the 1860s. Whilst the world dominance of production has gone, the USA is still the world's largest cotton exporter. Production is now automated with large mechanical cotton pickers. About three-quarters of output goes into the clothing industry. Cottonseed oil is used in margarine and salad dressing.

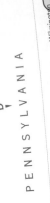

ATLANTIC OCEAN

Long Bay

Blues

Nashville and Memphis are both Tennessee cities with major musical connections. Memphis is the 'home of the blues', and its main music focus, Beale Street, is lined with blues clubs, stores and restaurants. Nashville is synonymous with the country music industry and thousands of country fans flock to the city every June for the Country Music Association (CMA) Music Festival.

THE BAHAMAS

Cape Romain
Lake Moultrie
Charleston
Lake Marion

Aiken
Savannah
Augusta
GEORGIA
Dublin
Macon
Oconee
Jesup
Brunswick
Cordele
Tifton
Valdosta

Clark Hill Reservoir

Jacksonville
St Augustine
FLORIDA
Lake George
Daytona Beach
Ocala
Gainesville
Lake City
Cape Canaveral
Melbourne
Orlando
Kissimmee
Lake Kissimmee
Fort Pierce
Lakeland
Lake Okeechobee
West Palm Beach
Tampa
Fort Lauderdale
Clearwater
Hollywood
St Petersburg
Everglades
Sarasota
Miami
Fort Myers
Cape Sable
Key West

Straits of Florida
Florida Keys

CUBA

The world's most-visited entertainment attraction, Walt Disney World near Orlando, Florida, provides a magical experience to over 17 million people every year.

ALABAMA
Anniston
Birmingham
La Grange
Columbus
Opelika
Tuscaloosa
Montgomery
Troy
Dothan
Selma
Panama City
Pensacola
Mobile
Tallahassee
Lake Seminole
Apalachee Bay
Cape San Blas

Gulf of Mexico

Chattahoochee
Alabama
Tombigbee
Mobile Bay

MISSISSIPPI
Grenada
Greenville
Columbus
Canton
Jackson
Meridian
Laurel
Brookhaven
Pascagoula
Pearl

LOUISIANA

Mississippi

The *Belle of Louisville* is the oldest operating steamboat in the USA, and the last true Mississippi steamboat still in operation. Built in 1914, and originally called the *Idlewild*, she worked both as a passenger ferry and for cargo haulage on the Mississippi River. Since 1963 she has operated out of Louisville to provide excursion cruises on the Ohio River.

0   100   200   300   400 km

One of only two alligator species, the American alligator lives only in the southern USA, with the largest populations in Florida and Louisiana. They can grow up to 4.4 m long and weigh over 450 kg. Florida is the only place in the world where alligators and crocodiles coexist. Crocodiles tend to live in brackish to salt water areas while alligators prefer fresh water.

Sharp!

CALIFORNIA

Tijuana
Mexicali

ARIZONA

NEW
MEXICO

Ensenada

Picacho
del Diablo
3096
San Felipe

Puerto
Peñasco

Nogales

Ciudad
Juárez

TEXAS

U.

Cabo
San Quintín
Lázaro
Cárdenas

Caborca

Cananea

El Barreal

Rosario

Benjamín
Hill

Nacozari
de García

Nuevo Casas
Grandes

Ojinaga

Guadalupe

Isla Ángel
de la Guarda

Madera

Buenaventura

Serranía
del Bur

Bahía Sebastián
Vizcaíno

Isla
Tiburón

Sonora

Hermosillo

Chihuahua

Isla
Cedros

Cuauhtémoc

Ciudad
Delicias

Bolsón
de Mapimí

Nueva R

Punta
Eugenia

Guaymas

Empalme

Yaqui

Conchos

Ciudad Camargo

Jiménez

Santa
Bárbara

Hidalgo
del Parral

Monclov

Sta
Rosalía

Esperanza

Ciudad Obregón

The 3,169 km-long
boundary between
Mexico and the USA
is the most frequently
crossed international
border in the world.

Punta San
Hipólito

Navojoa

Huatabampo

Presa
Miguel
Hidalgo

Tepehuanes

Gómez Palacio

San Pedro de
las Colonias

Isla
Carmen

Los Mochis

Torreón

Matamoros

Villa Insurgentes

Guasave

Nazas

Isla Santa
Margarita

Isla San José

Isla
Cerralvo

Costa Rica

Culiacán

Durango

Río Grande

Tropic of Cancer

La Paz

El Dorado

El Salto

Cabo
San Lucas

San José
del Cabo

Mazatlán

Fresnillo

Zacatecas

Tomatoes probably originated in
Mexico, with the first records of their
cultivation dating back to 500 BC.
Tortillas are part of most traditional
Mexican dishes. Wrapped around a
savoury filling they make a taco – the
best known of Mexico's 'fast food'.

Acaponeta

San Luis Po

Aguascalientes

Islas Marías

Tepic

M E X

Compostela

León

Puerto Vallarta

Tepatitlán

Irapuato

Islas
Revillagigedo
(Mex.)

I. San Benedicto

I. Socorro

Guadalajara

Salam

Cabo Corrientes

Laguna de Chapala

I. Clarión

Zacapu

Nev. de Colima
4339

Colima

Apatzingán

Mer

Manzanillo

Tecomán

Mexico

Mexico is washed by the sea on the east and west
coasts, and has borders with the USA in the north
and with Guatemala and Belize in the south. Most
of the country is high plateau, flanked by the Sierra
Madre Mountains. The climate is hot and humid
in the lowlands, warm on the plateau and cool
in the mountains. The north is arid, whilst the far south has heavy
rainfall. Many crops, such as grains, coffee, cotton and vegetables are
grown. Mexico City, the capital and largest city, has over 19 million
inhabitants. Mexico is the world's largest producer of silver and one
of the largest producers of oil. Mexico also has a growing tourist
industry; and is very popular with both other North American and
European tourists.

PACIFIC

OCEAN

Lázaro Cárdenas

Petatl

Impact!

The asteroid or comet impact that
caused the 180 km-wide Chicxulub
crater under the Yucatán peninsula
is thought to be linked to the mass
extinction of dinosaurs around
65 million years ago.

Although commonly associated with Mexico, it is believed that the piñata originated in China, arrived in Europe in the 14th century and was then introduced to Mexico in the 16th century. It is now a fun way to distribute party treats the world over, with themed piñatas available for all ages.

The Mayan temple of Chichén Itzá is one of the most visited archaeological sites in Mexico. Over a million people visit the ruins every year. Mexico is the tenth most visited country in the world with 22 million international visitors a year. As well as the Aztec and Mayan archaeological remains, tourists are drawn to the old Spanish colonial cities, adventure destinations and beach resorts. Most visitors are from the USA and Canada.

Mayan

S.   A.

Traditional

Mariachi is a traditional folk music from Mexico. The Spanish introduced the now characteristic guitars to the country – prior to Spanish colonization the indigenous population played with drums, rattles and shell-horns.

The alcoholic drink of tequila comes from the blue agave plant grown in the highlands of central Mexico. Extracted agave juice is fermented and distilled to produce the popular drink. Spirits branded 'tequila' can only be produced in Mexico, although some is shipped to the USA for bottling.

Mexico is the world's largest silver producer. Silver has been mined in the western range of the Sierra Madre mountains for 500 years, with Mexico being one of the world's leading silver producers for much of this time.

Map labels:

dad Acuña
E
4
Nuevo Laredo
Saldo
Rio Grande
Falcon Lake
inas
algo
Monterrey
Reynosa
Montemorelos
Matamoros
Linares
Laguna Madre
San Fernando
Jiménez
Co Peña Nevada 3644
Soto la Marina
Ciudad Victoria
oriental
Ciudad Mante
Ebano
Tampico
Cárdenas
Cd de Valles
Laguna de Tamiahua
Tantoyuca
Tamazunchale
Tuxpan
C O
Querétaro
Poza Rica
ya
Nautla
Pachuca
baro
MEXICO CITY
Xalapa
Toluca
5452
Puebla
Pico de Orizaba
Veracruz
Cuernavaca
Volcán Popocatepetl
5747
Orizaba
Córdoba
Iguala
tamirano
Tierra Blanca
Presa Miguel Alemán
Acayucan
Coatzacoalcos
San Juan Bautista Tuxtepec
Chilpancingo
Minatitlán
ierra Madre Del Sur
Oaxaca
Istmo de Tehuantepec
Presa Nezahualcóyotl
Tenosique
pulco
Ciudad Ixtepec
Tuxtla Gutiérrez
Comitán de Domínguez
Miahuatlán
Juchitán
Arriagá
Pinotepa Nacional
Salina Cruz
Tonalá
Puerto Escondido
Puerto Ángel
Gulf of Tehuantepec
Presa de la Angostura
GUATEMALA
E
Huixtla
1
Tapachula

Gulf of Mexico
G
Yucatan Channel
Cabo Catoche
3
Cancún
Mérida
Cozumel
Valladolid
I. de Cozumel
F
Campeche
Yucatán
B. de la Ascensión
Champotón
Banco Chinchorro
Laguna de Términos
Frontera
Ciudad del Carmen
Escárcega
Chetumal
Ambergris Caye
Villahermosa
BELIZE
2

0 100 200 300 400 km
F

Central America

Central America is a mountainous, volcanically active isthmus connecting North America to South America. The region is made up of the countries Belize, Guatemala, El Salvador Honduras, Nicaragua, Costa Rica and Panama, all of which have at some time been colonies and have gained independence. Many of these countries have strong economic links with the USA. International trade is very important in the region, demonstrated by the building of the Panama Canal, linking the Pacific and Atlantic Oceans. Completed in 1914, construction took thirty-four years, and cost over 30,000 lives.

Diverse

Costa Rica has a biodiversity level matched nowhere else on the planet. Covering 0.3 per cent of the world's surface, it has 5 per cent of its species.

Gulf of Mexico

Yucatán

Orange Walk
Belize
BELMOPAN
Turneffe Is
Flores
BELIZE
Dangriga
MEXICO
Maya Mountains
Punta Gorda
Islas de la Bahía
Trujillo
GUATEMALA
Puerto Barrios
La Ceiba
Cobán
Lago de Izabal
San Pedro Sula
Volcán de Tajumulco
El Progreso
HONDURA
4210
Quetzáltenango
Santa Rosa de Copán
Juticalpa
GUATEMALA CITY
Mazatenango
Jutiapa
Santa Ana
Sensuntepeque
TEGUCIGALPA
Danlí
SAN SALVADOR
San Vicente
San Miguel
Choluteca
Cord.
EL SALVADOR
Unión
Matagalpa
Golfo de Fonseca
León
Chinandega
Lago de Managua
MANAGUA
Granada
Riva
Cabo Santa Elena

PACIFIC OCEAN

Guatemala is the world's largest producer and exporter of cardamom. The Middle East is the main export destination, where it is used in cooking and mixed with coffee as a drink. Cardamom is the third most expensive spice after saffron and vanilla.

No worries

Small colourful Guatemalan worry dolls are given to Guatemalan children to put beneath their pillows at night. The belief is that if you tell your worries to the doll then both worries and doll will be gone in the morning. Being small and inexpensive, they are also a popular souvenir for tourists.

Most of the people in Central America are *mestizos*, of mixed descent from Europeans and indigenous Amerindians. Guatemala has the largest Mayan population of any of the countries, with over half the population of Mayan descent, and the indigenous culture there is particularly strong.

The quetzal, a rare bird of the Central American rainforests, is the national bird of Guatemala.

Isla de Coco (Costa Rica)

0   100   200   300   400 km

The Great Blue Hole, east of the Turneffe Islands off the coast of Belize, is an enormous submarine sinkhole, and a very desirable dive site for experienced divers. Measuring 305 m across and 145 m deep, it is almost perfectly circular. It is the depth of the water that gives it its deep blue colour.

Five native big cat species range throughout Central America – the jaguar, jaguarundi, margay, mountain lion and ocelot. The largest and most elusive is the Jaguar.

C U B A

JAMAICA

Islas del Cisne
(Swan Islands)
(Hond.)

C
a
r
i
b
b
e
a
n
S
e
a

◄3

A 'Banana republic' is a politically unstable country whose economy depends mainly upon a single crop. The term grew up from the heavy dependence of several Central American countries – especially Honduras and Guatemala – upon bananas in the late 19th and early 20th centuries.

Laguna de
Carátasca

Mosquitia

Coco

Cayos
Miskitos
(Nicaragua)

Puerto
Cabezas

Costa de Mosquitos

CARAGUA

Grande

Siquia

Mico

Bluefields

aragua

Punta de Perlas

Islas del Maíz
(Corn Is)
(Nicaragua)

◄2

Tree dwelling sloths live in the rainforests of Central and South America – although their reputation for sleepiness is partly unfounded. Once thought to be one of the sleepiest animals, studies have since shown that they sleep for just under 10 hours a day – more than humans but less than record-breaking brown bats at 20 hours or even cats at about 12 hours. With a diet of only leaves they do, however, need economy measures to conserve their energy so they move only when necessary, and then only slowly.

San Juan

OSTA RICA

Alajuela

Puerto Limón

D

COLOMBIA

ula
oya

SAN JOSÉ

Chirripó
3819

Golfo de
Nicoya

Bahía de
Coronado

Volcán
Barú
3475

Bocas
del Toro

Golfo de los
Mosquitos

Colón

Panamá
Canal

PANAMA
CITY

La Chorrera

Golfo del
Darién

Península
de Osa

La Concepción

David

P A N A M A

s t h m u s

Aguadulce

Archipiélago
de las Perlas

La Palma

◄1

Puerto
Armuelles

Santiago

Chitré

Golfo de
Chiriquí

Las Tablas

Gulf of
Panama

Península
de Azuero

Punta
Mala

Isla de Coiba

Punta
Mariato

1►

Panama has great strategic importance at the narrowest crossing point between the Pacific Ocean and Atlantic Ocean. Built between 1880 and 1914, the 80 km-long Panama Canal provides a shortcut between the Pacific Ocean and Atlantic Ocean and the revenue from canal tolls is a vital source of income for Panama.

Cuba is famous for its cigars. Many are still rolled by hand for the luxury market. An experienced cigar-roller is able to make hundreds of nearly identical cigars a day and is well-respected in society.

Maracas are characteristic of Cuban music, especially at celebrations or special events. The diversity of seed or dried bean fillings means that different sets of maracas can produce unique sounds.

Black Pearl, on the island of Grand Cayman, is the largest outdoor skate park in the western hemisphere. Next to the skate park is the world's largest wave pool, with a 3.3 m high swell for surfing.

The West Indies cricket team is an amalgamation of players from fifteen of the Caribbean islands. It was, from the mid 1970s until the early 1990s, the most feared of all the cricket playing nations with batsmen of devastating potential and a battery of some of the fastest bowlers in Test history.

Junkanoo is a very colourful cultural festival held in towns across The Bahamas every Boxing Day and New Year's Day. Featuring street parades, music and costume competitions, everyone is invited to join the party. The origins are uncertain although it is believed to have evolved from the celebrations of African plantation slaves when they were given holiday time at Christmas.

Gulf of Mexico

U.S.A.

Grand Bahama

Little Abaco

Freeport City

Great Abaco

THE BAHAMAS

Berry Is

Eleuthera

Straits of Florida

NASSAU
New Providence

Cat Island

Andros

Exuma Sound

S. Salvad

Tropic of Cancer

HAVANA

Matanzas

Archipélago de Sabana

Great Exuma

Artemisa

Pinar del Río

Sagua la Grande

Long Island

Guane

Golfo de Batabanó

Santa Clara

Archipélago de Camagüey

Crooked I.

Cabo San Antonio

Cienfuegos

CUBA

Isla de la Juventud

MEXICO

Trinidad

Sancti Spiritus

Ciego de Ávila

Camagüey

Nuevitas

Archipélago de los Jardines de la Reina

Las Tunas

Holguin

Golfo de Guacanayabo

Manzanillo

Bayamo

Ba

Cayman Islands (UK)

Little Cayman

Cabo Cruz

Sierra Maestra

Guanta

GEORGE TOWN

Cayman Brac

1994 Turquino

Santiago de Cuba

Grand Cayman

Windw

Jamaica Channel

Montego Bay

St Ann's Bay

Jé

JAMAICA

KINGSTON

Great Pedro Bluff

Spanish Town

Caribbean

SCORE   BATSMEN NO. RUNS
WKTS
OVERS   1ST
         2ND

Docile and beautifully coloured, the Antilles pinktoe tarantula is a sought-after spider pet in many countries. In its native lands of Guadeloupe and Martinique it is a tropical tree-dweller, creating strong webs and eating crickets, beetles, moths and even small lizards.

Caribbean Islands

The Caribbean region is made up of over 7,000 islands, reefs and cays. The climate is mostly tropical with year round sunshine, attracting many tourists. However, the region is also prone to hurricanes. The Puerto Rico trench, an ocean channel, plunges more than 8 kilometres below sea level, and is the deepest point in the Atlantic Ocean. Many of the islands have a history linked to European settlement and African slavery. The largest of these islands is Cuba. Whilst very close to the US mainland, the two countries had a difficult relationship for many years, due to Cuba's close alliance with the former Soviet Union.

Oldest!

Santo Domingo, the capital of the Dominican Republic, is the largest city in the Caribbean. It was founded in 1496 by Bartholomew Columbus – the younger brother of Christopher Columbus – and is the oldest continuously inhabited European settlement in the Caribbean.

The 7.0 magnitude earthquake that struck Port-au-Prince, the capital of Haiti, in 2010 killed an estimated 220,000 people and left over a million people homeless. Already one of the world's poorest countries, the earthquake was a major challenge to the nation's emergency services and triggered a massive global response of humanitarian aid.

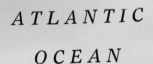

Several Caribbean locations featured in the filming of the *Pirates of the Caribbean* film series. St Vincent and the Grenadines served as the production base, and the fictional island of Cruces was filmed in Dominica and the Bahamas.

Tropic of Cancer

ked Island

Mayaguana

klins and

Caicos Is

Turks and Caicos Islands (UK)

GRAND TURK

Turks Is

ATLANTIC OCEAN

Great Inagua

Hispaniola

Cap-Haïtien

Monte Cristi

Puerto Plata

Port-de-Paix

Santiago

Gonaïves

San Francisco de Macoris

de la onâve

HAITI

Pico Duarte 3175 ▲

DOMINICAN REPUBLIC

La Romana

SAN JUAN

Virgin Is (USA)

ROAD TOWN

Anegada (UK)

Anguilla (UK)

ORT-AU-PRINCE

Les Cayes

2680 ▲

La Selle

Barahona

SANTO DOMINGO

Aguadilla

Mayagüez

Co de Punta ▲ 1338

Ponce

Virgin Is (UK)

THE VALLEY

St-Martin (Fr.)

Isla Beata

C. Beata

Isla Mona

PUERTO RICO (USA)

Vieques

St Croix

CHARLOTTE AMALIE

St Maarten (Neth.)

St-Barthélemy (Fr.)

St Eustatius (Neth.)

BASSETERRE

ST KITTS AND NEVIS

BRADES

Barbuda

ANTIGUA AND BARBUDA

ST JOHN'S

Antigua

Montserrat (UK)

Guadeloupe (Fr.)

Pointe-à-Pitre

BASSE-TERRE

Marie-Galante (Fr.)

DOMINICA

ROSEAU

Martinique (Fr.)

FORT-DE-FRANCE

ST LUCIA

CASTRIES

KINGSTOWN

BRIDGETOWN

ST VINCENT & THE GRENADINES

BARBADOS

GRENADA

ST GEORGE'S

Leeward Islands

Lesser Antilles

Windward Islands

Mona Passage

A n t i l l e s

Sea

Lesser Antilles

Aruba (Neth.)

ORANJESTAD

Curaçao (Neth.)

WILLEMSTAD

Bonaire (Neth.)

TRINIDAD AND TOBAGO

Tobago

Scarborough

PORT OF SPAIN

Arima

Trinidad

San Fernando

0   100   200   300   400 km

South America

Caribbean Sea

Barranquilla   Maracaibo   Caracas   Port of Spain
                                        TRINIDAD
                                        AND TOBAGO

VENEZUELA

Medellín   Georgetown
                              GUYANA   Paramaribo
        Bogotá   SURINAME   Cayenne
Cali   FRENCH
COLOMBIA   GUIANA

Quito   Equator
ECUADOR

Galapagos   Guayaquil   Belém
Islands
(Ecuador)   Iquitos   Manaus   São Luís

                                                                        Fortaleza
                                        B R A Z I L   Natal

Trujillo
        PERU   Recife

                                                                Aracaju
Lima
                    Lake   Salvador
                    Titicaca
PACIFIC   BOLIVIA   Brasília
        Arequipa   La Paz

OCEAN   Sucre   Belo Horizonte

                                          PARAGUAY   Rio de
                                                            Janeiro
                    Antofagasta   São Paulo   Tropic of Capricorn
                                          Asunción
                                                          Curitiba

                                                                    ATLANTIC

Juan Fernandez   OCEAN
Islands
(Chile)   Valparaíso   Porto Alegre
        Santiago   URUGUAY
                              Buenos
Concepción   Aires   Montevideo

                    A R G E N T I N A

                              Mar del Plata

                                          Falkland
                                          Islands
                                          (UK)
Punta   Tierra
Arenas   del   South Georgia
                Fuego   (UK)

                              South Orkney
                              Islands
                              (UK)

0   500   1000   1500   2000 km

24

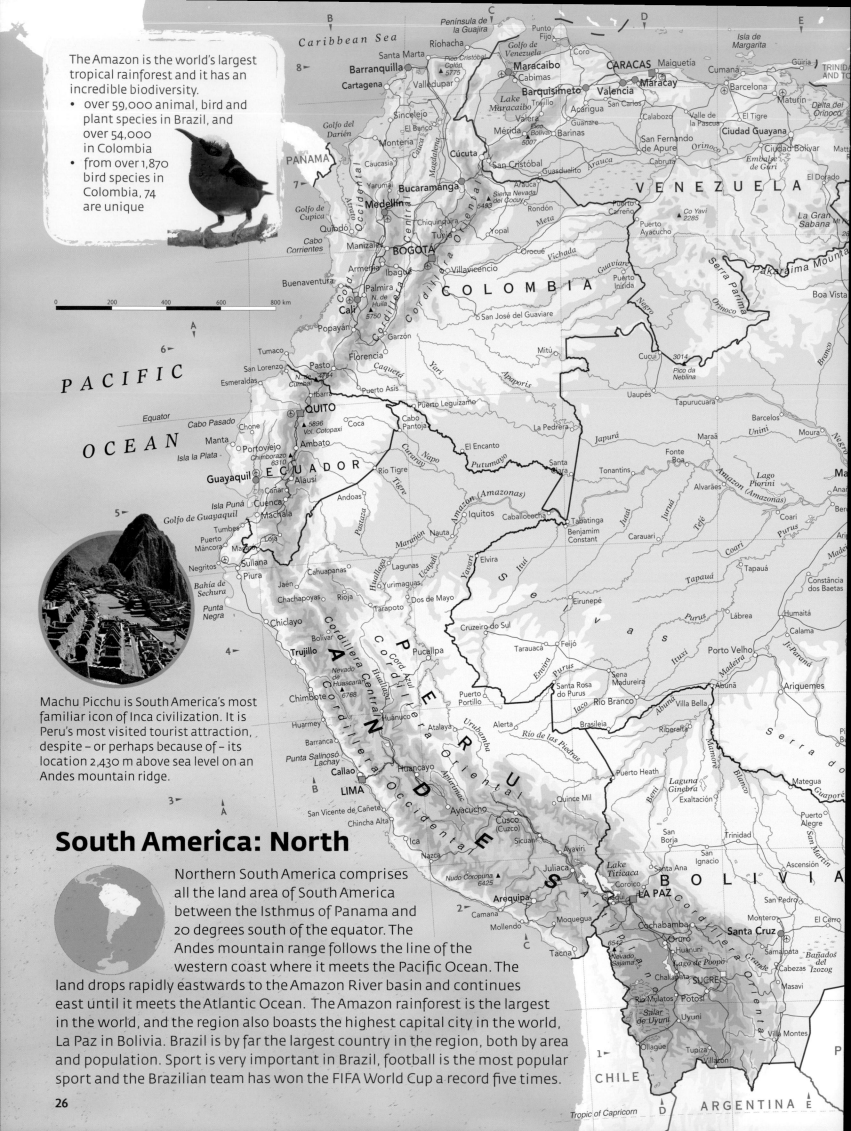

The Amazon is the world's largest tropical rainforest and it has an incredible biodiversity.
- over 59,000 animal, bird and plant species in Brazil, and over 54,000 in Colombia
- from over 1,870 bird species in Colombia, 74 are unique

Machu Picchu is South America's most familiar icon of Inca civilization. It is Peru's most visited tourist attraction, despite – or perhaps because of – its location 2,430 m above sea level on an Andes mountain ridge.

South America: North

Northern South America comprises all the land area of South America between the Isthmus of Panama and 20 degrees south of the equator. The Andes mountain range follows the line of the western coast where it meets the Pacific Ocean. The land drops rapidly eastwards to the Amazon River basin and continues east until it meets the Atlantic Ocean. The Amazon rainforest is the largest in the world, and the region also boasts the highest capital city in the world, La Paz in Bolivia. Brazil is by far the largest country in the region, both by area and population. Sport is very important in Brazil, football is the most popular sport and the Brazilian team has won the FIFA World Cup a record five times.

Reserves

Although not the largest producer of oil in the world, Venezuela holds the largest reserves. Most deposits are in the north of the country, around Lake Maracaibo, the Gulf of Venezuela and in the Orinoco river basin.

Largest!

The Amazon river contains a staggering fifth of the world's river flow. Over 1,000 streams and rivers flow into it, making it the world's largest drainage basin.

- during the wet season the Amazon river can reach a width of 190 km in places
- ocean-going ships can sail upstream as far as the city of Manaus, nearly 1,500 km from the river mouth

Over half the world's emeralds are mined in Colombia. Deep in the hills of the eastern Andes there are several large mines.

Brazil is the second largest producer of soybeans after the USA. Over 70 million tonnes of beans are harvested each year between January and April.

Brightly coloured poison dart frogs live among the leaves of the rainforest. Special sticky pads on the tips of their toes stop them falling to the forest floor. The most deadly is the golden poison arrow frog, which lives in Colombia

ATLANTIC OCEAN

BRAZIL

SURINAME

FRENCH GUIANA

GEORGETOWN

PARAMARIBO

Polo

Argentina is a dominant power in international polo and is globally recognised for its breeding of fine polo ponies. Breeding is closely controlled to retain qualities of speed, agility and strength.

The Atacama desert is commonly known as the driest place in the world. Some areas have less than 1 mm of rain a year and other areas have not had any rainfall at all for over 400 years.

Driest

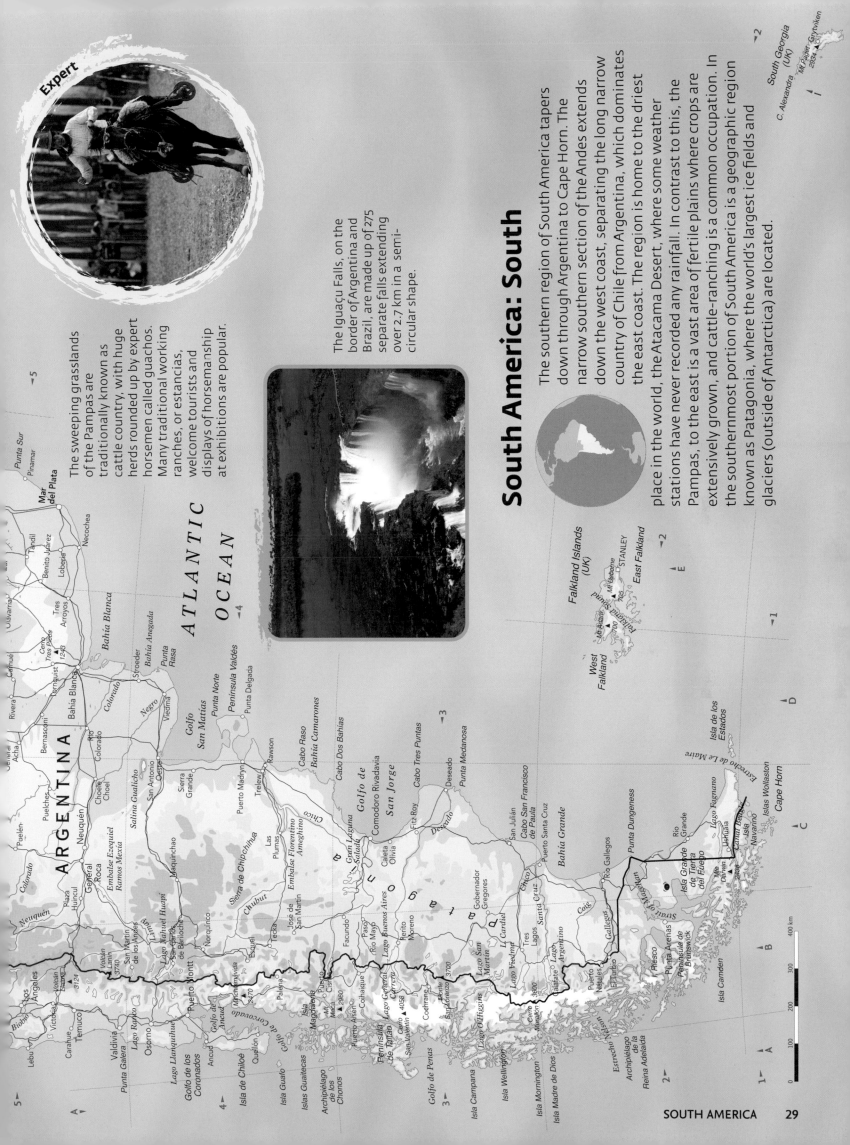

Expert

The sweeping grasslands of the Pampas are traditionally known as cattle country, with huge herds rounded up by expert horsemen called gauchos. Many traditional working ranches, or estancias, welcome tourists and displays of horsemanship at exhibitions are popular.

The Iguaçu Falls, on the border of Argentina and Brazil, are made up of 275 separate falls extending over 2.7 km in a semicircular shape.

South America: South

The southern region of South America tapers down through Argentina to Cape Horn. The narrow southern section of the Andes extends down the west coast, separating the long narrow country of Chile from Argentina, which dominates the east coast. The region is home to the driest place in the world, the Atacama Desert, where some weather stations have never recorded any rainfall. In contrast to this, the Pampas, to the east is a vast area of fertile plains where crops are extensively grown, and cattle-ranching is a common occupation. In the southernmost portion of South America is a geographic region known as Patagonia, where the world's largest ice fields and glaciers (outside of Antarctica) are located.

ATLANTIC OCEAN

ARGENTINA

Falkland Islands (UK)

West Falkland
East Falkland
STANLEY

South Georgia (UK)
C. Alexandra
Mt Paget-Grytviken
2934

Cape Horn

Strait of Magellan
Tierra del Fuego
Isla Grande de Tierra del Fuego

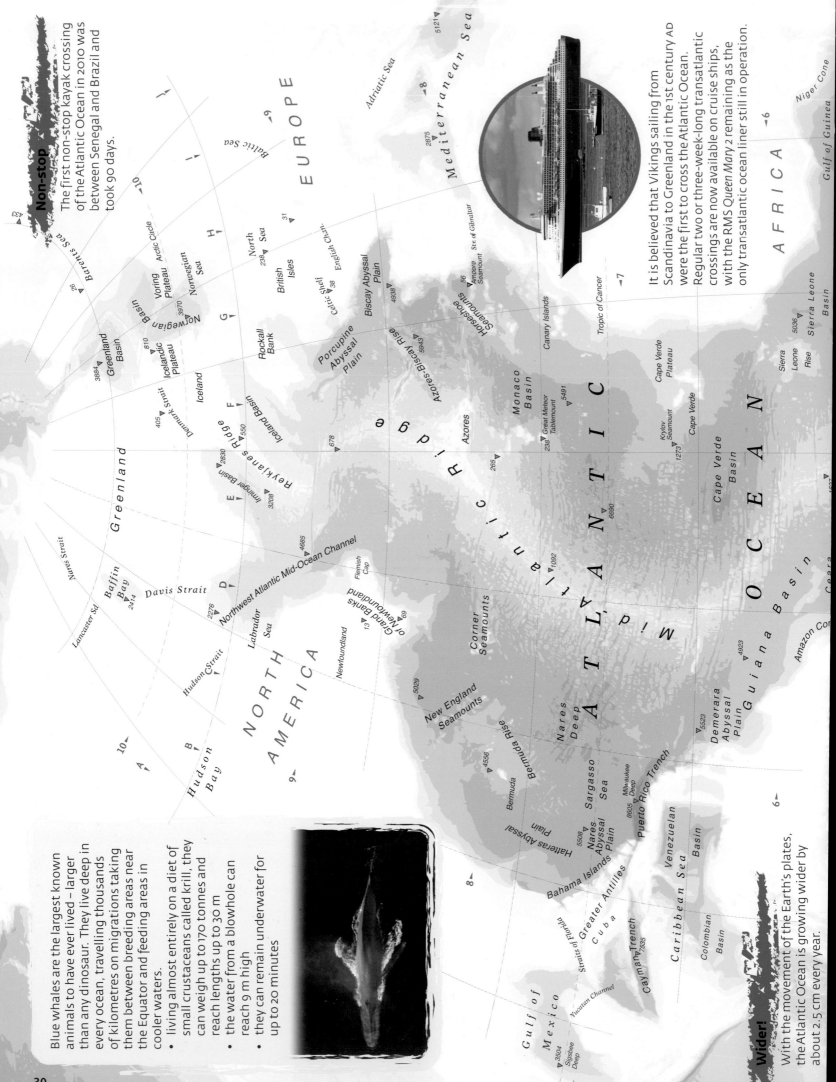

Non-stop

The first non-stop kayak crossing of the Atlantic Ocean in 2010 was between Senegal and Brazil and took 90 days.

Blue whales are the largest known animals to have ever lived – larger than any dinosaur. They live deep in every ocean, travelling thousands of kilometres on migrations taking them between breeding areas near the Equator and feeding areas in cooler waters.

- living almost entirely on a diet of small crustaceans called krill, they can weigh up to 170 tonnes and reach lengths up to 30 m
- the water from a blowhole can reach 9 m high
- they can remain underwater for up to 20 minutes

It is believed that Vikings sailing from Scandinavia to Greenland in the 1st century AD were the first to cross the Atlantic Ocean. Regular two or three-week-long transatlantic crossings are now available on cruise ships, with the RMS Queen Mary 2 remaining as the only transatlantic ocean liner still in operation.

Wider!

With the movement of the Earth's plates, the Atlantic Ocean is growing wider by about 2.5 cm every year.

Map labels

EUROPE

AFRICA

NORTH AMERICA

ATLANTIC OCEAN

Mid-Atlantic Ridge

Mediterranean Sea

Adriatic Sea

Baltic Sea

Barents Sea

North Sea

British Isles

English Chan.

Celtic Shelf

Str. of Gibraltar

Norwegian Sea

Voring Plateau

Arctic Circle

Iceland

Icelandic Plateau

Denmark Strait

Greenland Basin

Greenland

Reykjanes Ridge

Iceland Basin

Irminger Basin

Rockall Bank

Porcupine Abyssal Plain

Biscay Abyssal Plain

Azores-Biscay Rise

Azores

Ampere Seamount

Horseshoe Seamounts

Canary Islands

Great Meteor Tablemount

Krylov Seamount

Cape Verde Plateau

Cape Verde

Cape Verde Basin

Tropic of Cancer

Monaco Basin

Sierra Leone Rise

Sierra Leone Basin

Niger Cone

Gulf of Guinea

Guiana Basin

Amazon Cone

Demerara Abyssal Plain

Ceara

Venezuelan Basin

Colombian Basin

Caribbean Sea

Greater Antilles

Cuba

Bahama Islands

Puerto Rico Trench

Milwaukee Deep

Sargasso Sea

Nares Abyssal Plain

Nares Deep

Hatteras Abyssal Plain

Bermuda

Bermuda Rise

New England Seamounts

Corner Seamounts

Cayman Trench

Yucatan Channel

Straits of Florida

Gulf of Mexico

Sigsbee Deep

Grand Banks of Newfoundland

Flemish Cap

Newfoundland

Northwest Atlantic Mid-Ocean Channel

Labrador Sea

Hudson Strait

Hudson Bay

Davis Strait

Baffin Bay

Nares Strait

Lancaster Sd.

Nares Deep

Depth figures

433

26

3884

810

3970

405

2830

9205

550

678

4938

5943

56

238

5121

2875

1273

1092

6690

4923

5523

4556

5608

8605

7535

3504

2414

2276

4685

13

69

265

5036

38

31

238

5491

Atlantic Ocean

The Atlantic Ocean stretches down between North and South America in the west, and Europe and Africa in the east. All of the seas in Europe are in fact branches of the Atlantic Ocean, which covers around twenty per cent of the Earth's surface. Several archipelagos stretch out within the Atlantic Ocean along its length, including the Caribbean islands to the west. Many of those in the east, such as the Canary Islands, are European territories. Historically, the Atlantic Ocean has played an important part in the expansion of North and South America; the term 'black Atlantic' was coined in reference to its prominence in the slave trade between Africa and America.

In 1912 the RMS *Titanic* sank in the North Atlantic on its maiden voyage after colliding with an iceberg about 600 km south of Newfoundland.

Mystery

The Bermuda Triangle is an undefined triangular area in the North Atlantic Ocean, southwest of Bermuda, where many ships and aircraft have reputedly mysteriously disappeared over the years. Various supernatural explanations have been proposed but it is in a busy shipping area, prone to tropical storms, meaning that verified disappearances may actually be no more than expected for such an area.

Fast!

In 1858 the first transatlantic telegraph cable, between Ireland and Newfoundland, Canada, reduced the time it took to send a message across the Atlantic Ocean from 10 days or more to just a few minutes.

Predator

The creature that may have inspired the film *Alien* lives in all the world's oceans. Like the creatures from the film, *Phronima* is a fierce predator, but unlike the film version it is only 2.5 cm long.

PACIFIC OCEAN

SOUTH AMERICA

ANTARCTICA

SOUTHERN OCEAN

Congo Cone

Orange Cone

Tropic of Capricorn

Cape of Good Hope

Agulhas Basin

Angola Basin

Walvis Ridge

Namibia Abyssal Plain

Vema Seamount

Cape Basin

Agulhas Ridge

Agulhas Seamounts

St Helena

Discovery Seamounts

Shona Ridge

Atlantic-Indian Ridge

Enderby Abyssal Plain

Gunnerus Indian Antarctic Basin

Antarctic Circle

Ascension

Mid-Atlantic Ridge

Tristan da Cunha

Atlantic-Indian Antarctic Basin

Maud Seamount

American-Antarctic Ridge

Pernambuco Plain

Brazil Basin

Rio Grande Rise

South Sandwich Trench

Weddell Abyssal Plain

Stocks Seamount

Vitória Seamount

Abrolhos Bank

Santos Plateau

Argentine Basin

Argentine Rise

Falkland Escarpment

Scotia Ridge

Scotia Sea

Scotia Ridge

Weddell Sea

Argentine Abyssal Plain

Falkland Plateau

Falkland Islands

Yaghan Basin

South Shetland Trough

Cape Horn

Drake Passage

Antarctic Circle

Africa

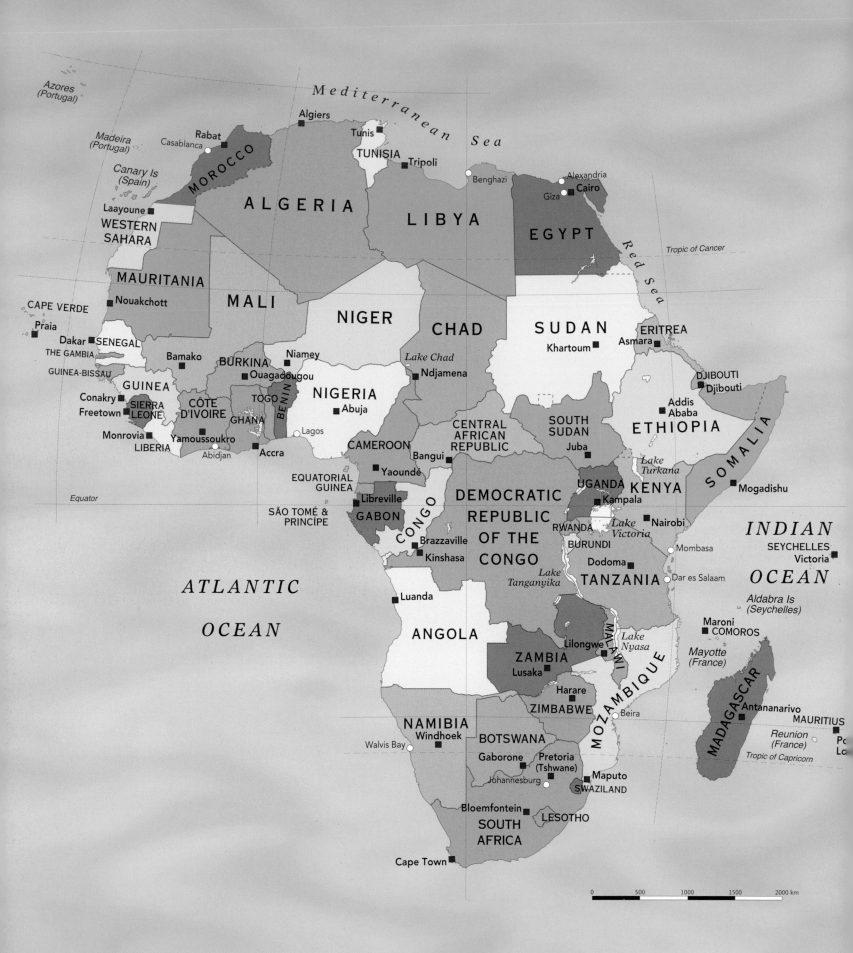

Azores
(Portugal)

Mediterranean Sea

Madeira
(Portugal)

Algiers
Tunis
TUNISIA
Tripoli
Benghazi
Alexandria
Cairo
Giza

Rabat
Casablanca
MOROCCO

Canary Is
(Spain)

Laayoune

WESTERN
SAHARA

ALGERIA

LIBYA

EGYPT

Tropic of Cancer

Red Sea

MAURITANIA

CAPE VERDE

Nouakchott

MALI

NIGER

CHAD

SUDAN

ERITREA

Praia

Dakar
THE GAMBIA
GUINEA-BISSAU

SENEGAL

Bamako

BURKINA

Niamey

Khartoum

Asmara

DJIBOUTI
Djibouti

Ouagadougou

Lake Chad

Ndjamena

Conakry
Freetown

GUINEA

SIERRA
LEONE

CÔTE
D'IVOIRE

GHANA

TOGO
BENIN

NIGERIA

Abuja

Addis
Ababa

ETHIOPIA

Monrovia
LIBERIA

Yamoussoukro

Abidjan

Accra

Lagos

CAMEROON

CENTRAL
AFRICAN
REPUBLIC

Bangui

SOUTH
SUDAN

Juba

Lake
Turkana

SOMALIA

Equator

EQUATORIAL
GUINEA

SÃO TOMÉ &
PRINCÍPE

Yaoundé

Libreville

GABON

CONGO

Brazzaville

Kinshasa

DEMOCRATIC
REPUBLIC
OF THE
CONGO

UGANDA
Kampala

RWANDA

BURUNDI

Lake
Victoria

KENYA

Nairobi

Dodoma

Mombasa

Mogadishu

INDIAN

SEYCHELLES
Victoria

OCEAN

ATLANTIC

OCEAN

Luanda

ANGOLA

Lake
Tanganyika

TANZANIA

Dar es Salaam

Aldabra Is
(Seychelles)

Maroni
COMOROS

Lilongwe

MALAWI

Lake
Nyasa

Mayotte
(France)

ZAMBIA

Lusaka

Harare

MOZAMBIQUE

MADAGASCAR

Antananarivo

MAURITIUS

NAMIBIA

Windhoek

ZIMBABWE

Beira

Reunion
(France)

Po
Lo

Walvis Bay

BOTSWANA

Gaborone

Pretoria
(Tshwane)

Johannesburg

Maputo

SWAZILAND

Tropic of Capricorn

Bloemfontein

LESOTHO

SOUTH
AFRICA

Cape Town

0   500   1000   1500   2000 km

Northwest Africa

Northwest Africa is the region of Northern Africa west of Egypt and the Nile Valley. Very few people live in the inhospitable interior and the most populous parts of the region are found along the milder Atlantic and Mediterranean coasts. The desert plains and hills of the Sahara dominate the landscape along with the rocky uplands of the Atlas Mountains in the north. There are huge oil and natural gas reserves in the deserts of Algeria and Libya, which are essential to these countries economically. The tourist industry is also very important to the economy of many of the coastal countries, particularly Morocco and Tunisia. This has recently been greatly affected by ongoing political and civil unrest in the region.

Steaming food is highly practical in areas with a limited water supply. Painted or glazed *tagines* are traditional clay pots used in Morocco to slow-cook rich stews of meat, chicken or fish. The base of the *tagine* is used for cooking and serving, and the conical top is removed for serving.

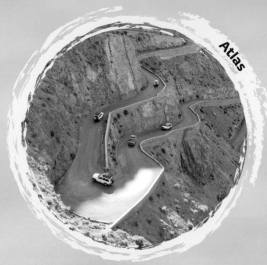

The Atlas Mountains extend across Morocco, northern Algeria and Tunisia. The highest point at 4,167 m is Jbel Toubkal. In Morocco a twisting drive between Marrakech and Ouarzazate crosses the mountain range, with the section winding up to Tizi N'tichka including a pass with nearly a hundred dizzying bends in only 30 km.

Map labels:

ATLANTIC OCEAN
Canary Islands (Spain)
La Palma
Tenerife
Santa Cruz de Tenerife
Gran Canaria
Las Palmas de Gran Canaria
Lanzarote
Fuerteventura
Tangier · Ceuta (Sp.) · Tétouan · Melilla (Sp.) · Oran · Ech Chélif
RABAT · Kénitra · Fez (Fès) · Oujda · Sidi Bel Abbès · Tlemcen
Casablanca · Meknès
El Jadida · Settat
Safi · Beni Mellal · Aïn Sefra · Bouârfa · Gha
Marrakesh · Er Rachidia · Béchar
Jbel Toubkal 4167 · Ouarzazate · Abadla
Agadir · MOROCCO
Tiznit · Atlas · El Goléa
Guelmine · Ksabi
Boujdour · Tindouf · ALGER
Reggane · In Sa
LAÂYOUNE
Galat Zemmour
WESTERN SAHARA · MAURITANIA · 'Erg Chech · S
Ad Dakhla · Administered by Morocco · Tropic of Cancer · Ar
Nouâdhibou · MALI
Râs Nouâdhibou

0 200 400 600 800 km

Precarious!

Ksars are fortified clay-built villages that are found across Morocco, Algeria and Libya. Often they included storage areas for grain, accessed by precarious external staircases. In southern Tunisia several became the location for the city of Mos Espa, the childhood home of Anakin Skywalker in the film *StarWars: The Phantom Menace*.

There is a strong tourist industry in Morocco and Tunisia. Holidaymakers are drawn to the warm, palm-fringed Mediterranean coastline as well as to the variety of culture, scenery and adventure on offer from countries bordering the Sahara.

Football

Football is by far the most popular sport for both spectating and playing in northwest Africa. Although access to sports facilities may be limited in remote areas, children can still enjoy a fun game anywhere outdoors.

Oil and gas provides about half of Libya's wealth. The Bouri field lies about 120 km offshore from Tripoli and is the largest producing oilfield in the Mediterranean Sea.

Plagues of desert locusts have repeatedly devastated crops in all the northwest African countries over many centuries.
- Swarms can travel up to 200 km daily
- Locusts can jump 70 cm. This is like a human jumping 18 m

Fez, in northern Morocco, has the oldest leather tannery in the world. Hides are processed by hand in stone vessels, softened, dyed and made into high-quality leather items like shoes, bags and slippers – all using methods and materials that have hardly changed for nine hundred years.

Lowest

The Sahara has one of the lowest population densities in the world. In about 9 million square kilometres there are only about 2.5 million people. Many people are nomadic, moving about in search of better living conditions. The Bedouin, meaning 'desert dweller', is an Arabian ethnic group that is divided into many different tribal clans that live right across northern Africa and the Middle East.

The spectacular ruins of Leptis Magna lie on the coast east of Tripoli in Libya. During Roman times it was the third most important city in Africa, rivalled only by Carthage and Alexandria. It is now one of the best-preserved yet least-visited Roman cities in the world.

AFRICA

Northeast and East Africa

The dominant physical feature of the northeast African continent is the fertile river valley of the Nile, the world's longest river at 6,695 kilometres in length. Lying next to this are the mountainous Ethiopian Highlands and the Horn of Africa, a peninsula jutting hundreds of kilometres into the Arabian Sea. There is a large Arab influence in the region, shown by the spread of Islam and the rich historic heritage of mosques. The Danakil Desert, home to the Afar people, lies in northeast Ethiopia, southern Eritrea and Djibouti and is one of the hottest places on earth. Many countries in this region have been devastated by civil wars and periods of drought, crop failure and famine.

Largest

Cairo, the capital of Egypt, is the largest city in Africa and also the largest city in the Arab world. Its strategic location upstream of the Nile delta made it an ancient stronghold. Al-Azhar University was founded there in AD 970 as a centre of Islamic learning and is one of the oldest universities in the world. About 20 km southwest of Cairo is Giza, also on the banks of the Nile. This is the site of the Great Pyramid of Giza – the largest and oldest of the Egyptian pyramids and the tallest man-made structure in the world until 1889.

Lake Assal is a saltwater crater lake in central Djibouti. At 155 m below sea level it is the lowest point in Africa. The hot climate causes high evaporation levels, and it holds the world's largest salt reserves. Most commercial extraction is from deposits on the shores of the lake.

Although Egypt is famous for its mighty pyramids there are actually more pyramids in north Sudan than there are in Egypt, although they are built on a much smaller scale.

- The most extensive site of Nubian pyramids is the ancient city of Meroe, north of Atbara on the eastern bank of the Nile. There are over 200 pyramids there and although most are in ruins, some have been reconstructed.
- At least thirty-five small, densely packed pyramids, together with graves, were discovered by archaeologists between 2009 and 2012 at Sedeinga, near the border with Egypt.

The Nile is the world's longest river, with a history of providing water, fertile soil and a transport route for over 2,500 years. It used to flood each year in late summer, bringing water and nutrients from melting snow and heavy rain in the Ethiopian Highlands down to the Nile floodplain and delta – this ceased with the construction of the Aswan Dam in 1970.

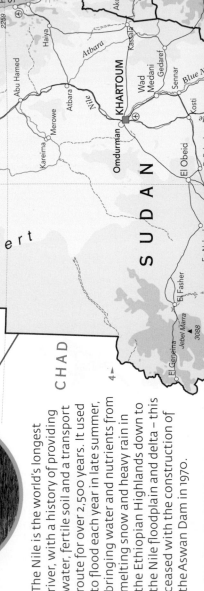

Vast flocks of flamingos on the shores of Lake Nakuru in the Rift Valley of Kenya makes one of the world's most amazing wildlife spectacles. An abundance of blue-green algae – created by their droppings mixed with the warm alkaline water – makes the lake the single most important feeding site for the lesser flamingo.

Every year over a million wildebeest, 500,000 Thomson's gazelles and 200,000 zebras migrate north from the Serengeti plains of Tanzania to Kenya in search of new grazing, returning again several months later. With a total of up to 2 million animals covering over 2,800 km it is one of wildlife's most incredible mass migrations.

Malaria

Infected mosquitoes cause malaria. About 95 per cent of the world's malaria-related deaths are in Africa, with Uganda and Kenya suffering the highest number of deaths.

Lake Tanganyika is Africa's deepest lake. It contains at least 400 species of fish, many of which are sensitive to pollution. The most brightly coloured cichlids are popular with aquarium owners and many are exported worldwide for breeding. Setting up a 'Lake Tanganyika biotope' to simulate the chemistry and temperature conditions in the lake is popular with aquarists.

Zebra

The plains zebra is the most common of Africa's zebras, ranging from Ethiopia to South Africa. Their striped patterns are distinctive.

- stripe patterns are unique to each zebra – no two animals have exactly the same pattern
- evidence shows that the zebra is a black animal with white stripes rather than a white animal with black stripes
- vertical stripes are useful for camouflage, blending with the grass of the savanna

West Africa

West Africa is densely populated and made up of many small countries, making it very culturally and ethnically diverse. Most of the region's biggest cities are found along the Atlantic coast. Stretching across the north of the region is the Sahel, an area of dry savannah grassland which is often a productive agricultural area but suffers from periodic droughts and famine. Agriculture forms the basis of most economies in the region, although significant oil and gas deposits have been found around the coasts of Côte d'Ivoire and the Niger delta.

Prototype

Africa's first house made of plastic bottles was built in the village of Sabon Yelwa in northern Nigeria in 2011. An estimated 14,000 discarded bottles were filled with sand, stacked on their sides on top of each other, and bound together with mud. The result was a durable, bullet-proof, environmentally-friendly and cost-effective building which became a prototype for further housing.

Drought, deforestation and overgrazing can all cause desertification, and the Sahel region of West Africa is especially vulnerable. Nouakchott, the capital of Mauritania, continually suffers as sand dunes encroach from the east. Over time cultivated land has been lost and homes have been abandoned.

From the 16th to the 19th century the coast of West Africa was one of the most important centres for the export of slaves from Africa to the Americas. Between 2 and 3 million slaves were traded from the region. Several former slave ports, such as Fort Elmina, near Sekondi in Ghana, have become popular tourist destinations, particularly for African-Americans wanting to pay their respects to their ancestors.

Côte d'Ivoire and Ghana together produce over half of the world's cocoa beans. Most cocoa trees are grown by smallholder farmers. Pods are harvested when ripe and the beans are extracted for fermentation and drying. They are then sold on for worldwide export to processors and major chocolate producing companies – mainly in Europe and the USA.

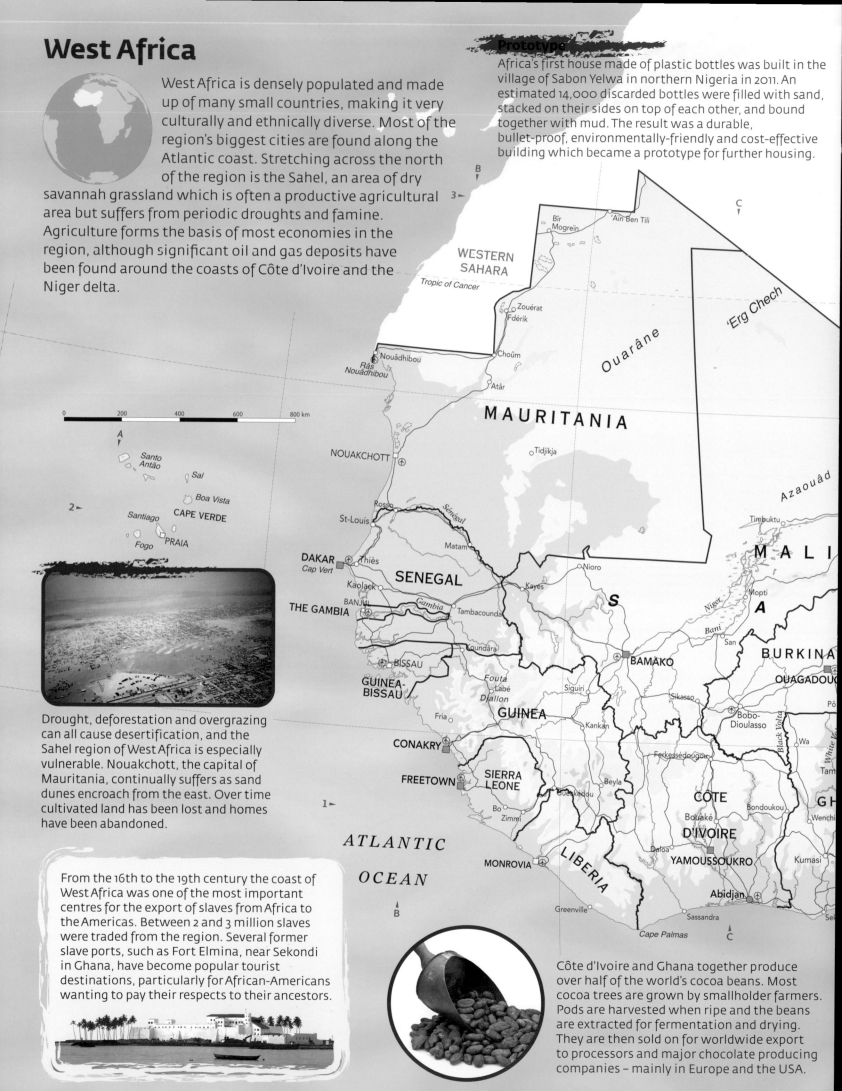

38

The Great Mosque of Djenné in southern Mali is the largest adobe building in the world. Constructed from sun-dried bricks of sand, clay, water and a binding substance, it is a completely natural building material. The thick walls insulate the building from heat during the day and keep it warm through the night – making this 1907 building a very eco-friendly construction.

With government commitment to education, and the help of foreign aid, literacy levels are improving – but are still low in many parts of West Africa.
- secondary school enrolment is only 20 per cent
- in Burkina Faso, Niger, Mali, Chad, Sierra Leone and Senegal the adult rate of illiteracy is over 60 per cent
- for women the rates are even worse – in Burkina Faso and Niger only about 15 per cent of women can read and write

Education

West Africa is known for its musical heritage, with traditional drumming playing an important part in ceremonies and festivities. Originating in Mali, the djembe is a carved wooden drum, covered with goatskin. It can produce a wide variety of sounds, and is a loud instrument. Traditionally the djembe is played only by men.

One of the world's most ancient religions, voodoo originated in West Africa and is practised by several peoples of southern Benin, Togo and Nigeria. The word 'voodoo' comes from a West African word meaning 'spirit'. The Akodessewa Fetish Market in Togo's capital, Lomé, sells all kinds of animal parts required by traditional healers to make medicines

Construction of the Akosombo dam on the Volta river in Ghana in 1965 created the world's largest man-made lake, Lake Volta. Covering over 8,500 square kilometres, the hydroelectricity generated supplies the majority of Ghana's needs and also electricity for export to Togo and Benin.

Central Africa

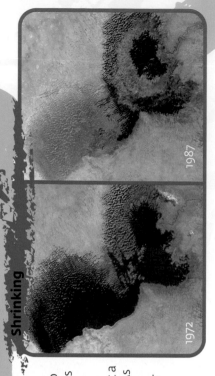

Shrinking

1972

1987

Central Africa is a core region of the African continent dominated by the vast Congo Basin. The Great Rift Valley that runs through Africa passes through the east of this region. Along this part of the valley there is a string of lakes, as well as a number of volcanoes.

The huge diversity of wildlife in Central Africa helps to support the tourist industry; many areas are designated as protected in order to reduce the threat of extinction for the region's most endangered species.

Lake Chad varies in size from year to year but the general trend recently is that it is shrinking. Once one of Africa's largest lakes, it is now estimated by NASA to be only about a fifth of the size it was in the 1970s. As well as suffering from low rainfall levels, water has also been taken for massive irrigation projects

The Gaboon viper lives in the rainforests of central Africa. It is a slow-moving snake, well-coloured for camouflage, and it hunts by ambush. Bites are rare, but as this snake produces the largest quantities of venom of any snake then any bite to a human is potentially fatal.

The bright green gemstone of malachite is mined at several locations in the Democratic Republic of the Congo, but the richest deposits are in the 'copperbelt' region of Katanga in the southeast. Sliced and polished to bring out the beautiful banding, malachite has also been used to make jewellery for thousands of years.

Ongoing conflict in the east of the Democratic Republic of the Congo has displaced over 2.4 million people within the country, and over 400,000 have also become refugees in neighbouring countries.

Cassava is a staple food crop in central Africa. Providing a high yield of carbohydrates per cultivated area, it supplies about half of all food energy requirements in the Central African Republic and the Democratic Republic of the Congo. The plant is perennial, very drought-tolerant, grows well in poor soils and has a long harvesting season – all factors that make it vital as both a subsistence and a cash crop.

Volcanoes

The 'Cameroon line' is a 1,000 km-long chain of extinct volcanoes that extends across land and sea from near Lake Chad through the mountains in Cameroon out into the Gulf of Guinea. It includes the islands of Bioco and São Tomé and Príncipe.

NIGER

CHAD

SUDAN

NIGERIA

Tibesti

Zouar

Emi Koussi
3415

Bodélé

Koro
Toro

Massif Ennedi

Erdi

Ouaddi

Abéché

Ati

Massakory

NDJAMENA

Lake Chad

Maroua

Garoua

Kelo

Moundou

Doba

Sarh

Ndélé

CENTRAL AFRICAN

B

C

4

5

4

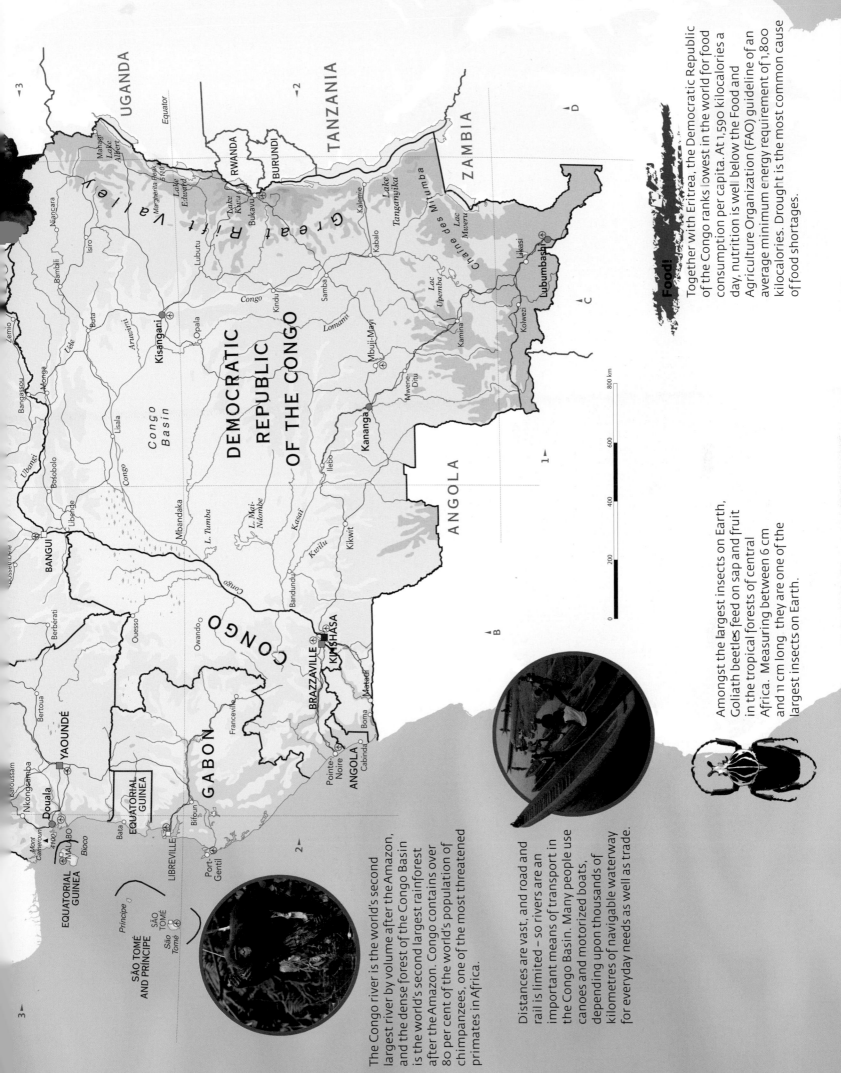

UGANDA

TANZANIA

RWANDA

BURUNDI

ZAMBIA

Margherita Peak
5110

Mahagi
Lake
Albert

Niangara

Lake
Edward

Bunia

Isiro

Bambili

Bukavu
Lake
Kivu

Lubutu

Buta

Üéle

Aruwimi

Uele

Kisangani

Opala

Congo

Kindu

Lubumbashi

Kabalo

Lake
Tanganyika

Kalemie

Lac
Mweru

Likasi

Kolwezi

Kamina

Kabalo

Lac
Upemba

Samba

Lomami

Mbuji-Mayi

Mwene-
Ditu

Kananga

Ilebo

Kasai

Zemio

Bangassou

Monga

Bosobolo

Lisala

Libenge

Mbandaka

L. Tumba

L. Mai-
Ndombe

Bandundu

Kwilu

Kikwit

DEMOCRATIC

REPUBLIC

OF THE CONGO

*Congo
Basin*

Ubangi

Congo

BANGUI

Berbérati

Ouesso

Owando

Congo

CONGO

BRAZZAVILLE
KINSHASA

Matadi

Boma

ANGOLA
Cabinda

Pointe-
Noire

ANGOLA

Bertoua

Bifoun

Franceville

Port-
Gentil

GABON

LIBREVILLE

YAOUNDÉ

Nkongsamba

Douala

Mont
Cameroun
4100

MALABO
Bioko

Bata

EQUATORIAL
GUINEA

**EQUATORIAL
GUINEA**

Príncipe

SÃO
TOMÉ

São
Tomé

**SÃO TOMÉ
AND PRÍNCIPE**

Great Rift Valley

Chaîne des Mitumba

Equator

0   200   400   600   800 km

The Congo river is the world's second largest river by volume after the Amazon, and the dense forest of the Congo Basin is the world's second largest rainforest after the Amazon. Congo contains over 80 per cent of the world's population of chimpanzees, one of the most threatened primates in Africa.

Distances are vast, and road and rail is limited – so rivers are an important means of transport in the Congo Basin. Many people use canoes and motorized boats, depending upon thousands of kilometres of navigable waterway for everyday needs as well as trade.

Food!

Together with Eritrea, the Democratic Republic of the Congo ranks lowest in the world for food consumption per capita. At 1,590 kilocalories a day, nutrition is well below the Food and Agriculture Organization (FAO) guideline of an average minimum energy requirement of 1,800 kilocalories. Drought is the most common cause of food shortages.

Amongst the largest insects on Earth, Goliath beetles feed on sap and fruit in the tropical forests of central Africa. Measuring between 6 cm and 11 cm long, they are one of the largest insects on Earth.

AFRICA   41

Up to 1.5 million people were killed in the Angolan war which lasted 27 years and ended in 2002. In the city of Kuito alone over 30,000 people were killed in a siege. Despite high publicity and efforts to clear landmines, Angola still remains one of the most heavily mined countries in the world.

By capacity the FNB Stadium (Soccer City) in the Soweto area of Johannesburg is the largest sports stadium in Africa. It was enlarged to hold 94,736 to host the 2010 FIFA World Cup, the first time an African country had hosted the World Cup. It also hosted the 2013 final of the Africa Cup of Nations.

The fynbos is a biome unique to South Africa. It has a high level of biodiversity, and the highest concentration of plant species of any floral kingdom. The best known of its plants is the King protea, South Africa's national flower.

Impressive

Rising to over 300 m, the southern Namib Desert in Namibia has some of the world's highest and most impressive sand dunes.

On the Zambezi river, at the border between Zimbabwe and Zambia, the Victoria Falls is the largest curtain of water in the world.

DEMOCRATIC REPUBLIC OF THE CONGO

M'banza Congo

Uíge

LUANDA

N'dalatando · Malanje
Dondo · Cuanza

Quibala

Saurimo

ANGOLA

Luau

Lobito
Benguela
Huambo
Kuito
Luena
Solwezi
Chingola
Kitwe

ZAMB

Menongue
Cuando
Mongu
LUSAKA
Kabw

Namibe
Lubango
Cubango
Zambezi
Pemba
K

Tombua
Cunene
Ondjiva
Katima Mulilo
Livingstone
Victoria Falls
ZIMB

Kaokoveld
Oshakati
Ovamboland
Rundu
Caprivi Strip
Okavango Delta
Maun
Nata
Makgadikgadi
Bul

Etosha Pan
Tsumeb
Francistown

Otjiwarongo

NAMIBIA
Damaraland
WINDHOEK
Gobabis
BOTSWANA
Serowe
Kalahari Desert
Polokw

Swakopmund
Walvis Bay
Namib Desert
Tsumis Park
Mochudi
GABORONE
Kanye
Mmabatho
PRETORIA
Mar
Soweto
Carletonville
Johann
Evaton

Mariental

Great Namaqualand
Keetmanshoop
Molopo
Vaal

Lüderitz

SOUTH AFRICA
Welkom
Lad

Karasburg
Orange
Upington
Kimberley
BLOEMFONTEIN
Mangaung
MASERU
Thabana Ntlenyar
LESOTHO
Drakens

Britstown
Orange
Umtata

Great Karoo
Mdantsa

ATLANTIC
St Helena Bay
Beaufort West
Bisho
East Le

OCEAN
Saldanha
Little Karoo
Grahamstown
CAPE TOWN
Worcester
KwaNobuhle
Port Elizabeth
Khayelitsha
Mossel Bay
Cape of Good Hope
Cape Agulhas

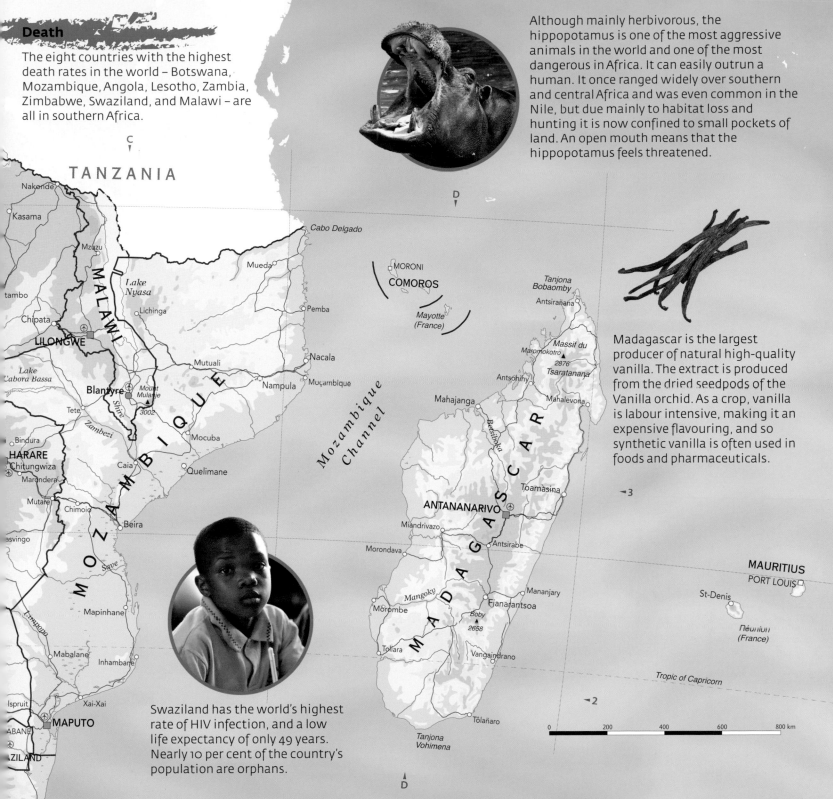

Death

The eight countries with the highest death rates in the world – Botswana, Mozambique, Angola, Lesotho, Zambia, Zimbabwe, Swaziland, and Malawi – are all in southern Africa.

Although mainly herbivorous, the hippopotamus is one of the most aggressive animals in the world and one of the most dangerous in Africa. It can easily outrun a human. It once ranged widely over southern and central Africa and was even common in the Nile, but due mainly to habitat loss and hunting it is now confined to small pockets of land. An open mouth means that the hippopotamus feels threatened.

Madagascar is the largest producer of natural high-quality vanilla. The extract is produced from the dried seedpods of the Vanilla orchid. As a crop, vanilla is labour intensive, making it an expensive flavouring, and so synthetic vanilla is often used in foods and pharmaceuticals.

Swaziland has the world's highest rate of HIV infection, and a low life expectancy of only 49 years. Nearly 10 per cent of the country's population are orphans.

Southern Africa

Southern Africa has a varied landscape, ranging from forest and grasslands to deserts. The region has both low-lying coastal areas, mountains and the extensive desert areas of the Namib and Kalahari. Namibia lies on the Atlantic coast and the landlocked states of Zambia, Zimbabwe and Botswana extend through to Mozambique on the Indian Ocean coast. In northeast Botswana the Okavango Delta, one of the world's largest inland deltas, is formed where the Okavango river empties into a swamp area in the northern Kalahari Desert. South Africa is an important country politically and economically in the region. It is ethnically and culturally diverse, and has eleven official languages. The independent kingdom of Lesotho is entirely enclosed within South Africa.

Cape Town is Africa's most popular tourist destination, and one of the most multicultural cities in the world.

Map labels:

TANZANIA

Nakonde
Kasama
tambo
Chipata
Mzuzu
LILONGWE
Lake Nyasa
Lichinga
Lake Cabora Bassa
Blantyre
Mount Mulanje 3002
Tete
Bindura
HARARE
Chitungwiza
Marondera
Mutare
Chimoio
asvingo
Mapinhane
Mabalane
Inhambane
Is\pruit
Xai-Xai
ABANE
MAPUTO
AZILAND
aritzburg
waMashu
urban

MALAWI
MOZAMBIQUE
Zambezi
Shire
Save
Limpopo

Cabo Delgado
Mueda
Pemba
Mutuali
Nacala
Nampula
Muçambique
Mocuba
Caia
Quelimane
Beira

MORONI
COMOROS
Mayotte (France)

Mozambique Channel

Tanjona Bobaomby
Antsiranana
Massif du Maromokotro 2876 Tsaratanana
Antsohihy
Mahajanga
Mahalevona
Toamasina
Betsiboka
ANTANANARIVO
Miandrivazo
Antsirabe
Morondava
Mangoky
Morombe
Mananjary
Fianarantsoa
Boby 2658
Toliara
Vangaindrano
Tôlañaro
Tanjona Vohimena

MADAGASCAR

MAURITIUS
PORT LOUIS
St-Denis
Réunion (France)

Tropic of Capricorn

0   200   400   600   800 km

INDIAN
OCEAN

Europe

ARCTIC OCEAN

Spitsbergen

Novaya Zemlya

Jan Mayen (Norway)

Arctic Circle

ICELAND
■ Reykjavik

ATLANTIC
OCEAN

Faroe Islands (Denmark)

White Sea

N O R W A Y

S W E D E N

F I N L A N D

Gulf of Bothnia

Helsinki

■ Oslo

Stockholm

Tallinn

ESTONIA

St Petersburg

RUSSIAN
FEDERATION

■ Moscow

North Sea

Edinburgh

Belfast

UNITED
KINGDOM

Dublin

IRELAND

London

DENMARK
Copenhagen

Baltic Sea

LATVIA

Riga

LITHUANIA

11

Vilnius

Minsk

BELARUS

Volgograd

NETHERLANDS

Berlin

Warsaw

English Channel

BELGIUM

GERMANY

POLAND

Kiev

UKRAINE

1

Prague

CZECH REPUBLIC

SLOVAKIA

Paris

Munich

Vienna

Bratislava

10

Chişinău

FRANCE

AUSTRIA

Budapest

Odesa

Bay of Biscay

Lyon

2

3

HUNGARY

ROMANIA

Milan

SAN MARINO

4

5

Zagreb

Belgrade

Bucharest

Corsica

MONACO

ITALY

6

SERBIA

BULGARIA

Caspian Sea

ANDORRA

Adriatic Sea

7

8

Sofia

Black Sea

Madrid

Barcelona

Rome

Skopje

9

Istanbul

Lisbon

PORTUGAL

SPAIN

Balearic Islands

Sardinia

Tirana

ALBANIA

TURKEY

Palma de Mallorca

Aegean Sea

Gibraltar (UK)

GREECE

Athens

Strait of Gibraltar

Sicily

Crete

Rhodes

MALTA

Mediterranean Sea

0   250   500   750   1000 km

1   LUXEMBOURG
2   SWITZERLAND
3   LIECHTENSTEIN
4   SLOVENIA
5   CROATIA
6   BOSNIA AND HERZEGOVINA
7   MONTENEGRO
8   KOSOVO
9   MACEDONIA (F.Y.R.O.M.) *
10 MOLDOVA
11 PART OF RUSSIAN FEDERATION

* FORMER YUGOSLAV
REPUBLIC OF MACEDONIA

Scandinavia

Scandinavia is a historical region in northern Europe, which is today often taken to include Norway, Sweden, Denmark, Finland and Iceland. The region shares much of their cultural history, dating back thousands of years.

Both Norway's and Iceland's economies have historically been highly dependent on fishing, and although this has lessened in recent years, fishing remains important. All of the Scandinavian countries speak very closely related languages, except Finland, which is quite distinct from the others. Denmark is the smallest of the nations by area, but the Faroe Islands and Greenland are also included within the Danish Kingdom.

Swedes love liquorice. Lakritsfestivalen is an annual festival of liquorice held in Stockholm that celebrates the flavour of the popular sweet. Salty liquorice is a particular favourite in Scandinavia although its tongue-numbing qualities are said to be an acquired taste!

Surprisingly, considering the cool climate, Scandinavian countries are all amongst the world's top consumers of ice cream.

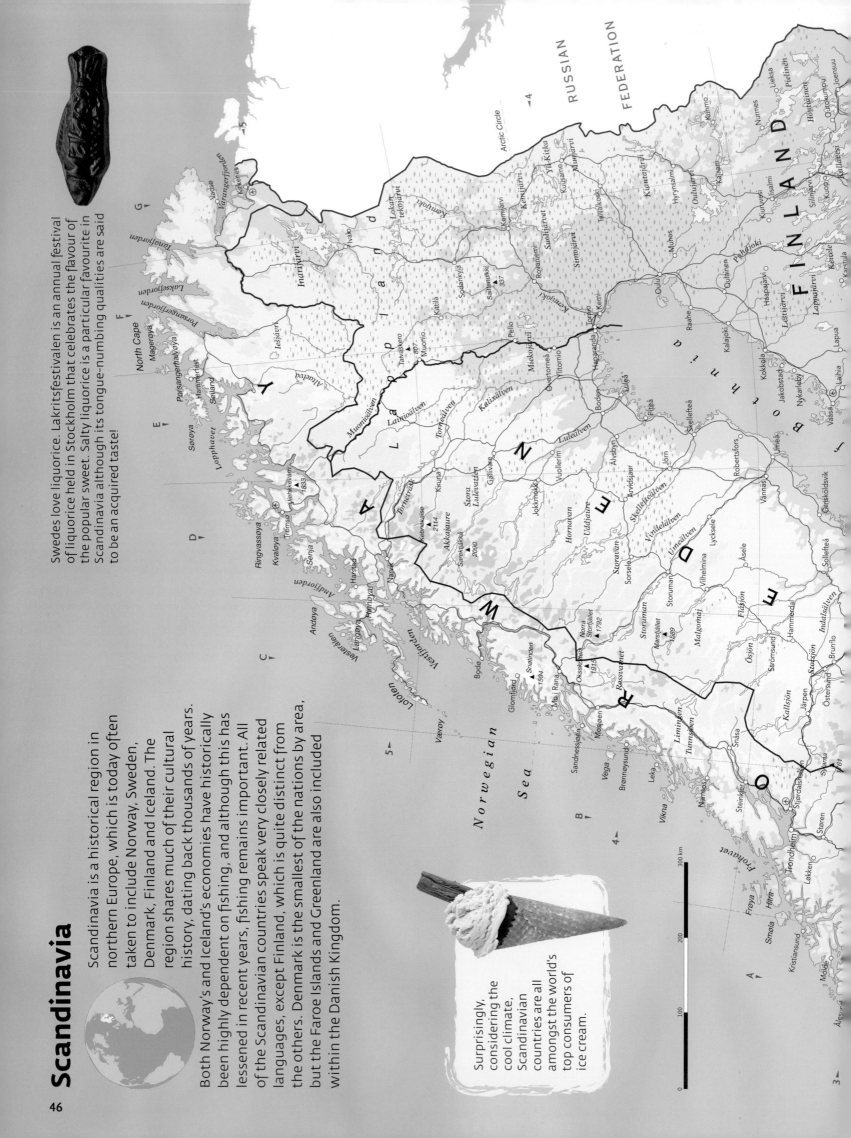

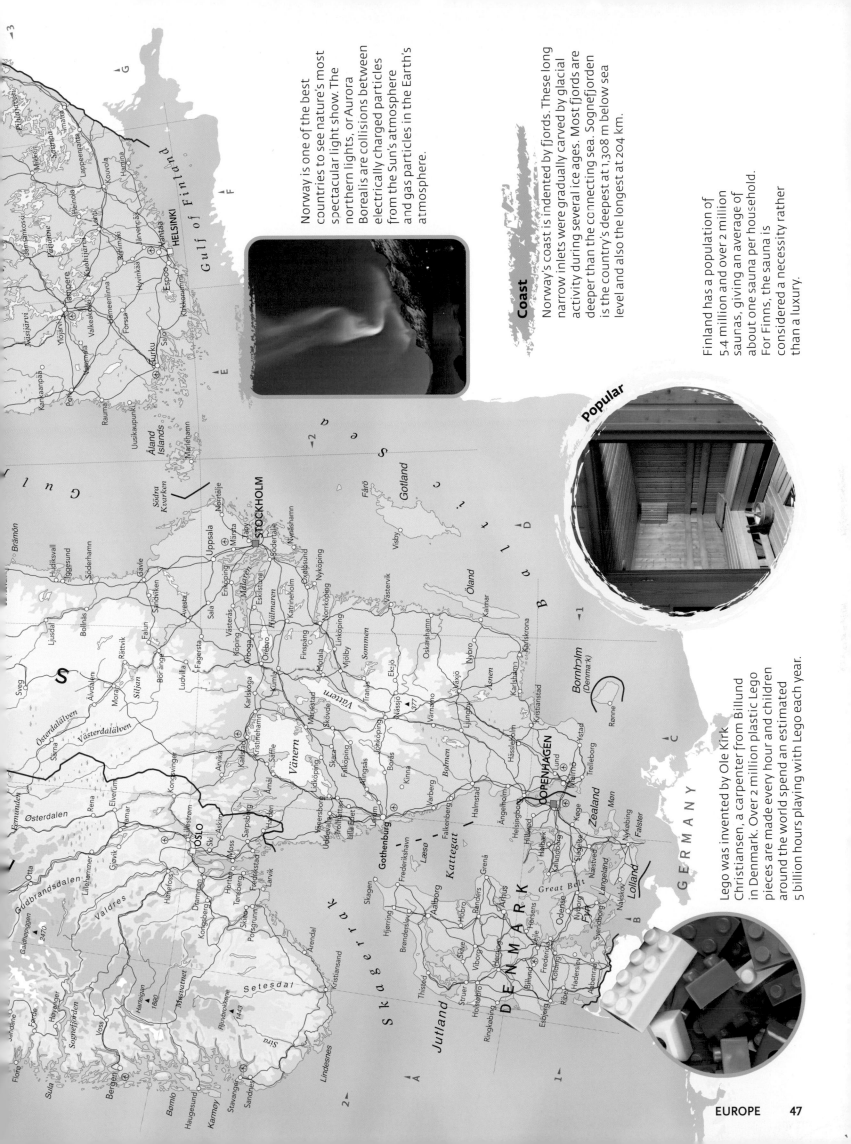

Norway is one of the best countries to see nature's most spectacular light show. The northern lights, or Aurora Borealis are collisions between electrically charged particles from the Sun's atmosphere and gas particles in the Earth's atmosphere.

Coast

Norway's coast is indented by fjords. These long narrow inlets were gradually carved by glacial activity during several ice ages. Most fjords are deeper than the connecting sea. Sognefjorden is the country's deepest at 1,308 m below sea level and also the longest at 204 km.

Popular

Finland has a population of 5.4 million and over 2 million saunas, giving an average of about one sauna per household. For Finns, the sauna is considered a necessity rather than a luxury.

Lego was invented by Ole Kirk Christiansen, a carpenter from Billund in Denmark. Over 2 million plastic Lego pieces are made every hour and children around the world spend an estimated 5 billion hours playing with Lego each year.

United Kingdom and Ireland

The UK and Ireland are spread across two large and many much smaller islands on the northwest of the European continent. The United Kingdom comprises England, Scotland and Wales, as well as Northern Ireland. London is the capital, and is one of the world's major tourist centres. The Republic of Ireland comprises around eighty percent of the island of Ireland. Nearly sixty per cent of the population live in urban areas, and there is a diminishing reliance on agriculture, which has traditionally been very important. Areas on the west coast of Ireland are often very wet, as it is heavily affected by North Atlantic drift ocean current. There are traditionally strong historical ties, but also political conflicts between the UK and Ireland.

An English aristocrat from Kent, the 4th Earl of Sandwich, is famed for having given his name to the sandwich in 1726 when he required an easy-to-hold snack at the gambling table. Although he may have popularised the eating of meat or cheese between slices of bread, the concept of eating some form of bread together with other foods probably goes back over 2,000 years.

Irish people drink more tea on average than anybody else in the world, with the British drinking the next most.

Teal

Smallest

With a population of less than 2,000, the village of St David's in Pembrokeshire, Wales, is also the smallest cathedral city in the world. The 12th century cathedral contains the remains of St David, the patron saint of Wales.

Although not the largest exporter, the UK is the country that produces the most varieties of cheese – over 700 compared to about 400 for France. Well-known varieties named after English cheese-producing regions are Cheddar, Shropshire and Wensleydale.

North Sea

ATLANTIC
OCEAN

SCOTLAND

North West Highlands

Grampian Mountains

UNITED

Southern Uplands

Orkney Islands

Shetland Islands

Outer Hebrides

Inner Hebrides

The London London Underground was the world's first underground railway, opening in 1863. It now carries over a billion passengers a year, more than the country's national rail network.

The 1066 Norman invasion began a much more extensive period of castle building than had been seen before in Britain. Wales, as 'the land of castles', has some of Europe's finest surviving examples of medieval castle construction – with Beaumaris, Caernarfon (see below), and Conwy as the most impressive.

Netherlands, Belgium and Luxembourg

The Netherlands, Belgium and Luxembourg are traditionally grouped together as 'the low countries', given their low-lying position. Indeed, some areas of the Netherlands are below sea level. The Netherlands and Belgium have small economic but intensive agricultural sectors. The Netherlands has a reputation for producing ornamental plants, bulbs and flowers, whilst Belgium is famous for its chocolate. The headquarters of the European Union is located in the Belgian capital, Brussels. Luxembourg lies in the south of the region, and is a major world banking sector. Together, all three form Benelux, an economic agreement which has been in force since the Second World War. The region has a very strong cycling tradition, producing many great cyclists over the years.

Belgium, the Netherlands and Luxembourg were three of the original six countries that established the beginnings of what is now the European Union (EU), and the headquarters of the EU is in Belgium. The 12 golden stars in a circle on the flag is a symbol of unity amongst the people of Europe, and does not relate to the number of member countries.

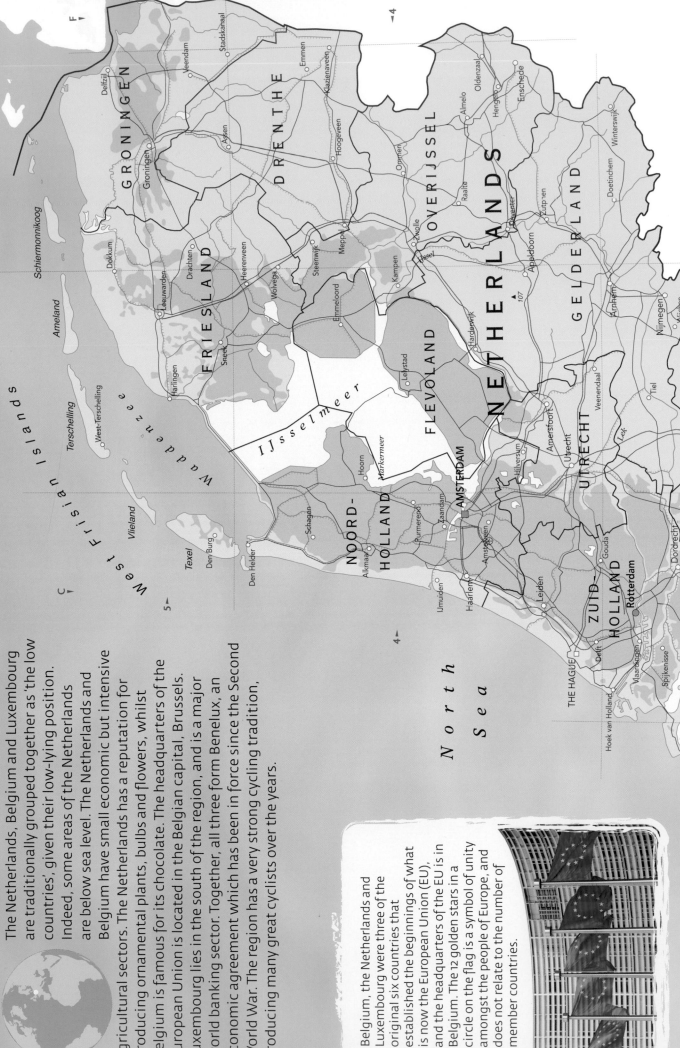

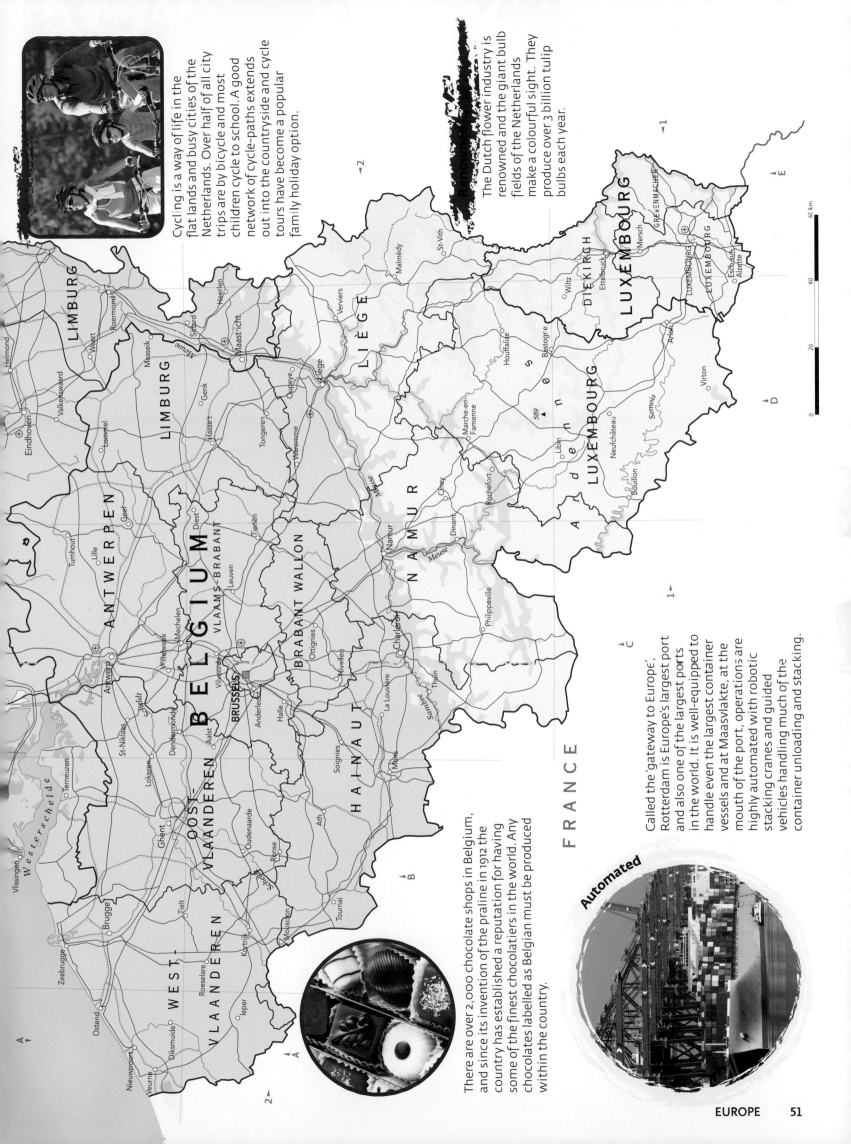

Cycling is a way of life in the flat lands and busy cities of the Netherlands. Over half of all city trips are by bicycle and most children cycle to school. A good network of cycle-paths extends out into the countryside and cycle tours have become a popular family holiday option.

Renowned

The Dutch flower industry is renowned and the giant bulb fields of the Netherlands make a colourful sight. They produce over 3 billion tulip bulbs each year.

There are over 2,000 chocolate shops in Belgium, and since its invention of the praline in 1912 the country has established a reputation for having some of the finest chocolatiers in the world. Any chocolates labelled as Belgian must be produced within the country.

Automated

Called the 'gateway to Europe', Rotterdam is Europe's largest port and also one of the largest ports in the world. It is well-equipped to handle even the largest container vessels and at Maasvlakte, at the mouth of the port, operations are highly automated with robotic stacking cranes and guided vehicles handling much of the container unloading and stacking.

France

France lies in Western Europe, with coastlines on the Atlantic Ocean and the Mediterranean Sea. It's southern and eastern borders are made up of mountain ranges; in particular the Alps and the Pyrenees. Over 80 per cent of the population live in urban areas, with almost a sixth of the population living in the Paris department. The economy has an important agricultural base, and France is a major producer of both fresh and processed food. There are coal reserves, and some oil and gas, but nuclear and hydroelectric power and imported fuels are vital. Tourism is very important to France. Paris has a reputation as one of the most romantic cities in the world, and is particularly well known for the Eiffel Tower.

The annual Tour de France, is divided into 21 daily stages along a course that varies each year. The overall race leader at the end of each stage is awarded a ceremonial yellow jersey. Since the first Tour de France in 1903 there have been over 2,000 yellow jerseys awarded to over 270 different riders. The winner of the race is the rider that receives the yellow jersey after the last stage of the race.

Although denim jeans may have originated in Italy, the cotton material of denim was first made in Nîmes, France. Developed as a strong sturdy fabric for workers, it was called 'serge de Nîmes'. The warp thread of denim is dyed indigo blue whilst the weft threads are white – this gives the characteristic lighter colour on the inside of jeans.

The Formula One Monaco Grand Prix is one of the world's most prestigious motor races. At 260.5 km over 78 laps, it is the only Grand Prix that does not adhere to the Fédération Internationale de l'Automobile (FIA) stipulated 300 km minimum race distance.

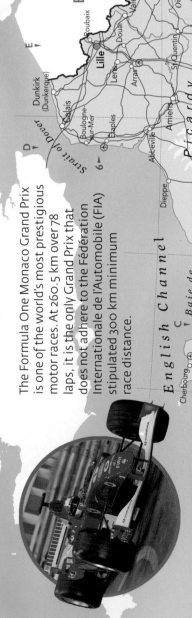

The 500 year-old painting of *Mona Lisa* by Leonardo da Vinci is one of the most famous works of art. About 6 million people each year visit the Louvre Museum in Paris to see it.

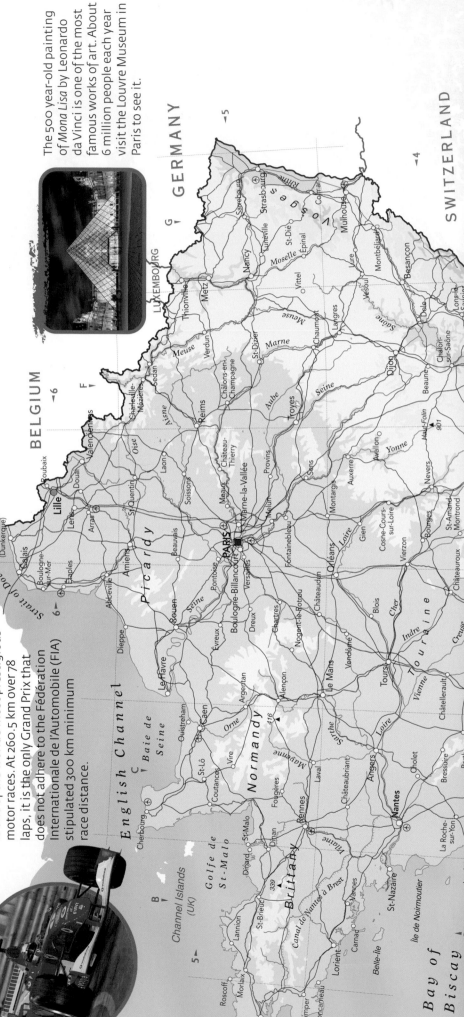

High-speed

France has one of the highest density transportation networks in the world. It led the world in high-speed train technology with the first TGV in 1983.

Energy

Renewable resources are important in France where the world's first large scale tidal power station opened on the Rance estuary in Brittany in 1966. It is still the world's largest tidal power station in terms of installed capacity. France is a high investor in nuclear technology, with over three-quarters of the country's energy derived from nuclear power.

Nestled between Spain and France in the Pyrenees mountain range, Andorra is a land of steep valleys, gorges and rugged mountains. At a height of 1,023 m Andorra la Vella, the capital of Andorra, is the highest capital city in Europe.

When it opened in 1889, the 324 m high Eiffel Tower in Paris was the highest structure in the world. It needs to be repainted with 55 tonnes of paint every seven years to protect it against corrosion. It is the most visited paid tourist attraction in the world.

Highest

Mont Blanc, in the French Alps, is the highest mountain in Western Europe.

- over 20,000 people climb the 4,810 m peak each year
- the mountain has been the scene of two fatal air crashes, in 1950 and 1966, with a combined death toll of 165 people
- an observatory was built at the summit in 1892 but it had to be abandoned in 1909 when a crevasse opened up underneath it

SPAIN

ITALY

ANDORRA

Corsica
(France)

Sardinia
(Italy)

Ligurian
Sea

Gulf of Lions

Côte d'Azur

ANDORRA LA VELLA

The beautiful Lipizzaner, a classical dressage horse, can be traced back to 1565 when the emperor of Austria bred Arabian stallions with Spanish mares in Lipica, now in Slovenia. Foals are born brown or black, and gradually lighten until they are pure white at the age of ten. Young stallions begin training at Vienna's Spanish Riding School when they are aged four. Once trained, they are the ballet dancers of the horse world, leaping, pirouetting and performing finely choreographed routines.

BERLIN

After dividing the city of Berlin since 1961, the Berlin Wall was finally dismantled in 1990, paving the way for the unification of West Germany and East Germany the same year. Fragments of the wall were sold as souvenirs all round the world. A short section remains as a memorial and art gallery.

Longest

Although not with the largest indoor ski area, at 640 m Bottrop in Germany does have the longest indoor ski run.

Oktoberfest brings the crowds to Munich in Germany every September and October to join in with a 16-day celebration of beer. With 14 large beer tents, over 6 million visitors and over 4,000 items in lost property, it is the world's largest annual fair.

Liechtenstein is one of only two doubly-landlocked countries in the world (the other is Uzbekistan) – meaning that it is a landlocked country surrounded by other landlocked countries.

POLAND

DENMARK

NETHERLANDS

BELGIUM

CZECH REPUBLIC

GERMANY

North Sea

Kap Arkona

Rügen

Sassnitz

Greifswald

Stralsund

Rostock

Güstrow

Wismar

Schwerin

Lübeck

Fehmarn

Mecklenburger Bucht

Kieler Bucht

Kiel

Neumünster

Schleswig

Flensburg

Husum

North Frisian Islands

Helgoländer Bucht

East Frisian Islands

Cuxhaven

Bremerhaven

Wilhelmshaven

Emden

Bocholt

Oldenburg

Bremen

Nienburg

Osnabrück

Münster

Hamm

Dortmund

Gelsenkirchen

Bottrop

Duisburg

Essen

Krefeld

Düsseldorf

Leverkusen

Bergisch Gladbach

Cologne

Bonn

Aachen

Siegen

Hagen

Arnsberg

Bielefeld

Paderborn

Marburg an der Lahn

Gießen

Fulda

Kassel

Göttingen

Mühlhausen

Gotha

Erfurt

Suhl

Meiningen

Nordhausen

Hildesheim

Hannover

Celle

Salzgitter

Braunschweig

Wolfsburg

Uelzen

Lüneburg

Nordenstedt

Neumünster

Ludwigslust

Neustrelitz

Neuruppin

Eberswalde

Finow

Rathenow

Brandenburg

Magdeburg

Dessau

Wittenberge

Perleberg

Schwedt an der Oder

Frankfurt an der Oder

Eisenhüttenstadt

Cottbus

Hoyerswerda

Bautzen

Görlitz

BERLIN

Potsdam

Lutherstadt Wittenberg

Halle

Leipzig

Dessau

Riesa

Meißen

Dresden

Chemnitz

Zwickau

Gera

Jena

Plauen

Lauchhammer

Erzgebirge

Elbe

Oder

Spree

Havel

Müritz

Mulde

Saale

Weser

Aller

Ems

Rhine

950

623

A B C D E

1 2 3 4 5 6

54

Germany, Austria and Slovenia

Germany, Austria, Liechtenstein and Slovenia are all alpine states that have strong historical and cultural ties. Germany has the major economy of the four, and German is an official language in all but Slovenia. Austria is landlocked, and relies heavily on Germany for trade links. Austria is particularly famous for skiing and has produced many world champions in the sport and boasts some of the best ski resorts in the world. In between the two is Liechtenstein, a tiny mountainous principality, whose economy is heavily based on the banking industry. Slovenia lies to the southeast of the region and is at the crossroads of many cultural and trading routes.

The 19th-century fairytale castle of Neuschwanstein, near Füssen in southwest Germany, was the inspiration for Disneyland's Sleeping Beauty Castle. It is one of the most-visited of all European castles and palaces.

Viennese balls date back for over 400 years. They are grand events, with many taking place in Vienna's Hofburg Palace. Each year there are over 450 balls in the 'ball season', many hosted by different trades such as the pharmacists' ball, the engineers and technicians ball and the lawyers ball, as well as the most famous Vienna Opera Ball.

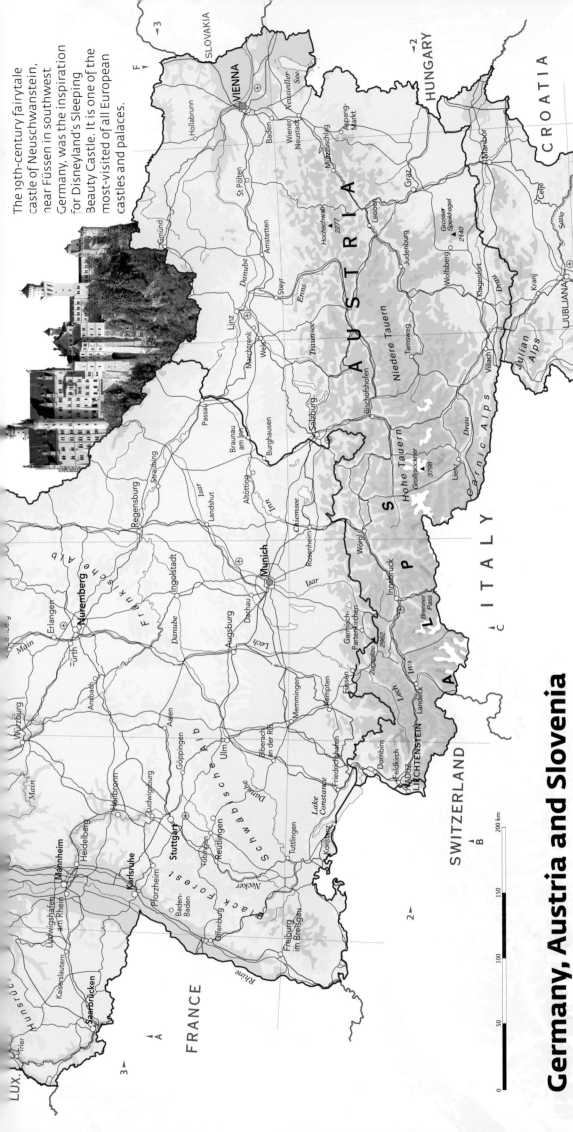

Fishing is long-established in Portugal, where per capita fish consumption rates are one of the highest in the world. Over three-quarters of fishing vessels are still small, traditional boats – although their catch is small they do bring in high-value species such as octopus, hake and conger eel.

Spain is the world's leading olive producer, supplying over a third of the world's olives and nearly 30 per cent of its olive oil.
- the Picual olive is the most widely grown, accounting for nearly a half of Spanish olive production
- green olives are those harvested before ripening whereas black olives are those harvested when fully ripe

Spain and Portugal

Spain and Portugal make up the historic Iberian Peninsula in the southwest of Europe. Many historical figures of maritime exploration have come from this region, and the maritime economy, such as fishing, remains very important to it. Spain comprises many regions that claim to have a distinct cultural heritage, such as the Basque region in the north. Spain is famous for its bullfighting heritage, which remains popular in the south of the country. Portugal lies on the west coast of the peninsula, and has only one political border, with Spain. Over a third of the country is forested, providing many resources to be exported around the EU. The majority of Portuguese people live along the coast, particularly around the capital, Lisbon.

MOROCCO

0   50   100   150   200 km

Gulf of
Gascony

FRANCE

ANDORRA

Gulf of
Lions

Irún
Donostia-San Sebastián
Bilbao
Vitoria-Gasteiz
Pamplona
Logroño
Soria
Ebro
Aragón
Jaca
3404 Aneto
Huesca
Sa de Guara
Tudela
Zaragoza
Calatayud
Monzón
Lleida
Manresa
Terrassa
Vic
Girona
Figueres
Cataluña
Costa Brava
Sabadell
Mataró
Barcelona
L'Hospitalet de Llobregat
1201
Reus
Tarragona
Calamocha
Alcañiz
Aragon
Guadalope
Tortosa
Golf de Sant Jordi
Jalón
Ebro
Serranía de Cuenca
Caimodorro 1920
2020
Cuenca
Millárs
Castelló de la Plana
Segorbe
Turia
Cabriel
Utiel
Valencia
Júcar
Cullera
Gandia
Villarrobledo
Albacete
La Mancha
Almansa
Alcoy-Alcoi
Cabo de la Nao
Villena
Elda
Hellín
Benidorm
Segura
1997
Elche-Elx
Alicante
Caravaca de la Cruz
La Sagra 2832
Murcia
Torrevieja
Costa Blanca
Lorca
Cartagena
Cabo de Palos
Baza
Huércal-Overa
Águilas
Vera
Almería
Cabo de Gata
Alborán

N

Balearic Islands

Minorca
Ciutadella de Menorca
Mahón
Puig Major 1445
Alcúdia
Palma de Mallorca
Mánacor
Majorca

Golfo de Valencia

Ibiza
Ibiza
Formentera

Mediterranean
Sea

ALGERIA

Originating in Andalucia, flamenco combines guitar playing and handclapping in a colourful musical dance style. With contemporary variations, it has spread worldwide and there are now more flamenco schools in Japan than there are in Spain.

Spain has the two richest football clubs in the world – Madrid and Barcelona. Rivalry between the two teams is long-standing and strong, with any matches between them called El Clásico.

The palace and fortress of Alhambra in Granada, is one of Spain's most treasured sites. It was built as a fortress and converted to a royal palace in 1333.

Italy and Switzerland

Italy occupies a peninsula in southern Europe extending out into the Mediterranean Sea. The Alps share the border with Switzerland in the north, and the Apennines run along the peninsula. The majority of Italians live in the north of the country, whilst the capital, Rome, lies centrally, on the Mediterranean coast. Italy is world famous for its wine, fashion and cars. The Vatican City, within Rome, is both an independent city-state, and the official residence of the Pope, the head of the Roman Catholic Church. Whilst the Vatican City has no official army, the Pope is protected by the Swiss Guard. Switzerland has a reputation for being politically neutral and is not an EU member. The Alps provide a major tourist attraction in both winter and summer.

Venetian glass is renowned worldwide for its colour and skilled craftsmanship. Production is centred on the island of Murano where centuries-old traditions of glass making continue to produce goblets, vases, jewellery, chandeliers and other decorative glasswork for tourists and collectors.

Fondue is promoted as the Swiss national dish but it originally came from an area covering Switzerland, France and Italy. Traditionally bread is dipped into cheese that has been melted in a communal pot, but fondues have since been expanded to include meat, and also chocolate-dipped fruit.

Highest

The Jungfrau Railway in Switzerland takes passengers to Europe's highest railway station, climbing a height of 1.4 km in 50 minutes.

Volcano

Southern Italy has the only three active volcanoes in Europe outside of Iceland. Etna and Stromboli experience continuous activity whilst Mount Vesuvius – the only active volcano on mainland Europe – last erupted in 1944.

Italy is the world's largest producer of grapes. It is also the world's second largest producer of wine, closely following France.

Strait of Otranto

I o n i a n   S e a

Pasta ranks top as 'the world's favourite food', and is the basis of many family favourites such as spaghetti Bolognese and lasagne. Easy to transport, quick to cook, and with a long shelf life, it is a useful and versatile food. Italy is the world's top pasta producer and it is also the top pasta consumer, with an average consumption of 26 kg per person a year – far outranking the second highest, Venezuela, at 12 kg.

Gulf of Taranto

T y r r h e n i a n   S e a

M e d i t e r r a n e a n   S e a

Italy is renowned as a manufacturer of luxury sports cars. Italian-designed concept cars showcasing new styling or technology are regularly unveiled at motor shows worldwide. It also has a leading reputation as a centre of fashion and textile design, with two Italian cities – Milan and Rome – amongst the 'big five' global fashion capitals of the world.

Sicily

Sardinia
(Italy)

A-maze-ing!

Covering 7 hectares, a labyrinth at Fontanellato, near Parma in Italy, is the largest bamboo maze in the world. The design is based on mazes depicted in Roman mosaics.

The AD 80 Colosseum of Rome, where gladiators fought to the death, was the largest amphitheatre in the Roman Empire. It seated around 50,000 people – about the same as many modern football stadiums.

0   50   100   150   200 km

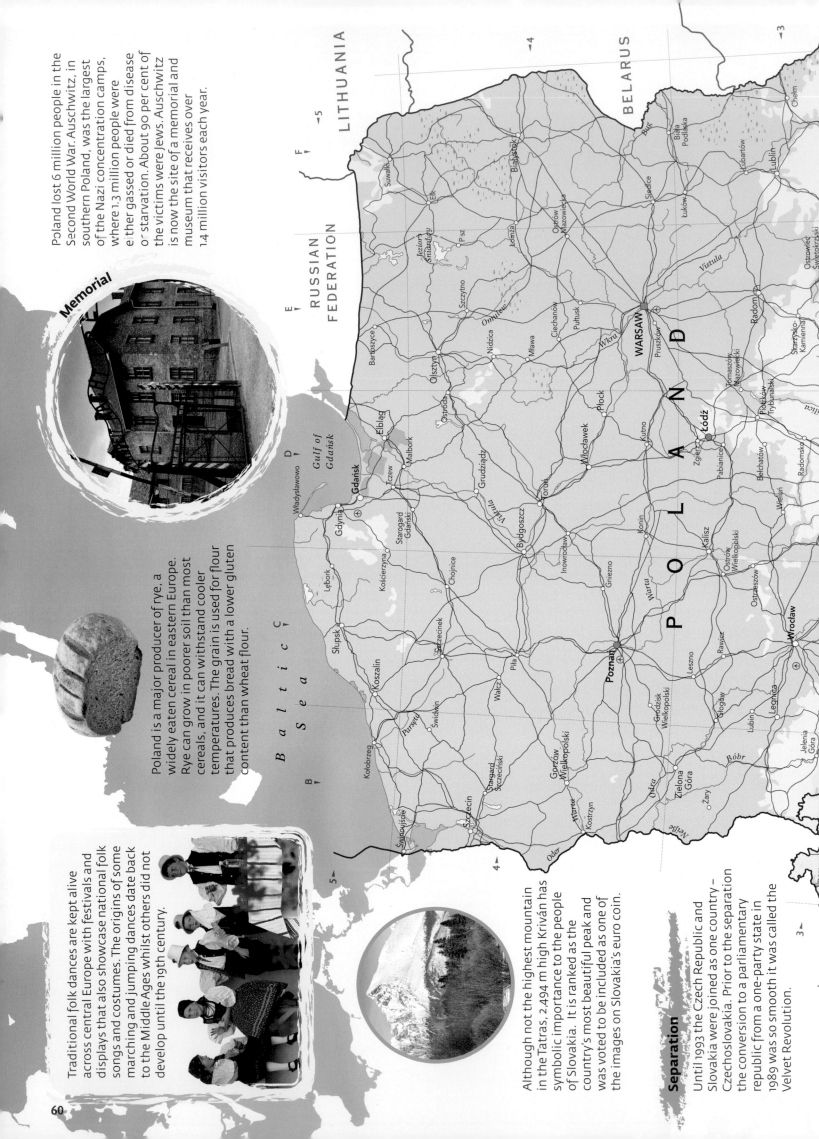

Poland lost 6 million people in the Second World War. Auschwitz, in southern Poland, was the largest of the Nazi concentration camps, where 1.3 million people were either gassed or died from disease or starvation. About 90 per cent of the victims were Jews. Auschwitz is now the site of a memorial and museum that receives over 1.4 million visitors each year.

Memorial

Poland is a major producer of rye, a widely eaten cereal in eastern Europe. Rye can grow in poorer soil than most cereals, and it can withstand cooler temperatures. The grain is used for flour that produces bread with a lower gluten content than wheat flour.

Traditional folk dances are kept alive across central Europe with festivals and displays that also showcase national folk songs and costumes. The origins of some marching and jumping dances date back to the Middle Ages whilst others did not develop until the 19th century.

Although not the highest mountain in the Tatras, 2,494 m high Kriváň has symbolic importance to the people of Slovakia. It is ranked as the country's most beautiful peak and was voted to be included as one of the images on Slovakia's euro coin.

Separation

Until 1993 the Czech Republic and Slovakia were joined as one country – Czechoslovakia. Prior to the separation the conversion to a parliamentary republic from a one-party state in 1989 was so smooth it was called the Velvet Revolution.

LITHUANIA

BELARUS

RUSSIAN FEDERATION

GERMANY

POLAND

Baltic Sea

Gulf of Gdańsk

Vistula

Oder

WARSAW

Gdańsk

Gdynia

Łódź

Poznań

Wrocław

Suwałki

Białystok

Ełk

Olsztyn

Elbląg

Malbork

Tczew

Władysławowo

Lębork

Kościerzyna

Słupsk

Koszalin

Kołobrzeg

Szczecinek

Chojnice

Bydgoszcz

Toruń

Grudziądz

Starogard Gdański

Inowrocław

Gniezno

Konin

Kalisz

Ostrów Wielkopolski

Leszno

Głogów

Legnica

Lubin

Zielona Góra

Żary

Gorzów Wielkopolski

Świdwin

Wałcz

Piła

Stargard Szczeciński

Szczecin

Kostrzyn

Gryfino

Świnoujście

Nidzica

Szczytno

Mława

Ciechanów

Pułtusk

Płock

Włocławek

Kutno

Zgierz

Pabianice

Bełchatów

Radomsko

Piotrków Trybunalski

Tomaszów Mazowiecki

Radom

Skarżysko-Kamienna

Kielce

Częstochowa

Wieluń

Ostrzeszów

Rawicz

Jelenia Góra

Wałbrzych

Świdnica

Ostrów Mazowiecka

Łomża

Siedlce

Łuków

Lubartów

Lublin

Biała Podlaska

Chełm

Zamość

Ostrowiec Świętokrzyski

Jezioro Śniardwy

Omulew

Wkra

Pilica

Warta

Warta

Bóbr

Odra

Nysa

Neisse

Parsęta

Liberec

Děčín

Bug

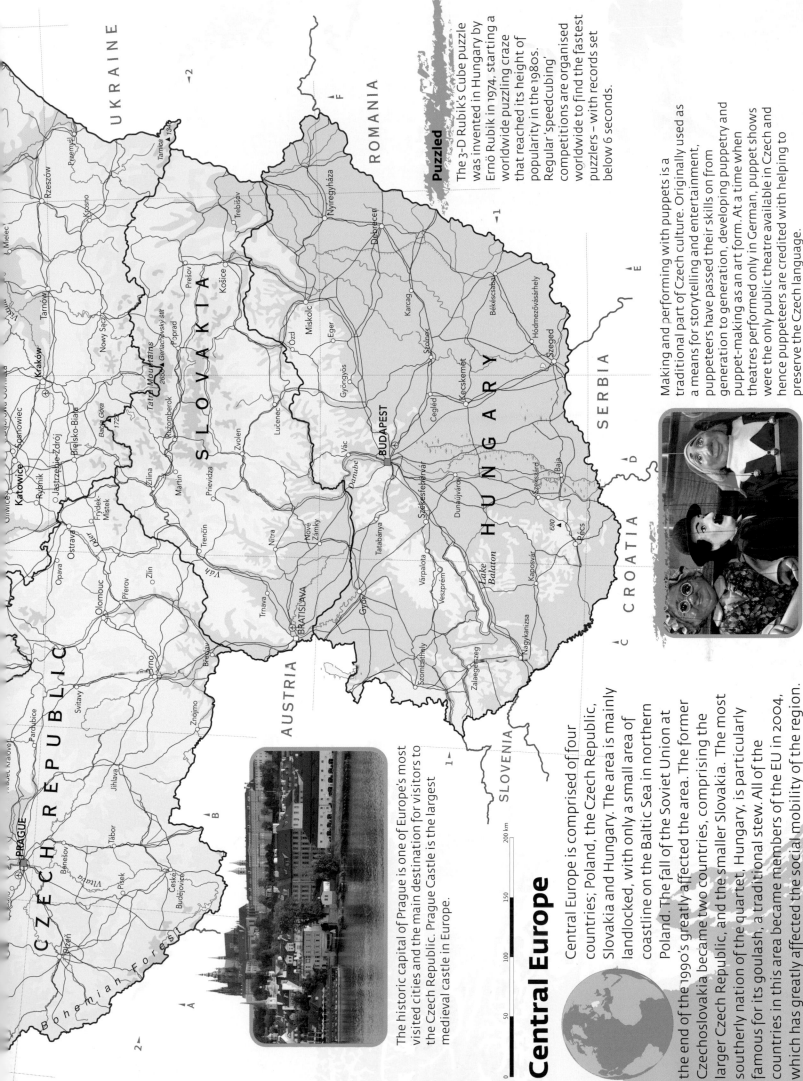

Central Europe

Central Europe is comprised of four countries; Poland, the Czech Republic, Slovakia and Hungary. The area is mainly landlocked, with only a small area of coastline on the Baltic Sea in northern Poland. The fall of the Soviet Union at the end of the 1990's greatly affected the area. The former Czechoslovakia became two countries, comprising the larger Czech Republic, and the smaller Slovakia. The most southerly nation of the quartet, Hungary, is particularly famous for its goulash, a traditional stew. All of the countries in this area became members of the EU in 2004, which has greatly affected the social mobility of the region.

The historic capital of Prague is one of Europe's most visited cities and the main destination for visitors to the Czech Republic. Prague Castle is the largest medieval castle in Europe.

Puzzled

The 3-D Rubik's Cube puzzle was invented in Hungary by Ernö Rubik in 1974, starting a worldwide puzzling craze that reached its height of popularity in the 1980s. Regular 'speedcubing' competitions are organised worldwide to find the fastest puzzlers – with records set below 6 seconds.

Making and performing with puppets is a traditional part of Czech culture. Originally used as a means for storytelling and entertainment, puppeteers have passed their skills on from generation to generation, developing puppetry and puppet-making as an art form. At a time when theatres performed only in German, puppet shows were the only public theatre available in Czech and hence puppeteers are credited with helping to preserve the Czech language.

Southeast Europe

The region of Southeast Europe is notable for the large number of countries which are now incorporated into it, partly as a result of the break-up of Yugoslavia in the 1990s. At the present time, seven independent countries make up the region. The political situation in the area is tense and evolving, with Kosovo becoming an independent nation as late as 2008. However, it is still unrecognized by Serbia, in which it was formerly incorporated. The 1990s were marked by conflict and civil war in the region, which cost hundreds of thousands of lives. The UN is still deeply involved in Southeast Europe. Nevertheless, the region has a fast-developing tourism industry, on which it is becoming more reliant.

A popular black or brown-spotted pet, the Dalmatian dog is believed to come from the Dalmatia region of Croatia, although its exact origin is uncertain. Puppies are born with plain white coats and the spots develop when they are about three weeks old.

A rebuilt bridge in Mostar symbolises hope for the future, and is one of the most recognizable landmarks of Bosnia and Herzegovina. The original 16th-century bridge was destroyed by tank-fire in 1993 during the Croat-Bosniak War and the replacement was built with the help of international funding.

Serbia is a major producer and exporter of high-quality raspberries. Intensive plantations give high yields, providing valuable income and employment in rural areas. About 90 per cent of production is frozen for export, with the remainder sold either fresh or processed.

BULGARIA

KOSOVO

PRIŠTINA

Kuršumlija
Leskovac
Vranje
Novi Pazar
Kosovska
Mitrovica
Peć
Bijelo Polje

MONTENEGRO

2522

Nikšić
PODGORICA
Cetinje
Bar
Lake Skutari
Shkodër
2694
Maja Jezercë

Tara

Metković
Dubrovnik

Korčula
Mljet

C

Adriatic Sea

MACEDONIA
(F.Y.R.O.M.)

SKOPJE
Tetovo
Gostivar
Kičevo
Veles
Kumanovo
Kočani
Strumica
Vardar
Prilep
Bitola
Gevgelija
2650
Bistra

Prizren
Debar
Ohrid
Lake Ohrid
Lake Prespa

ALBANIA

TIRANA
Lezhë
Durrës
Lushnjë
Elbasan
Peshkopi
Berat
Patos
Vlorë
Korçë
Gjirokastër
Sarandë

GREECE

ITALY

Strait of Otranto

Deepest

At 1,300 m deep the Tara River Canyon in Montenegro is the deepest river canyon in Europe. High levels of water flow and roaring cascades make it an adventurous destination for white-water rafting.

Croatia's high-quality stone provided the white limestone columns of the White House in Washington D.C., USA. Most of the stone for export comes from quarries on the Adriatic coast.

There are over 1,300 islands in the Adriatic Sea, and about 95 per cent belong to Croatia – although many of them are only small rocks or islets.

Dubrovnik is the jewel of Croatia's coast, and one of the best-known tourist destinations on the Adriatic Sea. One of the world's most complete medieval walled cities, it nevertheless suffered from shelling between 1991 and 1992 as part of the Croatian War of Independence.

Celebration

National folklore is strong in Albania. Song and dance is celebrated at international festivals and every five years the Gjirokastër National Folklore Festival takes place in southern Albania. Regarded as the most important event in Albanian culture, it celebrates music dance and national costume with demonstrations and competitions.

0   50   100   150 km

Bulgaria and Greece

For hundreds of years, Bulgaria and Greece were bound together as part of the Turkish Ottoman Empire, which ruled the region until the nineteenth century. Now distinct nations, both are predominated by Christian orthodox religions.

Bulgaria has a strong agricultural tradition, but also a growing tourism trade, as the country boasts some of Europe's most extensive unspoilt beaches. It is an important transportation route between Europe and Asia. Greece is on the southern coast of Europe, and is made up of a mainland, as well as many small islands surrounding its extensive coast. A third of Greeks live around the capital, Athens. Greece gained early importance in classical times in the fields of science, politics and philosophy.

Historic

The first known evidence of the yo-yo is from ancient Greece, making it possibly the oldest known toy in history after the doll. It has since become a popular game in many cultures, with different names, such as 'walking the dog', for different techniques and tricks. As with many toys it has undergone rises and falls in popularity, but current yo-yo culture embraces the toy with international competitions and on-going technical advances in construction.

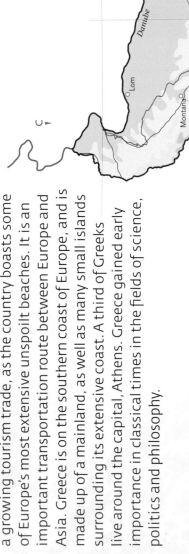

Presenting bread and salt to welcome guests is a Slavic tradition with variations across many countries. In Bulgaria most meals are accompanied by bread but special, flat bread called pogacha is used to express hospitality. It is usually presented by women, and guests are expected to take a piece and dip it in salt before eating it.

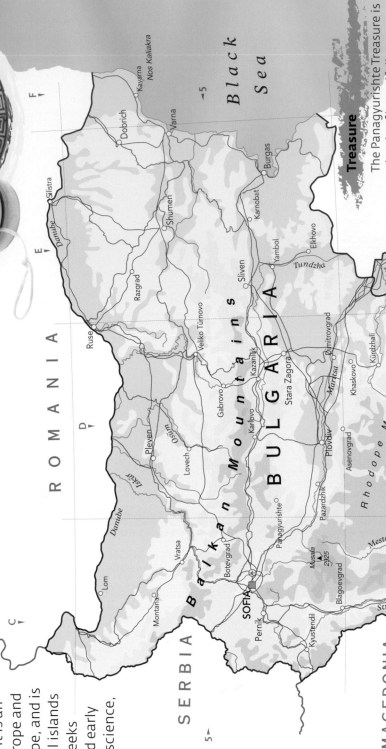

Treasure

The Panagyurishte Treasure is a horde of beautifully decorated golden artefacts discovered by three brothers in central Bulgaria in 1949. Dating back over 2,000 years, it is one of the most valuable collections in Bulgaria's National Museum of History. In 2012 many more golden treasures of a similar age were found by archaeologists in northern Bulgaria, including rings, snake-head bracelets and buttons.

Black Sea

ROMANIA

SERBIA

Balkan Mountains

BULGARIA

SOFIA

Rhodope Mountains

MACEDONIA
(F.Y.R.O.M.)

ALBANIA

Nos Kaliakra
Kavarna
Dobrich
Varna
Silistra
Shumen
Burgas
Karnobat
Razgrad
Sliven
Elkhovo
Ruse
Veliko Turnovo
Yambol
Tundzha
Gabrovo
Kazanlŭk
Stara Zagora
Dimitrovgrad
Ardas
Karlovo
Maritsa
Kŭrdzhali
Komotini
Pleven
Lovech
Osŭm
Panagyurishte
Plovdiv
Khaskovo
Xanthi
Alexandroupoli
Lom
Vratsa
Botevgrad
Pazardzhik
Asenovgrad
Smolyan
Drama
Thasos
Montana
Pernik
Blagoevgrad
Mesta
Serres
Kavala
Samothraki
Thrakiko Pelagos
Kyustendil
Struma
Petrich
Sandanski
Strimonas
Akra Arapis
Musala
2925
Iskŭr
Danube
Kilkis
Polykastro
Thessaloníki
Polygyros
Kalamaria
Edessa
Veroia
Lake Prespa
Floŗina
Kastoria
Kozani
Katerini
Aliakmonas

64

Straits

GREECE

Aegean

Cyclades

Dodecanese

Ionian Sea

Ionian Islands

Krytiko Pelagos

Mediterranean Sea

Pindus Mountains

Corfu
Kerkyra
Igoumenitsa
Ioannina
Preveza
Arta
Lefkada
Cephalonia
Zakynthos
Zakynthos
Kyparissia
Pylos
Pyrgos
Patras
Mesolongi
Karpenisi
Karditsa
Trikala
Larisa
Volos
1978
Olti 2152
Lamia
Amfissa
Levadeia
Parnassos 2457
Agios Konstantinos
Chalkida
Maliakos Kolpos
Acheloos
Pinelos
Patraikos Kolpos
Gulf of Corinth
Corinth
Megara
Nea Ionia
Piraeus
ATHENS
Agios Dimitrios
Marathonas
Akra Kalifreas
Evvoia
Skopelos
Voreioi Sporades
Skyros
Agios Efstatios
Lesbos
Mytilini
Chios
Chios
Psara
Izmir Körfezi
Samos
Ikaria
Amorgos
Naxos
Ios
Thira (Santorini)
Paros
Syros
Ermoupoli
Tinos
Andros
Kea
Kythnos
Milos
Kyllini 2376
Tripoli
Sparti
Kalamata
Na'plio
Aigina
Neapoli
Akra Maleas
Lakonikos Kolpos
Akra Tainaro
Messiniakos Kolpos
Kythira
Antikythira
Kos
Rhodes
Rhodes
Lindos
Karpathos
Kasos
Crete
Iraklion
Agios Nikolaos
Siteia
Rethymno
Chania
Kasteli
Akra Spatha
Idi 2456
Daras

150 km
0 50 100

Santorini, also known as Thira, is the most visited Greek island, followed by Crete and Corfu.

An acropolis is a fortress built on high ground to protect a settlement – and the Acropolis above Athens is the world's most famous example. Containing several ancient buildings, including the 438 BC temple of the Parthenon, it stands as a symbol of Greece's golden age.

Crumbly white feta is a traditional Greek cheese made from sheep's milk. Within the European Union only cheeses produced in a traditional way made from sheep's milk, or a mixture of sheep's and goat's milk, in certain parts of Greece, may use the name 'feta'.

Ukraine, Moldova and Romania

Both Ukraine and Romania border the northern coast of the Black Sea, whilst Moldova is land locked between them. All three have become democracies with the last twenty five years. The Ukraine and Moldova retain strong cultural and economic links with Russia as a result of their history within the Soviet Union. The Ukraine is generally flatland, and is the world's largest producer of sunflower seeds. Moldova is largely defined in physiology by rivers, with the Prut in the west, and the Dniester in the east. Below Moldova, and on Romania's border with the Ukraine, is the Danube Delta, the best-preserved wetland in Europe. This is very important to Romania's agriculture industry, as well as hosting over 300 species of birds, and being a designated UNESCO World Heritage site.

Although named after the Ukrainian city, chicken Kiev was invented in Moscow. The popular dish consists of chicken filled with garlic butter and coated in breadcrumbs.

The Painted Monasteries of Bucavina in northeast Romania are marvels of Byzantine art. The 15th and 16th century frescoes depict saints, prophets, angels and demons in a harmonious blend of colours.

The Sea of Azov, which is shared between Ukraine and the Russian Federation, is the shallowest sea in the world.

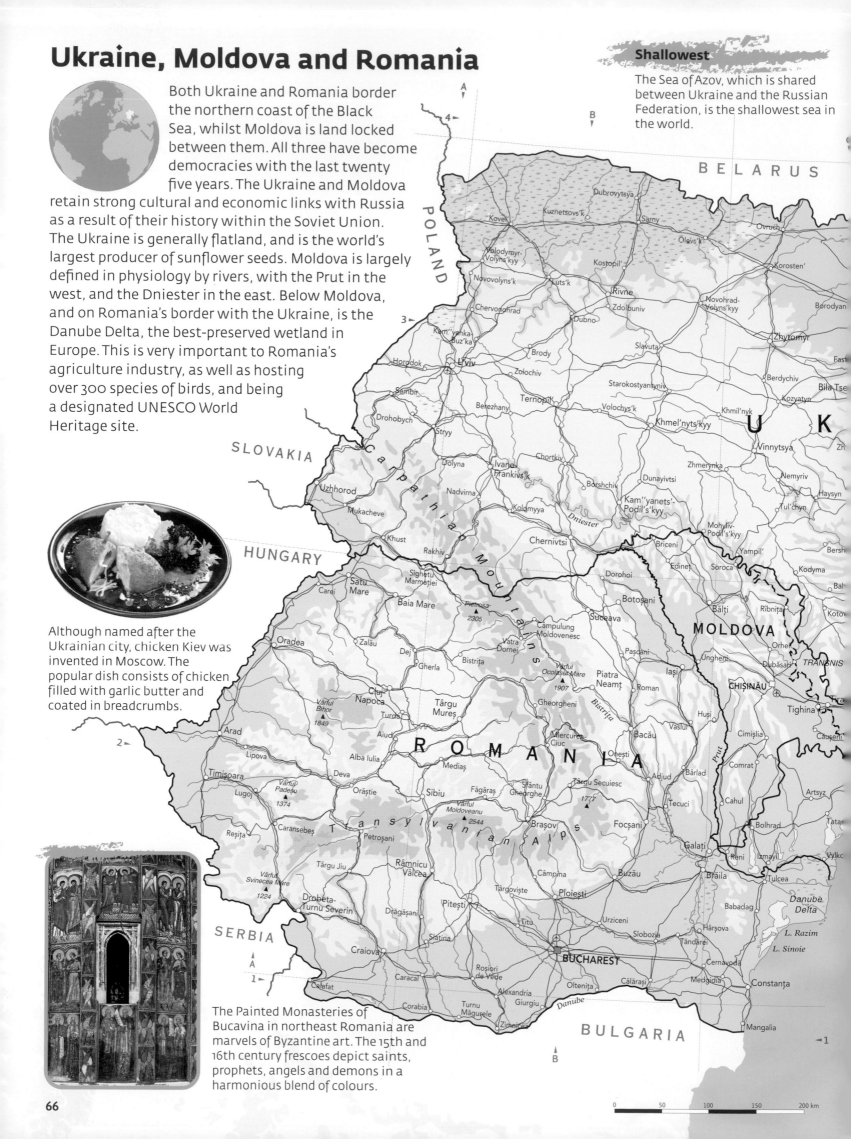

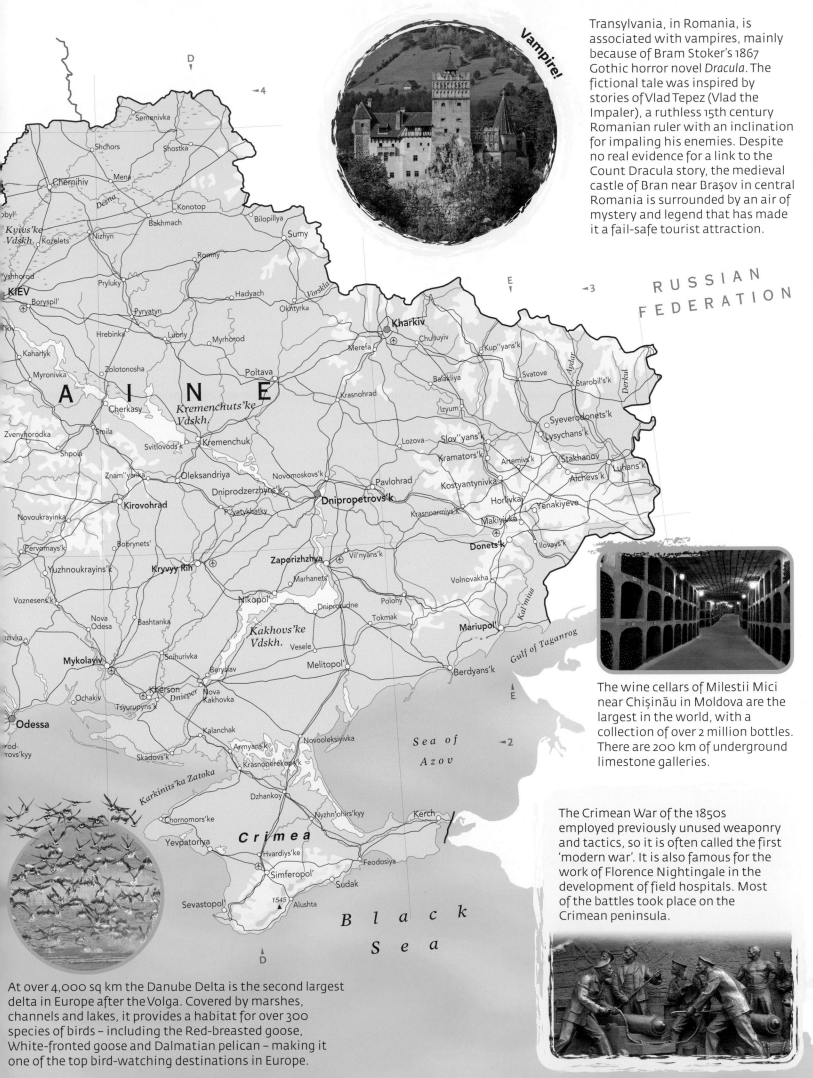

Vampire!

Transylvania, in Romania, is associated with vampires, mainly because of Bram Stoker's 1867 Gothic horror novel *Dracula*. The fictional tale was inspired by stories of Vlad Tepez (Vlad the Impaler), a ruthless 15th century Romanian ruler with an inclination for impaling his enemies. Despite no real evidence for a link to the Count Dracula story, the medieval castle of Bran near Braşov in central Romania is surrounded by an air of mystery and legend that has made it a fail-safe tourist attraction.

RUSSIAN FEDERATION

The wine cellars of Milestii Mici near Chişinău in Moldova are the largest in the world, with a collection of over 2 million bottles. There are 200 km of underground limestone galleries.

The Crimean War of the 1850s employed previously unused weaponry and tactics, so it is often called the first 'modern war'. It is also famous for the work of Florence Nightingale in the development of field hospitals. Most of the battles took place on the Crimean peninsula.

At over 4,000 sq km the Danube Delta is the second largest delta in Europe after the Volga. Covered by marshes, channels and lakes, it provides a habitat for over 300 species of birds – including the Red-breasted goose, White-fronted goose and Dalmatian pelican – making it one of the top bird-watching destinations in Europe.

The European bison, or wisent, is the national animal of Belarus. Historically ranging all over central Europe and the Caucasus, they were hunted to extinction in the wild by 1919 and there are no pure-bred bison left. Some animals survived in zoos and following reintroduction herds of them once again roam semi-free, although they are artificially fed with hay in the winter.

Hunted!

Amber is fossilized tree resin formed millions of years ago. The Baltic region has the largest known deposits in the world, containing about 80 per cent of the world's known amber. Although best known for making jewellery and other decorative items, amber has many other uses.
- to make varnishes and lacquers
- to burn as incense
- as an ingredient in perfumes
- in folk medicine

The Kaali impact crater on the Estonian island of Saaremaa was probably formed when a meteorite hit Earth between about 4,000 and 7,000 years ago. There is a main crater about 110 m wide containing a circular lake, and eight smaller craters created by the bombardment of broken meteorite pieces.

Lithuanian cuisine prides itself on its wide use of wild berries and mushrooms. There are over 400 varieties of edible mushrooms in the forests of Lithuania and whole families often go mushrooming together. The most prized variety is the King boletus which is used fresh, dried, salted or marinated, often in soups or sauces.

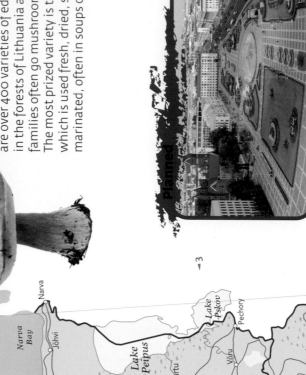

Planned

Minsk came under particularly heavy attack in the Second World War, losing roads, public buildings and over three-quarters of its housing. The rebuilt city stands as a monument to Soviet urban planning, with wide avenues, parks and squares.

Longest

The world's longest pipeline passes right across southern Belarus, transporting oil and gas from the Russian Federation to Poland, Germany, Ukraine, Slovakia, the Czech Republic and Hungary.

RUSSIAN FEDERATION

FINLAND

SWEDEN

Gulf of Finland

Baltic Sea

ESTONIA

LATVIA

Gulf of Riga

TALLINN
Narva
Narva Bay
Jõhvi
Rakvere
Lake Peipus
Tartu
Jõgeva
Paide
Võrtsjärv
Võru
Lake Pskov
Pechory
Rēzekne
Gulbene
Lubānas ēzers
Madona
Daugava
Ērgļi
Jēkabpils
Bauska
Garkalne
RIGA
Valmiera
Valka
Limbaži
Staicele
Karksi-Nuia
Viljandi
Haapsalu
Pärnu
Zvejniekciems
Jūrmala
Jelgava
Saldus
Mažeikiai
Liepāja
Ventspils
Kuldīga
Roja
Kolkasrags
Ruhnu (Estonia)
Saaremaa (Estonia)
Kuressaare
Orissaare
Hiiumaa
Kärdla
Käina
Vormsi

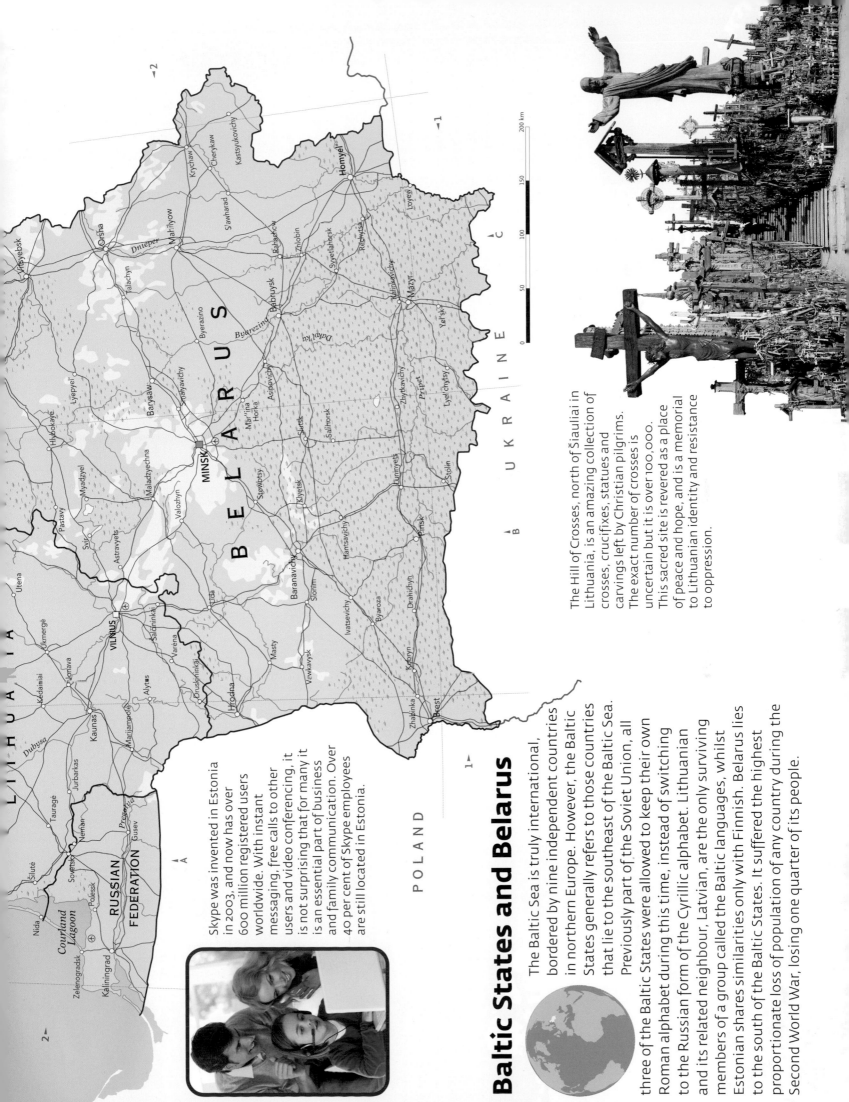

Baltic States and Belarus

The Baltic Sea is truly international, bordered by nine independent countries in northern Europe. However, the Baltic States generally refers to those countries that lie to the southeast of the Baltic Sea. Previously part of the Soviet Union, all three of the Baltic States were allowed to keep their own Roman alphabet during this time, instead of switching to the Russian form of the Cyrillic alphabet. Lithuanian and its related neighbour, Latvian, are the only surviving members of a group called the Baltic languages, whilst Estonian shares similarities only with Finnish. Belarus lies to the south of the Baltic States. It suffered the highest proportionate loss of population of any country during the Second World War, losing one quarter of its people.

Skype was invented in Estonia in 2003, and now has over 600 million registered users worldwide. With instant messaging, free calls to other users and video conferencing, it is not surprising that for many it is an essential part of business and family communication. Over 40 per cent of Skype employees are still located in Estonia.

The Hill of Crosses, north of Šiauliai in Lithuania, is an amazing collection of crosses, crucifixes, statues and carvings left by Christian pilgrims. The exact number of crosses is uncertain but it is over 100,000. This sacred site is revered as a place of peace and hope, and is a memorial to Lithuanian identity and resistance to oppression.

Asia

Arctic Circle

ARCTIC   OCEAN

RUSSIAN FEDERATION

- St Petersburg
- Moscow
- Perm
- Yakutsk
- Sea of Okhotsk
- Sakhalin

- Volgograd
- Chelyabinsk
- Omsk
- Novosibirsk
- Irkutsk
- Lake Baikal

Black Sea

GEORGIA
Ankara
TURKEY
ARMENIA
CYPRUS
LEBANON
SYRIA
AZERBAIJAN
ISRAEL
JORDAN
Baghdad
IRAQ
KUWAIT
Kuwait
Riyadh
SAUDI ARABIA
BAHRAIN
QATAR
UNITED ARAB EMIRATES
Muscat
OMAN
YEMEN
San'a
Aden
Socotra (Yemen)

Caspian Sea

KAZAKHSTAN
Astana
Aral Sea
Lake Balkhash
Almaty
Ürümqi

UZBEKISTAN
Tashkent
TURKMENISTAN
Ashgabat
KYRGYZSTAN
TAJIKISTAN

Tehran
IRAN
Kabul
AFGHANISTAN
Islamabad
Lahore
PAKISTAN
Delhi
New Delhi
Karachi

MONGOLIA
Ulan Bator

Shenyang
Harbin

Beijing
Tianjin

Lanzhou
Xi'an

CHINA

Chongqing

NORTH KOREA
Pyongyang
Sea of Japan (East Sea)
Seoul
SOUTH KOREA
Kobe
Fukuoka
Osaka

JAPAN
Sapporo
Tokyo

Nanjing
Shanghai
Wuhan

T'aipei
TAIWAN
Tropic of Cancer

Guangzhou
Hong Kong

PACIFIC OCEAN

NEPAL
BHUTAN
INDIA
BANGLADESH
Dhaka
Kolkata

MYANMAR (BURMA)
Nay Pyi Taw
Yangon

Hanoi
LAOS
Vientiane
VIETNAM

Manila
PHILIPPINES
Luzon

Mindanao
Davao

Mumbai
Hyderabad

Bay of Bengal

THAILAND
Bangkok
CAMBODIA
Phnom Penh
Ho Chi Minh City

South China Sea

Arabian Sea

Chennai

Sri Jayewardenepura Kotte
SRI LANKA
Colombo

MALDIVES

MALAYSIA
BRUNEI
Kuala Lumpur
Singapore
SINGAPORE
Putrajaya
Sumatra
INDONESIA
Borneo
Celebes
Makassar

Dili
EAST TIMOR

INDIAN OCEAN

Jakarta
Java
Surabaya

Equator

Red Sea

0   500   1000   1500   2000 km

Russian Federation

The Russian Federation consists of a huge northern sub-region of Asia, and a smaller area which lies in Europe to the west of the Ural Mountains. It is easily the largest country in the world, sparsely populated in the northern and eastern regions, densely populated in the west, and bordering fourteen different countries. Russia boasts a well-developed rail network system, which includes the iconic Trans-Siberian Railway, the longest railway in the world. The capital Moscow and the city of St Petersburg are favourite tourist destinations.

Matryoshka nesting dolls are sets of hollow wooden Russian dolls that fit inside each other. The first known set was carved in 1890. The outer doll is traditionally a woman but the dolls inside can be male or female. The innermost doll is usually a baby turned from a small solid wooden piece. Elaborately painted and brightly coloured, they make popular souvenirs for tourists.

Incredibly colourful, St Basil's Cathedral in Red Square, Moscow, is now a museum. Built in the 16th century, the city has grown up around it. Originally it was white to match the nearby Kremlin but in 1860 it had a makeover and has dazzled Moscow with its vivid colour scheme ever since.

Siberian, or Amur tigers are the world's largest cats. Once found throughout northern China, eastern Russia and the Korean peninsula, they were reduced by hunting and habitat loss to only about 50 animals in the 1940s. Conservation projects and anti-poaching efforts have helped increase numbers to nearly 500.

Largest

The coniferous forest of Siberia is the largest expanse of forest in the world.

Lake Baikal is the deepest lake in the world. The Baikal seal, unique to this lake, is the only true freshwater seal species.

Touring

Russian ballet is world-renowned. The Mariinsky Ballet (formerly Kirov) and the Bolshoi Ballet are both world-leading ballet companies, touring the world with classical performances and showcasing some of the world's finest dancers.

Connected

Istanbul is the only city in the world to straddle two continents. Two suspension bridges span the Bosporus, connecting Europe and Asia.

B l a c k   S e a

At over 550 years old, the Grand Bazaar in Istanbul is one of the oldest, and largest, covered markets in the world. Over 3,000 shops sell jewellery, carpets, clothing, furniture, spices and souvenirs to both locals and tourists.

BULGARIA

GREECE

İğneada Burnu

Edirne
Kırklareli
Babaeski
Lüleburgaz
Saray
Uzunköprü
Çorlu
Keşan
Tekirdağ
Şarköy
Gallipoli
Gökçeada
İmroz
Ezine
Çanakkale
Biga
Çan
Edremit
Balıkesir
Ayvalık
Bigadiç
Bergama
Soma
Akhisar
Aliağa
Menemen
Manisa
Turgutlu
İzmir
Bornova
Çeşme
Urla
Torbalı
Ödemiş
Kuşadası
Aydın
Nazilli
Söke
Milas
Bodrum
Muğla
Marmaris
Dalaman
Fethiye
Kaş

Saros Körfezi
Sea of Marmara
İstanbul
Bakırköy
Kartal
Yalova
Gemlik
Bursa
Mudanya
Bandırma
Mustafakemalpaşa
İnegöl
Susurluk
Simav
Kula
Uşak
Banaz
Sandıklı
Akşehir
Çivril
Pamukkale
Dinar
Denizli
Acıpayam
Bucak
Yatağan
Korkuteli
Kızılca Dağ 2591
Elmalı

Aegean Sea

Dardanelles

Sarıyer
Beykoz
Kadıköy
Kandıra
İzmit
Körfez
Gölcük
Adapazarı
Geyve
Göynük
Bilecik
Bozüyük
Sakarya
Eskişehir
Tavşanlı
Türkmen Dağı 1826
Kütahya
Altıntaş
Emirdağ
Afyon
Yunak
Akşehir Gölü
Gelincik Dağı 2799
Eğirdir Gölü
Isparta
Eğirdir
Beyşehir Gölü
Beyşehir
Seydişehir
Ilgın
İçeri
Bucak

Zonguldak
Ereğli
Düzce
Bolu
Mudurnu
Köroğlu Tepesi 2400
Gerede
Beypazarı
Polatlı
Sivrihisar 1819
Arayıt Dağı
ANKARA
Etimesgut
Kırıkkale
Keskin
Kaman
Şereflikoçhisar
Cihanbeyli
Lake Tuz
Karapınar
Konya
Beyşehir
Seydişehir
Karaman
Ereğli
Ulukışla
Kara Dağ 2288
Serik
Manavgat
Antalya
Alanya
Ermenek
Mut
Anamur

Antalya Körfezi

İnebolu
Bartın
Daday
Kastamonu
Karabük
Kurşunlu
Tosya
Çankırı
Kalecik
Yozgat
Yerköy
Akdağmadeni
Boğazlıyan
Mucur
Aksaray
Nevşehir
Hasan Dağı 3268
Niğde
Bor
Pozantı
Karaman
Tarsus
Mersin
Erdemli
Silifke

Sinop
Boyabat
Bafra
Samsun
Vezirköprü
Merzifon
Amasya
Çorum
Turhal
Tokat
Sungurlu
Kızılırmak
Delice
Kızılırmak
Kayseri
Erciyes Dağı 3917
Pınarbaşı
Binboğa Dağı 2917
Göksun
Feke
Kozan
Kadirli
Kahramanmaraş
Bahçe
Osmaniye
Gaziantep
Ceyhan
Adana
İskenderun
İskenderun Körfezi
Antakya
Samandağı
Kırıkhan

Yeşilırmak
Niksar

A n a t o l i a

T U R K E Y

P i s i d i a

Taurus   Mountains

0   50   100   150   200 km

Turkey and the Caucasus

Turkey occupies a large peninsula in southwest Asia. The south coast has a Mediterranean climate, but inland conditions are more extreme, with hot, dry summers and cold, snowy winters. The vast majority of the population is Sunni Muslim. Agriculture is still important to the economy, and Turkey is the world's largest producer of cherries, apricots and hazelnuts. The Caucasus region is to the east of Turkey, between the Black and Caspian Seas and has been the scene of some civic and political unrest. It comprises part of the Russian Federation, as well as Georgia, Azerbaijan and Armenia. The area is important for its biodiversity, boasting many different species of plants and animals.

ADMINISTERED AS NORTHERN CYPRUS
Cape Apostolos Andreas
Cape Arnauti
Kyrenia
NICOSIA
Mount Troödos 1951
Famagusta
Paphos
Larnaca
Limassol
CYPRUS

Mediterranean Sea

History

The origin of the term 'Caucasian', covering people from Europe, North Africa, Central Asia and South Asia, stems from the Caucasus as people from this region were believed to be the most typical example of the grouping.

Georgia is one of the world's oldest wine-producing regions, with archaeological evidence of viticulture dating back over 8,000 years. Climatic conditions are perfect for grape cultivation and many archaeologists believe that the region could be the source of the world's first cultivated grapevines.

Within Azerbaijan there are several hundred mud volcanoes on the coastal plain of the Caspian Sea – this is more than half of all the mud volcanoes in the world.

Turkish coffee is served dark, thick and very hot, and is drunk at most meals. The first coffeehouse in Istanbul is reported to have opened in the 1640s.

At the beginning of the 20th century Azerbaijan supplied nearly half of the world's oil. It now supplies less than 2 per cent but oil is still the mainstay of the economy and the basis of many heavy industries, accounting for the vast majority of the country's exports.

According to legend the soft flower-scented sweets of Turkish delight, or *rahat lokum*, were invented 500 years ago when the Sultan ordered a sweet-maker to create something for his harem. Usually served as cubes, they are flavoured with rosewater or citrus juice.

Mount Ararat, the highest peak in Turkey, is said to be the resting place of the biblical Noah's Ark after the flood subsided.

Mud

RUSSIAN FEDERATION

Caspian

Sea

ABKHAZIA
Sokhumi
Zugdidi
Kutaisi
Poti
Rioni
Bat'umi
Hopa
Borçka
Trabzon
Rize
Artvin
Giresun
Kaçkar Dağı 3932
Yusufeli
Şebinkarahisar
Gümüşhane
Bayburt
Tortum
Askale
Kara
Erzurum
Kelkit
Horasan
Ağrı
Erzincan
Tercan
Bingöl Dağı 3649
Karlıova
Hınıs
Malazgirt
Süphan Dağı 4058
Erciş
Arapgir
Tunceli
Keban Barajı
Murat
Elazığ
Kulp
Tatvan
Nemrut Dağı 2801
Lake Van
Van
Ergani
Silvan
Baykan
Başkale
Malatya
Adıyaman
Diyarbakır
Tigris
Batman
Kurtalan
Eruh
Hakkâri
Cilo Dağı 4168
Siverek
Karacalı Dağ 1957
Mardin
Cizre
Şanlıurfa
Viranşehir
Nusaybin
Akçakale

Caucasus

Tebulos Mt'a 4493
2379
Ivris Ughelt'ekhili
SOUTH OSSETIA
Tskhinvali

GEORGIA
T'BILISI
Kura
Rustavi
Balakän
Tashir
Alaverdi
Tovuz
Mingäçevir Su Anbari
Qax
Gora Bazardyuzyu 4466
Babadağ 3629
Quba
Siyäzän
Gyumri
Hrazdan
Sevan
Şämkir
Gäncä
Mingäçevir
Šamaxı
Sumqayıt
Çiloy Adası
ARMENIA
Art'ik
Ashtarak
Abovyan
Lake Sevan
Göygöl
Yevlax
Uçar
BAKU
Armavir
YEREVAN
Kälbäcär
AZERBAIJAN
Qazımämmäd
Şirvan
Mount Ararat 5165
Ararat
Yeghegnadzor
NAGORNO KARABAKH
CEASE-FIRE LINE 1994
Xankändi (Stepanakert)
İmişli
Muğan Düzü
Salyan
Dogubeyazit
Füzuli
Sisian
Läçin
Cälilabad
AZER.
Naxçıvan
Qazangödağ 3829
Kapan
Länkäran

Hirabit Dağ 3550
Artos Dağı 3537
Özalp
Mor Dağ 3807

IRAN

IRAQ

SYRIA

ASIA 75

Middle East

The Middle East is a region between Africa and mainland Asia that is often centred around the Arabian peninsula. It is made up of many countries, some of which are rich in natural resources such as oil. The largest country is Saudi Arabia, which is over 95 per cent desert. In the west of the country lie Mecca and Medina, Islam's holiest cities, which are visited each year by millions of Muslims on a pilgrimage known as the Hajj. To the north west of the region lies Israel, a majority Jewish state. It was created on Jewish holy land in 1948. Claims to the holy land by other world religions such as Islam and Christianity have led to much conflict in the region.

Evergreen

A highly symbolic evergreen tree, the Cedar of Lebanon is mentioned in the Bible more times than any other tree. It is named after the trees that grow on Mount Lebanon, where ancient groves are now preserved. As the Lebanese national emblem, it features on the country's flag and coat of arms. Over several thousand years the tree has had many and varied uses.

As one of the world's saltiest lakes, very little life can flourish in the Dead Sea – hence its name. Dead Sea mud is reputed to have therapeutic qualities. There are over 35 different minerals in the mud.

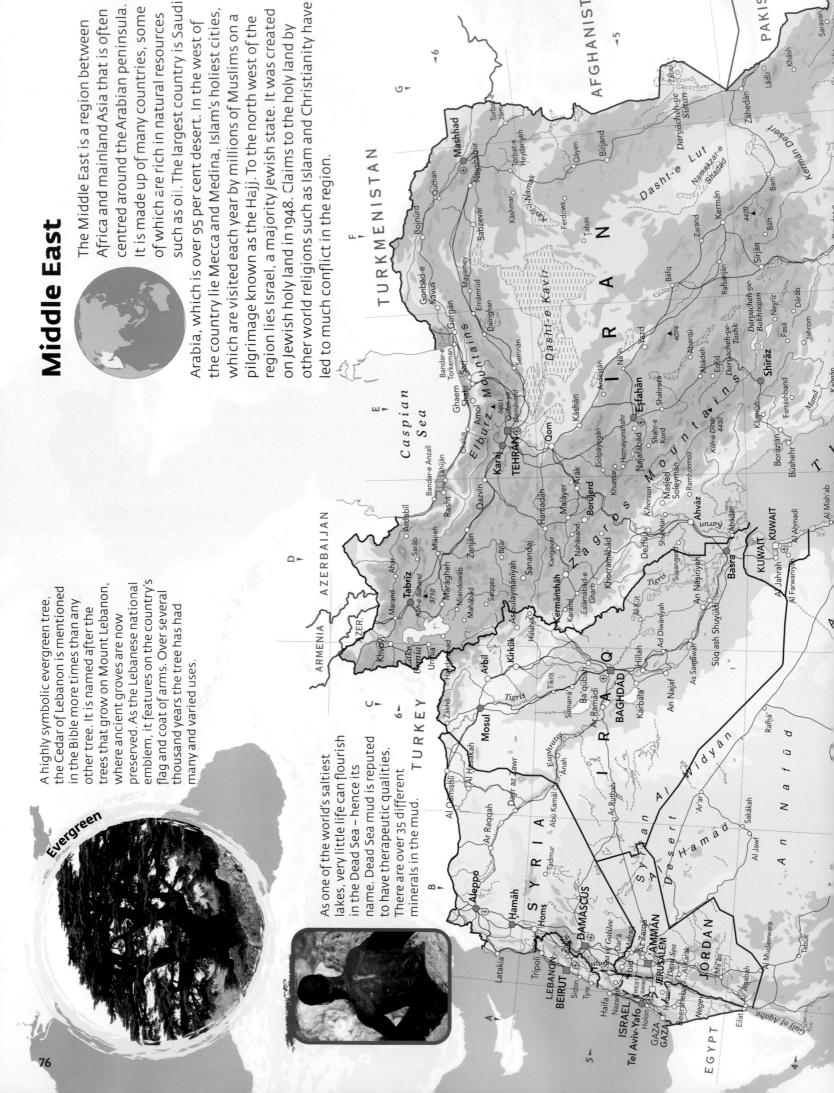

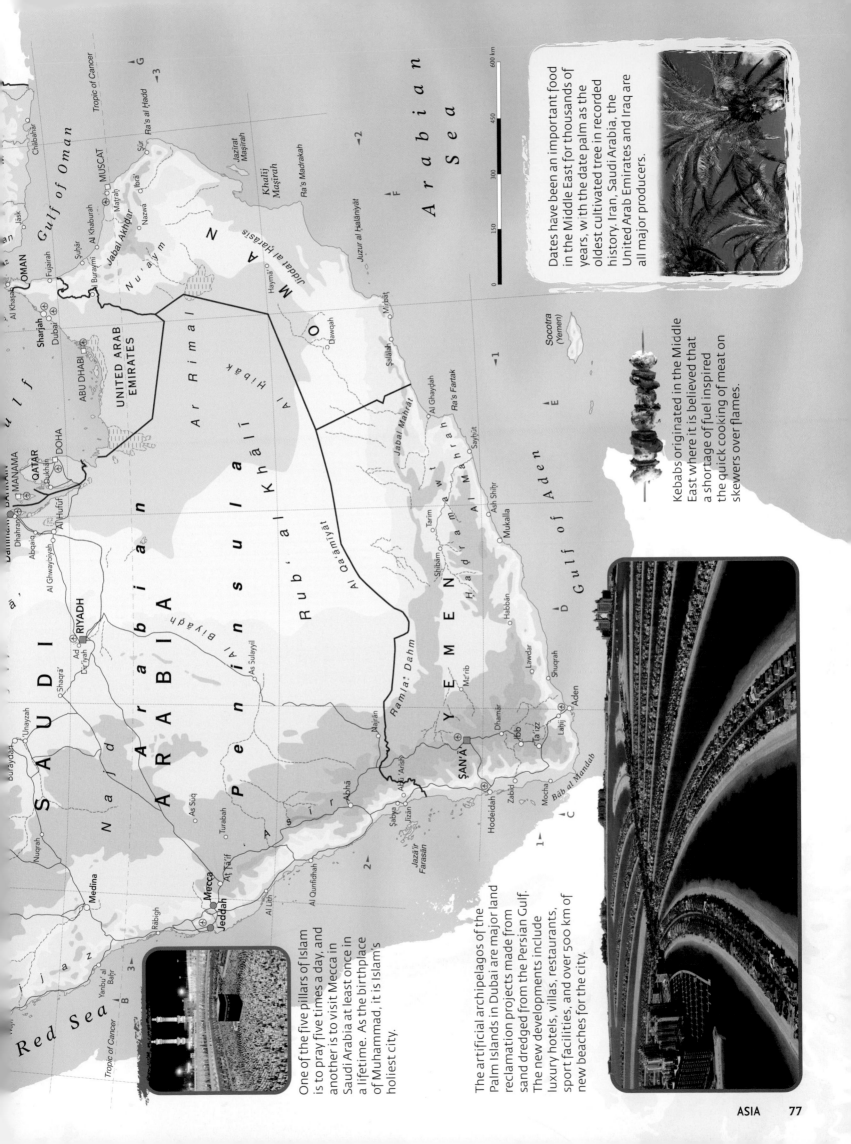

Dates have been an important food in the Middle East for thousands of years, with the date palm as the oldest cultivated tree in recorded history. Iran, Saudi Arabia, the United Arab Emirates and Iraq are all major producers.

Kebabs originated in the Middle East where it is believed that a shortage of fuel inspired the quick cooking of meat on skewers over flames.

One of the five pillars of Islam is to pray five times a day, and another is to visit Mecca in Saudi Arabia at least once in a lifetime. As the birthplace of Muhammad, it is Islam's holiest city.

The artificial archipelagos of the Palm Islands in Dubai are major land reclamation projects made from sand dredged from the Persian Gulf. The new developments include luxury hotels, villas, restaurants, sport facilities, and over 500 km of new beaches for the city.

Mosque

-stan
The six countries of central Asia all have the suffix '-stan' in their name, meaning 'the place of' or 'land'. The only other country with this suffix is neighbouring Pakistan.

The Silk Road is an historical network of trade routes that crossed central Asia between China and markets in western Asia and Europe. Silk and other goods such as gold and precious stones were traded. Many fine cities were built along the route. Samarqand, in Uzbekistan, was an important trading hub and is listed as a UNESCO World Heritage Site because of its importance at a crossroads of cultures, and for important buildings such as Bibi-Khanym Mosque, built in 1404.

Largest

Baykonyr Kosmodrome, in Kazakhstan, is the world's largest operational space launch facility. Sputnik 1, the world's first orbital spacecraft used Baykonyr, as did Vostok 1 in 1963 with Yuri Gagarin, the first man in space. It continues to be a well-used site with many scientific, military and commercial missions launched each year.

Ysyk-Köl, Kyrgyzstan's largest lake, is the second largest alpine lake in the world after Lake Titicaca, and the second largest saline lake in the world after the Caspian Sea. It never freezes, despite being surrounded by snow-covered mountains.

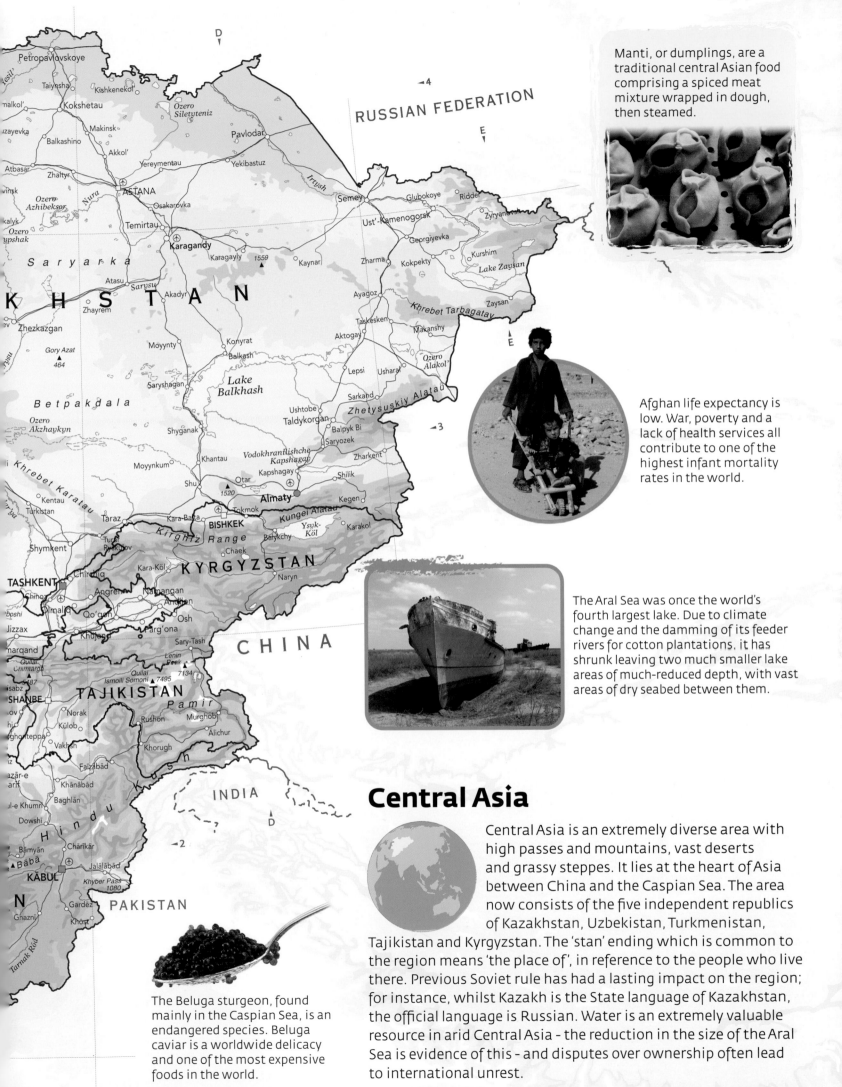

Manti, or dumplings, are a traditional central Asian food comprising a spiced meat mixture wrapped in dough, then steamed.

Afghan life expectancy is low. War, poverty and a lack of health services all contribute to one of the highest infant mortality rates in the world.

The Aral Sea was once the world's fourth largest lake. Due to climate change and the damming of its feeder rivers for cotton plantations, it has shrunk leaving two much smaller lake areas of much-reduced depth, with vast areas of dry seabed between them.

Central Asia

Central Asia is an extremely diverse area with high passes and mountains, vast deserts and grassy steppes. It lies at the heart of Asia between China and the Caspian Sea. The area now consists of the five independent republics of Kazakhstan, Uzbekistan, Turkmenistan, Tajikistan and Kyrgyzstan. The 'stan' ending which is common to the region means 'the place of', in reference to the people who live there. Previous Soviet rule has had a lasting impact on the region; for instance, whilst Kazakh is the State language of Kazakhstan, the official language is Russian. Water is an extremely valuable resource in arid Central Asia - the reduction in the size of the Aral Sea is evidence of this - and disputes over ownership often lead to international unrest.

The Beluga sturgeon, found mainly in the Caspian Sea, is an endangered species. Beluga caviar is a worldwide delicacy and one of the most expensive foods in the world.

Launched in 2012, the world's longest, fastest and steepest zip wire is in Pokhara, Nepal. At 1.8 km long with a vertical drop of nearly 610 m, it gives an adrenalin-packed 2 minute ride time at speeds of up to 140 km per hour – all with panoramic views of the Annapurna and Machhapuchare mountain ranges.

The Bengal tiger is the national animal of both India and Bangladesh. It is endangered with less than 2,500 left in the wild, over two-thirds of which are India and the remainder in Bangladesh, Nepal and Bhutan. One of the largest of the big cats, a male Bengal tiger weighs about three times more than an average human.

Highest

Eight of the world's ten highest peaks are in Nepal, including the world's highest mountain, Everest, at 8,848 m (29,028 ft) on the border between Nepal and China. Of the two most-used climbing routes up Everest, the southeast ridge from Nepal and the north ridge from China, it is the Nepalese route that is most frequently climbed. Over 3,000 individuals have climbed to the summit, with over three-quarters of ascents since 2000.

Indian pythons look threatening but they are not venomous. They kill their prey of small mammals, birds and reptiles by squeezing them, then after a heavy meal they may fast for several months - the longest recorded fasting period is 2 years.

South Asia

South Asia is bordered by multiple mountain ranges. The Himalaya in the north are the location of many of the highest mountains in the world. India is the largest and most populous country in South Asia, whilst the whole region is home to over 20 per cent of the total world population and is the most densely populated geographical region in the world. Although many countries have developed very quickly since the 1950s, poverty is still widespread across South Asia, particularly in rural areas where many rely on agriculture for their livelihood. South Asia has more than 2,000 ethnic groups, with populations ranging from hundreds of millions to small tribes.

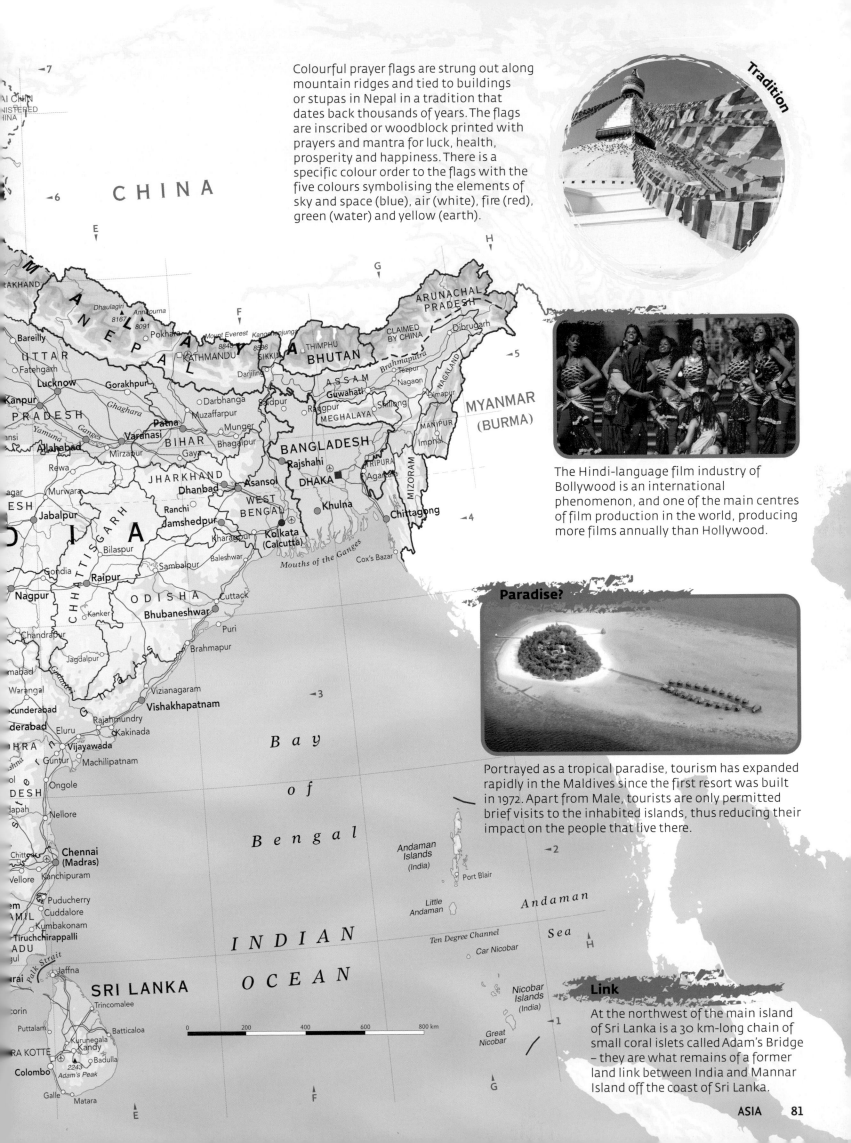

Colourful prayer flags are strung out along mountain ridges and tied to buildings or stupas in Nepal in a tradition that dates back thousands of years. The flags are inscribed or woodblock printed with prayers and mantra for luck, health, prosperity and happiness. There is a specific colour order to the flags with the five colours symbolising the elements of sky and space (blue), air (white), fire (red), green (water) and yellow (earth).

The Hindi-language film industry of Bollywood is an international phenomenon, and one of the main centres of film production in the world, producing more films annually than Hollywood.

Paradise?

Portrayed as a tropical paradise, tourism has expanded rapidly in the Maldives since the first resort was built in 1972. Apart from Male, tourists are only permitted brief visits to the inhabited islands, thus reducing their impact on the people that live there.

Link

At the northwest of the main island of Sri Lanka is a 30 km-long chain of small coral islets called Adam's Bridge – they are what remains of a former land link between India and Mannar Island off the coast of Sri Lanka.

Western China and Mongolia

The histories of China and Mongolia are closely linked, with Mongolia achieving independence from China only in the early twentieth century. The Gobi desert extends across the border between the two countries, and dominates southern Mongolia. Indeed, desertification is spreading in both countries, threatening both plant and animal habitats. As a result, the agricultural growing season is limited, and livestock is very important. Whilst Mongolia is the least densely populated country in the world, China is the most populous. Much of the population of western China and Mongolia is rural. In Mongolia, the rural landscape is characterized by nomadic herding using the traditional ger, or yurt – a heavy duty felt tent – as transportable accommodation.

Furthest

Within the Tarim Basin of the province of Xinjiang is the 'Eurasian pole of inaccessibility' – at 46° 17'N, 86° 40'E it is the point on Earth that is furthest from the sea.

KAZAKHSTAN

KYRGYZSTAN

TAJIKISTAN

AFGHANISTAN

PAKISTAN

INDIA

NEPAL

BHUTAN

MYANMAR (BURMA)

Altay Mountains

MON

Hövsgöl Nuur

Uvs Nuur

Har Us Nuur

Hyargas Nuur

Har Nuur

Döröö Nuur

Möron

Ulaangom

Altay

Uliastay

Tset

Bayanhong

Altay

Tacheng

Karamay

Pole of inaccessibility

Junggar Pendi

Ebinur Hu

Yining

Kuytun

Shihezi

Ürümqi

Qijiaojing

Turpan

Hami

Tien Shan

Aksu

Kuqa

Bohu

Bosten Hu

Kashi

XINJIANG UYGUR ZIZHIQU

Tarim Basin

Lop Nur

Anxi

Dunhuang

Yumen

GAN

Taklimakan Desert

Ruoqiang

C H I

Qilian Shan

Hotan

Qiemo

Altun Shan

Har Hu

Da Qaidam Zhen

Qinghai Hu

Kunlun Shan

K2 8611

AKSAI CHIN
ADMINISTERED BY CHINA

Golmud

QINGHAI

Plateau of Tibet

Derub

Gar

Yushu

H I M A L A Y A

Siling Co

Lharigarbo

X I Z A N G   Z I Z H I Q U

Nam Co

Qamdo

Salween

Mekong

Chang Jiang

Xigazê

Lhazê

Lhasa

Brahmaputra

Amdo

Mount Everest 8848

Kangmar

CLAIMED BY CHINA

INDIA

0 200 400 600 800 km

It may not be visible from outer space with the naked eye, as is often believed, but as the world's longest man-made structure the 8,852 km-long Great Wall of China is still an impressive structure.

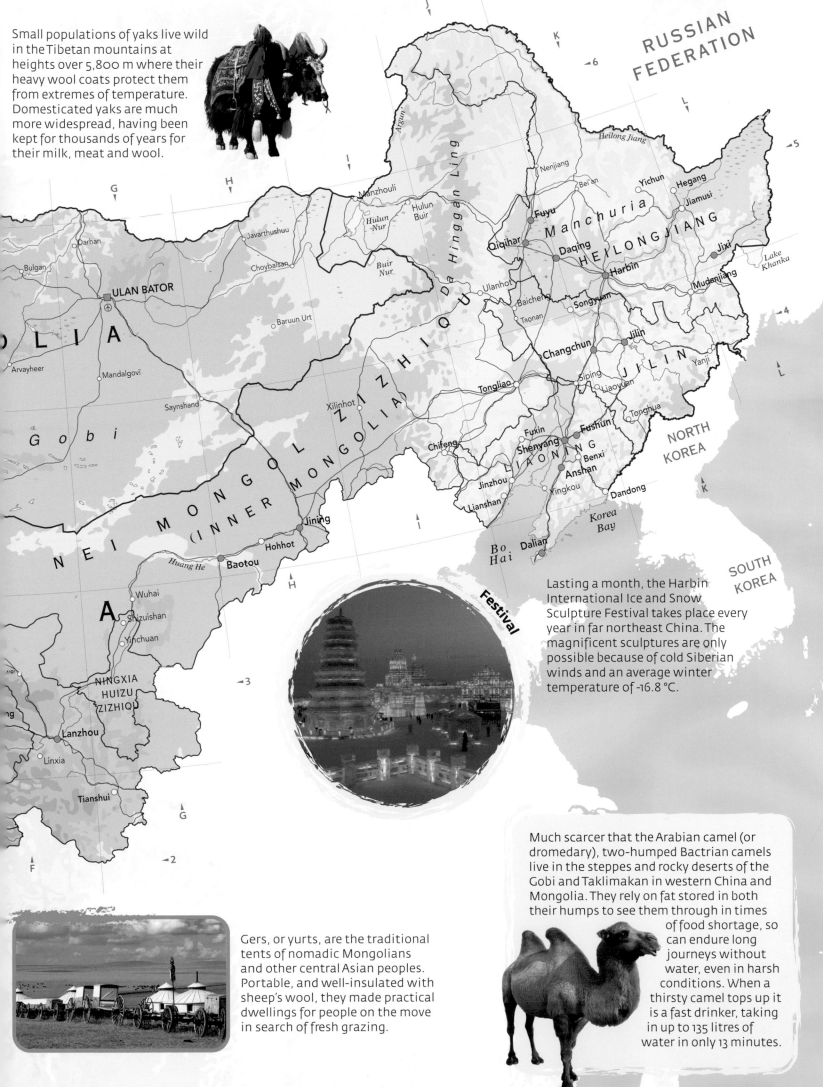

Small populations of yaks live wild in the Tibetan mountains at heights over 5,800 m where their heavy wool coats protect them from extremes of temperature. Domesticated yaks are much more widespread, having been kept for thousands of years for their milk, meat and wool.

RUSSIAN FEDERATION

Lasting a month, the Harbin International Ice and Snow Sculpture Festival takes place every year in far northeast China. The magnificent sculptures are only possible because of cold Siberian winds and an average winter temperature of -16.8 °C.

Gers, or yurts, are the traditional tents of nomadic Mongolians and other central Asian peoples. Portable, and well-insulated with sheep's wool, they made practical dwellings for people on the move in search of fresh grazing.

Much scarcer that the Arabian camel (or dromedary), two-humped Bactrian camels live in the steppes and rocky deserts of the Gobi and Taklimakan in western China and Mongolia. They rely on fat stored in both their humps to see them through in times of food shortage, so can endure long journeys without water, even in harsh conditions. When a thirsty camel tops up it is a fast drinker, taking in up to 135 litres of water in only 13 minutes.

Eastern China

Eastern China is a fast developing area. With an expanding infrastructure of roads and railways and also the construction of the Three Gorges Dam for hydroelectric power, the area is building on economic growth. The southeastern coastline is regularly affected by typhoons and drought is not uncommon in the fertile coastal plains. This area contains thirteen cities with a population of over five million people but the area is still predominantly agricultural, providing necessary food supplies for their people. Since the re-absorption into China of Hong Kong and Macao, these semi-autonomous zones have been important to the economy, and retain their own currencies.

Unique

Discovered in the province of Shanxi, the Terracotta Army is an astounding collection of over 3,000 life-size clay soldiers, 130 horse-drawn chariots, plus other figures, dating from the late 3rd century BC. They were buried with Qin Shi Huang, the First Emperor of China, to protect him in the afterlife. Exhibitions of some of the soldiers from the collection have travelled the world, drawing crowds of the public to participating museums.

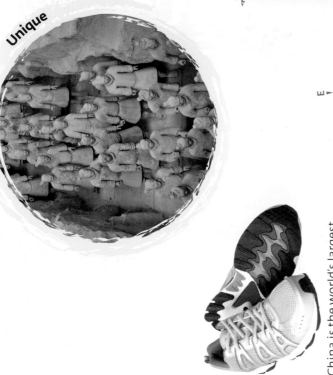

At the mouth of Chang Jiang (Yangtze), Shanghai is the world's busiest port. Over 2,000 container ships depart from its docks every month.

China is the world's largest producer of many consumer goods – including two-thirds of the world's shoes and 80 per cent of its toys.

Built in 2002, the Spring Temple Buddha in Henan province is the highest statue in the world at 128 m high.

Living in only a few mountainous areas of China, mainly in the province of Sichuan, the Giant panda has become an icon of international wildlife conservation. In the wild pandas require forests with a dense understory of bamboo, a habitat that has undergone serious decline.

NORTH KOREA

SOUTH KOREA

Yellow Sea

Bo Hai

Qinhuangdao
Tangshan
Chengde
BEIJING
Tianjin
Zhangjiakou
Datong
HEBEI
Baoding
Shijiazhuang
Taiyuan
SHANXI
Xingtai
Handan
Yangquan
Changzhi
Linfen
Baoji
Weinan
Xi'an
SHAANXI
Hanzhong
Huang He
Dezhou
Jinan
SHANDONG
Zibo
Weifang
Dongying
Shandong Bandao
Yantai
Weihai
Qingdao
Rizhao
Lianyungang
Zhangshu
Suqian
Yancheng
JIANGSU
Yangzhou
Suzhou
Bengbu
Huainan
Huaibei
ZHEJIANG
Shangqiu
Kaifeng
Zhengzhou
Anyang
Xinxiang
Jiaozuo
Luoyang
Pingdingshan
Nanyang
HENAN
Heze
Jining
Grand Canal
Linqing
Xintai
Zaozhuang
Tongshan
Fuyang
Nantong
CHINA
Jinsha Jiang

MYANMAR (BURMA)

LAOS

VIETNAM

PHILIPPINES

TAIWAN
China claims Taiwan as its 23rd province

Mobile
Hong Kong has highest percentage of mobile phone users, and one of the fastest average internet speeds in the world.

China is the world's largest manufacturer of fireworks. It is believed that they were invented in China about 2,000 years ago. Original firecrackers were bamboo shoots filled with gunpowder that were exploded to frighten away evil spirits. Liuyang, just east of Changsha in Hunan province is the modern focus of firework production, producing over half of China's output.

Although remote, the spectacular abstract patterns of terraced rice paddies draws photographers to Yuanyang in Yunnan province every year. Rice has been grown the same way there since the terraces were crafted over a thousand years ago.

ASIA 85

Japan and Korea

Japan is a volcanic mountainous island group off the coast of eastern Asia. It is made up of four main islands, with many smaller islands dotted around them. The area is also prone to earthquakes, with an earthquake in 2011 causing over 14,000 deaths. 98 per cent of the residents of Japan are ethnically Japanese, making it one of the most racially homogenous countries in the world. Most of the population is located on the largest island of Honshu. Japan has a huge technology sector, and boasts some of the biggest brands in the world. Before the Second World War a unified Korean state was controlled by Japan.

The 9.0 magnitude earthquake that struck Japan in 2011 was the most powerful quake ever known to hit the country, and the World Bank estimated it to be the costliest natural disaster in world history.

- it triggered a tsunami with waves over 40 m high
- it caused over 14,000 deaths, with thousands more injured or missing
- it moved the whole island of Honshu 2.4 m

Instant

The instant noodle was invented in Japan to combat severe food shortages after the Second World War. Originally considered a luxury item, the inventor, Momofuku Ando, went on to develop low-priced instant noodles in a cup in 1971 – and the 'pot noodle' was born.

Worldwide

Taekwon-do was developed in the 1950s in South Korea as a form of unarmed combat for the purpose of self-defence, and it has risen to become a highly respected form of martial arts worldwide.

Ginseng is widely cultivated in South Korea as a medicinal plant. The root is dried and used as a tonic.

Largest

Ocean Dome in Miyazaki, Japan is the world's largest indoor swimming pool. Measuring 300 m by 100 m, the sky-blue roof depicts clouds and there is a beach made of crushed marble.

CHINA

NORTH

P'YŎNGYANG

Sinŭiju
Huich'ŏn
Anju
Hyesan
Hamhŭng
Wŏnsan
Pukch'ŏng
Paektusan 2522
Kimch'aek
Ch'ŏngjin
Najin
Unggi
Tumen

La Pérouse Strait

Sea of Okhotsk

HOKKAIDŌ

Wakkanai
Monbetsu
Abashiri
Asahikawa
Kitami
Kushiro
Obihiro
Asahi-dake 2290
Hidaka-sanmyaku
Samani
Bibai
Yubari
Ishikari-wan
Tomakomai
Muroran
Sapporo
Otaru
Mori
Yakumo
Hakodate
Nemuro

Mutsu
Goshogawara
Hirosaki
Noshiro
Akita
Towada
Aomori
Hachinohe
Odate
Morioka
Miyako
Hanamaki
Kamaishi

Administered by
Rus. Fed.
Claimed by Japan

Sea of Japan

PACIFIC OCEAN

Divided

North Korea is technically at war with South Korea. The two Koreas are divided by the Demilitarized Zone (DMZ), a 4-km-wide strip of land that was established after the 1953 ceasefire of the Korean War. The DMZ is the most heavily militarized border in the world.

Japan is known for its high-speed 'bullet trains', which can reach top speeds of 442 km per hour, although the maximum operating speed is 320 km per hour.

In front of Shibuya station in Tokyo is one of the world's most famous, and busiest, pedestrian scramble crossings. When the lights turn red all traffic stops and pedestrians can cross in any direction.

The symmetrical peak of Mount Fuji, or Fuji-san, is Japan's highest mountain, and a well-known symbol of the country.

Scramble!

SOUTH KOREA

SEOUL
Kangnŭng
Ch'unch'ŏn
Ulchin
Kyŏnggi-man
Puch'ŏn
Inch'ŏn
Suwŏn
Andong
P'ohang
Songnam
Ch'ŏngju
Taegu
Pusan
Masan
Chinju
Ch'ŏnju
Kunsan
Taejŏn
Chŏnju
Chinju-san
1915
Kwangju
Mokp'o
Korea Strait

Cheju-haehyŏp
Cheju-do
Halla-san
1950

Ullŭng-do

Kyŏto
Niigata
Fukushima
Aizuwakamatsu
Kōriyama
Iwaki
Hitachi
Mito
Sadoga-shima
Nagaoka
Jōetsu
Utsunomiya
Maebashi
Ōyama
Tsuchiura
Kashiwazaki
Nagano
Ueda
Saitama
TŌKYŌ
Chiba
Kawasaki
Yokohama
Kōfu
Fuji-san
3776
Shirane-san
3192
Numazu
Shizuoka
O-shima
Izu-shotō
Hachijō-jima

Suzu
Nanao
Takaoka
Toyama
Matsumoto
Toyama-wan
Komatsu
Kanazawa
Fukui
Gifu
Nagoya
Toyota
Suzuka
Tsu
Ise
Hamamatsu
Tsuruga
Ōgaki
Kyōto
Ōsaka
Sakai
Matsusaka
Wakayama
Shingū
Biwa-ko
Kōbe
Maizuru
Wakasa-wan
Tottori
Matsue
Oki-shotō
Chūgoku-sanchi
Okayama
Hiroshima
Masuda
Shimonoseki
Tsushima
Hijashi-suidō
Iki
Kita-Kyūshū
Fukuoka
Kurume
Sasebo
Nagasaki
Ōmuta
Kumamoto
Kōchi-kaikyō
Seto-naikai
Takamatsu
Tokushima
Shikoku-sanchi
Kōchi
Uwajima
Kawatahama
Matsuyama
Shikoku
Kii-suidō
Ōita
Nobeoka
Kyūshū
Miyazaki
Kōra-gaku
1788
Kagoshima
Ōsumi-kaikyō
Ōsumi-shotō
Tanega-shima
Yaku-shima

Tokara-rettō

Amami-Ō-shima

Okinawa-shotō
Okinawa
Naha

Sakishima-shotō
Miyako-rettō

0   100   200   300   400 km

ASIA   87

Mainland Southeast Asia

Mainland Southeast Asia consists largely of two very prominent peninsulas: Indo-China, covering Vietnam, Laos and Cambodia; and the Malay Peninsula, occupied by Malaysia and by the southerly extensions of Thailand and Myanmar (Burma). The climate in

Southeast Asia is mainly tropical, hot and humid all year round with seasonal monsoon rainfall. The region is densely populated and the people are ethnically diverse and of mixed religion. Islam is widely practised by about 40 per cent of the population. The economy is heavily dependent on agriculture; however, manufacturing and service industries are fast becoming an important part of the economy. Tourism in particular is a key industry for the economic development of Southeast Asia.

The Mogok valley in northern Myanmar is the source of most of the world's finest rubies. They have been mined there for over a thousand years.

Thailand is the world's largest producer and exporter of natural rubber. Sticky white latex is collected from tapped rubber trees before being refined and processed. Over half of the rubber is used for wheel tyres and tubes.

Bangkok once had a network of canals, many of which have been filled in to make roads. Floating markets were once a way of life, but many now serve as tourist attractions. Vendors skillfully manoeuver their flat-bottomed canoes piled high with fruit, vegetables, prepared food and souvenirs, providing colourful photo opportunities to visitors as well as a traditional shopping experience.

Colourful

Water
Despite improving conditions, many women and children in Laos travel an average 10–15 km a day to fetch water, carrying up to 15 litres on each trip.

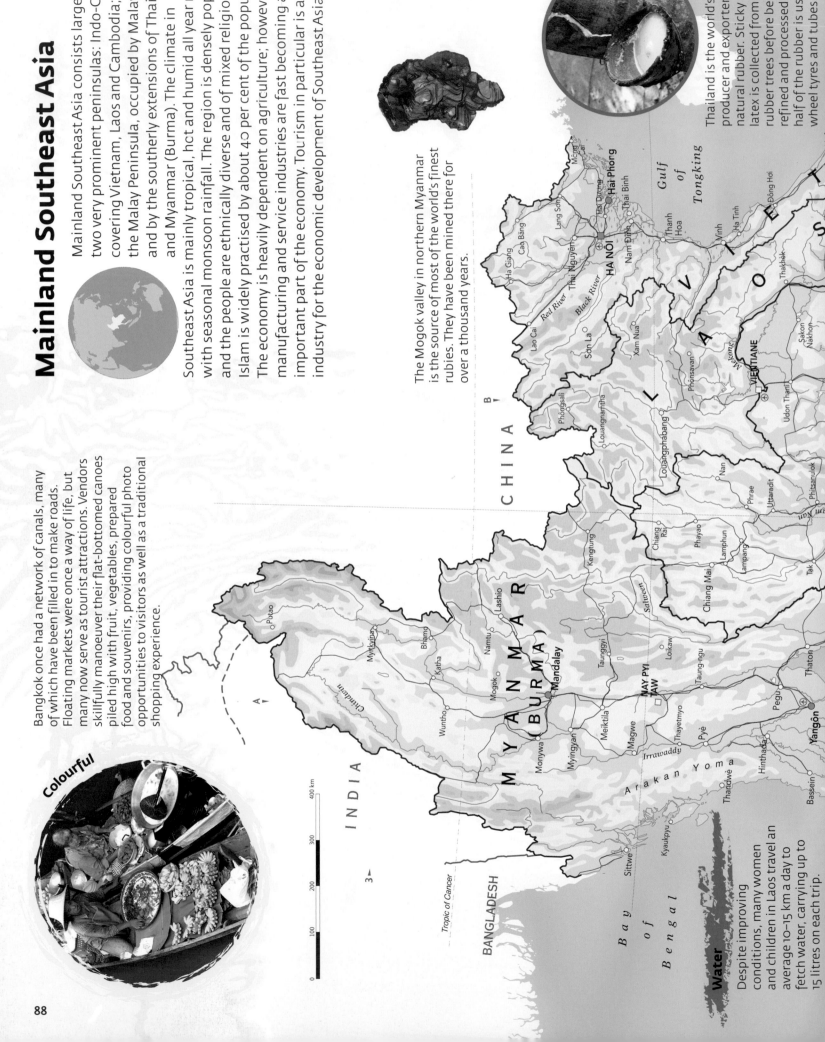

Over half of Thailand's cultivated land is used to produce rice. It is the world's largest rice exporter, with much of the yield being high-quality jasmine rice.

More humans depend on water buffalo than on any other animal. They were first domesticated in India about 5,000 years ago, and are now used widely across southern Asia, southeast Asia, and beyond. Although mechanization is increasing many animals are still vital on small family farms.

Seasonal

Monsoon rains cause changes in water levels that create an unusual seasonal cycle of water flow in and out of the Tonle Sap (Great Lake) in Cambodia. For almost half the year the river flows backwards into the lake, and for the rest of the time it flows the other way.

A traditional welcoming posture in parts of Southeast Asia is to press your palms together in front of the body and then bow. In Cambodia this is called a *sampeah* and it is traditional for younger or lower ranked people to initiate the gesture. In Thailand a very similar greeting is called a *wai*.

The 12th-century grand temple complex of Angkor Wat and Angkor Thom in Siem Reap, Cambodia is the world's largest group of religious buildings and is a major attraction for tourists. It features on the flag of Cambodia – the only building to feature on a country's flag.

Map labels

Quang Ngai
Quy Nhon
Tuy Hoa
Nha Trang
Buôn Ma Thuôt
Phan Rang-Thap Cham
Phan Thiêt
Đà Lat
Biên Hoà
Hô Chi Minh City
Tây Ninh
My Tho
Mouths of the Mekong

CAMBODIA
Stœng Trêng
Krâchéh
Kâmpóng Cham
Kâmpóng Thum
Prey Vêng
Siemréab (Siem Reap)
Tonle Sap
Bátdâmbâng
Poùthisât
Kâmpóng Chhnang
PHNOM PENH
Kâmpóng Spœ
Takêv
Kâmpôt
Long Xuyên
Cân Tho
Bac Liêu
Ca Mau
Mui Ca Mau

Ratchathani
Surin
Nakhon Ratchasima
Thiu Kaeo Phanom Dong Rak
Lop Buri
Sara Buri
Ayutthaya
BANGKOK
Rat Buri
Phet Buri
Chachoengsao
Chon Buri
Chanthaburi
Sihanoukville

Gulf of Thailand

Prachuap Khiri Khan
Chumphon
Isthmus of Kra
Surat Thani
Nakhon Si Thammarat
Phatthalung
Krabi
Phangnga
Takua Pa
Phuket
Songkhla
Hat Yai
Yala

Palaw
Myeik
Tenasserim
Rayong

Myerik Kyunzu (Mergui Archipelago)

Andaman Sea

MALAYSIA

Shadow puppets have a long history in southeast Asia. In Malaysia and Indonesia shadow puppet theatre is called 'wayang kulit'. Flat hand-painted puppets, made from thin sheets of buffalo leather, are manipulated by hand using rods connected to the puppet's moveable joints. The audience either watches from the other side of a screen to see a story unfold, or stays with the puppeteer to see the skill of puppetry in action.

The Philippines is the largest producer of pineapples in the world, as well as the second largest producer of coconuts and the third largest producer of bananas. Pineapples are a favourite fruit in many countries for eating, and for juice – but unlike many fruits, they do not ripen after they have been harvested.

Largest

Only a tenth of the population in Singapore owns a car, and the high demand for car ownership and usage is strictly controlled. Instead, an efficient Mass Rapid Transit rail system, with over 140 stations, is run in conjunction with bus and taxi services to provide a fully integrated public transport system.

East Timor became the first new country of the 21st century when it achieved independence in 2002. With over 40 per cent of the population below the poverty line, it is one of Asia's poorest nations.

South China Sea

Spratly Islands

Palawan

Brooke's Point

Balabac Strait

Bang

Kudat

Gunung Kinabalu
4095

Kota Kinabalu

SABAH

Lahad D

Sem

CAMBODIA

Andaman Sea

Gulf of Thailand

THAILAND

Kangar

Banda Aceh

Sigli

Bireun

Langsa

Pangkalansusu

Alor Star

Sungai Petani

George Town

Pinang

Butterworth

Taiping

Ipoh

Peninsular Malaysia

Kota Bharu

Pasir Putih

Kuala Terengganu

Dungun

Kuantan

MALAYSIA

BRUNEI
BANDAR SERI BEGAWAN

Miri

SARAWAK

Bintulu

Igan

Mukah

Sibu

Liku

Sambas

Kuching

Debak

Tanjungselor

Tanjungredeb

Medan

Tebingtinggi

Simeulue

Samosir

Prapat

Balige

Gunungsitoli

Nias

Sibolga

Temerluh

KUALA LUMPUR

PUTRAJAYA

Seremban

Melaka

Segamat

Keluang

Muar

Dumai

Minas

Johor Bahru

SINGAPORE
SINGAPORE

Natuna Besar (Indonesia)

Kepulauan Anambas (Indonesia)

Kepulauan Natuna (Indonesia)

Pemangkat

Serian

Sri Aman

Singkawang

Lubok Antu

Sangkulirang

Pulau-pulau Batu

Lubuksikaping

Payakumbuh

Pekanbaru

Kepulauan Riau

Kepulauan Tambelan

Mempawah

Pontianak

Borneo

Samarinda

Padang

Siberut

Sipura

Pagai Utara

Pagai Selatan

Kepulauan Mentawai

Pegunungan Barisan

G. Kerinci
3805

Sijunjung

Bangko

Jambi

Kepulauan Lingga

Belinyu

Sungailiat

Pangkalpinang

Bangka

Tanjungpandan

Belitung

Sukadana

Ketapang

Pangkalanbuun

Sampit

Amuntai

Balikpap

Kotabaru

Selat Karimata

INDIAN OCEAN

Sekayu

Palembang

Lahat

Toboali

Manggar

Banjarmasin

Laut

Bengkulu

G. Dempo
3159

Menggala

Tanjung Selatan

Bintuhan

Krui

Bandar Lampung

Java Sea

Enggano

Selat Sunda

Serang

JAKARTA

Bogor

Bandung

Cirebon

Bawean

IND

Madura

Kepulauan Kangean

Semarang

Surabaya

Surakarta

Cilacap

2608

3428

Probolinggo

Bali Sea

Yogyakarta

Malang

3676

3332

Jember

3142

Bali

Lombok
3726

G. T

Denpasar

Mataram

Su

Java

5443

Selat Lombok

Cocos Islands (Austr.)

Christmas Island (Austr.)

0   200   400   600 km

90

Maritime Southeast Asia

Almost all of Maritime Southeast Asia consists of a string of archipelagos which include the large islands of Java, Sumatra and Borneo. These archipelagos stretch west to east for almost 6,000 kilometres. The country of Malaysia is split between the mainland area, and the two territories of Sabah and Sarawak on the island of Borneo. Indonesia accounts for over 13,000 islands, many uninhabited. The Philippine islands make up the most northern group of islands in Maritime Southeast Asia. The entire region lies on the intersection of geological plates, and is one of the most volcanically active regions in the world. Both the Philippines and Indonesia are former colonies; the Philippines gained independence from the USA in 1946, whilst Indonesia achieved independence from the Netherlands in 1949.

Over half of Indonesians live on Java, making it the most heavily populated island in the world.

Komodo dragons are the largest, and most lethal, of all lizards, but less than 5,000 are left in the wild. They are found only on a few Indonesian islands, including Komodo, Rinca and Flores. Adults are over 3 m long, and can run at 24 km per hour, making them formidable predators that hunt and ambush their prey.

Wealthiest

Brunei is the wealthiest country in southeast Asia. It has the highest minimum wage, there are no taxes, and education and healthcare is free.

Deadliest

Found in the waters off Southeast Asia and Australia, Belcher's sea snake is the world's most venomous snake. Although it is docile and not all bites contain venom, those that do are enough to kill a human.

Map labels

Luzon Strait, Batan Islands (Philippines), Babuyan Islands, C. Engaño, Aparri, Tuguegarao, Ilagan, Bontoc, Bayombong, Pinatubo, Cabanatuan, Tarlac, Polillo Islands, PHILIPPINES, Quezon City, MANILA, San Pablo, Daet, Catanduanes, Batangas, Lucena, Naga, Calapan, Boac, Sorsogon, Mindoro, Legazpi, Irosin, Catarman, Romblon, Masbate, Catbalogan, Samar, Cuyo Islands, Pres. Manuel A Roxas, Tacloban, Panay, Iloilo, Bacolod, Cebu, Negros, Bohol, Tagbilaran, Surigao, Tanjay, Bohol Sea, Butuan, Dumaguete, Dapitan, Cagayan de Oro, Sulu Sea, Oroquieta, Pagadian, Mindanao, Cotabato, Davao, Zamboanga, Moro Gulf, Datu Piang, Mati, Isabela, Basilan, Davao Gulf, Jolo, General Santos, Tawi-Tawi, Sulu Archipelago, Celebes Sea

Philippine Sea, PACIFIC OCEAN, PALAU, MELEKEOK

Kepulauan Talaud (Indonesia), Kepulauan Sangir (Indonesia), Molucca Sea, Morotai, Tolitoli, Moutong, Manado, Tondano, Tobelo, Ternate, Halmahera, Sao-Siu, Gorontalo, Teluk Tomini, Kepulauan Togian, Labuna, Waigeo, Selat Dampir, Kwoka 3000, Manokwari, Biak, Tanjang d'Urville, Sarmi, Luwuk, Peleng, Bacan, Sorong, Jazirah Doberai, Numfoor, Yapen, Ransiki, Jayapura, Poso, Taliabu, Mangole, Obi, Misool, Salawati, Inanwatan, Teluk Cenderawasih, Memberamo, Celebes, Teluk Towori, Kepulauan Banggai, Kepulauan Sula, Dofa, Ceram Sea, Eafanlan, Teluk Berau, Babo, Tariku, Taritatu, Wotu, Malili, Seram, G. Binaija, Bula, Fakfak, Nabire, Pegunungan Maoke, Enarotali, New, PAPUA NEW GUINEA, Palopo, Piru 3019, Teluk Kamrau, Puncak Jaya 5030, Pk Trikora 4730, Pk Mandala 4700, Makale, Namlea, Ambon, Adi, Amamapare, Malamala, Manui, Buru, Anabanua, Kendari, Wowoni, Kepulauan Banda, Guinea, Kolaka, Kepulauan Kai, Wokam, Dobo, Kobroor, Makassar, Buton, Buton, Kepulauan Aru, Baubau, Kepulauan Tukangbesi, Banda Sea, Trangan, Sia, Pulau Selayar, Damar, Kepulauan Tanimbar, Pulau Dolok, Lompobattang 2871, Saumlakki, Tanjung Vals, Merauke, Flores Sea, Pulau Romang, Wetar, Babar, Selaru, Arafura Sea, Reo, Larantuka, Kalabahi, Alor, Huaki, Kepulauan Leti, Ruteng, Ende, EAST TIMOR, 2960 Foho Tatamailau, EAST TIMOR (TIMOR-LESTE), Savu Sea, 2427 G. Mutis, Kefamenanu, Timor, Timor Sea, Waingapu, Kupang, Sawu, Rote, AUSTRALIA

Indian Ocean

The Indian Ocean is the third largest of the oceans, containing approximately 20 per cent of the water on the Earth's surface. It is relatively warm and sheltered which made travel and trade across it easier than traversing the Atlantic or Pacific Oceans. Early traders made use of the seasonal monsoon winds to speed their sail craft between Africa and Asia. Today oil is the main commodity transported and the opening of the Suez Canal in 1869 shortened the journey to the west and made it safer than heading west around the Cape of Good Hope, or the Cape of Storms, as it used to be known. Safety has again become an issue with the increase in piracy off the coast of Somalia.

The 2004 Indian Ocean tsunami was the result of an earthquake off the west coast of Sumatra. It was the deadliest tsunami in recorded history, killing over 226,000 people in 14 countries, and leaving over a million homeless. Indonesia was the worst affected country, followed by Sri Lanka, India and Thailand.

oil

About 40 per cent of the world's offshore oil comes from the Indian Ocean, and its shipping lanes carry a heavy traffic of tankers from the oil fields, through the Gulf of Oman then all around the world.

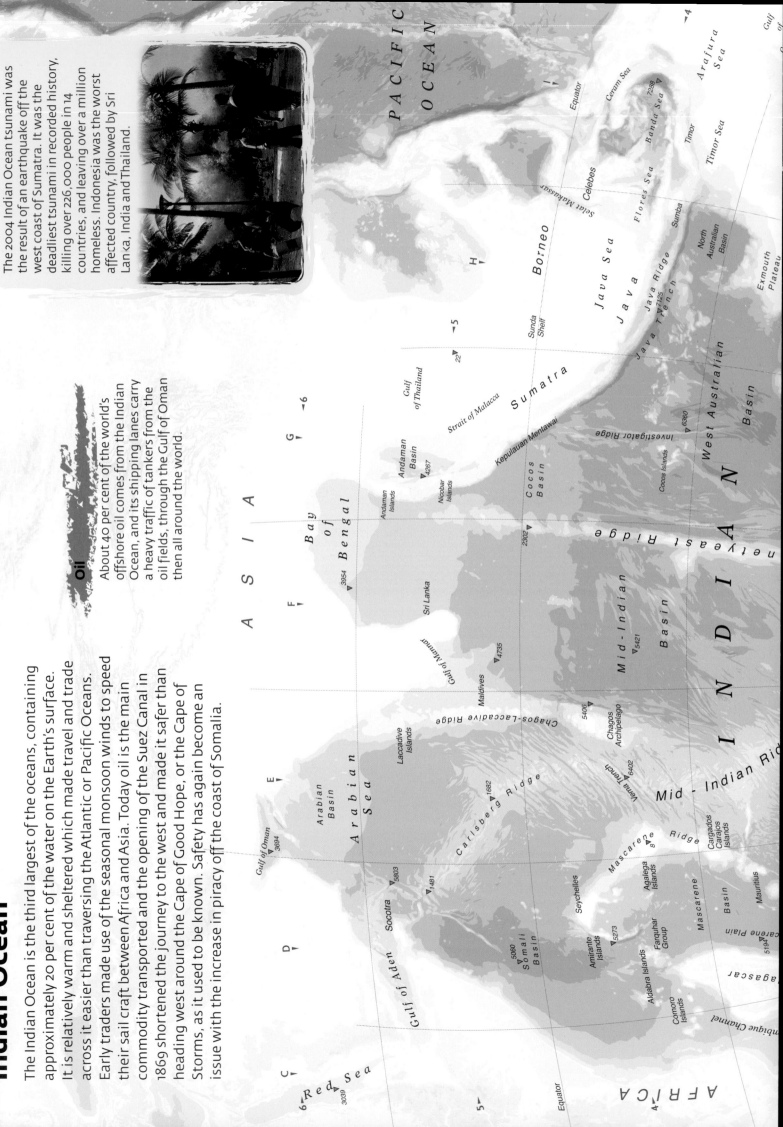

Warmest

The Indian Ocean is the warmest ocean, with the lowest oxygen content, making it less suited to marine life than any other ocean.

Several Indian Ocean islands – including the Seychelles and Maldives – provide all the ingredients for the 'destination wedding' market. White-sand beaches in a tropical climate, and a package that combines wedding and honeymoon – fulfils the dreams of many couples.

Piracy is a threat to international shipping, particularly off the Somali coast. Modern pirates target small boats, or larger cargo ships with small crews – and they are often as interested in the cash or personal belongings on board as much as the cargo. Multinational forces now operate counter-piracy operations.

Map labels

Tasman Sea

Tasman Basin

New Zealand

South Tasman Rise

Macquarie Ridge

Tasmania

Bass Strait

Tasman Abyssal Plain

▼770

Great Australian Bight

South Australian Basin

▼5670

O C E A N

Southeast Indian Ridge

Indian-Antarctic Ridge

▼3902

Perth Basin

▼5746

Naturaliste Plateau

Diamantina Deep 6602

▼7102

Broken Plateau

East

▼2067

▼3745

Australian - Antarctic Basin

▼1840

▼4181

▼4650

Fisher Bay

Antarctic Circle

Vincennes Bay

Davis Sea

Banzare Seamount ▼186

Kerguelen Plateau

Heard Island

McDonald Islands

Îles Kerguelen

A N T A R C T I C A

South Pole

Crozet Basin

▼5195

Iles Crozet

▼4590

Crozet Plateau

Prince Edward Islands

Conrad Rise 230

Enderby Abyssal Plain

6972▼

Lützow-Holm Bay

S O U T H E R N   O C E A N

Atlantic-Indian Antarctic Basin

Madagascar Ridge

Southwest Indian Ridge

Basin

Natal Basin

Mozambique Ridge

▼1207

▼6291

Agulhas Plateau

Agulhas Basin

▼6195

▼5371

Atlantic-Indian Ridge

Shona Ridge

Maud Seamount ▼1200

Antarctic Circle

5750▼

Oceania

Yaren
NAURU

KIRIBATI

New Guinea

PAPUA
NEW GUINEA
Lae

SOLOMON
ISLANDS

TUVALU

Arafura Sea

Port
Moresby

Honiara

Coral Sea

Timor Sea
Darwin

INDIAN

OCEAN

Cairns

Townsville

VANUATU

Port Vila

FIJI Suva

Alice
Springs

Rockhampton

New
Caledonia
(Fr.)
Nouméa

Tropic of Capricorn

A U S T R A L I A

Tropic of Capricorn

Brisbane
Gold Coast

P A C I F I C

Lake
Eyre

Kalgoorlie

Newcastle

O C E A N

Perth

Great
Australian Bight
Adelaide

Sydney

Canberra

Geelong Melbourne

Tasman Sea

North
Island

Auckland

Tasmania

NEW
ZEALAND

Hobart

Wellington

0   300   600   900   1200 km

Christchurch

South
Island
Dunedin

A · B · C · D

Atolls

In the 1940s and 1950s the two atolls of Bikini and Enewetak in the Marshall Islands were the sites of sixty-six US nuclear military tests.

Diverse

There are over 800 different languages in Papua New Guinea, making it one of the most culturally diverse countries in the world.

Guam (USA)   Rota

Northern Mariana Islands (USA)

MARSHALL
Bikini
ISLANDS

Yap

M i c r o n e s i a

Hall Is

Chuuk

Palikir
Pohnpei

Kosrae

C a r o l i n e
I s l a n d s

Mortlock
Islands

FEDERATED STATES
OF MICRONESIA

The unmistakeable rainbow lorikeet is one of the most colourful birds of the southwest Pacific. They are rainforest dwellers, feeding on flowers, insects and fruit.

Largest

The world's largest butterfly, the Queen Alexandra's birdwing, is disappearing from its only habitat in the coastal rainforests of northern Papua New Guinea. Habitat loss is the main reason for its decline.

NAU

Admiralty
Islands   St Matthias Group

Lihir
Group

New
Ireland

Namatanai

Bismarck Archipelago

Bismarck Sea

Rabaul

Cape St George

Bougainville
Island

Sohano

Arawa

Choiseul

SOLOMON
ISLANDS

Vanimo
Aitape
Wewak   Sepik

PAPUA

Kimbe

New Britain

Santa Isabel
Buala

Malu'u

Madang

Mt Wilhelm

Umboi

Solomon Sea

New Georgia Sound

Malaita

NEW

Sepik   Central Ra.

Mount Hagen
4088   4500   Goroka

Mendi

Lae

Morobe

New Georgia
Islands

HONIARA   Auuavu

GUINEA

Kikori

NEW GUINEA

Wau

D'Entrecasteaux

Guadalcanal

Kirakira

Balimo

Kerema

Mt
Victoria
4073

Islands

San Cristobal

Fly

Morehead

Bereina

Owen Stanley Range

Louisiade Archipelago

Daru

Gulf of
Papua   PORT
MORESBY   Kwikila   Abau

Torres Strait

The coconut palm grows widely across the tropics and subtropics. It likes sandy soil and tolerates salt so is ideal for colonizing the shores of the islands of the southwest Pacific.

AUSTRALIA

Coral Sea

Coral Sea
Islands
Territory
(Australia)

Îles Chesterfield
(France)

Grand Passage

Using the stars, winds and wave directions for navigation, Polynesians used to travel vast areas of the Pacific Ocean by outrigger canoe. Sea-going skills have been passed down for generations, often in the form of stories or songs.

Koumac

New Caledonia
(France)

0   200   400   600   800 km

Southwest Pacific

Until the early 20th century stick charts were made in the Marshall Islands and used as a form of map, often with shells tied to the framework to represent islands.

The southwest Pacific region is traditionally divided into three separate island groupings: Micronesia, Melanesia, and Polynesia. The Pacific islands were originally inhabited by adventurous seafarers from Asia. Many of the Islands in this region became independent in the twentieth century, after long term rule from the United States and Europe. Many of the islands, such as the Cook Islands owe their current names to European explorers. Many political borders in the area remain unsettled, and several islands still remain as US dependencies.

Samoans are the second largest Polynesian group after the Maori. Traditional ways are very important to Samoans and social status is more important than material possessions. The 'aiga', or family, is highly valued.

Most visited

Fiji is the most visited Pacific island country. Nadi International Airport, on the main island of Viti Levu, was developed as an airfield in the 1940s, becoming critical as a refuelling stop. It has since been greatly expanded and it remains as an important regional hub for travel to the southwest Pacific.

Ratak Chain

DALAP-ULIGA-DARRIT

KIRIBATI

BAIRIKI Gilbert Islands

Banaba

Kingsmill Group

PACIFIC OCEAN

Melanesia

Nanumea

Nui

Nukufetau Vaitupu

TUVALU Funafuti

VAIAKU

Nukulaelae

Howland Island (USA)

Baker Island (USA)

Equator

KIRIBATI

Kanton

McKean Rawaki

Phoenix Islands

Nikumaroro Manra

Orona

Atafu

Tokelau Nukunonu

(New Zealand) Fakaofo

Polynesia

Santa Cruz Islands

Banks Islands

vémasana

Norsup

VANUATU

ula Shepherd Is

PORT VILA

romango

Tanna

Îles Loyauté (France)

Ceva-i-Ra (Conway Reef)

Wallis and Futuna Islands (France)

MATĀ'UTU

Savai'i

SAMOA APIA

'Upolu

Niuatoputapu

Manu'a Islands

Tutuila (USA)

American Samoa (USA)

Pukapuka

Nassau

Rose Island

Suwarrow

Yasawa Group Great Sea Reef Vanua Levu

Labasa

Lautoka Tomanivi ▲1324

Viti Levu SUVA

FIJI

Kadavu Passage

Koro Sea

Tafahi

Vava'u Group

TONGA

ALOFI

Niue (New Zealand)

Palmerston Island

Ono-i-Lau

NUKU'ALOFA

Tongatapu Group

Ata

Tropic of Capricorn

Aitutaki

Hervey Islands Atiu

Cook Islands (New Zealand) Mauke

Rarotonga

Mangaia

Australia

Australia is an island continent between the Pacific and Indian Oceans. The nation of Australia also includes the island of Tasmania to the southeast, and many smaller islands around the coast. Australia has one of the lowest population densities in the world, although it has been growing rapidly since 1945. The majority of the population live on the coast and nearly a quarter of the country's population was born overseas. Two of the most famous natural features are Uluru, also known as Ayers Rock, and the Great Barrier Reef. Australia is prone to extreme climatic conditions, with both heat waves and flooding causing much damage and many deaths in recent years. Adventure sports are an important part of the tourism sector. Australia also has a large agricultural community, and is the world's largest exporter of wool.

World-class waves crash into the coasts of Australia, creating some awesome surfing opportunities.

The red kangaroo is Australia's largest mammal. It lives in scrubland, grass and desert across most of western and central Australia. A powerful animal, it can:
- jump nearly 2 m in a single leap
- hop at over 48 km per hour

Bushfires are common in the Australian outback. Eucalyptus trees – known as gum trees - are fast-growing and re-establish themselves quickly after forest fires.

With over 860 different kinds of snakes, lizards, turtles and crocodiles, Australia has more reptile species than any other country. Often measuring over 6m long, the saltwater crocodile is native to Australia and is the largest reptile in the world.

Sacred

Uluru, or Ayers Rock in the Northern Territory is one of Australia's most recognised icons. At 867 m it is not high, but rising from the desert it stands imposing and isolated and is sacred to Aboriginal people. At the base of the rock are shallow caves containing ancient Aboriginal paintings.

Map labels:

Timor Sea
Melville Island
Bathurst Island
Ashmore and Cartier Islands (Australia)
Darwin
Jabiru
Cape Londonderry
Joseph Bonaparte Gulf
Bonaparte Archipelago
Collier Bay
Cape Lévêque
Drysdale
Durack
Kununurra
Lake Argyle
Victoria
Daly
Mt Ord ▲ 936
Kimberley Plateau
King Leopold Ranges
Derby
Fitzroy Crossing
Halls Creek
Roebuck Bay
Broome
Eighty Mile Beach
Great Sandy Desert
Lake White
Lake Wills
Lake Mackay
Mt Zeil
Macdonnell
NORTHERN TERRITORY
Tanami Desert
Port Hedland
Karratha
Roebourne
Barrow Island
North West Cape
Chichester Range
Hamersley Range
1250
Newman
Oakover
Lake Disappointment
WESTERN
Paraburdoo
Ashburton
Gibson Desert
Lake Amadeus
Uluru (Ayers Rock) ▲ 867
INDIAN OCEAN
Lake MacLeod
Mt Augustus ▲ 1106
Gascoyne
Murchison
Robinson Ranges
AUST
Musgrave
1440 ▲ Mt Woodroffe
Everard R
Shark Bay
Dirk Hartog Island
Meekatharra
Lake Carnegie
AUSTRALIA
Kalbarri
Mount Magnet
Laverton
Lake Carey
Great Victoria Desert
Lake Barlee
Leonora
Geraldton
Dongara
Lake Moore
Kalgoorlie
Nullarbor Plain
Yanchep
Merredin
Lake Cowan
Perth
Fremantle
York
Norseman
Great Australian Bight
Mandurah
Bunbury
Katanning
Esperance
Margaret River
Hood Point
Cape Leeuwin
Point D'Entrecasteaux
Denmark
Albany

Isolated

Anna Creek Station in South Australia is the largest working cattle station in the world at 24,000 sq km. The isolated homestead has mail delivered twice a week, and stockmen now round up cattle using trail bikes rather than horses.

Variety

The Great Barrier Reef is the world's largest coral reef system. Home to an amazing variety of animals, there are:

- 1,625 species of fish
- over 400 species of coral
- 30 species of whales and dolphins
- 6 out of 7 of the world's total species of marine turtle

The indigenous people of Australia are one of the oldest surviving cultures in the world. Traditionally hunters and gatherers, they lived off the land and found all they needed from plants and animals.

Largest

Sydney is Australia's largest city. With its iconic Harbour Bridge and Opera House, Sydney Harbour is a premier cruise ship destination.

New Zealand

New Zealand is made up of two main islands, known as North Island and South Island. It was settled over a thousand years ago by the Maoris, but became a colony of the British Empire with the signing of the Waitangi treaty in 1840. Today, the Maori population numbers between 10 and 15 per cent of the total. Around 20 per cent of the population were born overseas. Much of the land on both islands is mountainous, although there is more pastureland on the North Island. Farming and agriculture are very important to the economy; with a population of only four million, New Zealand has over forty million sheep. There are about 14,000 earthquakes every year in New Zealand, although most cannot be felt.

Although New Zealand is the world's leading producer, the kiwi fruit originated in China. They were introduced to New Zealand in the 1900s and until the 1960s were known as 'Chinese gooseberries' before being named after New Zealand's most famous bird.

Pohutu is the largest active geyser in the southern hemisphere, and is one of the most visited geysers in the Rotorua area of geothermal activity. It erupts up to twenty times each day, sending a jet of hot water and steam up to 30 m into the air.

Maori

Maori are the indigenous Polynesian people of New Zealand. They have their own language and traditions, and a rich culture of music, dance and crafts such as carving. The haka is a lively posture dance, performed as a war challenge or in celebration, with one form now well-known as the pre-match ritual for New Zealand's rugby team.

Ancient

New Zealand's largest lake, and the second largest freshwater lake in Oceania, Lake Taupo lies in the caldera of a massive volcanic eruption that occurred over 26,000 years ago.

In 1982 when the number of sheep in New Zealand peaked at over 70 million there was an impressive ratio of 22 sheep for every person.

Map labels

Three Kings Islands
Cape Maria van Diemen
North Cape
Te Paki
Parengarenga Harbour
Ninety Mile Beach
Ahipara Bay
Tauroa Point
Hokianga Harbour
Cape Karikari
Doubtless Bay
Kaitaia
Kerikeri
Russell
Cape Brett
Poor Knights Islands
Kawakawa
Whangarei
Dargaville
Maungatapere
Bream Bay
Little Barrier
Great Barrier Island
North Head
Kaipara Harbour
Warkworth
Orewa
Helensford
Waiheke I.
Hauraki Gulf
Coromandel Peninsula
Coromandel Range
Colville Chan.
Whitianga
Mayor Island
Whakaari (White I.)
Cape Runaway
East Cape
Mawhai Point
Hicks Bay
Te Araroa
Hikurangi 1754
Raukumara
Ra
Waipaoa
Gisborne
Poverty Bay
Table Cape
Mahia Peninsula
Waiora
Hawke Bay
Cape Kidnappers
Napier
Hastings
Waipawa
Waipukurau
Cape Turnagain
Pongaroa
Ruahine Ra.
Tikokino
Takapau
Dannevirke
Woodville
Norsewood
Mt Ruapehu
2797
Ohakune
Waiouru
Taihape
Raetihi
Taumarunui
Ongarue
Mangakino
Tokoroa
Putaruru
Matamata
Te Aroha
Paeroa
Waihi
Waihou
Kaimai Ra.
Tauranga
Te Puke
Bay of Plenty
Whakatane
Opotiki
Matakana Island
Maketu
Rotorua
Lake Rotorua
Kawerau
Murupara
Ahimanawa Ra.
Kaweka Range
1369
Huiarau Range
Kaimanawa Mts
Lake Taupo
Turangi
Tongariro
Hauhungaroa
1078
Mt Tongariro
2518
Kuratau
Hauhungaroa
Kawhia Harbour
Waitomo
Te Kuiti
Otorohanga
Te Awamutu
Cambridge
Hamilton
Ngaruawahia
Huntly
Waikato
Morrinsville
Te Kauwhata
Waikato
Meremere
Waiuku
Manukau Harbour
Manukau
Papakura
Papatoetoe
Takapuna
Auckland
Thames
Paeroa
Waiotahi
Mangawhai
Taupiri
Raglan
Stratford
Cape Egmont
Mt Taranaki (Egmont) 2518
New Plymouth
Waitara
Opunake
Hawera
Patea
Waverley
Wanganui
Marton
Feilding
Palmerston North
Foxton
Levin
Otaki
North Taranaki Bight
South Taranaki Bight
Rangitikei
Manawatu
Pahiatua
North Island
Farewell Spit
Golden Bay
Separation Point
Cape Farewell
Kahurangi Point
Tasman
Whanganui
Ruahine Ra.
Wairarapa

TASMAN
SEA

C
D
E
F
G
5
6
7

The flightless and nocturnal kakapo is one of the rarest parrots in the world. As a ground-dwelling bird it made easy hunting for the Maori, who valued it for both its meat and its feathers. There are less than 130 left and all live in New Zealand, aided by the Kakapo Recovery Programme. Most live on the three predator-free islands of Codfish, Little Barrier and Anchor, and all are closely monitored.

- the kakapo is the world's heaviest parrot, and it is also the world's only flightless parrot
- it has a subsonic mating boom that can travel several kilometres

World's first

The world's first commercial bungee jumping site, Kawarau Bridge near Queenstown, launched bungy (bungee) jumping as an international sport phenomenon in 1988, and helped establish Queenstown as the adventure capital of the world. The Ledge Bungy is a newer jump that provides thrill-seekers with a panoramic viewpoint 400 m above Queenstown.

A statue of Sir Edmund Hillary permanently gazes towards New Zealand's highest peak, 3,754 m high Aoraki (Mount Cook). The New Zealand-born mountaineer gained worldwide recognition in 1953 as one of the first two climbers to reach the summit of Mount Everest.

GIANT MOA

New Zealand

50c

A flightless bird endemic to New Zealand, the moa was hunted to extinction by 1400. Until the arrival of human settlers its only predator had been Haast's eagle – the largest eagle ever known – which also became extinct in about 1400 when it lost the moa as its main food source.

Produced from nectar from the manuka tree in New Zealand and Australia, manuka honey has a strong flavour and a long tradition as a 'healing' honey with antibacterial properties.

PACIFIC OCEAN

South Island

Canterbury Bight

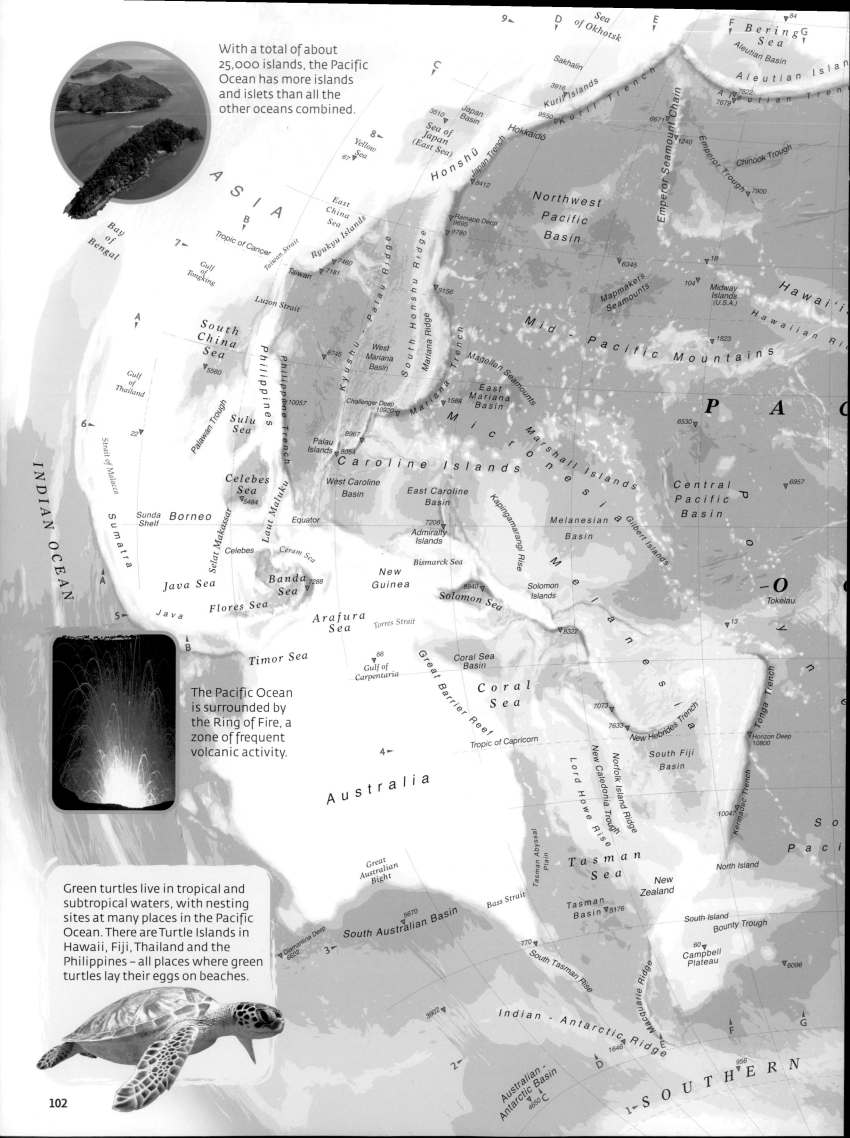

With a total of about 25,000 islands, the Pacific Ocean has more islands and islets than all the other oceans combined.

The Pacific Ocean is surrounded by the Ring of Fire, a zone of frequent volcanic activity.

Green turtles live in tropical and subtropical waters, with nesting sites at many places in the Pacific Ocean. There are Turtle Islands in Hawaii, Fiji, Thailand and the Philippines – all places where green turtles lay their eggs on beaches.

ASIA

Bay of Bengal

Tropic of Cancer

Gulf of Tongking

Strait of Malacca

INDIAN OCEAN

Sumatra

Gulf of Thailand

South China Sea

Luzon Strait

Taiwan Strait

Taiwan

Philippines

Palawan Trough

Philippine Trough

Sulu Sea

Celebes Sea

Borneo

Sunda Shelf

Selat Makassar

Celebes

Laut Maluku

Ceram Sea

Banda Sea

Java Sea

Flores Sea

Java

Arafura Sea

Timor Sea

Torres Strait

Gulf of Carpentaria

Great Australian Bight

Great Barrier Reef

South Australian Basin

Australia

Bass Strait

Diamantina Deep 6602

Sea of Okhotsk

Sakhalin

Kuril Islands

Japan Basin

Sea of Japan (East Sea)

Hokkaido

Honshū

Japan Trench

Ramapo Deep

Yellow Sea

East China Sea

Ryukyu Islands

Kyushu - Palau Ridge

South Honshu Ridge

West Mariana Basin

Mariana Ridge

Mariana Trench

Challenger Deep 10920

Palau Islands

Caroline Islands

West Caroline Basin

East Caroline Basin

Equator

Admiralty Islands

Bismarck Sea

New Guinea

Solomon Sea

Solomon Islands

Coral Sea Basin

Coral Sea

Tropic of Capricorn

Bering Sea

Aleutian Basin

Aleutian Islands

Aleutian Trench

Emperor Seamount Chain

Emperor Trough

Chinook Trough

Northwest Pacific Basin

Mapmakers Seamounts

Midway Islands (U.S.A.)

Mid - Pacific Mountains

Hawaiian Ridge

Magellan Seamounts

East Mariana Basin

Micronesia

Marshall Islands

Gilbert Islands

Kapingamarangi Rise

Melanesian Basin

Melanesia

Central Pacific Basin

PACIFIC

Tokelau

New Hebrides Trench

New Caledonia Trough

Norfolk Island Ridge

South Fiji Basin

Tonga Trench

Horizon Deep 10800

Kermadec Trench

Lord Howe Rise

Tasman Abyssal Plain

Tasman Sea

Tasman Basin

New Zealand

North Island

South Island

Bounty Trough

Campbell Plateau

Macquarie Ridge

Indian - Antarctic Ridge

South Tasman Rise

Australian - Antarctic Basin

SOUTHERN

Pacific Ocean

The Pacific Ocean is the largest of all the oceans, covering about a third of the Earth's surface. It extends from the Bering Sea in the north, south to join the Southern Ocean and from Asia across to the Americas. It is a geologically active area as the shoreline generally matches the edges of a large tectonic plate. This is known as the Ring of Fire and movement of this plate causes activity in the form of volcanoes, earthquakes and tsunami , with the result the Pacific Ocean is gradually shrinking in size. The deepest point on Earth occurs in the Mariana Trench in the west, where Challenger Deep measures 10,920 metres.

Lowest

The lowest known point on Earth is Challenger Deep at 10,920 m. It is over 2,000 m deeper than Mount Everest is high and it lies in the Mariana Trench, east of the Philippines, at the boundary of two crustal plates. It is named after HMS Challenger which made the first recordings of its depth in the 1870s. So far there have been only four descents of the depression.

Largest

Covering more than a third of the Earth's surface, the Pacific Ocean is larger in extent than the total land area of the world.

Over half the world's total fish catch comes from the Pacific Ocean. The main species are tuna, sardines, herring, swordfish, snapper and shellfish.

The Great Pacific Garbage Patch exists, but not as many people visualise it. A vast floating sea of discarded bottles and other debris is a myth, but what does exist is a vortex of mostly small plastic particles suspended near the surface of the water. To the naked eye it is not noticeable yet in some areas the amount of plastic outweighs the amount of plankton by six times.

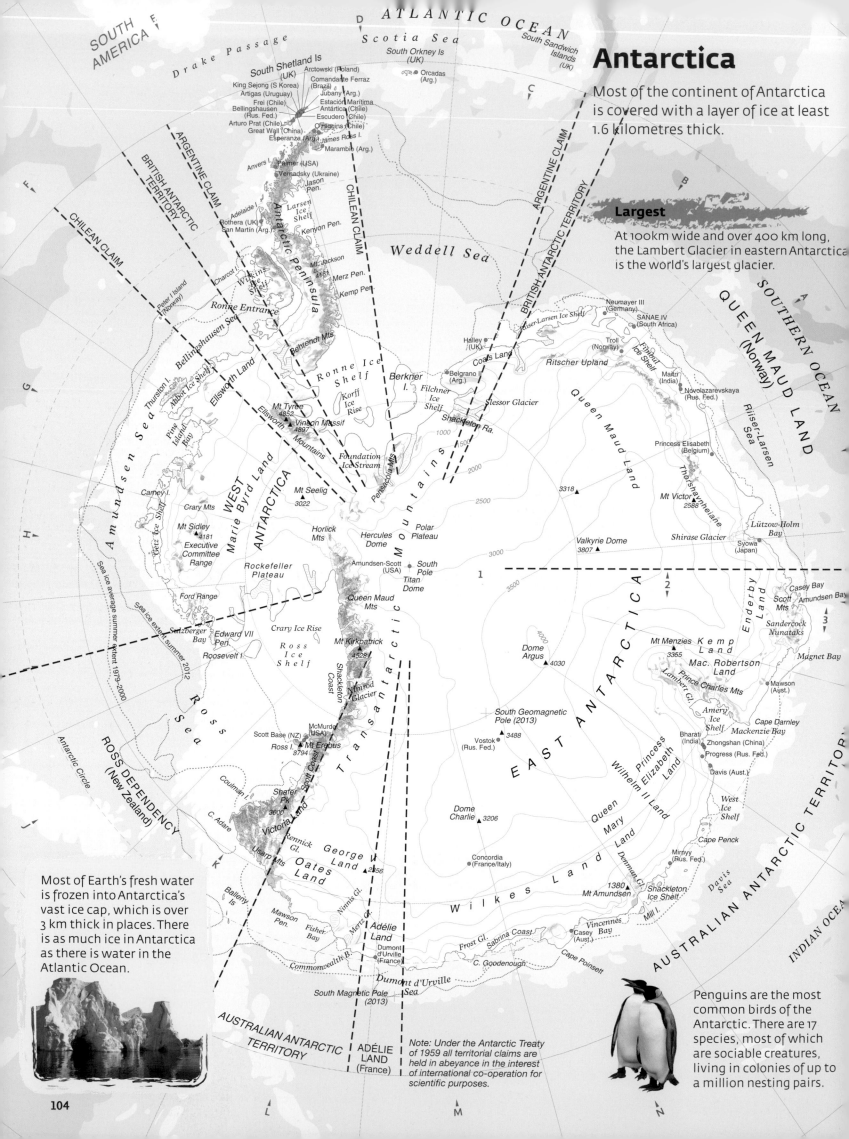

Antarctica

Most of the continent of Antarctica is covered with a layer of ice at least 1.6 kilometres thick.

Largest

At 100km wide and over 400 km long, the Lambert Glacier in eastern Antarctica is the world's largest glacier.

Most of Earth's fresh water is frozen into Antarctica's vast ice cap, which is over 3 km thick in places. There is as much ice in Antarctica as there is water in the Atlantic Ocean.

Note: Under the Antarctic Treaty of 1959 all territorial claims are held in abeyance in the interest of international co-operation for scientific purposes.

Penguins are the most common birds of the Antarctic. There are 17 species, most of which are sociable creatures, living in colonies of up to a million nesting pairs.

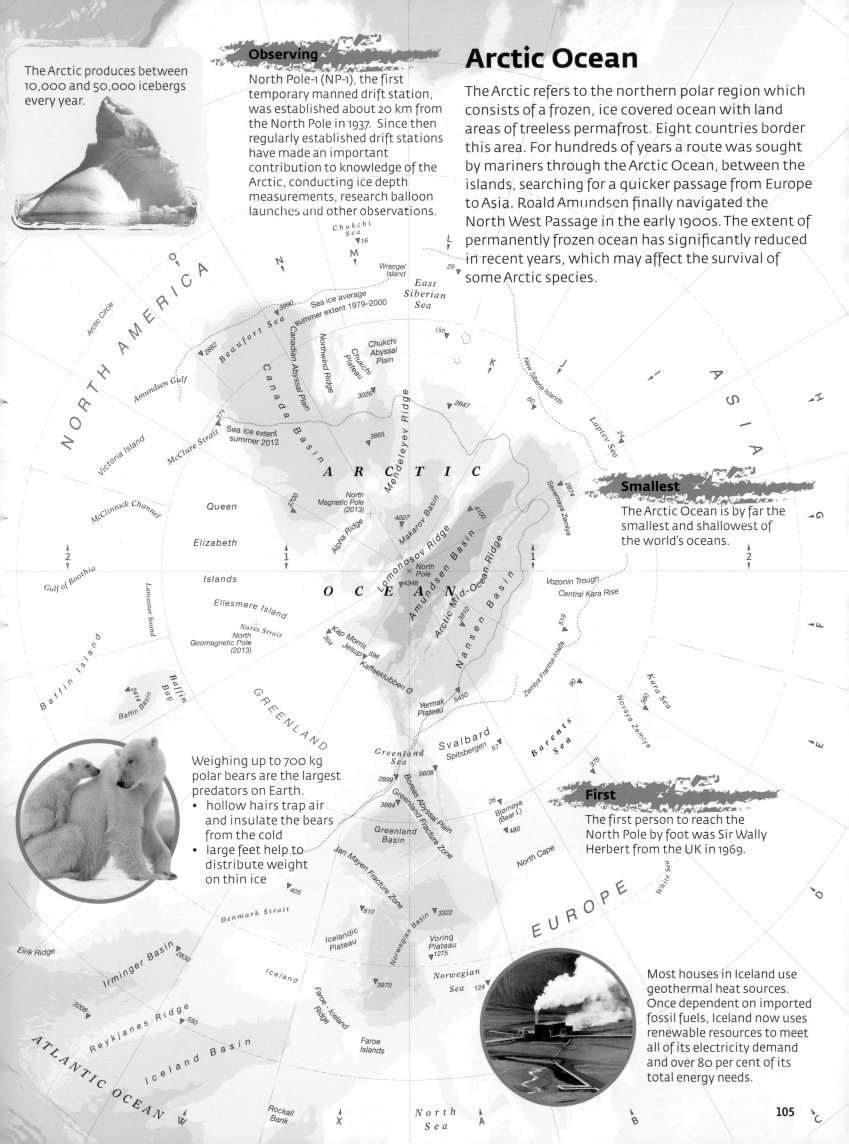

The Arctic produces between 10,000 and 50,000 icebergs every year.

Observing

North Pole-1 (NP-1), the first temporary manned drift station, was established about 20 km from the North Pole in 1937. Since then regularly established drift stations have made an important contribution to knowledge of the Arctic, conducting ice depth measurements, research balloon launches and other observations.

Arctic Ocean

The Arctic refers to the northern polar region which consists of a frozen, ice covered ocean with land areas of treeless permafrost. Eight countries border this area. For hundreds of years a route was sought by mariners through the Arctic Ocean, between the islands, searching for a quicker passage from Europe to Asia. Roald Amundsen finally navigated the North West Passage in the early 1900s. The extent of permanently frozen ocean has significantly reduced in recent years, which may affect the survival of some Arctic species.

Smallest

The Arctic Ocean is by far the smallest and shallowest of the world's oceans.

Weighing up to 700 kg polar bears are the largest predators on Earth.
- hollow hairs trap air and insulate the bears from the cold
- large feet help to distribute weight on thin ice

First

The first person to reach the North Pole by foot was Sir Wally Herbert from the UK in 1969.

Most houses in Iceland use geothermal heat sources. Once dependent on imported fossil fuels, Iceland now uses renewable resources to meet all of its electricity demand and over 80 per cent of its total energy needs.

Map labels

NORTH AMERICA
Arctic Circle
Chukchi Sea ▼16
N
M
Wrangel Island
East Siberian Sea
29 ▼
L
ASIA
H
Sea ice average summer extent 1979–2000
Beaufort Sea
▼3990
▼2882
Northwind Ridge
Chukchi Plateau
Chukchi Abyssal Plain
155 ▼
New Siberia Islands
K
J
Laptev Sea
24 ▼
60 ▼
Amundsen Gulf
Canadian Abyssal Plain
Canada Basin
3026 ▼
▼2647
Victoria Island
McClure Strait
371
Sea ice extent summer 2012
3665 ▼
Mendeleyev Ridge
ARCTIC
Severnaya Zemlya
2874 ▲
G
McClintock Channel
Queen
▼3700
North Magnetic Pole (2013) +
4007 ▼
Alpha Ridge
Makarov Basin
Amundsen Basin
4100 ▲
Arctic Mid-Ocean Ridge
2
1
1
2
Gulf of Boothia
Elizabeth
Lomonosov Ridge
North Pole ▼4346
Vozonin Trough
Central Kara Rise
Islands
OCEAN
Nansen Basin
3910 ▼
519 ▲
F
Ellesmere Island
Baffin Island
Lancaster Sound
Nares Strait
North Geomagnetic Pole (2013) +
Kap Morris
304
Jesup 596
Kaffeeklubben Ø
Zemlya Frantsa-Iosifa
90 ▲
Kara Sea
Novaya Zemlya
380 ▲
E
Baffin Bay
2414 ▲
Baffin Basin
GREENLAND
Yermak Plateau
5450 ▼
Svalbard
Spitsbergen 57 ▲
Barents Sea
375 ▼
Greenland Sea
2899 ▼
Boreas Basin
5608 ▼
Greenland Fracture Zone
3884 ▼
Greenland Basin
26 ▼
Bjørnøya (Bear I.)
480 ▼
First
North Cape
White Sea
D
Jan Mayen Fracture Zone
405 ▼
EUROPE
Eirik Ridge
Irminger Basin
2830 ▼
Denmark Strait
810 ▼
Norwegian Basin ▼3322
Voring Plateau ▼1275
3208 ▲
Reykjanes Ridge
550 ▼
Iceland
Iceland Basin
Icelandic Plateau
3970 ▼
Faroe-Iceland Ridge
Faroe Islands
Norwegian Sea 124 ▼
ATLANTIC OCEAN
W
Rockall Bank
X
North Sea
A
B
C

Country Indicators

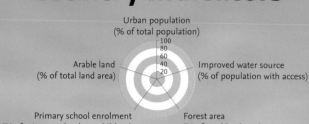

Urban population
(% of total population)

Arable land
(% of total land area)

Improved water source
(% of population with access)

Primary school enrolment
(% of primary school age children)

Forest area
(% of total land area)

Country area (square kilometres)
Country population (2012)
Human Development Index – HDI (2012)

Continent

Africa

Asia

Europe

North America

Oceania

South America

Afghanistan

Area: 652 225 sq km
Population: 32 358 000
HDI: 0.374

Albania

Area: 28 748 sq km
Population: 3 216 000
HDI: 0.749

Algeria

Area: 2 381 741 sq km
Population: 35 980 00●
HDI: 0.713

Angola

Area: 1 246 700 sq km
Population: 19 618 000
HDI: 0.508

Argentina

Area: 2 766 889 sq km
Population: 40 765 000
HDI: 0.811

Armenia

Area: 29 800 sq km
Population: 3 100 000
HDI: 0.729

Australia

Area: 7 692 024 sq km
Population: 22 606 000
HDI: 0.938

Austria

Area: 83 855 sq km
Population: 8 413 000
HDI: 0.895

Azerbaijan

Area: 86 600 sq km
Population: 9 306 00●
HDI: 0.734

The Bahamas

Area: 13 939 sq km
Population: 347 000
HDI: 0.794

Bahrain

Area: 691 sq km
Population: 1 324 000
HDI: 0.796

Bangladesh

Area: 143 998 sq km
Population: 150 494 000
HDI: 0.515

Belarus

Area: 207 600 sq km
Population: 9 559 000
HDI: 0.793

Belgium

Area: 30 520 sq km
Population: 10 754 000
HDI: 0.897

Belize

Area: 22 965 sq km
Population: 318 00●
HDI: 0.702

Benin

Area: 112 620 sq km
Population: 9 100 000
HDI: 0.436

Bhutan

Area: 46 620 sq km
Population: 738 000
HDI: 0.538

Bolivia

Area: 1 098 581 sq km
Population: 10 088 000
HDI: 0.675

Bosnia and Herzegovina

Area: 51 130 sq km
Population: 3 752 000
HDI: 0.735

Botswana

Area: 581 370 sq km
Population: 2 031 000
HDI: 0.634

Brazil

Area: 8 514 879 sq km
Population: 196 655 ●
HDI: 0.730

Brunei

Area: 5 765 sq km
Population: 406 000
HDI: 0.855

Bulgaria

Area: 110 994 sq km
Population: 7 446 000
HDI: 0.782

Burkina Faso

Area: 274 200 sq km
Population: 16 968 000
HDI: 0.343

Burundi

Area: 27 835 sq km
Population: 8 575 000
HDI: 0.355

Cambodia

Area: 181 035 sq km
Population: 14 305 000
HDI: 0.543

Cameroon

Area: 475 442 sq km
Population: 20 030 0●
HDI: 0.495

Canada

Area: 9 984 670 sq km
Population: 34 350 000
HDI: 0.911

Cape Verde

Area: 4 033 sq km
Population: 501 000
HDI: 0.586

Central African Republic

Area: 622 436 sq km
Population: 4 487 000
HDI: 0.352

Chad

Area: 1 284 000 sq km
Population: 11 525 000
HDI: 0.340

Chile

Area: 756 945 sq km
Population: 17 270 000
HDI: 0.819

China

Area: 9 584 492 sq km
Population: 1 332 079 000
HDI: 0.699

Colombia

Area: 1 141 748 sq km
Population: 46 927 000
HDI: 0.719

Comoros

Area: 1 862 sq km
Population: 754 000
HDI: 0.429

Congo

Area: 342 000 sq km
Population: 4 140 000
HDI: 0.534

Democratic Republic of the Congo

Area: 2 345 410 sq km
Population: 67 758 000
HDI: 0.304

Costa Rica

Area: 51 100 sq km
Population: 4 727 000
HDI: 0.773

Côte d'Ivoire

Area: 322 463 sq km
Population: 20 153 000
HDI: 0.432

Croatia

Area: 56 538 sq km
Population: 4 396 000
HDI: 0.805

Cuba

Area: 110 860 sq km
Population: 11 254 000
HDI: 0.780

Cyprus

Area: 9 251 sq km
Population: 1 117 000
HDI: 0.848

Czech Republic

Area: 78 864 sq km
Population: 10 534 000
HDI: 0.873

Denmark

Area: 43 075 sq km
Population: 5 573 000
HDI: 0.901

Djibouti

Area: 23 200 sq km
Population: 906 000
HDI: 0.445

Dominican Republic

Area: 48 442 sq km
Population: 10 056 000
HDI: 0.702

East Timor

Area: 14 874 sq km
Population: 1 154 000
HDI: 0.576

Ecuador

Area: 272 045 sq km
Population: 14 666 000
HDI: 0.724

Egypt

Area: 1 001 450 sq km
Population: 82 537 000
HDI: 0.662

El Salvador

Area: 21 041 sq km
Population: 6 227 000
HDI: 0.680

Equatorial Guinea

Area: 28 051 sq km
Population: 720 000
HDI: 0.554

Eritrea

Area: 117 400 sq km
Population: 5 415 000
HDI: 0.351

Estonia

Area: 45 200 sq km
Population: 1 341 000
HDI: 0.846

Ethiopia

Area: 1 133 880 sq km
Population: 84 734 000
HDI: 0.396

Fiji

Area: 18 330 sq km
Population: 868 000
HDI: 0.702

Finland

Area: 338 145 sq km
Population: 5 385 000
HDI: 0.892

France

Area: 543 965 sq km
Population: 63 126 000
HDI: 0.893

Country Indicators

Gabon

Area: 267 667 sq km
Population: 1 534 000
HDI: 0.683

The Gambia

Area: 11 295 sq km
Population: 1 776 000
HDI: 0.439

Georgia

Area: 69 700 sq km
Population: 4 329 000
HDI: 0.745

Germany

Area: 357 022 sq km
Population: 82 163 000
HDI: 0.920

Ghana

Area: 238 537 sq km
Population: 24 966 000
HDI: 0.558

Greece

Area: 131 957 sq km
Population: 11 390 00
HDI: 0.860

Guatemala

Area: 108 890 sq km
Population: 14 757 000
HDI: 0.581

Guinea

Area: 245 857 sq km
Population: 10 222 000
HDI: 0.355

Guinea-Bissau

Area: 36 125 sq km
Population: 1 547 000
HDI: 0.364

Guyana

Area: 214 969 sq km
Population: 756 000
HDI: 0.636

Haiti

Area: 27 750 sq km
Population: 10 124 000
HDI: 0.456

Honduras

Area: 112 088 sq km
Population: 7 755 00
HDI: 0.632

Hungary

Area: 93 030 sq km
Population: 9 966 000
HDI: 0.831

Iceland

Area: 102 820 sq km
Population: 324 000
HDI: 0.906

India

Area: 3 064 898 sq km
Population: 1 241 492 000
HDI: 0.554

Indonesia

Area: 1 919 445 sq km
Population: 242 326 000
HDI: 0.629

Iran

Area: 1 648 000 sq km
Population: 74 799 000
HDI: 0.742

Iraq

Area: 438 317 sq km
Population: 32 665 0
HDI: 0.590

Ireland

Area: 70 282 sq km
Population: 4 526 000
HDI: 0.916

Israel

Area: 22 072 sq km
Population: 7 562 000
HDI: 0.900

Italy

Area: 301 245 sq km
Population: 60 789 000
HDI: 0.881

Jamaica

Area: 10 991 sq km
Population: 2 751 000
HDI: 0.730

Japan

Area: 377 727 sq km
Population: 126 497 000
HDI: 0.912

Jordan

Area: 89 206 sq km
Population: 6 330 00
HDI: 0.700

Kazakhstan

Area: 2 717 300 sq km
Population: 16 207 000
HDI: 0.754

Kenya

Area: 582 646 sq km
Population: 41 610 000
HDI: 0.519

Kosovo

Area: 10 908 sq km
Population: 2 180 686
HDI: no data

Kuwait

Area: 17 818 sq km
Population: 2 818 000
HDI: 0.790

Kyrgyzstan

Area: 198 500 sq km
Population: 5 393 000
HDI: 0.622

Laos

Area: 236 800 sq km
Population: 6 288 00
HDI: 0.543

Latvia

Area: 64 589 sq km
Population: 2 243 000
HDI: 0.814

Lebanon

Area: 10 452 sq km
Population: 4 259 000
HDI: 0.745

Lesotho

Area: 30 355 sq km
Population: 2 194 000
HDI: 0.461

Liberia

Area: 111 369 sq km
Population: 4 129 000
HDI: 0.388

Libya

Area: 1 759 540 sq km
Population: 6 423 000
HDI: 0.769

Liechtenstein
Area: 160 sq km
Population: 36 000
HDI: 0.883

Lithuania

Area: 65 200 sq km
Population: 3 307 000
HDI: 0.818

Luxembourg

Area: 2 586 sq km
Population: 516 000
HDI: 0.875

Macedonia

Area: 25 713 sq km
Population: 2 064 000
HDI: 0.740

Madagascar

Area: 587 041 sq km
Population: 21 315 000
HDI: 0.483

Malawi

Area: 118 484 sq km
Population: 15 381 000
HDI: 0.418

Malaysia

Area: 332 965 sq km
Population: 28 859 000
HDI: 0.769

Mali

Area: 1 240 140 sq km
Population: 15 840 000
HDI: 0.344

Malta

Area: 316 sq km
Population: 418 000
HDI: 0.847

Mauritania

Area: 1 030 700 sq km
Population: 3 542 000
HDI: 0.467

Mauritius

Area: 2 040 sq km
Population: 1 307 000
HDI: 0.737

Mexico

Area: 1 972 545 sq km
Population: 114 793 000
HDI: 0.775

Moldova

Area: 33 700 sq km
Population: 3 545 000
HDI: 0.660

Monaco

Area: 2 sq km
Population: 35 000
HDI: no data

Mongolia

Area: 1 565 000 sq km
Population: 2 800 000
HDI: 0.675

Montenegro

Area: 13 812 sq km
Population: 632 000
HDI: 0.791

Morocco

Area: 446 550 sq km
Population: 32 273 000
HDI: 0.591

Mozambique

Area: 799 380 sq km
Population: 23 930 000
HDI: 0.327

Myanmar
Area: 676 577 sq km
Population: 48 337 000
HDI: 0.498

Namibia

Area: 824 292 sq km
Population: 2 324 000
HDI: 0.608

Nepal

Area: 147 181 sq km
Population: 30 486 000
HDI: 0.463

Netherlands

Area: 41 526 sq km
Population: 16 665 000
HDI: 0.921

New Zealand

Area: 270 534 sq km
Population: 4 415 000
HDI: 0.919

Nicaragua

Area: 130 000 sq km
Population: 5 870 000
HDI: 0.599

Niger

Area: 1 267 000 sq km
Population: 16 069 000
HDI: 0.304

Country Indicators

Nigeria

Area: 923 768 sq km
Population: 162 471 000
HDI: 0.471

North Korea

Area: 120 538 sq km
Population: 24 451 000
HDI: no data

Norway

Area: 323 878 sq km
Population: 4 925 000
HDI: 0.955

Oman

Area: 309 500 sq km
Population: 2 846 000
HDI: 0.731

Pakistan

Area: 803 940 sq km
Population: 176 745 000
HDI: 0.515

Palau

Area: 497 sq km
Population: 21 000
HDI: 0.791

Panama

Area: 77 082 sq km
Population: 3 571 000
HDI: 0.780

Papua New Guinea

Area: 462 840 sq km
Population: 7 014 000
HDI: 0.466

Paraguay

Area: 406 752 sq km
Population: 6 568 000
HDI: 0.669

Peru

Area: 1 285 216 sq km
Population: 29 400 000
HDI: 0.741

Philippines

Area: 300 000 sq km
Population: 94 852 000
HDI: 0.654

Poland

Area: 312 683 sq km
Population: 38 299 000
HDI: 0.821

Portugal

Area: 88 940 sq km
Population: 10 690 000
HDI: 0.816

Qatar

Area: 11 437 sq km
Population: 1 870 000
HDI: 0.834

Romania

Area: 237 500 sq km
Population: 21 436 000
HDI: 0.786

Russian Federation

Area: 17 075 400 sq km
Population: 142 836 000
HDI: 0.788

Rwanda

Area: 26 338 sq km
Population: 10 943 000
HDI: 0.434

Samoa

Area: 2 831 sq km
Population: 184 000
HDI: 0.702

São Tomé and Príncipe

Area: 964 sq km
Population: 169 000
HDI: 0.525

Saudi Arabia

Area: 2 200 000 sq km
Population: 28 083 000
HDI: 0.782

Senegal

Area: 196 720 sq km
Population: 12 768 000
HDI: 0.470

Serbia

Area: 77 453 sq km
Population: 7 306 677
HDI: 0.769

Sierra Leone

Area: 71 740 sq km
Population: 5 997 000
HDI: 0.359

Singapore

Area: 639 sq km
Population: 5 188 000
HDI: 0.895

Slovakia

Area: 49 035 sq km
Population: 5 472 000
HDI: 0.840

Slovenia

Area: 20 251 sq km
Population: 2 035 000
HD 0.892

Solomon Islands

Area: 28 370 sq km
Population: 552 000
HDI: 0.530

Somalia

Area: 637 657 sq km
Population: 9 557 000
HDI: no data

South Africa

Area: 1 219 090 sq km
Population: 50 460 000
HDI: 0.629

South Korea

Area: 99 274 sq km
Population: 48 391 000
HDI: 0.909

South Sudan

Area: 644 329 sq km
Population: 8 260 490
HDI: no data

Spain

Area: 504 782 sq km
Population: 46 455 000
HDI: 0.885

Sri Lanka

Area: 65 610 sq km
Population: 21 045 000
HDI: 0.715

Sudan

Area: 1 861 484 sq km
Population: 36 371 510
HDI: 0.414

Suriname

Area: 163 820 sq km
Population: 529 000
HDI: 0.684

Swaziland

Area: 17 364 sq km
Population: 1 203 000
HDI: 0.536

Sweden

Area: 449 964 sq km
Population: 9 441 000
HDI: 0.916

Switzerland

Area: 41 293 sq km
Population: 7 702 000
HDI: 0.913

Syria

Area: 184 026 sq km
Population: 20 766 000
HDI: 0.648

Tajikistan

Area: 143 100 sq km
Population: 6 977 000
HDI: 0.622

Tanzania

Area: 945 087 sq km
Population: 46 218 000
HDI: 0.476

Thailand

Area: 513 115 sq km
Population: 69 519 000
HDI: 0.690

Togo

Area: 56 785 sq km
Population: 6 155 000
HDI: 0.459

Trinidad and Tobago

Area: 5 130 sq km
Population: 1 346 000
HDI: 0.760

Tunisia

Area: 164 150 sq km
Population: 10 594 000
HDI: 0.712

Turkey

Area: 779 452 sq km
Population: 73 640 000
HDI: 0.722

Turkmenistan

Area: 488 100 sq km
Population: 5 105 000
HDI: 0.698

Uganda

Area: 241 038 sq km
Population: 34 509 000
HDI: 0.456

Ukraine

Area: 603 700 sq km
Population: 45 190 000
HDI: 0.740

United Arab Emirates

Area: 77 700 sq km
Population: 7 891 000
HDI: 0.818

United Kingdom

Area: 243 609 sq km
Population: 62 417 000
HDI: 0.875

**United States
of America**

Area: 9 826 635 sq km
Population: 313 085 000
HDI: 0.937

Uruguay

Area: 176 215 sq km
Population: 3 380 000
HDI: 0.792

Uzbekistan

Area: 447 400 sq km
Population: 27 760 000
HDI: 0.654

Vanuatu

Area: 12 190 sq km
Population: 246 000
HDI: 0.626

Venezuela

Area: 912 050 sq km
Population: 29 437 000
HDI: 0.748

Vietnam

Area: 329 565 sq km
Population: 88 792 000
HDI: 0.617

Yemen

Area: 527 968 sq km
Population: 24 800 000
HDI: 0.458

Zambia

Area: 752 614 sq km
Population: 13 475 000
HDI: 0.448

Zimbabwe

Area: 390 759 sq km
Population: 12 754 000
HDI: 0.397

Index

How to use the index

The best way to find the location of a place or a feature in an atlas is to use the index. All the names are listed in alphabetical order. Each entry gives the country or region of the world in which the name is located followed by the page number and its map grid reference. Area names included in the index are referenced to the centre of the feature. In the case of rivers, the mouth or confluence is taken as the point of reference. It may therefore be necessary to follow the river upstream from this point to find its name on the map.

To help distinguish the different part of each entry different styles of type are used.

| place name | description (if any) | country name or region name | page number | map grid reference |

Ardennes *plateau* Belgium **51** C1

Names of physical features such as rivers, capes, mountains etc. are followed by a description. The descriptions are usually shortened to one or two letters. Abbreviations are shown on the right. Town names are followed by a description only when the name may be confused with that of a physical feature.

Alice Springs *town* Australia **98** C3

Altamura Italy 59 F4
Altay China 82 C5
Altay Mongolia 82 E5
Altıntaş Turkey 74 B2
Altiplano plain Bolivia 26 D2
Alto Garças Brazil 27 G2
Altoona U.S.A. 14 B2
Altötting Germany 55 D3
Altun Shan mts China 82 C3
Alturas U.S.A. 9 A3
Altus U.S.A. 10 C2
Alushta Ukraine 67 D2
Alva U.S.A. 10 C3
Alvarães Brazil 26 E5
Älvdalen Sweden 47 C3
Älvsbyn Sweden 46 E4
Al Wajh Saudi Arabia 77 B4
Al Widyān plateau Iraq/Saudi Arabia 76 C5
Alyangula Australia 99 C4
Alytus Lithuania 69 B2
Amadeus, Lake salt flat Australia 98 C3
Amadjuak Lake Canada 5 K3
Amadora Portugal 56 A3
Åmål Sweden 47 C2
Amamapare Indon. 91 E2
Amami-Ō-shima i. Japan 87 A2
Amankel'dy Kazakh. 78 C4
Amarillo U.S.A. 10 B3
Amasya Turkey 74 C3
Amazon, Mouths of the Brazil 27 H6
Ambarchik Rus. Fed. 73 O3
Ambato Ecuador 26 B5
Ambergris Caye i. Belize 19 G2
Ambon Indon. 91 D2
Amdo China 82 D1
Ameland i. Netherlands 50 D5
American Samoa territory
  Pacific Ocean 97 G2
Amersfoort Netherlands 50 D4
Amfissa Greece 65 C3
Amgun' r. Rus. Fed. 73 L2
Amiens France 52 E5
Amistad Reservoir Mexico/U.S.A. 10 B1
'Ammān Jordan 76 B5
Amol Iran 76 E6
Amorgos i. Greece 65 D2
Amos Canada 6 C1
Amravati India 80 D4
Amritsar India 80 C6
Amstelveen Netherlands 50 C4
Amsterdam Netherlands 50 C4
Amstetten Austria 55 E3
Amudar'ya r. Asia 78 C3
Amund Ringnes Island Canada 5 I4
Amundsen Gulf Canada 4 F4
Amundsen Sea Antarctica 104 H2
Amuntai Indon. 90 C2
Amur r. Rus. Fed. 73 M2
Anabanua Indon. 91 D2
Anabar r. Rus. Fed. 73 J4
Anadolu Dağları mts Turkey 74 D3
Anadyr' Rus. Fed. 73 P3
Anadyrskiy Zaliv bay Rus. Fed. 73 Q3
'Ānah Iraq 76 C5
Anamã Brazil 26 E5
Anambas, Kepulauan is Indon. 90 B3
Anamur Turkey 74 C2
Anápolis Brazil 27 H2
Anatolia f. Turkey 74 B2
Añatuya Argentina 28 D7
Anchorage U.S.A. 4 D3
Ancona Italy 58 D5
Ancud Chile 29 B4
Ancud, Golfo de Chile 29 B4
Åndalsnes Norway 46 A3
Andalucia f. Spain 56 C2
Andaman Islands India 92 G5
Andaman Islands India 81 H2
Andaman Sea Asia 89 A2
Andaman Sea Indian Ocean 81 H2
Anderlecht Belgium 51 C2
Anderson r. Canada 4 F3
Anderson U.S.A. 4 D3
Andfjorden strait Norway 46 D5
Andhra Pradesh admin div. India 81 D3
Andijon Uzbek. 79 D3
Andoas Peru 26 B5
Andong South Korea 87 A4
Andorra Europe 53 D2
Andorra la Vella Andorra 53 D2
Andøya i. Norway 46 C5

Andrews U.S.A. 10 B2
Andria Italy 59 F4
Andros i. Greece 65 D2
Andros i. The Bahamas 22 C3
Andújar Spain 56 C3
Anéfis Mali 39 D2
Anegada i. Virgin Is (U.K.) 23 F2
Anegada, Bahía bay Argentina 29 D4
Aneto mt. Spain 57 F5
Angara r. Rus. Fed. 73 H2
Ånge Sweden 47 C3
Ángel de la Guarda, Isla i. Mexico 18 B4
Ängelholm Sweden 47 C2
Angers France 52 C4
Anglesey i. U.K. 49 D3
Angola Africa 42 A3
Angoulême France 53 D3
Angren Uzbek. 79 D3
Anguilla territory Caribbean Sea 23 F2
Anhui admin div. China 85 E4
Anhumas Brazil 27 G2
Anjū North Korea 86 A4
Ankara Turkey 74 C2
Annaba Algeria 35 C2
An Nafūd desert Saudi Arabia 76 C4
An Najaf Iraq 76 C5
Annapurna mt. Nepal 81 E5
Ann Arbor U.S.A. 13 E2
An Nāşirīyah Iraq 76 D5
Annecy France 53 G3
Anniston U.S.A. 17 B3
An Nu'ayrīyah Saudi Arabia 76 D4
Ansbach Germany 55 C3
Anshan China 83 J4
Anshun China 85 C3
Antakya Turkey 74 D2
Antalya Turkey 74 B2
Antalya Körfezi gulf Turkey 74 B2
Antananarivo Madagascar 43 D3
Antarctic Peninsula Antarctica 104 E3
An Teallach mt. U.K. 48 D5
Antequera Spain 56 C2
Antibes France 53 G2
Anticosti, Île d' i. Canada 7 D1
Antigua i. Antigua and Barbuda 23 F2
Antigua and Barbuda Caribbean Sea 23 F2
Antikythira i. Greece 65 C1
Antofagasta Chile 28 B8
Antofalla, Volcán volcano Argentina 28 C7
Antrim Hills U.K. 48 C4
Antsirabe Madagascar 43 D3
Antsirañana Madagascar 43 D3
Antsohihy Madagascar 43 D3
Antwerp Belgium 51 C3
Antwerpen admin div. Belgium 51 C3
Anxi China 82 E4
Anyang China 84 D5
Anzhero-Sudzhensk Rus. Fed. 72 G2
Aomori Japan 86 D5
Aoraki mt. New Zealand 101 C3
Aosta Italy 58 A6
Apalachee Bay U.S.A. 17 C2
Apaporis r. Colombia 26 C6
Aparri Phil. 91 D4
Apatzingán Mexico 18 D2
Apeldoorn Netherlands 50 D4
Apennines mts Italy 58 B6
Apia Samoa 96 F2
Apoera Suriname 27 F7
Apostolos Andreas, Cape Cyprus 74 C1
Appalachian Mountains U.S.A. 16 C4
Appleton U.S.A. 13 D2
Apucarana Brazil 28 F8
Apurímac r. Peru 26 C3
Aqaba, Gulf of Asia 76 A4
Arabian Peninsula Asia 77 C3
Arabian Sea Indian Ocean 80 B3
Aracaju Brazil 27 J3
Araçatuba Brazil 28 F8
Aracena, Sierra de hills Spain 56 B2
Arad Romania 66 B2
Arafura Sea Australia/Indon. 91 E2
Aragon f. Spain 57 E4
Aragón r. Spain 57 E5
Araguaia r. Brazil 27 H4
Araguaína Brazil 27 H4
Araguari Brazil 27 H2
Araguatins Brazil 27 H4
Arak Algeria 34 C1
Arāk Iran 76 D5
Arakan Yoma mts Myanmar 88 A3
Aral Sea lake Kazakh./Uzbek. 78 B3

Aral'sk Kazakh. 78 C3
Aranda de Duero Spain 56 D4
Aran Islands Ireland 49 B3
Aranjuez Spain 56 D4
Aransas Pass U.S.A. 11 C1
Arapgir Turkey 75 D2
Arapiraca Brazil 27 J4
Arapis, Akra pt Greece 64 D4
Araras Brazil 27 G4
Ararat Armenia 75 F2
Ararat, Mount Turkey 75 F2
Arauca Colombia 26 C7
Arauca r. Venez. 26 D7
Arawa P.N.G. 96 C3
Arayıt Dağı mt. Turkey 74 B2
Araz r. Azer. 75 G3
Arbīl Iraq 76 C6
Arboga Sweden 47 C2
Arbroath U.K. 48 E5
Arcachon France 53 C3
Archangel Rus. Fed. 72 C3
Arctic Bay town Canada 5 J4
Arctic Ocean 105 A1
Arctic Red r. Canada 4 E3
Ardabīl Iran 76 D6
Ardahan Turkey 75 E3
Ardas r. Greece 64 E4
Ardèche r. France 53 F3
Ardennes plateau Belgium 51 C1
Ardestān Iran 76 E5
Ardila r. Portugal 56 B3
Ardmore U.S.A. 11 C2
Arena, Point U.S.A. 9 A2
Arendal Norway 47 B2
Arequipa Peru 26 C2
Arere Brazil 27 G5
Arezzo Italy 58 C5
Arganda Spain 56 D4
Argentan France 52 C5
Argentina S. America 29 C5
Argentino, Lago lake Argentina 29 B2
Argenton-sur-Creuse France 52 D4
Argun' r. China/Rus. Fed. 73 K2
Argyle, Lake Australia 98 B4
Århus Denmark 47 B2
Arica Chile 28 B9
Arima Trinidad and Tobago 23 F1
Arinos Brazil 27 H2
Aripuanã Brazil 27 F3
Aripuanã r. Brazil 26 E4
Ariquemes Brazil 26 E4
Arizaro, Salar de salt flat Argentina 28 C8
Arizona admin div. U.S.A. 9 C1
Arkadelphia U.S.A. 11 D2
Arkalyk Kazakh. 79 C4
Arkansas admin div. U.S.A. 11 D2
Arkansas r. U.S.A. 11 D2
Arklow Ireland 49 C3
Arkona, Kap cape Germany 54 D6
Arles France 53 F2
Arlit Niger 39 D2
Arlon Belgium 51 D1
Armagh U.K. 49 C5
Armavir Armenia 75 F3
Armenia Asia 75 F3
Armenia town Colombia 26 B6
Armidale Australia 99 E2
Armyans'k Ukraine 67 D2
Arnauti, Cape Cyprus 74 C1
Arnhem Netherlands 50 D3
Arnhem, Cape Australia 99 C4
Arnhem Land f. Australia 98 C4
Arno r. Italy 58 C5
Arnsberg Germany 54 B4
Ar Ramādī Iraq 76 C5
Arran i. U.K. 48 D4
Ar Raqqah Syria 76 B6
Arras France 52 E6
Arriagá Mexico 19 F2
Ar Rimāl f. Saudi Arabia 77 E3
Arrowsmith, Mount New Zealand 101 C3
Ar Ruţbah Iraq 76 C5
Arta Greece 65 B3
Artemisa Cuba 22 B3
Artemivs'k Ukraine 67 E3
Artigas Uruguay 28 E6
Art'ik Armenia 75 F3
Artos Dağı mt. Turkey 75 E2
Artova Turkey 74 D3
Artsyz Ukraine 66 C2
Artvin Turkey 75 E3
Aru, Kepulauan is Indon. 91 E2

Aruanã Brazil 27 G3
Aruba i. Caribbean Sea 23 D1
Arunachal Pradesh admin div. India 81 G5
Arusha Tanzania 37 B2
Aruwimi r. Dem. Rep. Congo 41 C3
Arvayheer Mongolia 83 F5
Arviat Canada 5 I3
Arvidsjaur Sweden 46 D4
Arvika Sweden 47 C2
Arzamas Rus. Fed. 72 C2
Asahi-dake volcano Japan 86 D5
Asahikawa Japan 86 D5
Asansol India 81 F4
Ascencion i. S. Atlantic Ocean 31 G6
Ascensión Bolivia 26 E2
Ascensión, Bahía de la bay Mexico 19 G2
Ascoli Piceno Italy 58 D5
Åsele Sweden 46 D4
Asenovgrad Bulgaria 64 D5
Aşgabat Turkm. 78 B2
Ashburton r. Australia 98 A3
Ashburton New Zealand 101 C3
Asheville U.S.A. 16 C4
Ashford U.K. 49 G2
Ashland U.S.A. 13 C3
Ashmore and Cartier Islands territory Australia 98 B4
Ash Shiḩr Yemen 77 D1
Ashtarak Armenia 75 F3
Asia 70
Asinara, Golfo dell' bay Italy 59 B4
Asipovichy Belarus 69 B2
'Asīr f. Saudi Arabia 77 C3
Aşkale Turkey 75 E2
Askim Norway 47 B2
Asmara Eritrea 36 B4
Åsnen lake Sweden 47 C2
Aspang-Markt Austria 55 F2
Aspiring, Mount New Zealand 101 B2
Assab Eritrea 36 C4
Assal, Lake Djibouti 36 C4
Assam admin div. India 81 G5
As Samāwah Iraq 76 D5
As Sarīr f. Libya 35 E1
Assen Netherlands 50 E5
Assiniboine, Mount Canada 4 G2
Assis Brazil 28 F8
As Sulaymānīyah Iraq 76 D6
As Sulayyil Saudi Arabia 77 D3
As Sūq Saudi Arabia 77 C3
Astana Kazakh. 79 D4
Asti Italy 58 B6
Astorga Spain 56 B5
Astoria U.S.A. 8 A4
Astrakhan' Rus. Fed. 72 C1
Astravyets Belarus 69 B2
Asunción Para. 28 E7
Aswān Egypt 36 B5
Asyūţ Egypt 36 B5
Ata i. Tonga 96 F1
Atacama, Desierto de desert Chile see Atacama Desert
Atacama, Salar de salt flat Chile 28 C8
Atacama Desert Chile 28 C8
Atafu atoll Tokelau 96 F3
Atalaya Peru 26 C3
Atamyrat Turkm. 78 C2
Atâr Mauritania 38 B3
Atasu Kazakh. 79 D3
Atbara Sudan 36 B4
Atbara r. Sudan 36 B4
Atbasar Kazakh. 79 C4
Ath Belgium 51 B2
Athabasca r. Canada 4 G2
Athabasca, Lake Canada 5 H2
Athens Greece 65 C2
Athens Georgia U.S.A. 17 C3
Athens Texas U.S.A. 11 C2
Athlone Ireland 49 C3
Athos mt. Greece 64 D4
Ati Chad 40 B4
Atiu i. Cook Is 97 H2
Atlanta U.S.A. 17 C3
Atlantic City U.S.A. 14 C1
Atlantic Ocean 49 B5
Atlas Mountains Africa 34 B2
Atlas Saharien mts Algeria 34 C2
Atrato r. Colombia 26 B7
Aţ Ţā'if Saudi Arabia 77 C3
Atyrau Kazakh. 78 B3
Aube r. France 52 E5
Auburn U.S.A. 14 B2
Auckland New Zealand 100 E6
Augsburg Germany 55 C3

Augusta Georgia U.S.A. 17 C3
Augusta Maine U.S.A. 15 D2
Augustus, Mount Australia 98 A3
Aurangabad India 80 D3
Aurora Colorado U.S.A. 9 E2
Aurora Illinois U.S.A. 13 D2
Austin Nevada U.S.A. 9 B2
Austin Texas U.S.A. 11 C2
Australia Oceania 98
Australian Capital Territory admin div. Australia 99 D2
Austria Europe 55 D2
Auvergne, Monts d' mts France 53 E3
Auxerre France 52 E4
Avallon France 52 E4
Aveiro Brazil 27 F5
Aveiro Portugal 56 A4
Avellino Italy 59 E4
Avesta Sweden 47 D3
Aveyron r. France 53 D3
Avezzano Italy 59 D5
Aviemore U.K. 48 E5
Avignon France 53 F2
Ávila Spain 56 C4
Avilés Spain 56 C5
Avon r. England U.K. 49 E2
Avon r. England U.K. 49 F3
Avuavu Solomon Is 96 D3
Awarua Point New Zealand 101 B2
Āwash Ethiopia 37 C3
Awatere r. New Zealand 101 D4
Awbārī Libya 35 D1
Axel Heiberg Island Canada 5 I4
Ayacucho Peru 26 C3
Ayagoz Kazakh. 79 E3
Ayan Rus. Fed. 73 L2
Ayaviri Peru 26 C3
Aybas Kazakh. 78 A3
Aydar r. Ukraine 67 E3
Aydarkoʻl koʻli lake Uzbek. 78 C3
Aydın Turkey 74 A2
Ayers Rock hill Australia see Uluru
Ayr U.K. 48 D4
Ayteke Bi Kazakh. 78 C3
Ayutthaya Thailand 89 B2
Ayvalık Turkey 74 A2
Azaouâd f. Mali 38 C2
Azat, Gory hill Kazakh. 79 C3
Azerbaijan Asia 75 G3
Azhibeksor, Ozero lake Kazakh. 79 C4
Azores territory N. Atlantic Ocean 30 F8
Azov, Sea of Rus. Fed./Ukraine 67 E2
Azov, Sea of Rus. Fed./Ukraine 72 B1
Azuero, Península de Panama 21 C1
Azul Argentina 29 D5
Azul, Cordillera mts Peru 26 B4
Az Zarqā' Jordan 76 B5

B

Baardheere Somalia 37 C3
Bābā, Kōh-e mts Afgh. 79 C2
Babadağ mt. Azer. 75 G3
Babadag Romania 66 C2
Babaeski Turkey 74 A3
Bāb al Mandab strait Djibouti/Yemen 77 C1
Babar i. Indon. 91 D2
Babo Indon. 91 E2
Babruysk Belarus 69 C2
Babuyan Islands Phil. 91 D4
Bacabal Brazil 27 I5
Bacan i. Indon. 91 D2
Bacău Romania 66 B2
Back r. Canada 5 I3
Bac Liêu Vietnam 89 B1
Bacolod Phil. 91 D4
Badajoz Spain 56 B3
Baden Austria 55 F3
Baden-Baden Germany 55 B3
Badu Island Australia 99 D4
Badulla Sri Lanka 81 E1
Bafang Bay bay Canada 5 L4
Baffin Island Canada 5 L3
Bafoussam Cameroon 41 B3
Bāfq Iran 76 F5
Bafra Turkey 74 C3
Bāft Iran 76 F4
Bagé Brazil 28 F6
Baghdād Iraq 76 C5
Baghlān Afgh. 79 C2
Baguio Phil. 91 D4

113

Bahamas, The Caribbean Sea 22 C4
Baharly Turkm. 78 B2
Bahawalpur Pakistan 80 C5
Bahçe Turkey 74 D2
Bahía, Islas de la is Honduras 20 B3
Bahía Blanca Argentina 29 D5
Bahía Negra Para. 28 E8
Bahrain Asia 77 E4
Baia Mare Romania 66 A2
Baicheng China 83 J5
Baikal, Lake Rus. Fed. 73 I2
Bairiki Kiribati 97 F4
Bairnsdale Australia 99 D2
Baja Hungary 61 D1
Baja California peninsula Mexico
    18 B4
Baker U.S.A. 8 B3
Baker, Mount volcano U.S.A. 8 A4
Baker Island territory Pacific Ocean
    96 F4
Baker Lake Canada 5 I3
Bakersfield U.S.A. 9 B2
Bakhmach Ukraine 67 D3
Bakhtegan, Daryācheh-ye lake Iran
    76 E4
Bakırköy Turkey 74 B3
Baku Azer. 75 G3
Balabac Strait Malaysia/Philippines
    90 C3
Balakän Azer. 75 F3
Balakliya Ukraine 67 E3
Bala Lake U.K. 49 E3
Bālā Murghāb Afgh. 78 C2
Balanga Phil. 91 D4
Balaton, Lake Hungary 61 C1
Balbina, Represa de reservoir Brazil
    27 F5
Balclutha New Zealand 100 B1
Baldy Peak U.S.A. 9 D1
Balearic Islands Spain 57 F3
Baleia, Ponta da pt Brazil 27 J2
Baleine, Rivière à la r. Canada 7 D2
Baleshwar India 81 F4
Balestrieri, Punta mt. Italy 59 B4
Bali i. Indon. 90 C2
Balige Indon. 90 A3
Balıkesir Turkey 74 A2
Balikpapan Indon. 90 C2
Balimo P.N.G. 96 B3
Bali Sea Indon. 90 C2
Balkanabat Turkm. 78 B2
Balkan Mountains Bulgaria/Serbia
    64 C5
Balkash Kazakh. 79 D3
Balkashino Kazakh. 79 C4
Balkhash, Lake Kazakh. 78 D3
Ballarat Australia 99 D2
Ballena, Punta pt Chile 28 B7
Ballina Australia 99 E3
Ballina Ireland 49 B4
Ballinger U.S.A. 10 C2
Ballymena U.K. 48 C4
Balochistan f. Pakistan 80 A5
Balpyk Bi Kazakh. 79 D3
Balsas Brazil 27 H4
Balta Ukraine 66 C2
Bălţi Moldova 66 B2
Baltic Sea Europe 47 D1
Baltimore U.S.A. 16 C4
Balykchy Kyrg. 79 D3
Balykshi Kazakh. 78 B3
Bam Iran 76 F4
Bamako Mali 38 C2
Bamberg Germany 55 C3
Bambili Dem. Rep. Congo 41 C3
Bambouti C.A.R. 41 C3
Bāmyān Afgh. 79 C2
Banaba i. Kiribati 97 D3
Banabuiu, Açude reservoir Brazil 27 J4
Bananal, Ilha do i. Brazil 27 G3
Banaz Turkey 74 B2
Banda, Kepulauan is Indon. 91 D2
Banda Aceh Indon. 90 A3
Bandar-e ʿAbbās Iran 76 F4
Bandar-e Anzalī Iran 76 D6
Bandar-e Lengeh Iran 77 E4
Bandar-e Torkeman Iran 76 E6
Bandar Lampung Indon. 90 B2
Bandar Seri Begawan Brunei 90 C3
Banda Sea Indon. 91 E2
Bandirma Turkey 74 A3
Bandundu Dem. Rep. Congo 41 B2
Bandung Indon. 90 B2
Banff Canada 4 G2
Banff U.K. 48 E5

Bangalore India 80 D2
Bangassou C.A.R. 41 C3
Banggai, Kepulauan is Indon. 91 D2
Banggi i. Malaysia 90 C3
Bangka i. Indon. 90 B2
Bangko Indon. 90 B2
Bangkok Thailand 89 B2
Bangladesh Asia 81 F4
Bangor Northern Ireland U.K. 49 D4
Bangor Wales U.K. 49 D3
Bangor U.S.A. 15 D2
Bangui C.A.R. 41 B3
Bangweulu, Lake Zambia 42 B3
Bani r. Mali 38 C2
Banja Luka Bos. Herz. 62 C4
Banjarmasin Indon. 90 C2
Banjul The Gambia 38 B2
Banks Island Canada 4 F4
Banks Islands Vanuatu 97 D2
Banks Peninsula New Zealand 101 D3
Bann r. U.K. 48 C4
Bantry Ireland 49 B2
Baoding China 84 E5
Baoji China 84 C4
Baoshan China 85 A3
Baotou China 83 H4
Ba'qūbah Iraq 76 C5
Bar Montenegro 63 D3
Baracoa Cuba 22 D3
Barahona Dom. Rep. 23 D2
Baranavichy Belarus 69 B2
Barbacena Brazil 27 I1
Barbados Caribbean Sea 23 G1
Barbuda i. Antigua and Barbuda 23 F2
Barcaldine Australia 99 D3
Barcelona Spain 57 G4
Barcelona Venez. 26 E8
Barcelos Brazil 26 E5
Bareilly India 81 D5
Barents Sea Rus. Fed./Norway 72 B4
Bar Harbor U.S.A. 15 D2
Bari Italy 59 F4
Barinas Venez. 26 C7
Barisan, Pegunungan mts Indon.
    90 B2
Barkly Tableland f. Australia 99 C4
Bârlad Romania 66 B2
Barlee, Lake salt flat Australia 98 A3
Barletta Italy 59 F4
Barmer India 80 C5
Barnaul Rus. Fed. 72 G2
Barnstaple U.K. 49 D2
Barquisimeto Venez. 26 D8
Barra Brazil 27 I3
Barra i. U.K. 48 C5
Barra do Corda Brazil 27 H4
Barra do Garças Brazil 27 G2
Barranca Peru 26 B3
Barranquilla Colombia 26 C8
Barreal, El lake Mexico 18 C5
Barreiras Brazil 27 I3
Barretos Brazil 27 H1
Barrow r. Ireland 49 C3
Barrow U.S.A. 4 C4
Barrow, Point U.S.A. 4 C4
Barrow-in-Furness U.K. 49 E4
Barrow Island Australia 98 A3
Bartica Guyana 27 F7
Bartın Turkey 74 C3
Bartle Frere, Mount Australia 99 D4
Bartlesville U.S.A. 11 C3
Bartoszyce Poland 60 E5
Baruun-Urt Mongolia 83 H5
Barwon r. Australia 99 D2
Barysaw Belarus 69 C2
Basel Switz. 58 A7
Bashtanka Ukraine 67 D2
Basilan i. Phil. 91 D3
Basildon U.K. 49 G2
Basingstoke U.K. 49 F2
Başkale Turkey 75 F2
Basra Iraq 76 D5
Bassein Myanmar 88 A2
Basse-Terre Guadeloupe 23 F2
Basseterre St Kitts and Nevis 23 F2
Bass Strait Australia 99 D2
Bastak Iran 76 E4
Bastia France 53 H2
Bastogne Belgium 51 D2
Bastrop U.S.A. 11 D2
Bata Equat. Guinea 41 A3
Batabanó, Golfo de bay Cuba 22 B3
Batang China 85 A4
Batangas Phil. 91 D4
Batan Islands Phil. 91 D5

Batavia U.S.A. 14 B2
Bătdâmbâng Cambodia 89 B2
Batemans Bay town Australia 99 E2
Batesville U.S.A. 11 D3
Bath U.K. 49 E2
Bathurst Australia 99 D2
Bathurst Canada 7 D1
Bathurst Inlet Canada 5 H3
Bathurst Island Australia 98 C4
Bathurst Island Canada 5 I4
Batman Turkey 75 E2
Batna Algeria 35 C2
Baton Rouge U.S.A. 11 D2
Batticaloa Sri Lanka 81 E1
Batu, Pulau-pulau is Indon. 90 A2
Bat'umi Georgia 75 E3
Baubau Indon. 91 D2
Bauchi Nigeria 39 D2
Bauru Brazil 27 H1
Bauska Latvia 68 B3
Bautzen Germany 54 E4
Bawean i. Indon. 90 C2
Bayamo Cuba 22 C3
Bayanhongor Mongolia 82 F5
Bayb. Turkey 75 E3
Bay City Michigan U.S.A. 13 E2
Bay City Texas U.S.A. 11 C1
Baydaratskaya Guba bay Rus. Fed.
    72 E3
Baykan Turkey 75 E2
Baykonyr Kazakh. 78 C3
Bayombong Phil. 91 D4
Bayonne France 53 C2
Bayramaly Turkm. 78 C2
Bayreuth Germany 55 C3
Baza Spain 57 D2
Bazardyuzyu, Gora mt. Azer./Rus. Fed.
    75 F3
Beachy Head U.K. 49 G2
Beagle, Canal strait Argentina 29 C2
Bear Island Svalbard see Bjørnoya
Bear Paw Mountain U.S.A. 8 D4
Beata, Cabo cape Dom. Rep. 23 D2
Beata, Isla i. Dom. Rep. 23 D2
Beaufort Sea Canada/U.S.A. 4 D4
Beaufort West South Africa 42 B1
Beaumont U.S.A. 11 D2
Beaune France 52 F4
Beauvais France 52 E5
Beaver r. Canada 5 G2
Beaver U.S.A. 9 C2
Beaver Creek town Canada 4 D3
Becerreá Spain 56 B5
Béchar Algeria 34 B2
Beckley U.S.A. 16 C4
Bedelē Ethiopia 37 B3
Bedford U.K. 49 F3
Beenleigh Australia 99 E3
Beersheba Israel 76 A5
Beeville U.S.A. 11 C1
Bega Australia 99 D2
Béhague, Pointe pt French Guiana
    27 G6
Bei'an China 83 K5
Beihai China 85 C2
Beijing China 84 E5
Beira Mozambique 43 C3
Beirut Lebanon 76 B5
Beja Portugal 56 B3
Bejaïa Algeria 35 C2
Béjar Spain 56 C4
Békéscsaba Hungary 61 E1
Bela Pakistan 80 B5
Belarus Europe 69 B2
Belaya r. Rus. Fed. 73 P3
Bełchatów Poland 60 D3
Belcher Islands Canada 5 K2
Beledweyne Somalia 37 C3
Belém Brazil 27 H5
Belén Argentina 28 C7
Belen U.S.A. 9 D1
Belfast New Zealand 101 D3
Belfast U.K. 49 D4
Belfast U.S.A. 15 D2
Belgium Europe 51 C2
Belgorod Rus. Fed. 72 B2
Belgrade Serbia 62 E4
Belinyu Indon. 90 B2
Belitung i. Indon. 90 B2
Belize town Belize 20 B3
Belize N. America 20 B3
Bellac France 53 D4
Bellary India 80 D3
Belle-Île i. France 52 B4
Belle Isle, Strait of Canada 7 E2
Bellingham U.S.A. 8 A4

Bellinghausen Sea Antarctica 104 F2
Bellinzona Switz. 58 B7
Belluno Italy 58 D7
Belmonte Brazil 27 J2
Belmopan Belize 20 B3
Belo Horizonte Brazil 27 I2
Belukha, Gora mt. Kazakh./Rus. Fed.
    72 G1
Bemidji U.S.A. 12 C3
Benavente Spain 56 C5
Bend U.S.A. 8 A3
Bendigo Australia 99 D2
Benesov Czech Rep. 61 B2
Bengal, Bay of sea Indian Ocean
    81 F3
Bengbu China 84 E4
Benghazi Libya 35 E2
Bengkulu Indon. 90 B2
Benguela Angola 42 A3
Beni r. Bolivia 26 D3
Benidorm Spain 57 E3
Beni Mellal Morocco 34 B2
Benin Africa 39 D2
Benin, Bight of Africa 39 D1
Benin City Nigeria 39 D1
Benito Juárez Argentina 29 E5
Benjamim Constant Brazil 26 D5
Benjamín Hill town Mexico 18 B5
Ben Lawers mt. U.K. 48 D5
Ben Macdui mt. U.K. 48 E5
Ben More mt. U.K. 48 D5
Benmore, Lake New Zealand 101 C2
Ben Nevis mt. U.K. 48 D5
Bentonville U.S.A. 11 D3
Benue r. Nigeria 39 D1
Ben Wyvis mt. U.K. 48 D5
Benxi China 83 J4
Berat Albania 63 D2
Berau, Teluk bay Indon. 91 E2
Berbera Somalia 37 C4
Berbérati C.A.R. 41 B3
Berdyans'k Ukraine 67 E2
Berdychiv Ukraine 66 C3
Bereina P.N.G. 96 B3
Bereket Turkm. 78 B2
Berens River town Canada 5 I2
Berezhany Ukraine 66 B3
Berezivka Ukraine 67 C2
Berezniki Rus. Fed. 72 E3
Bergama Turkey 74 A2
Bergamo Italy 58 B6
Bergen Norway 47 B4
Bergerac France 53 D3
Bergisch Gladbach Germany 54 A4
Bering Strait Rus. Fed./U.S.A. 73 Q3
Berkeley U.S.A. 9 A3
Berkner Island Antarctica 104 D2
Berlin Germany 54 D5
Berlin U.S.A. 15 C2
Bermejo r. Argentina/Bolivia 28 D8
Bern Switz. 58 A7
Bernasconi Argentina 29 D5
Berry Islands The Bahamas 22 C4
Bershad' Ukraine 66 C3
Bertoua Cameroon 41 B3
Beruri Brazil 26 E5
Berwick-upon-Tweed U.K. 48 E4
Beryslav Ukraine 67 D2
Besançon France 52 G4
Besshoky, Gora hill Kazakh. 78 B3
Betanzos Spain 56 A5
Betpakdala plain Kazakh. 79 D3
Betsiboka r. Madagascar 43 D3
Beykoz Turkey 74 B3
Beyla Guinea 38 C1
Beyneu Kazakh. 78 B3
Beypazarı Turkey 74 B3
Beyşehir Turkey 74 B2
Beyşehir Gölü lake Turkey 74 B2
Béziers France 53 E2
Bhagalpur India 81 F5
Bhamo Myanmar 88 A3
Bhavnagar India 80 C4
Bhima r. India 80 D3
Bhopal India 80 D4
Bhubaneshwar India 81 F4
Bhuj India 80 B4
Bhutan Asia 81 G5
Biaban mts Iran 77 F4
Biak Indon. 91 E2
Biak i. Indon. 91 E2
Biała Podlaska Poland 60 F4
Białystok Poland 60 F4
Biarritz France 53 C2
Bibai Japan 86 D5
Biberach an der Riß Germany 55 B3

Bidar India 80 D3
Biddeford U.S.A. 15 C2
Biel Switz. 58 A7
Bielefeld Germany 54 B5
Biella Italy 58 B6
Bielsko-Biała Poland 61 D2
Biên Hoa Vietnam 89 B2
Bifoun Gabon 41 B2
Biga Turkey 74 A3
Bigadiç Turkey 74 B2
Bighorn r. U.S.A. 8 D4
Bighorn Mountains U.S.A. 8 D3
Big Lake town U.S.A. 10 B2
Big Rapids town U.S.A. 13 D2
Big Spring U.S.A. 10 B2
Big Trout Lake town Canada 6 B2
Bihać Bos. Herz. 62 B4
Bihar admin div. India 81 F4
Bihor, Vârful mt. Romania 66 A2
Bijapur India 80 D3
Bījār Iran 76 D6
Bijeljina Bos. Herz. 62 D4
Bijelo Polje Montenegro 63 D3
Bikaner India 80 C5
Bikini atoll Marshall Is 97 D5
Bilaspur India 81 E4
Bila Tserkva Ukraine 66 C3
Bilbao Spain 57 D5
Bilecik Turkey 74 B3
Bilhorod-Dnistrovs'kyy Ukraine 67 C2
Billings U.S.A. 8 D4
Bill of Portland cape U.K. 49 E2
Billund Denmark 47 B1
Bilma, Grand Erg de desert Niger
    39 E3
Biloela Australia 99 E3
Bilopillya Ukraine 67 D3
Binaija, Gunung mt. Indon. 91 D2
Binboğa Daği mt. Turkey 74 D2
Bindura Zimbabwe 43 C3
Bingham U.S.A. 15 D3
Binghamton U.S.A. 14 C2
Bingol Daği mt. Turkey 75 E2
Bintuhan Indon. 90 B2
Bintulu Malaysia 90 C3
Biobío r. Chile 29 B5
Bioco i. Equat. Guinea 41 A3
Birecik Turkey 75 D2
Bireun Indon. 90 A3
Birhan mt. Ethiopia 37 B4
Birigüi Brazil 28 F8
Bîrjand Iran 76 F5
Birmingham U.K. 49 F3
Birmingham U.S.A. 17 B3
Bîr Mogreïn Mauritania 38 B3
Birnin Konni Niger 39 D2
Bisbee U.S.A. 9 D1
Biscay, Bay of sea France/Spain 53 B3
Bischofshofen Austria 55 D2
Bishkek Kyrg. 79 D3
Bisho South Africa 42 B1
Biskra Algeria 35 C2
Bismarck U.S.A. 12 A3
Bismarck Archipelago is P.N.G. 96 B3
Bismarck Sea P.N.G. 96 B3
Bissau Guinea-Bissau 38 B2
Bistra mt. Kosovo/Macedonia 63 E3
Bistriţa Romania 66 B2
Bistriţa r. Romania 66 B2
Bitola Macedonia 63 E2
Bitterroot Range mts U.S.A. 8 C4
Biwa-ko lake Japan 87 C4
Biysk Rus. Fed. 72 G2
Bizerte Tunisia 35 C2
Bjørnøya i. Svalbard 105 B2
Blackall Australia 99 D3
Blackburn U.K. 49 E3
Black Forest mts Germany 55 B2
Black Hills U.S.A. 12 A2
Blackpool U.K. 49 E3
Black River Vietnam 88 B3
Black Sea Asia 74 B3
Black Sea Asia/Europe 67 D1
Black Volta r. Africa 38 C1
Blagoevgrad Bulgaria 64 C5
Blagoveshchensk Rus. Fed. 73 K2
Blair U.S.A. 12 B2
Blair Atholl U.K. 48 E5
Blanc, Mont mt. France/Italy 53 G3
Blanca, Bahía bay Argentina 29 D5
Blanche, Lake salt flat Australia 99 C3
Blanco r. Argentina 28 C6
Blanco r. Bolivia 26 E3
Blanco, Cape U.S.A. 8 A3
Blantyre Malawi 43 C3
Blenheim New Zealand 101 D4

Blida Algeria 34 C2
Bloemfontein South Africa 42 B2
Blois France 52 D4
Bloomington U.S.A. 13 D2
Bluefields Nicaragua 21 C2
Blue Mountains U.S.A. 8 B4
Blue Nile r. Sudan 36 B4
Blue Ridge mts U.S.A. 16 C4
Bluff New Zealand 101 B1
Blumenau Brazil 28 G7
Blytheville U.S.A. 11 E3
Bo Sierra Leone 38 B1
Boac Phil. 91 D4
Boa Esperança, Açude reservoir Brazil
  27 I4
Boa Viagem Brazil 27 J4
Boa Vista Brazil 26 E6
Boa Vista i. Cape Verde 38 A2
Bobaomby, Tanjona cape Madagascar
  43 D3
Bobo-Dioulasso Burkina Faso 38 C2
Bóbr r. Poland 60 B4
Bobrynets' Ukraine 67 D3
Boby mt. Madagascar 43 D2
Bocas del Toro Panama 21 C1
Bocholt Germany 54 A4
Bodélé f. Chad 40 B4
Boden Sweden 46 E4
Bodmin U.K. 49 D2
Bodmin Moor f. U.K. 49 D2
Bodø Norway 46 C4
Bodrum Turkey 74 A2
Bogalusa U.S.A. 11 E2
Boğazlıyan Turkey 74 C3
Boggeragh Mountains Ireland 49 B3
Bognor Regis U.K. 49 F2
Bogor Indon. 90 B2
Bogotá Colombia 26 C6
Bo Hai gulf China 84 F5
Bohemian Forest mts Germany 61 A2
Bohol i. Indon. 91 D3
Bohol Sea Phil. 91 D3
Bohu China 82 C4
Boise U.S.A. 8 B3
Boise City U.S.A. 10 B3
Bojnürd Iran 76 F6
Bolhrad Ukraine 66 C2
Bolívar Peru 26 B4
Bolívar, Pico mt. Venez. 26 C7
Bolivia S. America 26 E2
Bollnäs Sweden 47 D3
Bolmen lake Sweden 47 C2
Bologna Italy 58 D4
Bolsena, Lago di lake Italy 58 C5
Bol'shevik, Ostrov i. Rus. Fed. 73 I4
Bol'shoy Aluy r. Rus. Fed. 73 N3
Bol'shoy Lyakhovskiy, Ostrov i.
  Rus. Fed. 73 M4
Bolton U.K. 49 E3
Bolu Turkey 74 B3
Bolzano Italy 58 C7
Boma Dem. Rep. Congo 41 B2
Bombay India see Mumbai
Bømlo i. Norway 47 A2
Bonaire i. Caribbean Sea 23 E1
Bonaparte Archipelago is Australia
  98 B4
Bonavista Canada 7 E1
Bondoukou Côte d'Ivoire 38 C1
Bonete, Cerro mt. Argentina 28 C7
Bonifacio France 53 H1
Bonifacio, Strait of France/Italy 5
  3 H1
Bonn Germany 54 A4
Bonners Ferry U.S.A. 8 B4
Bontoc Phil. 91 D4
Bontosunggu Indon. 91 C2
Boothia, Gulf of Canada 5 J3
Boothia Peninsula Canada 5 I4
Bor Turkey 74 C2
Borankul Kazakh. 78 B3
Borås Sweden 47 C2
Borāzjān Iran 76 E4
Borborema, Planalto da plateau Brazil
  27 J4
Borçka Turkey 75 E3
Bordeaux France 53 C3
Borden Island Canada 5 G4
Borden Peninsula Canada 5 J4
Bordj Omer Driss Algeria 35 C1
Borlänge Sweden 47 C3
Borneo i. Asia 90 C2
Bornholm i. Denmark 47 C1
Bornova Turkey 74 A2
Borodyanka Ukraine 66 C3
Borovskoy Kazakh. 78 C4

Borsakelmas sho'rxogi salt marsh
  Uzbek. 78 B3
Borshchiv Ukraine 66 B3
Borūjerd Iran 76 D5
Boryspil' Ukraine 67 C3
Borzya Rus. Fed. 73 J2
Bosanska Dubica Bos. Herz. 62 C4
Bose China 85 C2
Bosna r. Bos. Herz. 62 D4
Bosnia and Herzegovina Europe 62 C4
Bosobolo Dem. Rep. Congo 41 B3
Bosporus strait Turkey 74 B3
Bossembélé C.A.R. 41 B3
Bosten Hu lake China 82 C4
Boston U.K. 49 F3
Boston U.S.A. 15 C2
Boston Mountains U.S.A. 11 D3
Botevgrad Bulgaria 64 C5
Bothnia, Gulf of Finland/Sweden
  47 D3
Botoşani Romania 66 B2
Botswana Africa 42 B2
Botte Donato, Monte mt. Italy 59 F3
Bottrop Germany 54 A4
Bouaké Côte d'Ivoire 38 C1
Bouar C.A.R. 41 B3
Bouârfa Morocco 34 B2
Bougainville Island P.N.G. 96 C3
Bouillon Belgium 51 D1
Boulder U.S.A. 9 D3
Boulogne-Billancourt France 52 E5
Boulogne-sur-Mer France 52 D6
Bourg-en-Bresse France 53 F4
Bourges France 52 E4
Bourke Australia 99 D2
Bournemouth U.K. 49 F2
Bowen Australia 99 D4
Bowling Green U.S.A. 16 B4
Boxtel Netherlands 50 D3
Boyabat Turkey 74 C3
Boyne r. Ireland 49 C3
Brabant Wallon admin. div. Belgium
  51 C2
Brač i. Croatia 63 C3
Bradano r. Italy 59 F4
Brades Montserrat 23 F2
Bradford U.K. 49 F3
Brady U.S.A. 10 C1
Braga Portugal 56 A4
Bragança Brazil 27 H5
Bragança Portugal 56 B4
Brahmapur India 81 E3
Brahmaputra r. China/India 81 G4
Brăila Romania 66 B2
Brämön i. Sweden 47 D3
Branco r. Brazil 26 E5
Brandenburg Germany 54 D5
Brandon Canada 5 I1
Brasileia Brazil 26 D3
Brasília Brazil 27 H2
Braşov Romania 66 B2
Bratislava Slovakia 61 C2
Bratsk Rus. Fed. 73 I2
Braunau am Inn Austria 55 D3
Braunschweig Germany 54 C5
Bray Ireland 49 C3
Brazil S. America 27 G3
Brazos r. U.S.A. 10 C1
Brazzaville Congo 41 B2
Bream Bay New Zealand 100 E7
Břeclav Czech Rep. 61 C2
Brecon U.K. 49 E2
Brecon Beacons f. U.K. 49 E2
Breda Netherlands 50 D3
Bremen Germany 54 B5
Bremerhaven Germany 54 B5
Brenham U.S.A. 11 D2
Brenner Pass Austria/Italy 55 C3
Brescia Italy 58 C6
Bressanone Italy 58 C7
Bressay i. U.K. 48 B5
Bressuire France 52 C4
Brest Belarus 69 A2
Brest France 52 B5
Breton Sound bay U.S.A. 11 E1
Brett, Cape New Zealand 100 E7
Brewarrina Australia 99 D3
Bria C.A.R. 40 C3
Briançon France 53 G3
Briceni Moldova 66 B3
Bridgend U.K. 49 E2
Bridgeport U.S.A. 15 C2
Bridgetown Barbados 23 G1
Bridgwater U.K. 49 E2
Bridlington U.K. 49 F4
Brig Switz. 58 A7

Brighton New Zealand 101 C2
Brighton U.K. 49 F2
Brindisi Italy 59 F4
Brisbane Australia 99 E3
Bristol U.K. 49 E2
Bristol U.S.A. 16 C4
Bristol Bay U.S.A. 4 B2
Bristol Channel estuary U.K. 49 D2
British Columbia admin. div. Canada
  4 F2
British Empire Range mts Canada 5 J5
Britstown South Africa 42 B1
Brittany f. France 52 B5
Brive-la-Gaillarde France 53 D3
Brno Czech Rep. 61 C2
Broad r. U.S.A. 16 C3
Brock Island Canada 5 G4
Brockville U.S.A. 14 B2
Brodeur Peninsula Canada 5 J4
Brody Ukraine 66 B3
Broken Arrow U.S.A. 11 C3
Broken Hill town Australia 99 D2
Brønderslev Denmark 47 B2
Brønnøysund Norway 46 C4
Brooke's Point town Phil. 90 C3
Brookhaven U.S.A. 17 A3
Brookings U.S.A. 12 B3
Brooks Range mts U.S.A. 4 C3
Broom, Loch inlet U.K. 48 D5
Broome Australia 98 B4
Brownfield U.S.A. 10 B2
Brownsville U.S.A. 11 C1
Brownwood U.S.A. 10 C2
Brugge Belgium 51 B3
Brumado Brazil 27 I3
Brunei Asia 90 C3
Brunflo Sweden 46 C3
Brunner, Lake New Zealand 101 C3
Brunswick Georgia U.S.A. 17 C3
Brunswick Maine U.S.A. 15 D2
Brunswick, Península de Chile 29 B2
Brussels Belgium 51 C2
Bryan U.S.A. 11 D2
Bryansk Rus. Fed. 72 B2
Buala Solomon Is 96 C3
Bucak Turkey 74 B2
Bucaramanga Colombia 26 C7
Bucharest Romania 66 B2
Buckland Tableland f. Australia 99 D3
Budapest Hungary 61 D1
Bude U.K. 49 D2
Buenaventura Colombia 26 B6
Buenaventura Mexico 18 C4
Buenos Aires Argentina 28 E6
Buenos Aires, Lago lake Argentina/
  Chile 29 B3
Buffalo New York U.S.A. 14 B2
Buffalo Wyoming U.S.A. 8 D3
Bug r. Poland 60 F3
Buin Nur l. Mongolia 83 I5
Bujumbura Burundi 37 A2
Bukavu Dem. Rep. Congo 41 C2
Bukoba Tanzania 37 B2
Bula Indon. 91 E2
Bulawayo Zimbabwe 42 B2
Bulgan Mongolia 83 F5
Bulgaria Europe 64 D5
Buller r. New Zealand 101 D4
Bulun Rus. Fed. 73 K4
Bunbury Australia 98 A2
Bundaberg Australia 99 E3
Buôn Ma Thuôt Vietnam 89 B2
Bunbury Australia 98 A2
Buraydah Saudi Arabia 77 C4
Burdur Turkey 74 B2
Burē Ethiopia 37 B4
Burgas Bulgaria 64 E5
Burghausen Germany 55 D3
Burgos Spain 56 D5
Burhanpur India 80 D4
Burkina Faso Africa 38 C2
Burlington Colorado U.S.A. 9 E2
Burlington Iowa U.S.A. 13 D2
Burlington Vermont U.S.A. 15 C2
Burma Asia see Myanmar
Burnie Australia 99 D1
Burnley U.K. 49 E3
Burns U.S.A. 8 B3
Burns Lake town Canada 4 F2
Burra Australia 99 C2
Burro, Serranías del mts Mexico
  18 D4
Bursa Turkey 74 B3
Burton upon Trent U.K. 49 F3
Buru i. Indon. 91 D2
Burundi Africa 37 A2
Burwash Landing Canada 4 E3

Buryn' Ukraine 67 D3
Bury St Edmunds U.K. 49 G3
Büshehr Iran 76 E4
Buta Dem. Rep. Congo 41 C3
Butler U.S.A. 14 B2
Buton i. Indon. 91 D2
Butte U.S.A. 8 C4
Butterworth Malaysia 90 B3
Butt of Lewis cape U.K. 48 C6
Butuan Phil. 91 D3
Buxoro Uzbek. 78 C2
Buzău Romania 66 B2
Byarezina r. Belarus 69 C2
Byaroza Belarus 69 B2
Bydgoszcz Poland 60 D4
Byerazino Belarus 69 C2
Bylot Island Canada 5 K4
Byrranga, Gory mts Rus. Fed. 73 H4
Bytom Poland 61 D3

C

Caballococha Peru 26 C5
Cabanatuan Phil. 91 D4
Cabezas Bolivia 26 E2
Cabimas Venez. 26 C8
Cabinda Angola 41 B2
Cabora Bassa, Lake reservoir
  Mozambique 43 C3
Caborca Mexico 18 B5
Cabo San Lucas Mexico 18 C3
Cabot Strait Canada 7 E1
Cabrera, Sierra de la mts Spain 56 B5
Cabriel r. Spain 57 E3
Cabruta Venez. 26 D7
Cacapava do Sul Brazil 28 F6
Cáceres Brazil 27 F2
Cáceres Spain 56 B3
Cachi Argentina 28 C7
Cachi, Nevados de mts Argentina
  28 C8
Cachimbo, Serra do hills Brazil 27 G4
Cachoeiro de Itapemirim Brazil 27 I1
Cadillac U.S.A. 13 D2
Cádiz Spain 56 B2
Cádiz, Golfo de gulf Spain 56 B2
Caen France 52 C5
Caernarfon U.K. 49 D3
Caernarfon Bay U.K. 49 D3
Caerphilly U.K. 49 E2
Cafayate Argentina 28 C7
Cagayan de Oro Phil. 91 D3
Cagliari Italy 59 B3
Cagliari, Golfo di bay Italy 59 B3
Çagyl Turkm. 78 B3
Cahir Ireland 49 C3
Cahors France 53 D3
Cahuapanas Peru 26 B4
Cahul Moldova 66 C2
Caia Mozambique 43 C3
Caiabis, Serra dos hills Brazil 27 F3
Caiapó, Serra do mts Brazil 27 G2
Caicos Islands Turks and Caicos Is
  23 D3
Caimodorro mt. Spain 57 E4
Cairngorm Mountains U.K. 48 E5
Cairns Australia 99 D4
Cairo Egypt 36 B6
Calabar Nigeria 39 D1
Calabozo Venez. 26 D7
Calafat Romania 66 A2
Calafate Argentina 29 B2
Calais France 52 D6
Calais U.S.A. 15 D3
Calama Brazil 26 E4
Calama Chile 28 C8
Calamian Group is Phil. 91 C4
Calamocha Spain 57 E4
Calapan Phil. 91 D4
Călăraşi Romania 66 B2
Calatayud Spain 57 E4
Calcanhar, Ponta do pt Brazil 27 J4
Calçoene Brazil 27 G6
Calcutta India see Kolkata
Caldas da Rainha Portugal 56 A3
Caldera Chile 28 B7
Caleta Olivia Argentina 29 C3
Calgary Canada 4 G2
Cali Colombia 26 B6
California admin. div. U.S.A. 9 A2
California, Gulf of Mexico 18 B5
Cälilabad Azer. 75 G2
Callao Peru 26 B3

Caltanissetta Italy 59 E2
Calvi France 53 H2
Camagüey Cuba 22 C3
Camagüey, Archipiélago de is Cuba
  22 C3
Camana Peru 26 C2
Camarones, Bahía bay Argentina
  29 C4
Ca Mau Vietnam 89 B1
Ca Mau, Mui cape Vietnam 89 B1
Cambrian Mountains U.K. 49 E3
Cambridge New Zealand 100 E6
Cambridge U.K. 49 G3
Cambridge U.S.A. 16 D4
Cambridge Bay town Canada 5 H3
Camden U.S.A. 11 D2
Camden, Isla i. Chile 29 B2
Cameroon Africa 41 B3
Cameroun, Mont volcano Cameroon
  41 A3
Cametá Brazil 27 H5
Campana, Isla i. Chile 29 A3
Campbell, Cape New Zealand 101 E4
Campbell River town Canada 4 F2
Campbeltown U.K. 48 D4
Campeche Mexico 19 F2
Campeche, Bahía de gulf Mexico
  19 F2
Câmpina Romania 66 B2
Campina Grande Brazil 27 J4
Campinas Brazil 27 H1
Campobasso Italy 59 E4
Campo Grande Brazil 27 G1
Campos Brazil 27 I1
Câmpulung Moldovenesc Romania
  66 B2
Çan Turkey 74 A3
Canada N. America 4 G3
Canadian U.S.A. 10 B3
Canadian r. U.S.A. 10 B3
Çanakkale Turkey 74 A3
Cananea Mexico 18 C7
Cañar Ecuador 26 B5
Canary Islands N. Atlantic Ocean
  34 A1
Canaveral, Cape U.S.A. 17 C2
Canberra Australia 99 D2
Cancún Mexico 19 G3
Caniapiscau r. Canada 7 D2
Caniapiscau, Lac lake Canada 7 C2
Çankırı Turkey 74 C3
Cannes France 53 G2
Canoas Brazil 28 F7
Cantabrian Mountains Spain 56 C5
Canterbury U.K. 49 G2
Canterbury Bight bay New Zealand
  101 C2
Canterbury Plains New Zealand
  101 C3
Cân Thơ Vietnam 89 B2
Canto do Buriti Brazil 27 I4
Canton Mississippi U.S.A. 17 B3
Canton Ohio U.S.A. 13 E2
Canumã Brazil 27 F5
Canyon town U.S.A. 10 B3
Cao Bằng Vietnam 88 B3
Capbreton France 53 C2
Cape Breton Island Canada 7 D1
Cape Town South Africa 42 A1
Cape Verde N. Atlantic Ocean 38 A2
Cape York Peninsula Australia 99 D4
Cap-Haïtien Haiti 23 D3
Capim r. Brazil 27 H5
Capraia, Isola di i. Italy 58 B5
Caprera, Isola i. Italy 59 B4
Capri, Isola di i. Italy 59 E4
Capricorn Channel Australia 99 E3
Caprivi Strip f. Namibia 42 B3
Caquetá r. Colombia 26 B6
Caracal Romania 66 B2
Caracas Venez. 26 D8
Carahue Chile 29 B5
Caransebeş Romania 66 A2
Caratasca, Laguna de lagoon
  Honduras 21 C3
Caratinga Brazil 27 I2
Carauari Brazil 26 D5
Caravaca de la Cruz Spain 57 E3
Carazinho Brazil 28 F7
Carbonara, Capo cape Italy 59 B3
Carcassonne France 53 E2
Cárdenas Mexico 19 F3
Cardiel, Lago lake Argentina 29 B3
Cardiff U.K. 49 E2
Cardigan Bay U.K. 49 D3
Carei Romania 66 A2

Carey, Lake *salt flat* Australia **98** B3
Cargados Carajos Islands Mauritius **92** D3
Carhué Argentina **29** D5
Caribbean Sea Atlantic Ocean **22** C2
Caribou U.S.A. **15** D3
Caribou Mountains Canada **4** G2
Carinhanha *r.* Brazil **27** I3
Carletonville South Africa **42** B2
Carlisle U.K. **48** E4
Carlow Ireland **49** C3
Carlsbad U.S.A. **9** E1
Carmacks Canada **4** E3
Carmarthen U.K. **49** D2
Carmarthen Bay U.K. **49** D2
Carmen, Isla *i.* Mexico **18** B4
Carnac France **52** B4
Carnegie, Lake *salt flat* Australia **98** B3
Carnic Alps *mts* Italy **58** D7
Car Nicobar *i.* India **81** G1
Carnsore Point Ireland **49** C3
Carolina Brazil **27** H4
Caroline Islands Micronesia **96** B4
Caroline Peak New Zealand **101** A2
Carpathian Mountains Romania **66** A3
Carpentaria, Gulf of Australia **99** C4
Carpentras France **53** F3
Carrantuohill *mt.* Ireland **49** B2
Carranza, Cabo *cape* Chile **28** B5
Carrara Italy **58** C6
Carrick-on-Shannon Ireland **49** B3
Carrick-on-Suir Ireland **49** C3
Carrington U.S.A. **12** B3
Carrizo Springs *town* U.S.A. **10** C1
Carrizozo U.S.A. **9** D1
Carroll U.S.A. **12** C2
Carson City U.S.A. **9** B2
Cartagena Colombia **26** B8
Cartagena Spain **57** E2
Caruarú Brazil **27** J4
Casablanca Morocco **34** B2
Cascade Point New Zealand **101** B2
Cascade Range *mts* U.S.A. **8** A3
Cascavel Brazil **28** F8
Caserta Italy **59** E4
Casino Australia **99** E3
Casper U.S.A. **8** D3
Caspian Lowland Kazakh./Rus. Fed. **72** C1
Caspian Lowland Kazakh./Rus. Fed. **78** A3
Caspian Sea Asia/Europe **78** A3
Cassiar Mountains Canada **4** E3
Castanhal Brazil **27** H5
Castelló de la Plana Spain **57** E3
Castlebar Ireland **49** B3
Castle Douglas U.K. **48** E4
Castres France **53** E2
Castries St Lucia **23** F1
Castro Verde Portugal **56** A2
Cataluña *f.* Spain **57** F4
Catamarca Argentina **28** C7
Catanduanes *i.* Phil. **91** D4
Catania Italy **59** E2
Catanzaro Italy **59** F3
Catarman Phil. **91** D4
Catbalogan Phil. **91** D4
Cat Island The Bahamas **22** C3
Catoche, Cabo *cape* Mexico **19** G3
Catriló Argentina **29** D5
Catskill Mountains U.S.A. **14** C2
Cauca *r.* Colombia **26** C7
Caucasia Colombia **26** B7
Caucasus *mts* Georgia/Rus. Fed. **75** E3
Cauquenes Chile **28** B5
Căușeni Moldova **66** C2
Cavan Ireland **49** C3
Caxias Brazil **27** I5
Caxias do Sul Brazil **28** F7
Cayenne French Guiana **27** G6
Cayman Brac *i.* Cayman Is **22** C2
Cayman Islands *territory* Caribbean Sea **22** B2
Cebu Phil. **91** D4
Cedar Rapids *town* U.S.A. **13** C2
Cedros, Isla *i.* Mexico **18** A4
Ceduna Australia **98** C2
Cefalù Italy **59** E3
Cegléd Hungary **61** D1
Celaya Mexico **19** D3
Celebes *i.* Indon. **91** D2
Celebes Sea Indon./Philippines **91** D3
Celje Slovenia **55** E2
Celle Germany **54** C5
Cenderawasih, Teluk *bay* Indon. **91** E2
Central, Cordillera *mts* Colombia **26** B6
Central, Cordillera *mts* Peru **26** B4
Central African Republic Africa **40** B3
Central Range *mts* P.N.G. **96** B3
Central Siberian Plateau Rus. Fed. **73** J3
Central Valley *depression* U.S.A. **9** A2
Cephalonia *i.* Greece **65** B3
Ceram Sea Indon. **91** E2
Ceres Argentina **28** D7
Cernavodă Romania **66** C2
Cerralvo, Isla *i.* Mexico **18** C3
Cerritos Mexico **19** D3
Cervo Spain **56** B5
České Budějovice Czech Rep. **61** B2
Çeşme Turkey **74** A2
Cetinje Montenegro **63** D3
Ceuta N. Africa **56** C1
Ceva-i-Ra *reef* Fiji **97** E1
Cévennes *mts* France **53** E2
Ceyhan Turkey **74** C2
Chābahār Iran **77** G4
Chachapoyas Peru **26** B4
Chachoengsao Thailand **89** B2
Chad Africa **40** B4
Chad, Lake Africa **40** B4
Chadron U.S.A. **12** A2
Chaek Kyrg. **79** D3
Chagai Hills Afgh./Pakistan **80** A5
Chaghcharān Afgh. **78** C2
Chagos Archipelago *is* British Indian Ocean Terr. **92** E4
Chalkida Greece **65** C3
Chalky Inlet New Zealand **101** A1
Challapata Bolivia **26** D2
Challis U.S.A. **8** C3
Châlons-en-Champagne France **52** F5
Chalon-sur-Saône France **52** F4
Chālus Iran **76** E6
Chaman Pakistan **80** B6
Chambéry France **53** F3
Chamonix-Mont-Blanc France **53** G3
Champaign U.S.A. **13** D2
Champotón Mexico **19** F2
Chañaral Chile **28** B7
Chandalar *r.* U.S.A. **4** D3
Chandeleur Islands U.S.A. **11** E1
Chandigarh India **80** D6
Chandrapur India **81** D3
Changchun China **83** K4
Changde China **85** D3
Chang Jiang *r.* China **85** E4
Changsha China **85** D3
Changzhi China **84** D5
Changzhou China **84** E4
Chania Greece **65** D1
Channel Islands English Channel **49** E1
Channel Islands U.S.A. **9** B1
Channel-Port-aux-Basques Canada **7** E1
Chanthaburi Thailand **89** B2
Chapala, Laguna de *lake* Mexico **18** D3
Chapayevo Kazakh. **78** B4
Chapecó Brazil **28** F7
Chapleau Canada **6** B1
Chārīkār Afgh. **79** C2
Charleroi Belgium **51** C2
Charles, Cape U.S.A. **16** D4
Charleston *South Carolina* U.S.A. **17** D3
Charleston *West Virginia* U.S.A. **16** C4
Charleston Peak U.S.A. **9** B2
Charleville Australia **99** D3
Charleville-Mézières France **52** F5
Charlotte U.S.A. **16** C4
Charlotte Amalie Virgin Is (U.S.A.) **23** F2
Charlottesville U.S.A. **16** D4
Charlottetown Canada **7** D1
Charters Towers Australia **99** D3
Chartres France **52** D5
Chassiron, Pointe de *pt* France **53** C4
Châteaubriant France **52** C4
Châteaudun France **52** D5
Châteauroux France **52** D4
Château-Thierry France **52** E5
Châtellerault France **52** D4
Chattahoochee *r.* U.S.A. **17** C3
Chattanooga U.S.A. **16** B4
Chaumont France **52** F5
Chaves Brazil **27** H5
Cheb Czech Rep. **61** A3
Cheboksary Rus. Fed. **72** C2
Cheddar U.K. **49** E2
Chehalis U.S.A. **8** A4
Cheju-do *i.* South Korea **87** A3
Cheju-haehyŏp *strait* South Korea **87** A3
Chelan, Lake U.S.A. **8** A4
Chełm Poland **60** F3
Chelmer *r.* U.K. **49** G2
Chelmsford U.K. **49** G2
Cheltenham U.K. **49** E2
Chelyabinsk Rus. Fed. **72** E2
Chemnitz Germany **54** D4
Chengde China **84** E6
Chengdu China **85** B4
Chennai India **81** E2
Chenzhou China **85** D3
Cher *r.* France **52** D4
Cherbourg France **52** C5
Cherepovets Rus. Fed. **72** B2
Cherkasy Ukraine **67** D3
Chernihiv Ukraine **67** C3
Chernivtsi Ukraine **66** B3
Chernyshevskiy Rus. Fed. **73** J3
Cherskogo, Khrebet *mts* Rus. Fed. **73** M3
Chervonohrad Ukraine **66** B3
Cherwell *r.* U.K. **49** F2
Cherykaw Belarus **69** C2
Chesapeake Bay U.S.A. **16** D4
Chester U.K. **49** E3
Chester U.S.A. **13** D1
Chesterfield U.K. **49** F3
Chesterfield, Îles *is* New Caledonia **96** C2
Chesuncook Lake U.S.A. **15** D3
Chetumal Mexico **19** G2
Cheviot Hills U.K. **48** E4
Cheyenne U.S.A. **9** E3
Cheyenne *r.* U.S.A. **12** A2
Chhattisgarh *admin div.* India **81** E4
Chiang Mai Thailand **88** A2
Chiang Rai Thailand **88** A2
Chiba Japan **87** D4
Chibougamau Canada **6** C1
Chicago U.S.A. **13** D2
Chichester Range *mts* Australia **98** A3
Chickasha U.S.A. **11** C3
Chiclayo Peru **26** B4
Chico *r. Chubut* Argentina **29** C4
Chico *r. Santa Cruz* Argentina **29** C3
Chicoutimi Canada **7** C1
Chidley, Cape Canada **7** D3
Chiemsee *lake* Germany **55** D2
Chieti Italy **58** E5
Chifeng China **83** I4
Chifre, Serra do *mts* Brazil **27** I2
Chihuahua Mexico **18** C4
Childress U.S.A. **10** B2
Chile S. America **28** B6
Chillán Chile **29** B5
Chillicothe U.S.A. **13** E1
Chiloé, Isla de *i.* Chile **29** B4
Chilpancingo Mexico **19** E2
Chimborazo *mt.* Ecuador **26** B5
Chimbote Peru **26** B4
Chimboy Uzbek. **78** B3
Chimoio Mozambique **43** C3
Chimtargha, Qullai *mt.* Tajik. **79** C2
Chinandega Nicaragua **20** B2
Chincha Alta Peru **26** B3
Chinchorro, Banco *reef* Mexico **19** G2
Chindwin *r.* Myanmar **88** A3
Chingola Zambia **42** B3
Chinhoyi Zimbabwe **43** C3
Chinju South Korea **87** A4
Chinoz Uzbek. **79** C3
Chioggia Italy **58** D6
Chios Greece **65** E3
Chios *i.* Greece **65** D3
Chipata Zambia **43** C3
Chipchihua, Sierra de *mts* Argentina **29** C4
Chiquinquira Colombia **26** C7
Chirchiq Uzbek. **79** C3
Chiricahua Peak U.S.A. **9** D1
Chiriquí, Golfo de *bay* Panama **21** C1
Chiri-san *mt.* South Korea **87** A4
Chirripó *mt.* Costa Rica **21** C1
Chisasibi Canada **6** C2
Chișinău Moldova **66** C2
Chita Rus. Fed. **73** J2
Chitambo Zambia **43** C3
Chitradurga India **80** D2
Chitral Pakistan **80** C7
Chitré Panama **21** C1
Chittagong Bangladesh **81** G4
Chittoor India **81** D2
Chitungwiza Zimbabwe **43** C3
Choele Choel Argentina **29** C5
Choiseul *i.* Solomon Is **96** C3
Chojnice Poland **60** C4
Cholet France **52** C4
Choluteca Honduras **20** B2
Chomutov Czech Rep. **60** A3
Chon Buri Thailand **89** B2
Chone Ecuador **26** A5
Ch'ŏngjin North Korea **86** A5
Ch'ŏngju South Korea **87** A4
Chongqing China **85** C3
Chongqing *admin div.* China **85** C3
Chonos, Archipiélago de los *is* Chile **29** B3
Chornobyl' Ukraine **67** C3
Chornomors'ke Ukraine **67** D2
Chortkiv Ukraine **66** B3
Chōshi Japan **87** D4
Choûm Mauritania **38** B3
Choybalsan Mongolia **83** H5
Christchurch New Zealand **101** D3
Christmas Island *territory* Indian Ocean **90** B1
Chubut *r.* Argentina **29** C4
Chudniv Ukraine **66** C3
Chūgoku-sanchi *mts* Japan **87** B3
Chuhuyiv Ukraine **67** E3
Chukchi Sea Rus. Fed./U.S.A. **73** Q3
Chukotskiy Poluostrov *peninsula* Rus. Fed. **73** Q3
Chumbicha Argentina **28** C7
Chumphon Thailand **89** A2
Ch'unch'ŏn South Korea **87** A4
Chunya *r.* Rus. Fed. **73** H3
Chuquicamata Chile **28** C8
Chur Switz. **58** B7
Churchill Canada **5** I2
Churchill *r. Man.* Canada **5** I2
Churchill *r. Nfld. and Lab.* Canada **7** D2
Churchill, Cape Canada **5** I2
Chuuk *i.* Micronesia **96** C4
Chuxiong China **85** B3
Ciechanów Poland **60** E4
Ciego de Ávila Cuba **22** C3
Cienfuegos Cuba **22** B3
Cigüela *r.* Spain **57** D3
Cihanbeyli Turkey **74** C2
Cilacap Indon. **90** B2
Cilo Dağı *mt.* Turkey **75** F2
Çiloy Adası *i.* Azer. **75** G3
Cimișlia Moldova **66** C2
Cimone, Monte *mt.* Italy **58** C6
Cinca *r.* Spain **57** F4
Cincinnati U.S.A. **13** E1
Ciney Belgium **51** D2
Cinto, Monte *mt.* France **53** H2
Cirebon Indon. **90** B2
Cisne, Islas del Honduras **21** C3
Ciudad Acuña Mexico **19** D4
Ciudad Altamirano Mexico **19** D2
Ciudad Bolívar Venez. **26** E7
Ciudad Camargo Mexico **18** C4
Ciudad del Carmen Mexico **19** F2
Ciudad Delicias Mexico **18** C4
Ciudad de Valles Mexico **19** E3
Ciudad Guayana Venez. **26** E7
Ciudad Ixtepec Mexico **19** E2
Ciudad Juárez Mexico **18** C5
Ciudad Mante Mexico **19** E3
Ciudad Obregón Mexico **18** C4
Ciudad Real Spain **56** D3
Ciudad Rodrigo Spain **56** B4
Ciudad Victoria Mexico **19** E3
Ciutadella de Menorca Spain **57** G4
Civitavecchia Italy **59** C5
Çivril Turkey **74** B2
Cixi China **85** F4
Cizre Turkey **75** E2
Claremont U.S.A. **15** C2
Clarence New Zealand **101** D3
Clarence *r.* New Zealand **101** D3
Clarión, Isla *i.* Mexico **18** B2
Clark Hill Reservoir U.S.A. **17** C3
Clarksburg U.S.A. **16** C4
Clarksville *Arkansas* U.S.A. **11** D3
Clarksville *Tennessee* U.S.A. **16** B4
Claro *r.* Brazil **28** F9
Clear, Cape Ireland **49** B2
Clearwater U.S.A. **17** C2
Cleburne U.S.A. **11** C2
Clermont Australia **99** D3
Clermont-Ferrand France **53** E3
Cleveland U.S.A. **13** E2
Cleveland, Mount U.S.A. **8** C4
Clifton U.S.A. **9** D1
Clinton U.S.A. **10** C3
Clisham *hill* U.K. **48** C5
Cloncurry Australia **99** D3
Clonmel Ireland **49** C3
Cloud Peak U.S.A. **8** D3
Cloudy Bay New Zealand **101** E4
Clovis U.S.A. **9** E1
Cluj-Napoca Romania **66** A2
Clutha *r.* New Zealand **101** B2
Clwyd *r.* U.K. **49** E3
Clyde *r.* U.K. **48** D4
Clyde, Firth of *estuary* U.K. **48** D4
Clyde River *town* Canada **5** L4
Coari Brazil **26** E5
Coari *r.* Brazil **26** E4
Coast Mountains Canada **4** F2
Coast Ranges *mts* U.S.A. **9** A3
Coats Island Canada **5** J3
Coats Land *f.* Antarctica **104** C2
Coatzacoalcos Mexico **19** F2
Cobán Guat. **20** A3
Cobar Australia **99** D2
Cobh Ireland **49** B2
Coca Ecuador **26** B5
Cochabamba Bolivia **26** D2
Cochin India **80** D1
Cochrane Chile **29** B3
Coco *r.* Nicaragua/Hond. **21** C2
Coco, Isla de *i.* Costa Rica **20** B1
Cocos Islands *territory* Indian Ocean **90** A1
Cocuy, Sierra Nevada del *mt.* Colombia **26** C7
Cod, Cape U.S.A. **15** C2
Codfish Island New Zealand **101** A1
Codó Brazil **27** I5
Coffs Harbour *town* Australia **99** E2
Coiba, Isla de *i.* Panama **21** C1
Coig *r.* Argentina **29** C2
Coihaique Chile **29** B3
Coimbatore India **80** D2
Coimbra Portugal **56** A4
Colby U.S.A. **12** A1
Colchester U.K. **49** G2
Coldstream U.K. **48** E4
Coleman U.S.A. **10** C2
Coleraine U.K. **48** C4
Coleridge, Lake New Zealand **101** C3
Colima Mexico **18** D2
Colima, Nevado de *volcano* Mexico **18** D2
Coll *i.* U.K. **48** C5
Collier Bay Australia **98** B4
Colmar France **52** G5
Cologne Germany **54** A4
Colômbia Brazil **28** G8
Colombia S. America **26** C6
Colombo Sri Lanka **81** D1
Colón Argentina **28** E6
Colón Panama **21** D1
Colorado *r.* Argentina **29** D5
Colorado *r.* Mexico/U.S.A. **9** C1
Colorado *admin div.* U.S.A. **9** D2
Colorado *r.* U.S.A. **10** C1
Colorado Plateau U.S.A. **9** C2
Colorado Springs *town* U.S.A. **9** E2
Columbia *Missouri* U.S.A. **13** C1
Columbia *South Carolina* U.S.A. **17** C3
Columbia *r. Washington* U.S.A. **8** A4
Columbia, Mount Canada **4** G2
Columbia Plateau U.S.A. **8** B3
Columbus *Georgia* U.S.A. **17** C3
Columbus *Mississippi* U.S.A. **17** B3
Columbus *Nebraska* U.S.A. **12** B2
Columbus *Ohio* U.S.A. **13** E1
Colville *r.* U.S.A. **4** C4
Colville Channel New Zealand **100** E6
Colwyn Bay *town* U.K. **49** E3
Comacchio Italy **58** D6
Comandante Salas Argentina **28** C6
Comitán de Domínguez Mexico **19** F2
Como Italy **58** B6
Como, Lake Italy **58** B6
Comodoro Rivadavia Argentina **29** C3
Comoros Africa **43** D3
Compostela Mexico **18** D3
Comrat Moldova **66** C2
Conakry Guinea **38** B1
Concarneau France **52** B4
Conceição do Araguaia Brazil **27** H4
Concepción Argentina **28** C7
Concepción Chile **29** B5

118

Florida *admin div.* U.S.A. 17 C2
Florida, Straits of The Bahamas/U.S.A. 22 B3
Florida Keys *is* U.S.A. 17 C1
Florina Greece 64 B4
Florø Norway 47 A3
Fly *r.* P.N.G. 96 B3
Foča Bos. Herz. 62 D3
Focşani Romania 66 B2
Foggia Italy 59 E4
Fogo *i.* Cape Verde 38 A2
Foix France 53 D2
Foligno Italy 58 D5
Folkestone U.K. 49 G2
Fonseca, Golfo de *bay* El Salvador/Honduras 20 B2
Fontainebleau France 52 E5
Fonte Boa Brazil 26 D5
Førde Norway 47 A3
Fordyce U.S.A. 11 D2
Forfar U.K. 48 E5
Forlì Italy 58 D6
Formentera *i.* Spain 57 F3
Formosa Argentina 28 E7
Formosa Brazil 27 H2
Formosa, Serra *hills* Brazil 27 F3
Forrest City U.S.A. 11 D3
Forssa Finland 47 E3
Forsyth U.S.A. 8 D4
Fort Albany Canada 6 B2
Fortaleza Brazil 27 J5
Fort Augustus U.K. 48 D5
Fort Chipewyan Canada 5 G2
Fort-de-France Martinique 23 F1
Fort Frances Canada 6 A1
Fort Good Hope Canada 4 F3
Forth, Firth of *estuary* U.K. 48 E5
Fortín Capitán Demattei Para. 28 D8
Fortín General Mendoza Para. 28 D8
Fortín Pilcomayo Argentina 28 D8
Fort Lauderdale U.S.A. 17 C2
Fort Liard Canada 4 F3
Fort McMurray Canada 5 G2
Fort McPherson Canada 4 E3
Fort Myers U.S.A. 17 C2
Fort Nelson Canada 4 F2
Fort Peck Reservoir U.S.A. 8 D4
Fort Pierce U.S.A. 17 C2
Fortrose New Zealand 101 B1
Fort St John Canada 4 F2
Fort Scott U.S.A. 12 C1
Fort Severn Canada 6 B2
Fort-Shevchenko Kazakh. 78 B3
Fort Simpson Canada 4 F3
Fort Smith Canada 5 G2
Fort Smith U.S.A. 11 D3
Fort Stockton U.S.A. 10 B2
Fort Sumner U.S.A. 9 E1
Fort Wayne U.S.A. 13 D2
Fort William U.K. 48 D5
Fort Worth U.S.A. 11 C2
Foshan China 85 D2
Fossano Italy 58 A6
Fougères France 52 C5
Foulwind, Cape New Zealand 101 C4
Fouta Djallon *f.* Guinea 38 B2
Foveaux Strait New Zealand 101 A1
Foxe Basin *gulf* Canada 5 K3
Foxe Channel Canada 5 J3
Foxe Peninsula Canada 5 K3
Fox Islands U.S.A. 4 B2
Foxton New Zealand 100 E4
Foyle *r.* Ireland/U.K. 48 C4
Foyle, Lough *bay* Ireland/U.K. 48 C4
Foz do Iguaçu Brazil 28 F7
Franca Brazil 27 H1
France Europe 52 D4
Franceville Gabon 41 B2
Francis Case, Lake U.S.A. 12 B2
Francistown Botswana 42 B2
Frankfurt am Main Germany 54 B4
Frankfurt an der Oder Germany 54 E5
Fränkische Alb *hills* Germany 55 C3
Franklin U.S.A. 14 B2
Franklin D. Roosevelt Lake *reservoir* U.S.A. 8 B4
Franklin Mountains New Zealand 101 A2
Frantsa-Iosifa, Zemlya *is* Rus. Fed. 72 D4
Frasca, Capo della *cape* Italy 59 B3
Fraser *r.* Canada 4 F2
Fraserburgh U.K. 48 E5
Fraser Island Australia 99 E3
Fray Bentos Uruguay 28 E6

Fredericia Denmark 47 B1
Fredericksburg U.S.A. 10 C2
Fredericton Canada 7 D1
Frederikshavn Denmark 47 B2
Fredrikstad Norway 47 B2
Freeport U.S.A. 11 C1
Freeport City The Bahamas 22 C4
Freetown Sierra Leone 38 B1
Freiburg im Breisgau Germany 55 A3
Fréjus France 53 G2
Fremantle Australia 98 A2
French Guiana S. America 27 G6
Fresnillo Mexico 18 D3
Fresno U.S.A. 9 B2
Fria Guinea 38 B2
Friedrichshafen Germany 55 B2
Friesland *admin div.* Netherlands 50 D5
Frobisher Bay Canada 5 L3
Frohavet *bay* Norway 46 B3
Frome, Lake *salt flat* Australia 99 C2
Frontera Mexico 19 F2
Frosinone Italy 59 D4
Frøya *i.* Norway 46 B3
Frýdek-Místek Czech Rep. 61 D2
Fuenlabrada Spain 56 D4
Fuerteventura *i.* Canary Islands 34 A1
Fujairah United Arab Emirates 77 F4
Fujian *admin div.* China 85 E3
Fuji-san *volcano* Japan 87 C4
Fukui Japan 87 C4
Fukuoka Japan 87 B3
Fukushima Japan 87 D4
Fulda Germany 54 B4
Funafuti *atoll* Tuvalu 97 E3
Furnas, Represa *reservoir* Brazil 27 H1
Fürth Germany 55 C3
Fushun China 83 J4
Füssen Germany 55 C2
Fuxin China 83 J4
Fuyang China 84 E4
Fuyu China 83 J5
Fuzhou Fujian China 85 E3
Fuzhou Jiangxi China 85 E3
Füzuli Azer. 75 F2
Fyn *i.* Denmark 47 B1
Fyne, Loch *inlet* U.K. 48 D4

G

Gaalkacyo Somalia 37 C3
Gabès Tunisia 35 D2
Gabès, Gulf of *gulf* Tunisia 35 D2
Gabon Africa 41 B2
Gaborone Botswana 42 B2
Gabrovo Bulgaria 64 D5
Gadsden U.S.A. 17 B3
Gaeta Italy 59 D4
Gaeta, Golfo di *gulf* Italy 59 D4
Gafsa Tunisia 35 C2
Gagnon Canada 7 D2
Gainesville Florida U.S.A. 17 C2
Gainesville Georgia U.S.A. 16 C3
Gainesville Texas U.S.A. 11 C2
Gairdner, Lake *salt flat* Australia 99 C2
Galapagos Islands Pacific Ocean 103 L5
Galashiels U.K. 48 E4
Galaţi Romania 66 C2
Galdhøpiggen *mt.* Norway 47 B3
Galera, Punta *pt* Chile 29 B4
Galesburg U.S.A. 13 C2
Galilee, Sea of *lake* Israel 76 B5
Galle Sri Lanka 81 E1
Gallegos *r.* Argentina 29 B2
Gallipoli Italy 59 G4
Gallipoli Turkey 64 A4
Gällivare Sweden 46 E4
Gallup U.S.A. 9 D2
Galmudug *f.* Somalia 37 C3
Galtat Zemmour Western Sahara 34 A1
Galveston U.S.A. 11 D1
Galway Ireland 49 B3
Galway Bay Ireland 49 B3
Gambia *r.* The Gambia 38 B2
Gambia, The Africa 38 B2
Gäncä Azer. 75 F3
Gandadiwata, Bukit *mt.* Indon. 91 C2
Gander Canada 7 E1
Gandhidham India 80 C4
Gandhinagar India 80 C4

Gandía Spain 57 E3
Ganges *r.* Bangladesh/India 81 E5
Ganges, Mouths of the Bangladesh/India 81 F4
Gansu *admin div.* China 82 E3
Ganzhou China 85 D3
Gao Mali 39 C2
Gaoxiong Taiwan 85 F2
Gap France 53 G3
Gar China 82 B2
Garabil Belentligi *hills* Turkm. 78 C2
Garabogaz Turkm. 78 B3
Garabogazköl Turkm. 78 B3
Garabogazköl Aýlagy *bay* Turkm. 78 B3
Garanhuns Brazil 27 J4
Garcia Sola, Embalse de *reservoir* Spain 56 C3
Gard *r.* France 53 F2
Garda, Lake Italy 58 C6
Garden City U.S.A. 12 A1
Gardēz Afgh. 79 C2
Garissa Kenya 37 B2
Garkalne Latvia 68 B3
Garmisch-Partenkirchen Germany 55 C2
Garonne *r.* France 53 C3
Garoowe Somalia 37 C3
Garoua Cameroon 40 B3
Garré Argentina 29 C3
Garşy Turkm. 78 B3
Gary U.S.A. 13 D2
Garzón Colombia 26 B6
Gascony, Gulf of France 57 D5
Gascoyne *r.* Australia 98 A3
Gashua Nigeria 39 E2
Gaspé Canada 7 D1
Gaspé, Péninsule de *peninsula* Canada 7 D1
Gastonia U.S.A. 16 C4
Gata, Cabo de *cape* Spain 57 D2
Gatesville U.S.A. 11 C2
Gävle Sweden 47 D3
Gawler Australia 99 C2
Gaya India 81 E5
Gaya Niger 39 D2
Gaza *territory* Asia 76 A5
Gaza Gaza 76 A5
Gaziantep Turkey 74 D2
Gazojak Turkm. 78 C3
Gdańsk Poland 60 D5
Gdańsk, Gulf of Poland/Rus. Fed. 60 D5
Gdynia Poland 60 D5
Gedaref Sudan 36 B4
Geel Belgium 51 D3
Geelong Australia 99 D2
Gejiu China 85 B2
Gela Italy 59 E2
Gelderland *admin div.* Netherlands 50 E4
Gelincik Dağı *mt.* Turkey 74 B2
Gelsenkirchen Germany 54 A4
Gemlik Turkey 74 B3
General Acha Argentina 29 D5
General Alvear Argentina 28 C5
General Carrera, Lago *lake* Chile 29 B3
General Roca Argentina 29 C5
General Santos Phil. 91 D3
Genesee *r.* U.S.A. 14 B2
Geneva Switz. 58 A7
Geneva U.S.A. 14 B2
Geneva, Lake France/Switz. 52 G4
Genil *r.* Spain 56 C2
Genk Belgium 51 D2
Genoa Italy 58 B6
Genoa, Gulf of Italy 58 B5
George *r.* Canada 7 D2
George, Lake U.S.A. 17 C2
Georgetown Guyana 27 F7
George Town Malaysia 90 B3
Georgetown U.S.A. 11 C2
Georgia Asia 75 E3
Georgia *admin div.* U.S.A. 17 C3
Georgian Bay Canada 6 B1
Georgina *r.* Australia 99 C3
Georgiyevka Kazakh. 79 E3
Gera Germany 54 D4
Geral de Goiás, Serra *hills* Brazil 27 H3
Geraldine New Zealand 101 C2
Geraldton Australia 98 A3
Gerede Turkey 74 C3

Gerlachovský štit *mt.* Slovakia 61 E2
Germany Europe 54 B4
Gettysburg U.S.A. 12 B3
Gevgelija Macedonia 63 F2
Geyve Turkey 74 B3
Ghadāmis Libya 35 C2
Ghaem Shahr Iran 76 E6
Ghaghara *r.* India 81 E5
Ghana Africa 38 C1
Ghardaïa Algeria 34 C2
Ghāt Libya 35 D1
Ghaziabad India 80 D5
Ghazni Afgh. 79 C2
Ghent Belgium 51 B3
Gheorgheni Romania 66 B2
Gherla Romania 66 A2
Ghūrīān Afgh. 78 C2
Gibraltar Gibraltar 56 C2
Gibraltar, Strait of Morocco/Spain 56 B1
Gibson Desert Australia 98 B3
Gien France 52 E4
Gießen Germany 54 B4
Gifu Japan 87 C4
G'ijduvon Uzbek. 78 C3
Gijón-Xixón Spain 56 C5
Gila *r.* U.S.A. 9 C1
Gilbert Islands Kiribati 97 E4
Gilbués Brazil 27 H4
Gilgit Pak. 80 C7
Gillette U.S.A. 8 D3
Gillingham U.K. 49 G2
Ginebra, Laguna *lake* Bolivia 26 D3
Giresun Turkey 75 D3
Girishk Afgh. 78 C2
Girona Spain 57 G4
Gironde *estuary* France 53 C3
Girvan U.K. 48 D4
Gisborne New Zealand 100 G5
Giurgiu Romania 66 B1
Giza Egypt 36 B5
Gizhiga Rus. Fed. 73 O3
Gjirokastër Albania 63 E2
Gjøvik Norway 47 B3
Glacier Peak *volcano* U.S.A. 8 A4
Gladstone Australia 99 E3
Glasgow U.K. 48 D4
Glasgow U.S.A. 8 D4
Glendale U.S.A. 9 C1
Glendive U.S.A. 8 E4
Glen Innes Australia 99 E3
Glennallen U.S.A. 4 D3
Glenrothes U.K. 48 E5
Glens Falls *town* U.S.A. 14 C2
Glenwood Springs *town* U.S.A. 9 D2
Gliwice Poland 61 D2
Głogów Poland 60 C3
Glomfjord Norway 46 C4
Gloucester U.K. 49 E2
Glubokoye Kazakh. 79 E4
Gmünd Austria 55 E3
Gniezno Poland 60 C4
Goa *admin div.* India 80 B2
Goat Fell *hill* U.K. 48 D4
Gobabis Namibia 42 A2
Gobernador Gregores Argentina 29 B3
Gobi *desert* China/Mongolia 83 G4
Godavari *r.* India 80 C3
Goes Netherlands 51 B3
Goiânia Brazil 27 H2
Goiás Brazil 27 G2
Goiás *admin div.* Brazil 27 H3
Gökçeada *i.* Turkey 74 A3
Göksun Turkey 74 D2
Gölbaşı Turkey 74 D2
Gölcük Turkey 74 B3
Gold Coast *town* Australia 99 E3
Golden Bay New Zealand 100 D4
Göle Turkey 75 E3
Golmud China 82 D3
Golpāyegān Iran 76 E5
Gómez Palacio Mexico 18 D4
Gonaïves Haiti 23 D2
Gonâve, Île de la *i.* Haiti 23 D2
Gonbad-e Kavus Iran 76 F6
Gonder Ethiopia 36 B4
Gondia India 81 E4
Gongga Shan *mt.* China 85 B3
Good Hope, Cape of South Africa 42 A1
Goodwindi Australia 99 E3
Goose Lake U.S.A. 9 A3
Göppingen Germany 55 B3
Gorakhpur India 81 E5
Gora Narodnaya *mt.* Rus. Fed. 72 E3
Gorgān Iran 76 E6

Gorizia Italy 58 D6
Görlitz Germany 54 E4
Gornji Vakuf Bos. Herz. 62 C3
Goroka P.N.G. 96 B3
Gorontalo Indon. 91 D3
Gorry Kamen' *mt.* Rus. Fed. 73 H3
Gorzów Wielkopolski Poland 60 B4
Goshogawara Japan 86 D5
Gospić Croatia 62 B4
Gostivar Macedonia 63 E2
Gotha Germany 54 C4
Gothenburg Sweden 47 B2
Gotland *i.* Sweden 47 D2
Göttingen Germany 54 B4
Gouda Netherlands 50 C4
Gouin, Réservoir *reservoir* Canada 6 C1
Gourdon France 53 D3
Governador Valadares Brazil 27 I2
Göygöl Azer. 75 F3
Göynük Turkey 74 B3
Gozo *i.* Malta 59 E2
Grafton Australia 99 E3
Graham U.S.A. 10 C2
Grahamstown South Africa 42 B1
Grampian Mountains U.K. 48 D5
Granada Nicaragua 20 B2
Granada Spain 56 D2
Gran Canaria *i.* Canary Islands 34 A1
Gran Chaco *f.* Argentina/Paraguay 28 D7
Grand Bahama *i.* The Bahamas 22 C4
Grand Canal China 84 E5
Grand Canyon *gorge* U.S.A. 9 C2
Grand Canyon *town* U.S.A. 9 C2
Grand Cayman *i.* Cayman Is 22 B2
Grande *r.* Bolivia 26 E2
Grande *r.* Bahia Brazil 27 H3
Grande *r.* São Paulo Brazil 27 G1
Grande *r.* Nicaragua 21 C2
Grande, Bahía *bay* Argentina 29 C2
Grande Prairie Canada 4 G2
Grandes, Salinas *salt flat* Argentina 28 C6
Grand Falls - Windsor *town* Canada 7 E1
Grand Forks U.S.A. 12 B3
Grand Island *town* U.S.A. 12 B2
Grand Isle *town* U.S.A. 11 D1
Grand Junction U.S.A. 9 D2
Grândola Portugal 56 A3
Grand Passage New Caledonia 96 D2
Grand Rapids *town* Michigan U.S.A. 13 D2
Grand Rapids *town* Minnesota U.S.A. 13 C3
Grand Teton *mt.* U.S.A. 8 C3
Grand Turk Turks and Caicos Is 23 D3
Grangeville U.S.A. 8 C4
Granite Peak U.S.A. 8 D4
Gran Laguna Salada *lake* Argentina 29 C3
Gran Paradiso *mt.* Italy 58 A6
Grantham U.K. 49 F3
Grants U.S.A. 9 D2
Grants Pass U.S.A. 8 A3
Grasse France 53 G2
Grave, Pointe de *pt* France 53 C3
Graz Austria 55 E2
Great Abaco *i.* The Bahamas 22 C4
Great Australian Bight *gulf* Australia 98 B2
Great Barrier Island New Zealand 100 E6
Great Barrier Reef Australia 99 D4
Great Basin U.S.A. 9 B3
Great Bear Lake Canada 4 F3
Great Belt *strait* Denmark 47 B1
Great Bend U.S.A. 12 B1
Great Dividing Range *mts* Australia 99 D2
Greater Antilles *is* Caribbean Sea 22 B3
Great Exuma *i.* The Bahamas 22 C3
Great Falls *town* U.S.A. 8 C4
Great Inagua *i.* The Bahamas 23 D3
Great Karoo *plateau* South Africa 42 B1
Great Namaqualand *f.* Namibia 42 A2
Great Nicobar *i.* India 81 G1
Great Ouse *r.* U.K. 49 G3
Great Pedro Bluff *pt* Jamaica 22 C2
Great Plains U.S.A. 12 A3
Great Rift Valley *f.* Africa 37 B2
Great St Bernard Pass Italy/Switz. 58 A6

Great Salt Lake U.S.A. 9 C3
Great Sandy Desert Australia 98 B3
Great Sea Reef Fiji 97 E2
Great Slave Lake Canada 4 G3
Great Victoria Desert Australia 98 B3
Great Yarmouth U.K. 49 G3
Greco, Monte *mt.* Italy 59 D4
Gredos, Sierra de *mts* Spain 56 C4
Greece Europe 65 B3
Greeley U.S.A. 9 E3
Green *r.* U.S.A. 9 C2
Green Bay *town* U.S.A. 13 D2
Greenland *territory* N. America 105 V2
Greenock U.K. 48 D4
Green River *town* U.S.A. 9 D3
Greenville Liberia 38 C1
Greenville *Mississippi* U.S.A. 17 A3
Greenville *South Carolina* U.S.A. 16 C3
Greenville *Texas* U.S.A. 11 C2
Gregory Range *hills* Australia 99 D4
Greifswald Germany 54 D6
Grenå Denmark 47 B2
Grenada *town* U.S.A. 17 B3
Grenada 23 F1
Grenade France 53 D2
Grenoble France 53 F3
Grevena Greece 64 B4
Grevenmacher *admin div.* Lux. 51 E1
Grey *r.* New Zealand 101 C3
Greymouth New Zealand 101 C3
Grey Range *hills* Australia 99 D3
Grimsby U.K. 49 F3
Grodzisk Wielkopolski Poland 60 C4
Groningen Netherlands 50 E5
Groningen *admin div.* Netherlands 50 E5
Groote Eylandt *i.* Australia 99 C4
Grosser Speikkogel *mt.* Austria 55 E2
Grosseto Italy 58 C5
Großglockner *mt.* Austria 55 D2
Groundhog *r.* Canada 6 B1
Groznyy Rus. Fed. 72 C1
Grudziądz Poland 60 D4
Grytviken Atlantic Ocean 29 I2
Guacanayabo, Golfo de *bay* Cuba 22 C3
Guadajoz *r.* Spain 56 C2
Guadalajara Mexico 18 D3
Guadalajara Spain 57 D4
Guadalcanal *i.* Solomon Is 96 D3
Guadalete *r.* Spain 56 B2
Guadalope *r.* Spain 57 E4
Guadalquivir *r.* Spain 56 B2
Guadalupe *i.* Mexico 18 A4
Guadalupe, Sierra de *mts* Spain 56 C3
Guadalupe Peak U.S.A. 10 B2
Guadarrama, Sierra de *mts* Spain 56 C4
Guadeloupe *territory* Caribbean Sea 23 F2
Guadiana *r.* Portugal/Spain 56 B2
Guadix Spain 57 D2
Guafo, Isla *i.* Chile 29 B4
Guaíra Brazil 28 F8
Guaitecas, Islas *is* Chile 29 B4
Guajira, Península de la Colombia 26 C8
Gualeguay *r.* Argentina 28 E6
Gualicho, Salina *salt flat* Argentina 29 C4
Guam *territory* Pacific Ocean 96 B5
Guanambi Brazil 27 I3
Guanare Venez. 26 D7
Guane Cuba 22 B3
Guangdong *admin div.* China 85 D2
Guangxi Zhuangzu Zizhiqu *admin div.* China 85 C2
Guangyuan China 85 C4
Guangzhou China 85 D2
Guantánamo Cuba 22 C3
Guaporé *r.* Bolivia/Brazil 26 E3
Guaqui Bolivia 26 D2
Guara, Sierra de *mts* Spain 57 E5
Guarapuava Brazil 28 F7
Guarda Portugal 56 B4
Guasave Mexico 18 C4
Guasdualito Venez. 26 C7
Guatemala N. America 20 A3
Guatemala City Guat. 20 A2
Guaviare *r.* Colombia 26 D6
Guayaquil Ecuador 26 B5
Guayaquil, Golfo de *gulf* Ecuador 26 A5
Guaymas Mexico 18 B4
Guba Ethiopia 36 B4
Gudbrandsdalen *f.* Norway 47 B3
Guéckédou Guinea 38 B1
Guelmine Morocco 34 A1
Guéret France 53 D4
Guernsey *i.* Channel Is 49 E1
Guildford U.K. 49 F2
Guilin China 85 D3
Guinea Africa 38 B2
Guinea, Gulf of Africa 39 D1
Guinea-Bissau Africa 38 B2
Güiria Venez. 26 E8
Guiyang China 85 C3
Guizhou *admin div.* China 85 C3
Gujarat *admin div.* India 80 C4
Gujranwala Pakistan 80 C6
Gulbarga India 80 D3
Gulbene Latvia 68 B3
Gulu Uganda 37 B3
Gumdag Turkm. 78 B2
Gümüşhane Turkey 75 D3
Guna India 80 D4
Guntur India 81 E3
Gunungsitoli Indon. 90 A3
Gurgueia *r.* Brazil 27 I4
Guri, Embalse de *reservoir* Venez. 26 E7
Gürün Turkey 74 D2
Gurupi *r.* Brazil 27 H5
Gusau Nigeria 39 D2
Gusev Rus. Fed. 69 A2
Güstrow Germany 54 D5
Guwahati India 81 G5
Guyana S. America 27 F6
Guymon U.S.A. 10 B3
G'uzor Uzbek. 78 C2
Gwadar Pakistan 80 A5
Gwalior India 80 D5
Gwardafuy, Gees *cape* Somalia 36 D4
Gweru Zimbabwe 42 B3
Gympie Australia 99 E3
Gyöngyös Hungary 61 D1
Gyr Hungary 61 C1
Gypsumville Canada 5 I2
Gyumri Armenia 75 E3

H

Haapajärvi Finland 46 F3
Haapsalu Estonia 68 A3
Haarlem Netherlands 50 C4
Habbān Yemen 77 D1
Hachijo-jima *i.* Japan 87 C3
Hachinohe Japan 86 D5
Ḥadd, Ra's al *pt* Oman 77 F3
Haderslev Denmark 47 B1
Ḥaḍramawt *f.* Yemen 77 D2
Hadyach Ukraine 67 D3
Haeju North Korea 87 A4
Hagen Germany 54 A4
Hagerstown U.S.A. 16 D4
Ha Giang Vietnam 88 B3
Haida Gwaii *is* Canada 4 E2
Hai Dương Vietnam 88 B3
Haifa Israel 76 A5
Haikou China 85 D1
Ḥā'il Saudi Arabia 76 C4
Hainan *admin div.* China 85 C1
Hainaut *admin div.* Belgium 51 C2
Haines U.S.A. 4 E2
Hai Phong Vietnam 88 B3
Haiti Caribbean Sea 23 D2
Haiya Sudan 36 B4
Hakkâri Turkey 75 E2
Hakodate Japan 86 D5
Halabja Iraq 76 D6
Ḥalāniyāt, Juzur al *is* Oman 77 F2
Halden Norway 47 B2
Halifax Canada 7 D1
Halla-san *mt.* South Korea 87 A3
Hall Beach *town* Canada 5 J3
Halle Belgium 51 C2
Halle Germany 54 C4
Hall Islands Micronesia 96 C4
Halls Creek *town* Australia 98 B4
Halmahera *i.* Indon. 91 D3
Halmstad Sweden 47 C2
Hamadān Iran 76 D5
Ḥamāh Syria 76 B6
Hamamatsu Japan 87 C3
Hamar Norway 47 B3
Hamburg Germany 54 B5
Hämeenlinna Finland 47 F3
Hamersley Range *mts* Australia 98 A3
Hamhŭng North Korea 86 A4
Hami China 82 D4
Hamilton Canada 6 C1
Hamilton New Zealand 100 E6
Hamina Finland 47 F3
Hamm Germany 54 A4
Hammerdal Sweden 46 C3
Hammerfest Norway 46 E5
Hammond U.S.A. 11 D2
Hanamaki Japan 86 D4
Handan China 84 D5
Hangzhou China 85 F4
Hanmer Springs *town* New Zealand 101 D3
Hannover Germany 54 B5
Ha Nôi Vietnam 88 B3
Hantsavichy Belarus 69 B2
Hanzhong China 84 C4
Haparanda Sweden 46 F4
Happy Valley-Goose Bay *town* Canada 7 D2
Harare Zimbabwe 43 C3
Ḥarāsīs, Jiddat al *desert* Oman 77 F2
Harbin China 83 K5
Harderwijk Netherlands 50 D4
Hardin U.S.A. 8 D4
Hargeysa Somalia 37 C3
Har Hu *lake* China 82 E3
Harlingen Netherlands 50 D5
Harlingen U.S.A. 11 C1
Harlow U.K. 49 G2
Harney Basin U.S.A. 8 A3
Härnösand Sweden 47 D3
Har Nuur *lake* Mongolia 82 D5
Harricanaw *r.* Canada 6 C2
Harris *peninsula* U.K. 48 C5
Harrisburg U.S.A. 14 B2
Harrison U.S.A. 11 D3
Harrison, Cape Canada 7 E2
Harrisonburg U.S.A. 16 D4
Harrogate U.K. 49 F3
Harşit *r.* Turkey 75 D3
Hârşova Romania 66 B2
Harstad Norway 46 D5
Harteigan *mt.* Norway 47 A3
Hartford U.S.A. 15 C2
Hartland Point U.K. 49 D2
Hartwell Reservoir U.S.A. 16 C3
Har Us Nuur *lake* Mongolia 82 D5
Harwich U.K. 49 G2
Haryana *admin div.* India 80 D5
Hasan Dağı *mts* Turkey 74 C2
Hasselt Belgium 51 D2
Hassi Messaoud Algeria 35 C2
Hässleholm Sweden 47 C2
Hastings New Zealand 100 F5
Hastings U.K. 49 G2
Hastings U.S.A. 12 B2
Ha Tinh Vietnam 88 B2
Hatteras, Cape U.S.A. 16 D4
Hat Yai Thailand 89 B1
Haud *plain* Ethiopia 37 C3
Haugesund Norway 47 A2
Hauhungaroa *mt.* New Zealand 100 E5
Haukivesi *lake* Finland 47 G3
Hauraki Gulf New Zealand 100 E6
Hauroko, Lake New Zealand 101 A1
Haut Atlas *mts* Morocco 34 B2
Haut-Folin *hill* France 52 F4
Havana Cuba 22 B3
Haverfordwest U.K. 49 D2
Havre U.S.A. 8 D4
Havre-St-Pierre Canada 7 D2
Hawai'ian Islands N. Pacific Ocean 102 G7
Hawea, Lake New Zealand 101 B2
Hawera New Zealand 100 E5
Hawick U.K. 48 E4
Hawkdun Range *mts* New Zealand 101 B2
Hawke Bay New Zealand 100 F5
Hawthorne U.S.A. 9 B2
Hay Australia 99 D2
Hay *r.* Canada 4 G2
Haydarābad Iran 76 D6
Haymā' Oman 77 F2
Hayotboshi tog'i *mt.* Uzbek. 79 C3
Hay River *town* Canada 4 G3
Hays U.S.A. 12 B1
Haysyn Ukraine 66 C3
Hazleton U.S.A. 14 B2
Heard Island Indian Ocean 93 E1
Hebei *admin div.* China 84 E5
Hebron Israel 76 B5
Hecate Strait Canada 4 E2
Hechi China 85 C2
Hede Sweden 47 C3
Heerenveen Netherlands 50 D4
Heerlen Netherlands 51 D2
Hefei China 84 E4
Hegang China 83 L5
Heidelberg Germany 55 B3
Heilbronn Germany 55 B3
Heilongjiang *admin div.* China 83 K5
Heilong Jiang *r.* China 83 K5
Heinola Finland 47 F3
Helgoländer Bucht *gulf* Germany 54 B6
Hellín Spain 57 E3
Helmand *r.* Afgh. 78 C2
Helmond Netherlands 51 D3
Helmsdale U.K. 48 E6
Helsingborg Sweden 47 C2
Helsinki Finland 47 F3
Henan *admin div.* China 84 D4
Henares *r.* Spain 56 D4
Henderson *Nevada* U.S.A. 9 C2
Henderson *North Carolina* U.S.A. 16 D4
Henderson *Texas* U.S.A. 11 D2
Hengelo Netherlands 50 E4
Hengyang China 85 D3
Henrietta Maria, Cape Canada 6 B2
Herāt Afgh. 78 C2
Hereford U.K. 49 E3
Hereford U.S.A. 10 B2
Hermosillo Mexico 18 B4
Herning Denmark 47 B2
Hervey Islands Cook Is 97 H2
Heze China 84 E5
Hicks Bay *town* New Zealand 100 G6
Hidaka-sanmyaku *mts* Japan 86 D5
Hidalgo del Parral Mexico 18 C4
Higashi-suidō *strait* Japan 87 A3
High Peak *hills* U.K. 49 F3
Hiiumaa *i.* Estonia 68 A3
Hijaz *f.* Saudi Arabia 77 B4
Hikurangi *mt.* New Zealand 100 G6
Hildesheim Germany 54 B5
Hillah Iraq 76 C5
Hillerød Denmark 47 C1
Hillsboro U.S.A. 11 C2
Hilversum Netherlands 50 D4
Himachal Pradesh *admin div.* India 80 D6
Himalaya *mts* Asia 80 D6
Hindu Kush *mts* Afgh./Pakistan 79 C2
Hınıs Turkey 75 E2
Hinnøya *i.* Norway 46 C5
Hinthada Myanmar 88 A2
Hirabit Dağ *mt.* Turkey 75 F2
Hirosaki Japan 86 D5
Hiroshima Japan 87 B3
Hispaniola *i.* Caribbean Sea 23 D3
Hitachi Japan 87 D4
Hitra *i.* Norway 46 B3
Hjälmaren *lake* Sweden 47 C2
Hjørring Denmark 47 B2
Hlybokaye Belarus 69 B2
Hobart Australia 99 D1
Hobart U.S.A. 10 C3
Hobro Denmark 47 B2
Ho Chi Minh City Vietnam 89 B2
Hochschwab *mt.* Austria 55 E2
Hodeidah Yemen 77 C1
Hódmezővásárhely Hungary 61 E1
Hoek van Holland Netherlands 50 C3
Hof Germany 54 C4
Hohe Tauern *mts* Austria 55 D2
Hohhot China 83 H4
Hokianga Harbour New Zealand 100 D7
Hokitika New Zealand 101 C3
Hokkaidō *i.* Japan 86 D5
Holbæk Denmark 47 B1
Holbrook U.S.A. 9 C1
Holdrege U.S.A. 12 B2
Holguín Cuba 22 C3
Hollabrunn Austria 55 F3
Hollywood U.S.A. 17 C2
Holon Israel 76 A5
Holstebro Denmark 47 B2
Holston *r.* U.S.A. 16 C4
Holyhead U.K. 49 D3
Holy Island U.K. 48 F4
Homāyunshahr Iran 76 E5
Home Bay Canada 5 L3
Homs Syria 76 B5
Homyel' Belarus 69 C2
Hondo U.S.A. 10 C1
Honduras N. America 20 B3
Hønefoss Norway 47 B3
Hong Kong China 85 D2
Hong Kong *admin div.* China 85 D2
Honiara Solomon Is 96 C3
Honshū *i.* Japan 87 C4
Hood, Mount *volcano* U.S.A. 8 A4
Hood Point Australia 98 A2
Hoogeveen Netherlands 50 E4
Hoorn Netherlands 50 D4
Hopa Turkey 75 E3
Hope *r.* New Zealand 101 D3
Hope U.S.A. 11 D2
Hope, Point U.S.A. 4 B3
Hopedale Canada 7 D2
Hope Saddle *pass* New Zealand 101 D4
Horasan Turkey 75 E3
Horlivka Ukraine 67 E3
Hormuz, Strait of Iran/Oman 77 F4
Horn, Cape Chile 29 C1
Hornavan *lake* Sweden 46 D4
Horodok Ukraine 66 A3
Horsens Denmark 47 B1
Horsham Australia 99 D2
Horten Norway 47 B2
Hotan China 82 A3
Hot Springs *town Arkansas* U.S.A. 11 D2
Hot Springs *town South Dakota* U.S.A. 12 A2
Houffalize Belgium 51 D2
Houma U.S.A. 11 D1
Houston U.S.A. 11 C1
Hovd Mongolia 82 D5
Hövsgöl Nuur *lake* Mongolia 82 F6
Howe, Cape Australia 99 D2
Howland Island *territory* Pacific Ocean 96 F4
Hoy *i.* U.K. 48 E6
Høyanger Norway 47 A3
Hoyerswerda Germany 54 E4
Höytiäinen *lake* Finland 46 G3
Hradec Králové Czech Rep. 61 B3
Hrazdan Armenia 75 F3
Hrebinka Ukraine 67 D3
Hrodna Belarus 69 A2
Huaibei China 84 E4
Huainan China 84 E4
Huaki Indon. 91 D2
Huallaga *r.* Peru 26 B4
Huambo Angola 42 A3
Huancayo Peru 26 B3
Huang He *r.* China 83 G4
Huangshi China 85 E4
Huánuco Peru 26 B4
Huanuni Bolivia 26 D2
Huarmey Peru 26 B3
Huascarán, Nevado de *mt.* Peru 26 B4
Huasco Chile 28 B7
Huasco *r.* Chile 28 B7
Huatabampo Mexico 18 C4
Hubei *admin div.* China 85 D4
Hubli India 80 D3
Huddersfield U.K. 49 F3
Hudiksvall Sweden 47 D3
Hudson *r.* U.S.A. 14 C2
Hudson Bay *sea* Canada 5 J2
Hudson Strait Canada 7 C3
Huê Vietnam 88 B2
Huelva Spain 56 B2
Huércal-Overa Spain 57 E2
Huesca Spain 57 E5
Hugo U.S.A. 11 C2
Huiarau Range *mts* New Zealand 100 F5
Huich'ŏn North Korea 86 A5
Huila, Nevado de *volcano* Colombia 26 B6
Huixtla Mexico 19 F2
Huizhou China 85 D2
Hulun Buir China 83 I5
Hulun Nur *lake* China 83 I5
Humahuaca Argentina 28 C8
Humaitá Brazil 26 E4
Humber, Mouth of the U.K. 49 G3
Humboldt *r.* U.S.A. 9 B3
Humphreys Peak U.S.A. 9 C2
Hunan *admin div.* China 85 D3
Hungary Europe 61 D1
Hunsrück *hills* Germany 55 A3
Huntington U.S.A. 16 C4
Huntly New Zealand 100 E6
Huntly U.K. 48 E5
Huntsville *Alabama* U.S.A. 16 B3
Huntsville *Texas* U.S.A. 11 C2
Huron U.S.A. 12 B2
Huron, Lake Canada/U.S.A. 13 E2

Hurunui r. New Zealand 101 D3
Huşi Romania 66 C2
Husum Germany 54 B6
Huzhou China 85 F4
Hvar i. Croatia 63 C3
Hvardiys'ke Ukraine 67 D2
Hyargas Nuur lake Mongolia 82 D5
Hyderabad India 81 D3
Hyderabad Pakistan 80 B5
Hyères France 53 G2
Hyesan North Korea 86 A5
Hyrynsalmi Finland 46 G4
Hyvinkää Finland 47 F3

I

Iaco r. Brazil 26 D3
Iaçu Brazil 27 I3
Iaşi Romania 66 B2
Iba Phil. 91 C4
Ibadan Nigeria 39 D1
Ibagué Colombia 26 B6
Ibar r. Serbia 63 E3
Ibarra Ecuador 26 B6
Ibb Yemen 77 C1
Iberá, Esteros del marsh Argentina 28 E7
Ibiapaba, Serra da hills Brazil 27 I5
Ibiza Spain 57 F3
Ibiza i. Spain 57 F3
Ibotirama Brazil 27 I3
Ibrā' Oman 77 F3
Ica Peru 26 B3
Iceland Europe 44
Icinoseki Japan 86 D4
Idaho admin div. U.S.A. 8 C3
Idaho Falls town U.S.A. 8 C3
Idi mt. Greece 65 D1
Ieper Belgium 51 A2
Iešjávri lake Norway 46 F5
Ifôghas, Adrar des hills Mali 38 D2
Igan Malaysia 90 C3
Iggesund Sweden 47 D3
Iglesias Italy 59 B3
Iğneada Burnu pt Turkey 74 B3
Igoumenitsa Greece 65 B3
Iguaçu r. Brazil 28 F7
Iguala Mexico 19 E2
Iguape Brazil 28 G8
Iguatu Brazil 27 J4
Iisalmi Finland 46 F3
IJmuiden Netherlands 50 C4
IJssel r. Netherlands 50 C4
IJsselmeer lake Netherlands 50 D4
Ikaahuk Canada 4 F4
Ikaria i. Greece 65 E2
Iki i. Japan 87 A3
Ilagan Phil. 91 D4
Ilebo Dem. Rep. Congo 41 C2
Ilfracombe U.K. 49 D2
Ilgın Turkey 74 B2
Ilha Solteira, Represa reservoir Brazil 28 F8
Ilhéus Brazil 27 J3
Illinois admin div. U.S.A. 13 D2
Illinois r. U.S.A. 13 C1
Illizi Algeria 35 C1
Iloilo Phil. 91 D4
Ilorin Nigeria 39 D1
Ilovays'k Ukraine 67 E2
Imatra Finland 47 G3
İmişli Azer. 75 G2
Imola Italy 58 C6
Imperatriz Brazil 27 H4
Imphal India 81 G4
İmroz Turkey 74 A3
Inangahua Junction New Zealand 101 C4
Inanwatan Indon. 91 E2
Inarijärvi lake Finland 46 F5
Inch'ŏn South Korea 87 A4
Indalsälven r. Sweden 46 D3
Independence U.S.A. 12 C1
Inderbor Kazakh. 78 B3
India Asia 80 C4
Indiana admin div. U.S.A. 13 D2
Indianapolis U.S.A. 13 D1
Indian Ocean 92 F3
Indigirka r. Rus. Fed. 73 M3
Indonesia Asia 90 C2
Indore India 80 D4
Indre r. France 52 D4
Indus r. China/Pakistan 80 B4

Indus, Mouths of the Pakistan 80 B4
İnebolu Turkey 74 C3
İnegöl Turkey 74 B3
Infiernillo, Presa reservoir Mexico 18 D2
Infiesto Spain 56 C5
Ingolstadt Germany 55 C3
Inhambane Mozambique 43 C2
Inland Kaikoura Range mts New Zealand 101 D3
Inn r. Europe 55 C2
Inner Hebrides is U.K. 48 C5
Inner Mongolia admin div. China see Nei Mongol Zizhiqu
Innisfail Australia 99 D4
Innsbruck Austria 55 C2
Inowrocław Poland 60 D4
In Salah Algeria 34 C1
International Falls town U.S.A. 13 C3
Inukjuak Canada 6 C2
Inuvik Canada 4 E3
Inveraray U.K. 48 D5
Invercargill New Zealand 101 B1
Inverness U.K. 48 D5
Ioannina Greece 65 B3
Ionian Islands Greece 65 A3
Ionian Sea Greece/Italy 65 A3
Ios i. Greece 65 D2
Iowa admin div. U.S.A. 12 C2
Iowa City U.S.A. 13 C2
Ipatinga Brazil 27 I2
Ipoh Malaysia 90 B3
Ipswich Australia 99 E1
Iqaluit Canada 5 L3
Iquique Chile 28 B8
Iquitos Peru 26 C5
Iraklion Greece 65 D1
Iran Asia 76 E5
Īrānshahr Iran 76 G4
Irapuato Mexico 18 D3
Iraq Asia 76 C5
Irati Brazil 28 F7
Irbid Jordan 76 B5
Ireland Europe 49 C3
Iringa Tanzania 37 B2
Iriri r. Brazil 27 G5
Irish Sea Ireland/U.K. 49 D3
Irituia Brazil 27 H5
Irkutsk Rus. Fed. 73 I2
Iron Mountain town U.S.A. 13 D3
Irosin Phil. 91 D4
Irrawaddy r. China/Myanmar 88 A2
Irrawaddy, Mouths of the Myanmar 89 A2
Irtysh r. Kazakh./Rus. Fed. 72 E2
Irtysh r. Kazakh./Rus. Fed. 79 D4
Irún Spain 57 E5
Isabela Phil. 91 D3
Isabelia, Cordillera mts Nicaragua 20 B2
Isar r. Germany 55 D3
Ischia, Isola d' i. Italy 59 D4
Ise Japan 87 C3
Ishikari-wan bay Japan 86 D5
Ishinomaki Japan 87 D4
Isiro Dem. Rep. Congo 41 C3
İskenderun Turkey 74 D2
İskenderun Körfezi bay Turkey 74 C2
Iskŭr r. Bulgaria 64 D5
Islamabad Pakistan 80 C6
Islay i. U.K. 48 C4
Isle of Man i. Irish Sea 49 D4
Ismoili Somoní, Qullai mt. Tajik. 79 D2
Isparta Turkey 74 B2
Israel Asia 76 A5
İstanbul Turkey 74 B3
Istria peninsula Croatia 62 A5
Itabuna Brazil 27 J3
Itacoatiara Brazil 27 F5
Itaituba Brazil 27 F5
Itajaí Brazil 28 G7
Italy Europe 58 B6
Itamaraju Brazil 27 J2
Itapecuru Mirim Brazil 27 I5
Itapetininga Brazil 28 G8
Itararé Brazil 28 G8
Ithaca U.S.A. 14 B2
Itiquira r. Brazil 27 F2
Ituí r. Brazil 26 C4
Itumbiara Brazil 28 G9
Ituni Guyana 27 F7
Ituxi r. Brazil 26 D4
Iul'tin Rus. Fed. 73 Q3
Ivaí r. Brazil 28 F8

Ivalo Finland 46 F5
Ivano-Frankivs'k Ukraine 66 B3
Ivanovo Rus. Fed. 72 C2
Ivatsevichy Belarus 69 B2
Ivinheima r. Brazil 28 F8
Iwaki Japan 87 D4
Iwo Nigeria 39 D1
Izabal, Lago de lake Guat. 20 B3
Izhevsk Rus. Fed. 72 D2
Izmayil Ukraine 66 C2
İzmir Turkey 74 A2
İzmir Körfezi strait Greece/Turkey 65 E3
İzmit Turkey 74 B3
Izozog, Bañados del swamp Bolivia 26 E2
Izu-shotō is Japan 87 C3
Izyum Ukraine 67 E3

J

Jabalón r. Spain 56 C3
Jabalpur India 81 D4
Jabiru Australia 98 C4
Jaca Spain 57 E5
Jacareacanga Brazil 27 F4
Jackman U.S.A. 15 C3
Jackson Mississippi U.S.A. 17 A3
Jackson Tennessee U.S.A. 16 B4
Jacksonville Arkansas U.S.A. 11 D2
Jacksonville Florida U.S.A. 17 C3
Jacksonville North Carolina U.S.A. 16 D3
Jacksonville Texas U.S.A. 11 C2
Jacobabad Pakistan 80 B5
Jacuí r. Brazil 28 F6
Jaén Peru 26 B4
Jaén Spain 56 D2
Jaffa, Cape Australia 99 C2
Jaffna Sri Lanka 81 D1
Jagdalpur India 81 E3
Jahrom Iran 76 E4
Jaipur India 80 D5
Jaisalmer India 80 C5
Jajce Bos. Herz. 62 C4
Jakarta Indon. 90 B2
Jakobstad Finland 46 E3
Jalālābād Afgh. 79 D2
Jalgaon India 80 D4
Jalna India 80 D3
Jalón r. Spain 57 E4
Jālū Libya 35 E1
Jamaica Caribbean Sea 22 C2
Jamaica Channel Haiti/Jamaica 22 C2
Jamanxim r. Brazil 27 F4
Jambi Indon. 90 B2
James r. North Dakota/South Dakota U.S.A. 12 B3
James r. Virginia U.S.A. 16 D4
James Bay Canada 6 B2
James Peak New Zealand 101 B2
Jamestown Australia 99 C2
Jamestown New York U.S.A. 14 B2
Jamestown North Dakota U.S.A. 12 B3
Jammu India 80 C6
Jammu and Kashmir admin div. India 80 D7
Jamnagar India 80 C4
Jampur Pakistan 80 C5
Jämsänkoski Finland 47 F3
Jamshedpur India 81 F4
Janaúba Brazil 27 I2
Januária Brazil 27 I2
Japan Asia 87 B4
Japan, Sea of Asia 86 B5
Japurá r. Brazil 26 D5
Jardim Brazil 27 F1
Jardines de la Reina, Archipiélago de los is Cuba 22 C3
Järpen Sweden 46 C3
Järvenpää Finland 47 F3
Jäsk Iran 76 E4
Jasper Canada 4 G2
Jataí Brazil 27 G2
Java i. Indon. 90 B2
Java Sea Indon. 90 C2
Javarthushuu Mongolia 83 H5
Jawhar Somalia 37 C3
Jaya, Puncak mt. Indon. 91 E2
Jayapura Indon. 91 F2
Jaz Mūriān, Hāmūn-e lake Iran 76 F4
Jedburgh U.K. 48 E4

Jeddah Saudi Arabia 77 B3
Jefferson, Mount U.S.A. 9 B2
Jefferson City U.S.A. 13 C1
Jejuí Guazú r. Para. 28 E8
Jēkabpils Latvia 68 F3
Jelenia Góra Poland 60 B3
Jelgava Latvia 68 A3
Jember Indon. 90 C2
Jena Germany 54 C4
Jennings U.S.A. 11 D2
Jequié Brazil 27 I3
Jérémie Haiti 23 D2
Jerez de la Frontera Spain 56 B2
Jerid, Chott el lake Tunisia 35 C2
Jersey i. Channel Is 49 E1
Jerusalem Israel/West Bank 76 B5
Jesi Italy 58 D5
Jesup U.S.A. 17 C3
Jesús María Argentina 28 D6
Jhansi India 81 D5
Jharkhand admin div. India 81 F4
Jiamusi China 83 L5
Ji'an China 85 D3
Jiangmen China 85 D2
Jiangsu admin div. China 84 E4
Jiangxi admin div. China 85 D3
Jiaozuo China 84 D5
Jiaxing China 85 F4
Jiayi Taiwan 85 F2
Jiehkkevárri mt. Norway 46 D5
Jieyang China 85 E2
Jihlava Czech Rep. 61 B2
Jilib Somalia 37 C3
Jilin China 83 K4
Jilin admin div. China 83 K4
Jilong Taiwan 85 F3
Jīma Ethiopia 37 B3
Jiménez Chihuahua Mexico 18 D4
Jiménez Tamaulipas Mexico 19 E3
Jinan China 84 E5
Jingdezhen China 85 E3
Jinghong China 85 B2
Jingmen China 85 D4
Jingzhou China 85 D4
Jinhua China 85 E3
Jining Nei Mongol China 83 H4
Jining Shandong China 84 E5
Jinja Uganda 37 B3
Jinjiang China 85 E2
Jinsha Jiang r. China 85 B3
Jinzhou China 83 J4
Ji-Paraná r. Brazil 26 E4
Jiujiang China 85 E3
Jixi China 83 L5
Jīzān Saudi Arabia 77 C2
Jizzax Uzbek. 79 C3
João Maria, Albardão do coastal area Brazil 28 F6
João Pessoa Brazil 27 K4
Jodhpur India 80 C5
Joensuu Finland 46 G3
Jōetsu Japan 87 C4
Jõgeva Estonia 68 F3
Johannesburg South Africa 42 B2
John H. Kerr Reservoir U.S.A. 16 D4
John o'Groats U.K. 48 E6
Johor Bahru Malaysia 90 B3
Joinville Brazil 28 G7
Jokkmokk Sweden 46 D4
Jolo Phil. 91 D3
Jolo i. Phil. 91 D3
Jonava Lithuania 69 B2
Jonesboro U.S.A. 11 D2
Jones Sound strait Canada 5 J4
Jönköping Sweden 47 C2
Jonquière Canada 7 C1
Jordan Asia 76 B5
Jordan Valley town U.S.A. 8 B3
Jörn Sweden 46 E4
Jos Nigeria 39 D1
José de San Martín Argentina 29 B4
Joseph Bonaparte Gulf Australia 98 B4
Juazeiro Brazil 27 I4
Juazeiro do Norte Brazil 27 J4
Juba South Sudan 37 B3
Jubba r. Somalia 37 C3
Júcar r. Spain 57 E3
Juchitán Mexico 19 E2
Judenburg Austria 55 E2
Juigalpa Nicaragua 21 B2
Juiz de Fora Brazil 27 I1
Juliaca Peru 26 C2
Julian Alps mts Slovenia 55 D2
Juliana Top mt. Suriname 27 F6

Junction U.S.A. 10 C2
Junction City U.S.A. 12 B1
Juneau U.S.A. 4 E2
Jungfrau mt. Switz. 58 A7
Junggar Pendi basin China 82 C5
Juniata r. U.S.A. 14 B2
Jura mts France/Switz. 58 A6
Jura i. U.K. 48 D5
Jurbarkas Lithuania 69 A2
Jūrmala Latvia 68 A3
Juruá r. Brazil 26 D5
Juruena r. Brazil 27 F3
Jutaí r. Brazil 26 D5
Jutiapa Guat. 20 B2
Juticalpa Honduras 20 B2
Jutland peninsula Denmark 47 B2
Juventud, Isla de la i. Cuba 22 B3
Jyväskylä Finland 47 F3

K

K2 mt. India 82 A3
Kabalo Dem. Rep. Congo 41 C2
Kābul Afgh. 79 C2
Kabwe Zambia 42 B3
Kachchh, Gulf of India 80 B4
Kachug Rus. Fed. 73 I2
Kaçkar Dağı mt. Turkey 75 E3
Kadavu Passage Fiji 97 E2
Kadıköy Turkey 74 A2
Kadirli Turkey 74 D2
Kadugli Sudan 37 A4
Kaduna Nigeria 39 D2
Kaesŏng North Korea 87 A4
Kaffeklubben Ø i. Greenland 105 W1
Kafireas, Akra pt Greece 65 D3
Kaga Bandoro C.A.R. 40 B3
Kagoshima Japan 87 B3
Kaharlyk Ukraine 67 C3
Kaherekoau Mountains New Zealand 101 A2
Kahramanmaraş Turkey 74 D2
Kahurangi Point New Zealand 100 D4
Kai, Kepulauan is Indon. 91 E2
Kaifeng China 84 D4
Kaikoura New Zealand 101 D3
Kaikoura Peninsula New Zealand 101 D3
Kaimai Range hills New Zealand 100 E6
Kaimanawa Mountains New Zealand 100 E5
Käina Estonia 68 A3
Kaipara Harbour New Zealand 100 E6
Kairouan Tunisia 35 D2
Kaiserslautern Germany 55 A3
Kaitaia New Zealand 100 D7
Kaiyuan China 85 B2
Kajaani Finland 46 F4
Kaka Turkm. 78 B2
Kakanui Mountains New Zealand 101 C2
Kakhovs'ke Vodoskhovyshche reservoir Ukraine 67 D2
Kakinada India 81 E3
Kaktovik U.S.A. 4 F4
Kalabahi Indon. 91 D2
Kalahari Desert Africa 42 B2
Kalajoki Finland 46 E4
Kalamaria Greece 64 C4
Kalamata Greece 65 C2
Kalamazoo U.S.A. 13 D2
Kalanchak Ukraine 67 D2
Kälbäcär Azer. 75 F3
Kalbarri Australia 98 A3
Kalecik Turkey 74 C3
Kalemie Dem. Rep. Congo 41 C2
Kaliakra, Nos pt Bulgaria 64 F5
Kaliningrad Rus. Fed. 69 A2
Kalinkavichy Belarus 69 C2
Kalisz Poland 60 D3
Kalixälven r. Sweden 46 E4
Kallavesi lake Finland 46 F3
Kallsjön lake Sweden 46 C3
Kalmar Sweden 47 D2
Kal'mius r. Ukraine 67 E2
Kaltag U.S.A. 4 C3
Kaluga Rus. Fed. 72 B2
Kalundborg Denmark 47 B1
Kama r. Rus. Fed. 72 D2
Kamaishi Japan 86 D4
Kaman Turkey 74 C2
Kamchatka Peninsula Rus. Fed. 73 N2

Kamenskoye Rus. Fed. 73 O3
Kamensk-Ural'skiy Rus. Fed. 72 E2
Kamina Dem. Rep. Congo 41 C2
Kamloops Canada 4 F2
Kampala Uganda 37 B3
Kampen Netherlands 50 D4
Kâmpóng Cham Cambodia 89 B2
Kâmpóng Chhnăng Cambodia 89 B2
Kâmpóng Spœ Cambodia 89 B2
Kâmpóng Thum Cambodia 89 B2
Kâmpôt Cambodia 89 B2
Kamrau, Teluk bay Indon. 91 E2
Kam"yanets'-Podil's'kyy Ukraine
   66 B3
Kam"yanka-Buz'ka Ukraine 66 B3
Kamyshin Rus. Fed. 72 C2
Kananga Dem. Rep. Congo 41 C2
Kanawha r. U.S.A. 16 C4
Kanazawa Japan 87 C4
Kanchipuram India 81 D2
Kandahār Afgh. 78 C2
Kandıra Turkey 74 B3
Kandy Sri Lanka 81 E1
Kandyagash Kazakh. 78 B3
Kangal Turkey 74 D2
Kangān Iran 76 E4
Kangar Malaysia 90 B3
Kangaroo Island Australia 99 C2
Kangāvar Iran 76 D5
Kangchenjunga mt. India/Nepal
   81 F5
Kangding China 85 B4
Kangean, Kepulauan is Indon. 90 C2
Kangiqsualujjuaq Canada 7 D2
Kangiqsujuaq Canada 7 C3
Kangmar China 82 C1
Kangnŭng South Korea 87 A4
Kanin, Poluostrov peninsula Rus. Fed.
   72 C3
Kankaanpää Finland 47 E3
Kankakee U.S.A. 13 D2
Kankan Guinea 38 C2
Kanker India 81 E4
Kano Nigeria 39 D2
Kanpur India 81 E5
Kansas admin div. U.S.A. 12 B1
Kansas r. U.S.A. 12 B1
Kansas City U.S.A. 12 C1
Kansk Rus. Fed. 73 H2
Kantchari Burkina Faso 39 D2
Kanton atoll Kiribati 96 F3
Kanye Botswana 42 B2
Kaokoveld f. Namibia 42 A3
Kaolack Senegal 38 B2
Kapan Armenia 75 F2
Kapiti Island New Zealand 100 E4
Kap Morris Jesup pt Greenland
   105 V1
Kaposvár Hungary 61 C1
Kapshagay Kazakh. 79 D3
Kapshagay, Vodokhranilishche
   reservoir Kazakh. 79 D3
Kapuskasing Canada 6 B1
Kara r. Turkey 75 E2
Kara-Balta Kyrg. 79 D3
Karabalyk Kazakh. 78 C4
Karabük Turkey 74 C3
Karabutak Kazakh. 78 C3
Karacalı Dağ mt. Turkey 75 D2
Karachi Pakistan 80 B4
Kara Dağ mt. Turkey 74 C2
Karagandy Kazakh. 79 D3
Karagayly Kazakh. 79 D3
Karaginskiy Zaliv bay Rus. Fed. 73 O2
Karaj Iran 76 E6
Kara-Köl Kyrg. 79 D3
Karakol Kyrg. 79 D3
Karakoram Range mts Asia 80 C7
Karakum Desert Kazakh. 78 B3
Karakum Desert Turkm. 78 C2
Karaman Turkey 74 C2
Karamay China 82 B5
Karamea Bight bay New Zealand
   101 C4
Karand Iran 76 D5
Karapınar Turkey 74 C2
Karasburg Namibia 42 A2
Kara Sea Rus. Fed. 72 F4
Karasu r. Turkey 75 E2
Karasuk Rus. Fed. 72 F2
Karatau, Khrebet mts Kazakh. 79 C3
Karbalā' Iraq 76 C5
Karcag Hungary 61 E1
Karditsa Greece 65 B3
Kärdla Estonia 68 A3
Kareima Sudan 36 B4

Kariba, Lake reservoir Zambia/
   Zimbabwe 42 B3
Karikari, Cape New Zealand 100 D7
Karimata, Selat strait Indon. 90 B2
Karkinits'ka Zatoka gulf Ukraine
   67 D2
Karksi-Nuia Estonia 68 B3
Karlıova Turkey 75 E2
Karlovac Croatia 62 B4
Karlovo Bulgaria 64 D5
Karlovy Vary Czech Rep. 61 A3
Karlshamn Sweden 47 C2
Karlskoga Sweden 47 C2
Karlskrona Sweden 47 C2
Karlsruhe Germany 55 B3
Karlstad Sweden 47 C2
Karmøy i. Norway 47 A2
Karnataka admin div. India 80 D2
Karnobat Bulgaria 64 E5
Karora Eritrea 36 B4
Karpathos i. Greece 65 E1
Karpenisi Greece 65 B3
Karratha Australia 98 A3
Kars Turkey 75 E3
Karstula Finland 46 F3
Kartal Turkey 74 B3
Karun r. Iran 76 D5
Karymskoye Rus. Fed. 73 J2
Kaş Turkey 74 B2
Kasaï r. Dem. Rep. Congo 41 B2
Kasama Zambia 43 C3
Kasese Uganda 37 B3
Kāshān Iran 76 E5
Kashi China 82 A3
Kashiwazaki Japan 87 C4
Kāshmar Iran 76 F6
Kasos i. Greece 65 E1
Kassala Sudan 36 B4
Kassel Germany 54 B4
Kasserine Tunisia 35 C2
Kastamonu Turkey 74 C3
Kastelli Greece 65 C1
Kastoria Greece 64 B4
Kastsyukovichy Belarus 69 D2
Katahdin, Mount U.S.A. 15 D3
Katanning Australia 98 A2
Katerini Greece 64 C4
Kate's Needle mt. Canada/U.S.A. 4 E2
Katha Myanmar 88 A3
Kathmandu Nepal 81 F5
Katikati New Zealand 100 E6
Katima Mulilo Namibia 42 B3
Katowice Poland 61 D3
Katrineholm Sweden 47 D2
Katsina Nigeria 39 D2
Kattaqo'rg'on Uzbek. 78 C2
Kattegat strait Denmark/Sweden
   47 B2
Kauhajoki Finland 47 E3
Kaunas Lithuania 69 A2
Kaura-Namoda Nigeria 39 D2
Kavala Greece 64 D4
Kavarna Bulgaria 64 F5
Kavīr, Dasht-e desert Iran 76 E5
Kawakawa New Zealand 100 E7
Kawasaki Japan 87 C4
Kawerau New Zealand 100 F5
Kawhia Harbour New Zealand 100 E5
Kayes Mali 38 B2
Kaynar Rus. Fed. 79 D3
Kayseri Turkey 74 C2
Kazach'ye Rus. Fed. 73 L4
Kazakhskiy Zaliv bay Kazakh. 78 B3
Kazakhstan Asia 78 C3
Kazan' Rus. Fed. 72 C2
Kazanlŭk Bulgaria 64 D5
Kâzerün Iran 76 E4
Kea i. Greece 65 D2
Keban Barajı reservoir Turkey 75 D2
Kebnekaise mt. Sweden 46 D4
Kecskemét Hungary 61 D1
Kdainiai Lithuania 69 A2
Keetmanshoop Namibia 42 A2
Kefamenanu Indon. 91 D2
Kegen Kazakh. 79 D3
Keila Estonia 68 B3
Keitele lake Finland 46 F3
Kelif Uzboýy marsh Turkm. 78 C2
Kelkit r. Turkey 75 D3
Kellett, Cape Canada 4 F4
Kelo Chad 40 B3
Kelowna Canada 4 G1
Keluang Malaysia 90 B3
Kem' Rus. Fed. 72 B3
Kemerovo Rus. Fed. 72 G2
Kemi Finland 46 F4

Kemijärvi Finland 46 F4
Kemijärvi lake Finland 46 F4
Kemijoki r. Finland 46 F4
Kemp Land f. Antarctica 104 Q2
Kempten Germany 55 C2
Kenai U.S.A. 4 C3
Kendal U.K. 49 E4
Kendari Indon. 91 D2
Kengtung Myanmar 88 A3
Kénitra Morocco 34 B2
Kennebec r. U.S.A. 15 D2
Kennet r. U.K. 49 F2
Kenora Canada 6 A1
Kentau Kazakh. 79 C3
Kentucky admin div. U.S.A. 16 B4
Kentucky r. U.S.A. 16 B4
Kentucky Lake U.S.A. 16 B4
Kenya Africa 37 B3
Kenya, Mount Kenya 37 B2
Kerala admin div. India 80 D2
Kerch Ukraine 67 E2
Kerema P.N.G. 96 B3
Kerguelen, Îles is Indian Ocean 93 E1
Kerikeri New Zealand 100 D7
Kerinci, Gunung volcano Indon. 90 B2
Kerkyra Greece 65 A3
Kermān Iran 76 F5
Kermān Desert Iran 76 F4
Kermānshāh Iran 76 D5
Kerrville U.S.A. 10 C2
Keşan Turkey 74 A3
Kesennuma Japan 86 D4
Keskin Turkey 74 C2
Ketapang Indon. 90 C2
Ketchikan U.S.A. 4 E2
Kettering U.K. 49 F3
Key West U.S.A. 17 C1
Khabarovsk Rus. Fed. 73 L1
Khambhat, Gulf of India 80 C3
Khānābād Afgh. 79 C2
Khandwa India 80 D4
Khanka, Lake China/Rus. Fed. 73 L1
Khanpur Pakistan 80 C5
Khantau Kazakh. 79 D3
Khantayskoye, Ozero lake Rus. Fed.
   72 H3
Khanty-Mansiysk Rus. Fed. 72 E3
Kharagpur India 81 F4
Kharkiv Ukraine 67 E3
Khartoum Sudan 36 B4
Khāsh Iran 76 G4
Khaskovo Bulgaria 64 D4
Khatanga Rus. Fed. 73 I4
Khatangskiy Zaliv bay Rus. Fed. 73 I4
Khayelitsha South Africa 42 A1
Khersan r. Iran 76 D5
Kherson Ukraine 67 D2
Kheta r. Rus. Fed. 73 I4
Khmel'nyts'kyy Ukraine 66 B3
Khmil'nyk Ukraine 66 B3
Khon Kaen Thailand 88 B2
Khorramābād Iran 76 D5
Khorugh Tajik. 79 D2
Khōst Afgh. 79 C2
Khromtau Kazakh. 78 B4
Khŭjand Tajik. 79 C2
Khulna Bangladesh 81 F4
Khunsar Iran 76 E5
Khust Ukraine 66 A3
Khvoy Iran 76 C6
Khyber Pass Afgh./Pakistan 79 C2
Kiantajärvi lake Finland 46 G4
Kičevo Macedonia 63 E2
Kidnappers, Cape New Zealand
   100 F5
Kiel Germany 54 C6
Kielce Poland 61 E3
Kieler Bucht bay Germany 54 C6
Kiev Ukraine 67 C3
Kigali Rwanda 37 B2
Kigoma Tanzania 37 A2
Kii-suidō strait Japan 87 B3
Kikinda Serbia 62 E4
Kikori P.N.G. 96 B3
Kikwit Dem. Rep. Congo 41 B2
Kilgore U.S.A. 11 D2
Kilimanjaro volcano Tanzania 37 B2
Kilis Turkey 74 D2
Kilkee Ireland 49 B3
Kilkenny Ireland 49 C3
Kilkis Greece 64 C4
Killarney Ireland 49 B3
Killeen U.S.A. 11 C2
Kilmarnock U.K. 48 D4
Kimbe P.N.G. 96 C3
Kimberley South Africa 42 B2

Kimberley Plateau Australia 98 B4
Kimch'aek North Korea 86 A5
Kinabalu, Gunung mt. Malaysia 90 C3
Kindu Dem. Rep. Congo 41 C2
Kingaroy Australia 99 E3
King Island Australia 99 D2
King Leopold Ranges hills Australia
   98 B4
Kingman U.S.A. 9 C2
King's Lynn U.K. 49 G3
Kingsmill Group is Kiribati 97 E3
Kings Peak U.S.A. 9 C3
Kingston Canada 6 C1
Kingston Jamaica 22 C2
Kingston U.S.A. 14 C2
Kingston upon Hull U.K. 49 F3
Kingstown St Vincent 23 F1
Kingsville U.S.A. 11 C1
King William Island Canada 5 I3
Kinna Sweden 47 C2
Kinshasa Dem. Rep. Congo 41 B2
Kirakira Solomon Is 96 D2
Kirikhan Turkey 74 D2
Kırıkkale Turkey 74 C2
Kirkcaldy U.K. 48 E5
Kirkenes Norway 46 G5
Kirkkonummi Finland 47 F3
Kirkland Lake town Canada 6 B1
Kırklareli Turkey 74 A3
Kirkūk Iraq 76 C6
Kirkwall U.K. 48 E6
Kirovohrad Ukraine 67 D3
Kiruna Sweden 46 E4
Kisangani Dem. Rep. Congo 41 C3
Kishkenekol' Kazakh. 79 D4
Kismaayo Somalia 37 C2
Kissimmee U.S.A. 17 C2
Kissimmee, Lake U.S.A. 17 C2
Kisumu Kenya 37 B2
Kita-Kyūshū Japan 87 B3
Kitami Japan 86 D5
Kitimat Canada 4 F2
Kittilä Finland 46 F4
Kitty Hawk U.S.A. 16 D4
Kitwe Zambia 42 B3
Kiuruvesi Finland 46 F3
Kivu, Lake Dem. Rep. Congo/Rwanda
   41 C2
Kızılca Dağ mt. Turkey 74 B2
Kızıl Dağı mt. Turkey 75 D2
Kızılırmak Turkey 74 C3
Kızılırmak r. Turkey 74 C3
Kladno Czech Rep. 61 B3
Klagenfurt Austria 55 E2
Klaipėda Lithuania 69 A2
Klamath r. U.S.A. 8 A3
Klamath Falls town U.S.A. 8 A3
Klazienaveen Netherlands 50 E4
Kłodzko Poland 61 C3
Klyetsk Belarus 69 B2
Kluchevskaya, Sopka volcano
   Rus. Fed. 73 O2
Knin Croatia 62 C4
Knockadoon Head Ireland 49 C2
Knockmealdown Mountains Ireland
   49 B3
Knoxville U.S.A. 16 C4
Kobda Kazakh. 78 B4
Kōbe Japan 87 C3
Koblenz Germany 54 A4
Kobroör i. Indon. 91 E2
Kobryn Belarus 69 B2
Kočani Macedonia 63 F2
Kōchi Japan 87 B3
Kodiak U.S.A. 4 C2
Kodiak Island U.S.A. 4 C2
Kodyma Ukraine 66 C3
Kōfu Japan 87 C4
Køge Denmark 47 C1
Kokkola Finland 46 F3
Kokpekty Kazakh. 79 E3
Kokshetau Kazakh. 79 C4
Kolaka Indon. 91 D2
Kolding Denmark 47 B1
Kolguyev, Ostrov i. Rus. Fed. 72 C3
Kolhapur India 80 C3
Kolkasrags pt Latvia 68 A3
Kolkata India 81 F4
Kołobrzeg Poland 60 B5
Kolomyya Ukraine 66 B3
Kolwezi Dem. Rep. Congo 41 C1
Kolyma r. Rus. Fed. 73 N3

Kolymskiy, Khrebet mts Rus. Fed.
   73 O3
Komatsu Japan 87 C4
Komodo i. Indon. 91 C2
Komotini Greece 64 D4
Komsomolets, Ostrov i. Rus. Fed.
   73 H5
Komsomol'sk-na-Amure Rus. Fed.
   73 L2
Kongsberg Norway 47 B2
Kongsvinger Norway 47 C3
Konin Poland 60 D4
Konotop Ukraine 67 D3
Konstanz Germany 55 B2
Konya Turkey 74 C2
Konyrat Kazakh. 79 D3
Köping Sweden 47 D2
Koprivnica Croatia 62 C5
Korçë Albania 63 E2
Korčula i. Croatia 63 C3
Korea Bay China/North Korea 83 J3
Korea Strait Japan/South Korea 87 A3
Körfez Turkey 74 B3
Köriyama Japan 87 D4
Korkuteli Turkey 74 B2
Köroğlu Tepesi mt. Turkey 74 C3
Koro Sea Fiji 97 E2
Korosten' Ukraine 66 C3
Koro Toro Chad 40 B4
Korsakov Rus. Fed. 73 M1
Kortrijk Belgium 51 E2
Koryakskiy Khrebet mts Rus. Fed.
   73 P3
Kos i. Greece 65 E2
Kościerzyna Poland 60 C5
Kosciuszko, Mount Australia 99 D2
Košice Slovakia 61 E2
Kosovo Europe 63 E3
Kosovska Mitrovica Kosovo 63 E3
Kosrae i. Micronesia 96 D4
Kostanay Kazakh. 78 C4
Kosti Sudan 36 B4
Kostopil' Ukraine 66 B3
Kostroma Rus. Fed. 72 C2
Kostrzyn Poland 60 B4
Kostyantynivka Ukraine 67 E3
Koszalin Poland 60 C5
Kota India 80 D5
Kotabaru Indon. 90 C2
Kota Bharu Malaysia 90 B3
Kota Kinabalu Malaysia 90 C3
Kotel'nyy, Ostrov i. Rus. Fed. 73 L4
Kotlas Rus. Fed. 72 C3
Kotovs'k Ukraine 66 C2
Kotuy r. Rus. Fed. 73 I4
Kotzebue U.S.A. 4 B3
Kotzebue Sound strait U.S.A. 4 B3
Koumac New Caledonia 96 D1
Koundâra Guinea 38 B2
Kourou French Guiana 27 G7
Kouvola Finland 47 F3
Kovel' Ukraine 66 B3
Kowhitirangi New Zealand 101 C3
Kozan Turkey 74 C2
Kozani Greece 64 B4
Kozelets' Ukraine 67 D3
Kozhikode India 80 D2
Kozyatyn Ukraine 66 C3
Kra, Isthmus of Thailand 89 A1
Krabi Thailand 89 A1
Krâchéh Cambodia 89 B2
Kragujevac Serbia 62 E4
Kraków Poland 61 D3
Kramators'k Ukraine 67 E3
Kramfors Sweden 46 D3
Kranj Slovenia 55 E2
Krasino r. Rus. Fed. 72 D4
Krasnoarmiys'k Ukraine 67 E3
Krasnodar Rus. Fed. 72 B1
Krasnohrad Ukraine 67 D3
Krasnoperekops'k Ukraine 67 D2
Krasnoyarsk Rus. Fed. 72 H2
Krefeld Germany 54 A4
Kremenchuk Ukraine 67 D3
Kremenchuts'ke Vodoskhovyshche
   reservoir Ukraine 67 D3
Kretinga Lithuania 68 A2
Krishna r. India 80 D3
Kristiansand Norway 47 A2
Kristianstad Sweden 47 C2
Kristiansund Norway 46 A3
Kristinehamn Sweden 47 C2
Krk i. Croatia 62 B4
Krosno Poland 61 E2
Krui Indon. 90 B2
Kruševac Serbia 62 E3

Lodwar Kenya 37 B3
Łódź Poland 60 D3
Lofoten is Norway 46 C5
Logan, Mount Canada 4 D3
Logroño Spain 57 D5
Loikaw Myanmar 88 A2
Loire r. France 52 C4
Loja Ecuador 26 B5
Loja Spain 56 C2
Lokan tekojärvi reservoir Finland 46 F4
Lokeren Belgium 51 C3
Løkken Norway 46 B3
Lokoja Nigeria 39 D1
Lolland i. Denmark 47 B1
Lom Bulgaria 64 C5
Lomami r. Dem. Rep. Congo 41 C2
Lomas de Zamora Argentina 28 E6
Lombok i. Indon. 90 C2
Lombok, Selat strait Indon. 90 C2
Lomé Togo 39 D1
Lommel Belgium 51 D3
Lomond, Loch lake U.K. 48 D5
Lompobattang, Gunung mt. Indon. 91 C2
Łomża Poland 60 F4
London Canada 6 B1
London U.K. 49 F2
Londonderry U.K. 48 C4
Londonderry, Cape Australia 98 B4
Longa, Proliv strait Rus. Fed. 73 P4
Long Bay U.S.A. 17 D3
Long Beach town U.S.A. 9 B1
Longford Ireland 49 C3
Long Island The Bahamas 22 C3
Long Island U.S.A. 15 C2
Longlac Canada 6 B1
Long Point New Zealand 101 B1
Longreach Australia 99 D3
Longtown U.K. 48 E4
Longview U.S.A. 11 D2
Long Xuyên Vietnam 89 B2
Lons-le-Saunier France 52 F4
Lookout, Cape U.S.A. 16 D3
Loop Head Ireland 49 B3
Lop Buri Thailand 89 B2
Lop Nur salt flat China 82 D4
Lopphavet bay Norway 46 E5
Lorca Spain 57 E2
Lordsburg U.S.A. 9 D1
Lorient France 52 B4
Lorn, Firth of estuary U.K. 48 D5
Los Ángeles Chile 29 B5
Los Angeles U.S.A. 9 B1
Los Blancos Argentina 28 D8
Los Mochis Mexico 18 C4
Los Vientos Chile 28 C8
Los Vilos Chile 28 B6
Lot r. France 53 D3
Louangnamtha Laos 88 B3
Louangphabang Laos 88 B2
Loughborough U.K. 49 F3
Louisiade Archipelago is P.N.G. 96 C2
Louisiana admin div. U.S.A. 11 D2
Louisville U.S.A. 16 B4
Lourdes France 53 C2
Lovech Bulgaria 64 D5
Lovelock U.S.A. 9 B3
Lowell U.S.A. 15 C2
Lower Hutt New Zealand 101 E4
Lower Lough Erne lake U.K. 49 C4
Lowestoft U.K. 49 G3
Loyauté, Îles is New Caledonia 97 D1
Loyew Belarus 69 C1
Loznica Serbia 62 D4
Lozova Ukraine 67 E3
Lu'an China 84 E4
Luanda Angola 42 A4
Luarca Spain 56 C2
Luau Angola 42 B3
Lubānas ezers lake Latvia 68 B3
Lubango Angola 42 A3
Lubartów Poland 60 F3
Lubbock U.S.A. 10 B2
Lübeck Germany 54 C5
Lubin Poland 60 C3
Lublin Poland 60 F3
Lubny Ukraine 67 D3
Lubok Antu Malaysia 90 C3
Lubuksikaping Indon. 90 B3
Lubumbashi Dem. Rep. Congo 41 C1
Lubutu Dem. Rep. Congo 41 C2
Lucena Phil. 91 D4
Lucena Spain 56 C2
Lučenec Slovakia 61 D2
Lucerne Switz. 58 B7
Lucknow India 81 E5

Lüderitz Namibia 42 A2
Ludhiana India 80 D6
Ludvika Sweden 47 C3
Ludwigsburg Germany 55 B3
Ludwigshafen am Rhein Germany 55 B3
Ludwigslust Germany 54 C5
Luena Angola 42 A3
Lufeng China 85 E2
Lufkin U.S.A. 11 D2
Lugano Switz. 58 B7
Lugo Spain 56 B5
Lugoj Romania 66 A2
Luhans'k Ukraine 67 E3
Łuków Poland 60 F3
Luleå Sweden 46 E4
Luleälven r. Sweden 46 E4
Lüleburgaz Turkey 74 A3
Lumberton U.S.A. 16 D3
Lund Sweden 47 C1
Lundy i. U.K. 49 D2
Lüneburg Germany 54 C5
Lunéville France 52 G5
Luninyets Belarus 69 B2
Luoyang China 84 D4
Lupanshui China 85 B3
Lure France 52 G4
Lusaka Zambia 42 B3
Lushnjë Albania 63 D2
Lut, Dasht-e desert Iran 76 F5
Lutherstadt Wittenberg Germany 54 D4
Luton U.K. 49 F2
Luts'k Ukraine 66 B3
Luwuk Indon. 91 D2
Luxembourg admin div. Belgium 51 D2
Luxembourg Europe 51 E1
Luxembourg town Lux. 51 E1
Luxor Egypt 36 B5
Luzilândia Brazil 27 I5
Luzon i. Phil. 91 D4
Luzon Strait Phil. 91 D5
L'viv Ukraine 66 B3
Lycksele Sweden 46 D4
Lyel'chytsy Belarus 69 C1
Lyepyel' Belarus 69 C2
Lyme Bay U.K. 49 E2
Lynchburg U.S.A. 16 D4
Lynn Lake town Canada 5 H2
Lyon France 53 F3
Lysychans'k Ukraine 67 E3

M

Ma'ān Jordan 76 B5
Maas r. Netherlands 50 C3
Maaseik Belgium 51 D3
Maastricht Netherlands 51 D2
Mabalane Mozambique 43 C2
Mabaruma Guyana 27 F7
Macá, Monte mt. Chile 29 B3
Macao China 85 D2
Macapá Brazil 27 G6
Macará Ecuador 26 B5
Macau Brazil 27 J4
Macaúba Brazil 27 G3
Macclesfield U.K. 49 E3
Macdonnell Ranges mts Australia 98 C3
Macedo de Cavaleiros Portugal 56 B4
Macedonia Europe 63 E2
Maceió Brazil 27 J4
Mach Pakistan 80 B5
Machala Ecuador 26 B5
Machias U.S.A. 15 D2
Machilipatnam India 81 E3
Mackay Australia 99 D3
Mackay, Lake salt flat Australia 98 B3
Mackenzie r. Canada 4 E3
Mackenzie King Island Canada 5 G4
Mackenzie Mountains Canada 4 E3
MacLeod, Lake Australia 98 A3
Macomer Italy 59 B4
Mâcon France 53 F4
Macon U.S.A. 17 C3
Mac. Robertson Land f. Antarctica 104 P2
Macumba r. Australia 99 C3
Madadeni South Africa 42 C2
Madagascar Africa 43 D2
Madang P.N.G. 96 B3
Madeira r. Brazil 26 E4

Madera Mexico 18 C4
Madhya Pradesh admin div. India 81 D4
Madison U.S.A. 13 D2
Madison r. U.S.A. 8 C4
Madona Latvia 68 B3
Madrakah, Ra's cape Oman 77 F2
Madras India see Chennai
Madras U.S.A. 8 A3
Madre, Laguna lagoon Mexico 19 E4
Madre de Dios, Isla i. Chile 29 A2
Madre del Sur, Sierra mts Mexico 19 D2
Madre Occidental, Sierra mts Mexico 18 C4
Madre Oriental, Sierra mts Mexico 18 D4
Madrid Spain 56 D4
Madura i. Indon. 90 C2
Madurai India 81 D1
Maebashi Japan 87 C4
Maestra, Sierra mts Cuba 22 C3
Mafia Island Tanzania 37 B2
Mafra Brazil 28 G7
Mafraq Jordan 76 B5
Magadan Rus. Fed. 73 N2
Magdalena r. Colombia 26 C7
Magdalena, Isla i. Chile 29 B4
Magdeburg Germany 54 C5
Magellan, Strait of Chile 29 B2
Magerøya i. Norway 46 F5
Maggiorasca, Monte mt. Italy 58 B6
Maggiore, Lake Italy 58 B6
Magnitogorsk Rus. Fed. 72 D2
Magnolia U.S.A. 11 D2
Maguarinho, Cabo cape Brazil 27 H5
Magwe Myanmar 88 A3
Mahābād Iran 76 D6
Mahagi Dem. Rep. Congo 41 D3
Mahajanga Madagascar 43 D3
Mahalevona Madagascar 43 D3
Maharashtra admin div. India 80 D3
Maha Sarakham Thailand 88 B2
Mahia Peninsula New Zealand 100 F5
Mahilyow Belarus 69 C2
Mahón Spain 57 H3
Mahrāt, Jabal mt. Yemen 77 E2
Maidstone U.K. 49 G2
Maiduguri Nigeria 39 E2
Maīmanah Afgh. 78 C2
Main r. Germany 55 B3
Mai-Ndombe, Lac Dem. Rep. Congo 41 B2
Maine admin div. U.S.A. 15 D3
Mainland i. Orkney U.K. 48 E6
Mainland i. Shetland U.K. 48 E7
Mainz Germany 55 B4
Maiquetía Venez. 26 D8
Maíz, Islas del is Nicaragua 21 C2
Maizuru Japan 87 C4
Maja Jezercë mt. Albania 63 D3
Majene Indon. 91 C2
Major, Puig mt. Spain 57 G3
Majorca i. Spain 57 G3
Makale Indon. 91 C2
Makanshy Kazakh. 79 E3
Makarska Croatia 63 C3
Makassar Indon. 91 C2
Makassar, Selat strait Indon. 90 C2
Makat Kazakh. 78 B3
Makgadikgadi depression Botswana 42 B2
Makhachkala Rus. Fed. 72 C1
Makhambet Kazakh. 78 B3
Makinsk Kazakh. 79 D4
Makiyivka Ukraine 67 E3
Makran f. Iran/Pakistan 80 A5
Makurdi Nigeria 39 D1
Mala, Punta pt Panama 21 C1
Malabar Coast coast India 80 C2
Malabo Equat. Guinea 41 A3
Malacca, Strait of Indon./Malaysia 90 A3
Malad City U.S.A. 8 C3
Maladzyechna Belarus 69 B2
Málaga Spain 56 C2
Malaita i. Solomon Is 96 D3
Malakal South Sudan 37 B3
Malakula i. Vanuatu 97 D2
Malamala Indon. 91 D2
Malang Indon. 90 C2
Malanje Angola 42 A4
Mälaren lake Sweden 47 D2
Malargüe Argentina 28 C5
Malatya Turkey 75 D2
Malawi Africa 43 C3

Malāyer Iran 76 D5
Malaysia Asia 90 B3
Malazgirt Turkey 75 E2
Malbork Poland 60 D5
Maldives Indian Ocean 80 C1
Maldonado Uruguay 28 F6
Maleas, Akra pt Greece 65 C2
Malgomaj lake Sweden 46 D4
Mali Africa 38 C2
Malili Indon. 91 D2
Malin Head Ireland 48 C4
Mallaig U.K. 48 D5
Mallow Ireland 49 B3
Malmédy Belgium 51 E2
Malmö Sweden 47 C1
Måløy Norway 47 A3
Malta Europe 59 E1
Malta town U.S.A. 8 D4
Malu'u Solomon Is 96 D3
Malvern U.S.A. 11 D2
Malyy Anyuy r. Rus. Fed. 73 O3
Mama r. Rus. Fed. 73 M3
Mamelodi South Africa 42 B2
Mamoré r. Bolivia/Brazil 26 D3
Man, Isle of i. Irish Sea 49 D4
Manacor Spain 57 G3
Manado Indon. 91 D3
Managua Nicaragua 20 B2
Managua, Lago de lake Nicaragua 20 B2
Manakau mt. New Zealand 101 D3
Manama Bahrain 77 E4
Mananjary Madagascar 43 D2
Manapouri, Lake New Zealand 101 A2
Manatuto East Timor 91 D2
Manaus Brazil 26 E5
Manavgat Turkey 74 B2
Manawatu r. New Zealand 100 E4
Manchester U.K. 49 E3
Manchester U.S.A. 15 C2
Manchuria f. China 83 K5
Mand r. Iran 76 E4
Mandala, Puncak mt. Indon. 91 F2
Mandalay Myanmar 88 A3
Mandalgovĭ Mongolia 83 G5
Mandan U.S.A. 12 A3
Mandurah Australia 98 A2
Manfredonia Italy 59 F4
Manfredonia, Golfo di bay Italy 59 F4
Manga Brazil 27 I3
Mangaia i. Cook Is 97 H1
Mangakino New Zealand 100 E5
Mangalia Romania 66 C1
Mangalore India 80 C2
Mangaung South Africa 42 B2
Manggar Indon. 90 B2
Mangistau Kazakh. 78 B3
Mangoky r. Madagascar 43 D2
Mangole i. Indon. 91 D2
Manicouagan, Réservoir reservoir Canada 7 D2
Manila Phil. 91 D4
Manipur admin div. India 81 G4
Manisa Turkey 74 A2
Manitoba admin div. Canada 5 I2
Manitoba, Lake Canada 5 I2
Manizales Colombia 26 B7
Mankato U.S.A. 12 D2
Manmad India 80 C4
Mannheim Germany 55 B3
Manokwari Indon. 91 E2
Manra i. Kiribati 96 F3
Manresa Spain 57 F4
Mansa Zambia 42 B3
Mansel Island Canada 5 K3
Mansfield Louisiana U.S.A. 11 D2
Mansfield Ohio U.S.A. 13 E2
Manta Ecuador 26 A5
Mantiqueira, Serra da mts Brazil 27 H1
Mantua Italy 58 C6
Manu'a Islands American Samoa 97 G2
Manui i. Indon. 91 D2
Manukau New Zealand 100 E6
Manukau Harbour New Zealand 100 E6
Manzanares Spain 56 D3
Manzanillo Cuba 22 C3
Manzanillo Mexico 18 D2
Manzhouli China 83 I5
Maoke, Pegunungan mts Indon. 91 E2
Mapimí, Bolsón de desert Mexico 18 D4
Mapinhane Mozambique 43 C2

Mapuera r. Brazil 27 F5
Maputo Mozambique 43 C2
Maquinchao Argentina 29 C4
Maraã Brazil 26 D5
Marabá Brazil 27 H4
Maracá, Ilha de i. Brazil 27 G6
Maracaibo Venez. 26 C8
Maracaibo, Lake inlet Venez. 26 C7
Maracaju, Serra de hills Brazil 28 E8
Maracás, Chapada de hills Brazil 27 I3
Maracay Venez. 26 D8
Marādah Libya 35 D1
Maradi Niger 39 D2
Marāgheh Iran 76 D6
Marajó, Ilha de i. Brazil 27 H6
Marand Iran 76 D6
Marañón r. Peru 26 C5
Mararoa r. New Zealand 101 A2
Marathonas Greece 65 C3
Marbella Spain 56 C2
Marburg South Africa 43 C1
Marburg an der Lahn Germany 54 B4
Marche-en-Famenne Belgium 51 D2
Mar Chiquita, Laguna lake Argentina 28 D6
Marchtrenk Austria 55 E3
Marcy, Mount U.S.A. 14 C2
Mar del Plata Argentina 29 E5
Marfa U.S.A. 10 B2
Margaret River town Australia 98 A2
Margarita, Isla de i. Venez. 26 E8
Margherita Peak Dem. Rep. Congo/ Uganda 41 C3
Mārgō, Dasht-e desert Afgh. 78 C2
Marhanets' Ukraine 67 D2
Marías, Islas is Mexico 18 C3
Mariato, Punta pt Panama 21 C1
Maria van Diemen, Cape New Zealand 100 D7
Maribor Slovenia 58 F8
Marie Byrd Land f. Antarctica 104 H2
Marie-Galante i. Guadeloupe 23 F2
Mariehamn Finland 47 D3
Mariental Namibia 42 A2
Mariestad Sweden 47 C2
Marietta Georgia U.S.A. 17 C3
Marietta Ohio U.S.A. 13 E1
Marijampol Lithuania 69 A2
Marília Brazil 27 H1
Mar''ina Horka Belarus 69 C2
Maringá Brazil 28 F8
Marion, Lake U.S.A. 17 C3
Mariscal José Félix Estigarribia Para. 28 D8
Maritime Alps mts France/Italy 53 G3
Maritsa r. Bulgaria 64 D4
Mariupol' Ukraine 67 E2
Marka Somalia 37 C3
Markermeer lake Netherlands 50 D4
Markha r. Rus. Fed. 73 J3
Marksville U.S.A. 11 D2
Marmande France 53 D3
Marmara, Sea of Turkey 74 B3
Marmaris Turkey 74 B2
Marne r. France 52 E5
Marne-la-Vallée France 52 E5
Maromokotro mt. Madagascar 43 D3
Marondera Zimbabwe 43 C3
Maroni r. French Guiana 27 G7
Maroua Cameroon 40 B4
Marquette U.S.A. 13 D3
Marra, Jebel mt. Sudan 36 A4
Marrakesh Morocco 34 B2
Marsa al Burayqah Libya 35 D2
Marsabit Kenya 37 B3
Marsala Italy 59 D2
Marsá Maţrūḥ Egypt 36 A6
Marseille France 53 F2
Marsfjället mt. Sweden 46 C4
Marshall U.S.A. 11 D2
Marshall Islands Pacific Ocean 96 D5
Marsh Island U.S.A. 11 D1
Märsta Sweden 47 D2
Martaban, Gulf of Myanmar 88 A2
Martha's Vineyard i. U.S.A. 15 C2
Martin Slovakia 61 D2
Martinique territory Caribbean Sea 23 F1
Martok Kazakh. 78 B4
Marton New Zealand 100 E4
Maruia r. New Zealand 101 D3
Mary Turkm. 78 C2
Maryborough Australia 99 E3
Maryland admin div. U.S.A. 16 D4
Masan South Korea 87 A4

124

Masavi Bolivia 26 E2
Masbate Phil. 91 D4
Masbate i. Phil. 91 D4
Maseru Lesotho 42 B2
Mashhad Iran 76 F6
Mashkel, Hamun-i- f. Pakistan 80 A5
Maṣīrah, Jazīrat i. Oman 77 F3
Maṣīrah, Khalīj bay Oman 77 F2
Masjed Soleymān Iran 76 D5
Mask, Lough lake Ireland 49 B3
Mason Bay New Zealand 101 A1
Massachusetts admin div. U.S.A. 15 C2
Massachusetts Bay U.S.A. 15 C2
Massakory Chad 40 B4
Massawa Eritrea 36 B4
Massena U.S.A. 14 C2
Massif Central mts France 53 E3
Masterton New Zealand 100 E4
Masty Belarus 69 B2
Masuda Japan 87 B3
Masvingo Zimbabwe 43 C2
Matadi Dem. Rep. Congo 41 B2
Matagalpa Nicaragua 20 B2
Matagorda Island U.S.A. 11 C1
Matakana Island New Zealand 100 F6
Matam Senegal 38 B2
Matamoros Coahuila Mexico 18 D4
Matamoros Tamaulipas Mexico 19 E4
Matanzas Cuba 22 B3
Matara Sri Lanka 81 E1
Mataram Indon. 90 C2
Mataró Spain 57 G4
Mataura New Zealand 101 B1
Mataura r. New Zealand 101 B1
Matā'utu Wallis and Futuna Is 96 F2
Mategua Bolivia 26 E3
Matera Italy 59 F4
Mathis U.S.A. 11 C1
Mathura India 80 D5
Mati Phil. 91 D3
Maṭraḥ Oman 77 F3
Matsue Japan 87 B4
Matsumoto Japan 87 C4
Matsusaka Japan 87 C3
Matsu Tao i. Taiwan 85 F3
Matsuyama Japan 87 B3
Matterhorn mt. Italy/Switz. 58 A6
Matterhorn mt. U.S.A. 8 C4
Matthews Ridge Guyana 26 E7
Maturín Venez. 26 E7
Maués Brazil 27 G4
Mauke i. Cook Is 97 H1
Maun Botswana 42 B2
Mauritania Africa 38 B2
Mauritius Indian Ocean 43 E2
Mawhai Point New Zealand 100 G5
Mawlamyaing Myanmar 88 A2
Maya r. Rus. Fed. 73 L2
Mayaguana i. The Bahamas 23 D3
Mayagüez Puerto Rico 23 E2
Mayamey Iran 76 F6
Maya Mountains Belize/Guatemala 20 B3
Mayenne r. France 52 C4
Mayo Canada 4 E3
Mayor Island New Zealand 100 F6
Mayotte i. Africa 43 D3
Mazār-e Sharīf Afgh. 79 C2
Mazatenango Guat. 20 A2
Mazatlán Mexico 18 C3
Mažeikiai Lithuania 68 A3
Mazyr Belarus 69 C2
Mbabane Swaziland 43 C2
Mbandaka Dem. Rep. Congo 41 B2
M'banza Congo Angola 42 A4
Mbarara Uganda 37 B2
Mbeya Tanzania 37 B2
Mbuji-Mayi Dem. Rep. Congo 41 C2
McAlester U.S.A. 11 C2
McClintock Channel Canada 5 H4
McClure Strait Canada 4 F4
McConaughy, Lake U.S.A. 12 A2
McCook U.S.A. 12 A2
McDonald Islands Indian Ocean 93 E1
McDonald Peak U.S.A. 8 C4
McGrath U.S.A. 4 C3
McGuire, Mount U.S.A. 8 C4
McKean i. Kiribati 96 F3
McKinley, Mount U.S.A. 4 C3
Mdantsane South Africa 42 B1
Mead, Lake reservoir U.S.A. 9 C2
Meadville U.S.A. 14 A2
Meaux France 52 E5
Mecca Saudi Arabia 77 B3

Mechelen Belgium 51 C3
Mecklenburger Bucht bay Germany 54 C6
Medan Indon. 90 A3
Medanosa, Punta pt Argentina 29 C3
Medellín Colombia 26 B7
Medenine Tunisia 35 D2
Medford U.S.A. 8 A3
Medgidia Romania 66 C2
Medias Romania 66 B2
Medicine Bow Peak U.S.A. 9 D3
Medicine Hat Canada 5 G2
Medina Saudi Arabia 77 B3
Medina del Campo Spain 56 C4
Medvezh'yegorsk Rus. Fed. 72 B3
Meekatharra Australia 98 A3
Meerut India 80 D5
Megara Greece 65 C3
Meghalaya admin div. India 81 G5
Meiktila Myanmar 88 A3
Meiningen Germany 54 C4
Meißen Germany 54 D4
Meizhou China 85 E2
Mejicana mt. Argentina 28 C7
Mejillones Chile 28 B8
Meknès Morocco 34 B2
Mekong r. Asia 89 B2
Mekong r. China 85 B2
Mekong, Mouths of the Vietnam 89 B1
Melaka Malaysia 90 B3
Melanesia is Pacific Ocean 102 E5
Melbourne Australia 99 D2
Melbourne U.S.A. 17 C2
Melekeok Palau 91 E3
Melilla N. Africa 57 D1
Melitopol' Ukraine 67 D2
Melo Uruguay 28 F6
Melrhir, Chott lake Algeria 35 C2
Melun France 52 E5
Melville Canada 5 H2
Melville, Cape Australia 99 D4
Melville Island Australia 98 C4
Melville Island Canada 5 H4
Melville Peninsula Canada 5 J3
Memberamo r. Indon. 91 E2
Memmingen Germany 55 C2
Mempawah Indon. 90 B3
Memphis U.S.A. 16 A4
Mena Ukraine 67 D3
Mena U.S.A. 11 D2
Mende France 53 E3
Mendī Ethiopia 37 B3
Mendi P.N.G. 96 B3
Mendip Hills U.K. 49 E2
Mendoza Argentina 28 C6
Menemen Turkey 74 A2
Menggala Indon. 90 B2
Menongue Angola 42 A3
Mentawai, Kepulauan is Indon. 90 A2
Meppel Netherlands 50 E4
Merano Italy 58 C7
Merauke Indon. 91 F2
Mercedes Argentina 28 E7
Meredith, Lake U.S.A. 10 B3
Merefa Ukraine 67 E3
Mergui Archipelago is Myanmar 89 A2
Mérida Mexico 19 G3
Mérida Spain 56 B3
Mérida Venez. 26 C7
Meridian U.S.A. 17 B3
Merowe Sudan 36 B4
Merredin Australia 98 A2
Merrick hill U.K. 48 D4
Mersch Lux. 51 E1
Mersey estuary U.K. 49 E3
Mersin Turkey 74 C2
Merthyr Tydfil U.K. 49 E2
Mértola Portugal 56 B2
Mertvyy Kultuk, Sor lake Kazakh. 78 B3
Merzifon Turkey 74 C3
Mesa U.S.A. 9 C1
Mesolongi Greece 65 B3
Messina Italy 59 E3
Messiniakos Kolpos bay Greece 65 C2
Mesta r. Bulgaria 64 C4
Metán Argentina 28 C7
Metković Croatia 63 C3
Metlika Slovenia 55 E1
Metz France 52 G5
Meuse r. Belgium/France 51 D2
Mexicali Mexico 18 A5
Mexico N. America 18 D3

Mexico City Mexico 19 E2
Mezen' Rus. Fed. 72 C3
Miahuatlán Mexico 19 E2
Miami Florida U.S.A. 17 C2
Miami Oklahoma U.S.A. 11 D3
Miandowāb Iran 76 D6
Miandrivazo Madagascar 43 D3
Mīāneh Iran 76 D6
Miass Rus. Fed. 72 E2
Michigan admin div. U.S.A. 13 D3
Michigan, Lake U.S.A. 13 D2
Michurinsk Rus. Fed. 72 C2
Mico r. Nicaragua 21 C2
Micronesia is Pacific Ocean 102 E6
Middlesbrough U.K. 49 F4
Midi, Canal du France 53 E2
Midland U.S.A. 10 B2
Midway Islands territory N. Pacific Ocean 102 G7
Miekojärvi lake Finland 46 F4
Mielec Poland 61 E3
Miercurea-Ciuc Romania 66 B2
Miguel Alemán, Presa reservoir Mexico 19 E2
Miguel Hidalgo, Presa reservoir Mexico 18 C4
Mikkeli Finland 47 F3
Milan Italy 58 B6
Milas Turkey 74 A2
Milbank U.S.A. 12 B3
Mildura Australia 99 D2
Miles City U.S.A. 8 D4
Milford Haven U.K. 49 D2
Milford Sound inlet New Zealand 101 A2
Millárs r. Spain 57 E3
Millau France 53 E3
Mille Lacs lakes U.S.A. 13 C3
Milos i. Greece 65 D2
Milton New Zealand 101 B1
Milton Keynes U.K. 49 F3
Milwaukee U.S.A. 13 D2
Mimizan France 53 C3
Mīnāb Iran 76 F4
Minas Indon. 90 B3
Minatitlán Mexico 19 F2
Minchinmávida volcano Chile 29 B4
Mindanao i. Phil. 91 D3
Minden U.S.A. 11 D2
Mindoro i. Phil. 91 D4
Mineral Wells U.S.A. 10 C2
Mingäçevir Azer. 75 F3
Mingäçevir Su Anbarı reservoir Azer. 75 F3
Minna Nigeria 39 D1
Minneapolis U.S.A. 13 C2
Minnesota admin div. U.S.A. 12 C3
Minnesota r. U.S.A. 13 C2
Miño r. Portugal/Spain 56 A4
Minorca i. Spain 57 G4
Minot U.S.A. 12 A3
Minsk Belarus 69 B2
Miracema do Tocantins Brazil 27 H4
Miranda Brazil 27 F1
Miranda r. Brazil 28 E9
Miranda de Ebro Spain 57 D5
Mirandela Portugal 56 B4
Mirbāṭ Oman 77 E2
Miri Malaysia 90 C3
Mirim, Lagoa lake Brazil 28 F6
Mirnyy Rus. Fed. 73 J3
Mirpur Khas Pakistan 80 B5
Mirzapur India 81 E5
Miskitos, Cayos is Nicaragua 21 C2
Miskolc Hungary 61 E2
Misoöl i. Indon. 91 E2
Mişrātah Libya 35 D2
Missinaibi r. Canada 6 B2
Mississippi admin div. U.S.A. 17 A3
Mississippi r. U.S.A. 11 D2
Mississippi Delta U.S.A. 11 E1
Missoula U.S.A. 8 C4
Missouri admin div. U.S.A. 13 C1
Missouri r. U.S.A. 13 C1
Mistassini, Lac lake Canada 7 C2
Mistissini Canada 7 C2
Mitchell r. Australia 99 D4
Mitchell U.S.A. 12 B2
Mitchell, Mount U.S.A. 16 C4
Mito Japan 87 D4
Mitre mt. New Zealand 100 E4
Mittimatalik Canada 5 K4
Mitú Colombia 26 C6
Mitumba, Chaîne des mts Dem. Rep. Congo 41 C2
Miyako Japan 86 D4

Miyako-rettō is Japan 87 A1
Miyaly Kazakh. 78 B3
Miyazaki Japan 87 B3
Mizoram admin div. India 81 G4
Mjölby Sweden 47 C2
Mława Poland 60 E4
Mljet i. Croatia 63 C3
Mmabatho South Africa 42 B2
Moab U.S.A. 9 D2
Moa Island Australia 99 D4
Mobile U.S.A. 17 B3
Mobile Bay U.S.A. 17 B3
Moçambique Mozambique 43 D3
Mocha Yemen 77 C1
Mochudi Botswana 42 B2
Mocuba Mozambique 43 C3
Modena Italy 58 C6
Modesto U.S.A. 9 A2
Moe Australia 99 D2
Moeraki Point New Zealand 101 C2
Moffat U.K. 48 E4
Mogadishu Somalia 37 C3
Mogok Myanmar 88 A3
Mohaka r. New Zealand 100 F5
Mohawk r. U.S.A. 14 C2
Mohyliv-Podil's'kyy Ukraine 66 B3
Mo i Rana Norway 46 C4
Mojave Desert U.S.A. 9 B2
Mokau r. New Zealand 100 E5
Mokp'o South Korea 87 A3
Molde Norway 46 A3
Moldova Europe 66 C2
Moldoveanu, Vârful mt. Romania 66 B2
Mollendo Peru 26 C2
Molopo r. Botswana/South Africa 42 B2
Molucca Sea Indon. 91 D3
Mombasa Kenya 37 B2
Møn i. Denmark 47 C1
Mona, Isla i. Puerto Rico 23 E2
Monaco Europe 53 G2
Monaghan Ireland 49 C4
Mona Passage Dom. Rep./Puerto Rico 23 E2
Monbetsu Japan 86 D5
Monclova Mexico 18 D4
Moncton Canada 7 D1
Mondego r. Portugal 56 A4
Mondoví Italy 58 A6
Monforte de Lemos Spain 56 B5
Monga Dem. Rep. Congo 41 C3
Mông Cai Vietnam 88 B3
Mongolia Asia 82 E5
Mongu Zambia 42 B3
Monroe U.S.A. 11 D2
Monrovia Liberia 38 B1
Mons Belgium 51 B2
Montana Bulgaria 64 C5
Montana admin div. U.S.A. 8 C4
Montargis France 52 E4
Montauban France 53 D3
Montauk Point U.S.A. 15 C2
Montbéliard France 52 G4
Mont-de-Marsan France 53 C2
Monte Alegre Brazil 27 G5
Monte-Carlo Monaco 53 G2
Monte Caseros Argentina 28 E6
Monte Cristi Dom. Rep. 23 D2
Montecristo, Isola di i. Italy 58 C5
Montego Bay Jamaica 22 C2
Montélimar France 53 F3
Monte Lindo r. Para. 28 E8
Montemorelos Mexico 19 E4
Montenegro Europe 63 C3
Monterey Bay U.S.A. 9 A2
Montería Colombia 26 B7
Montero Bolivia 26 E2
Monterrey Mexico 19 D4
Monte Santu, Capo di cape Italy 59 B4
Montes Claros Brazil 27 I2
Montevideo Uruguay 28 E6
Montevideo U.S.A. 12 B3
Montgomery U.S.A. 17 B3
Monticello Arkansas U.S.A. 11 D2
Monticello Utah U.S.A. 9 D2
Montluçon France 53 E4
Monto Australia 99 E3
Montpelier U.S.A. 15 C2
Montpellier France 53 E2
Montréal Canada 7 C1
Montrose U.K. 48 E5
Montserrat territory Caribbean Sea 23 F2
Monywa Myanmar 88 A3
Monza Italy 58 B6

Monzón Spain 57 F4
Moore, Lake salt flat Australia 98 A3
Moorhead U.S.A. 12 B3
Moose r. Canada 6 B2
Moosehead Lake U.S.A. 15 D3
Moose Jaw Canada 5 H2
Moosonee Canada 6 B2
Mopti Mali 38 C2
Moquegua Peru 26 C2
Mora Sweden 47 C3
Moray Firth bay U.K. 48 D5
Mor Daği mt. Turkey 75 F2
Morden Canada 5 I1
Morecambe U.K. 49 E4
Morecambe Bay U.K. 49 E4
Moree Australia 99 D3
Morehead P.N.G. 96 B3
Morelia Mexico 18 D2
Morena, Sierra mts Spain 56 B2
Morgan City U.S.A. 11 D2
Morgantown U.S.A. 16 D4
Mori Japan 86 D5
Morioka Japan 86 D4
Morlaix France 52 B5
Mornington, Isla i. Chile 29 A3
Morocco Africa 34 B2
Morogoro Tanzania 37 B2
Moro Gulf Phil. 91 D3
Morombe Madagascar 43 D2
Mörön Mongolia 82 F5
Morondava Madagascar 43 D2
Morón de la Frontera Spain 56 C2
Moroni Comoros 43 D3
Morotai i. Indon. 91 D3
Morpeth U.K. 48 F4
Morris U.S.A. 12 B3
Morristown U.S.A. 16 C4
Morro, Punta pt Chile 28 B7
Morteros Argentina 28 D6
Mortlock Islands Micronesia 96 C4
Moscow Rus. Fed. 72 B2
Moscow U.S.A. 8 B4
Mosel r. Germany 55 A3
Moselle r. France 52 G5
Mosgiel New Zealand 101 C2
Moshi Tanzania 37 B2
Mosjøen Norway 46 C4
Mosquitia f. Honduras 21 C3
Mosquitos, Costa de coastal area Nicaragua 21 C2
Mosquitos, Golfo de los bay Panama 21 C1
Moss Norway 47 B2
Mossel Bay town South Africa 42 B1
Mossman Australia 99 D4
Mossoró Brazil 27 J4
Mostar Bos. Herz. 62 C3
Møsvatnet lake Norway 47 B2
Motala Sweden 47 C2
Motherwell U.K. 48 E4
Motril Spain 56 D2
Moulins France 52 E4
Moultrie, Lake U.S.A. 17 D3
Moundou Chad 40 B3
Mountain Home town Arkansas U.S.A. 11 D3
Mountain Home town Idaho U.S.A. 8 B3
Mount Gambier town Australia 99 D2
Mount Hagen town P.N.G. 96 B3
Mount Isa town Australia 99 C3
Mount Magnet town Australia 98 A3
Mount Pleasant town U.S.A. 11 D2
Mount Rushmore National Monument nat. park U.S.A. 12 A2
Mount Vernon town U.S.A. 13 D1
Moura Australia 99 D3
Moura Brazil 26 E5
Mourne Mountains U.K. 49 C4
Mouscron Belgium 51 B2
Moutong Indon. 91 D3
Moyale Ethiopia 37 B3
Mo'ynoq Uzbek. 78 B3
Moyynkum Kazakh. 79 D3
Moyynty Kazakh. 79 D3
Mozambique Africa 43 C2
Mozambique Channel Africa 43 D3
Mtwara Tanzania 37 C1
Muar Malaysia 90 B3
Mucur Turkey 74 C3
Mudanjiang China 83 K4
Mudanya Turkey 74 B3
Mudurnu Turkey 74 B3
Mueda Mozambique 43 C3

Muğan Düzü *lowland* Azer. 75 G2
Muğla Turkey 74 B2
Mühlhausen Germany 54 C4
Muhos Finland 46 F4
Mukacheve Ukraine 66 A3
Mukah Malaysia 90 C3
Mukalla Yemen 77 D1
Mulanje, Mount Malawi 43 C3
Mulde *r.* Germany 54 D4
Muleshoe U.S.A. 10 B2
Mulhacén *mt.* Spain 56 D2
Mulhouse France 52 G4
Mull *i.* U.K 48 D5
Mullingar Ireland 49 C3
Mull of Kintyre *cape* U.K. 48 D4
Mull of Oa *cape* U.K. 48 C4
Multan Pakistan 80 C6
Mumbai India 80 C3
Muna *r.* Rus. Fed. 73 K3
Munger India 81 F5
Munich Germany 55 C3
Münster Germany 54 A4
Muojärvi *lake* Finland 46 G4
Muonio Finland 46 F4
Muonioälven *r.* Finland/Sweden 46 E4
Murallón, Cerro *mt.* Chile 29 B3
Murat *r.* Turkey 75 E2
Murchison *r.* Australia 98 A3
Murcia Spain 57 E2
Muret France 53 D2
Murghob Tajik. 79 D2
Müritz *lake* Germany 54 D5
Murmansk Rus. Fed. 72 B3
Muroran Japan 86 D5
Murray *r.* Australia 99 C2
Murray, Lake U.S.A. 17 C3
Murray Bridge Australia 99 C2
Murupara New Zealand 100 F5
Murwara India 81 E4
Murwillumbah Australia 99 D1
Murzechirla Turkm. 78 C2
Murzūq Libya 35 D1
Mürzzuschlag Austria 55 E2
Musala *mt.* Bulgaria 64 C5
Muscat Oman 77 F3
Musgrave Ranges *mts* Australia 98 C3
Muskogee U.S.A. 11 C3
Musoma Tanzania 37 B2
Mustafakemalpaşa Turkey 74 B3
Müţ Egypt 36 A5
Mut Turkey 74 C2
Mutare Zimbabwe 43 C3
Mutis, Gunung *mt.* Indon. 91 D2
Mutsu Japan 86 D5
Mutuali Mozambique 43 C3
Muzaffarpur India 81 F5
Mwanza Tanzania 37 B2
Mwene-Ditu Dem. Rep. Congo 41 C2
Mweru, Lake Dem. Rep. Congo/ Zambia 41 C2
Myadzyel Belarus 69 B2
Myanmar Asia 88 A3
Myeik Myanmar 89 A2
Myeik Kyunzu *is* Myanmar 89 A2
Myingyan Myanmar 88 A3
Myitkyina Myanmar 88 A3
Mykolayiv Ukraine 67 D2
Myrhorod Ukraine 67 D3
Myronivka Ukraine 67 C3
Mysore India 80 D2
My Tho Vietnam 89 B2
Mytilini Greece 65 E3
Mzuzu Malawi 43 C3

N

Naas Ireland 49 C3
Naberezhnyye Chelny Rus. Fed. 72 D2
Nabire Indon. 91 E2
Nacala Mozambique 43 D3
Nacogdoches U.S.A. 11 D2
Nacozari de García Mexico 18 C5
Nadvirna Ukraine 66 B3
Nadym Rus. Fed. 72 F3
Næstved Denmark 47 B1
Nafplio Greece 65 C2
Naga Phil. 91 D4
Nagaland *admin div.* India 81 G5
Nagano Japan 87 C4
Nagaoka Japan 87 C4
Nagaon India 81 G5
Nagasaki Japan 87 A3
Nagercoil India 80 D1

Nagorno-Karabakh *territory* Azer. 75 F2
Nagoya Japan 87 C4
Nagpur India 81 D4
Nagurskoye Rus. Fed. 72 C5
Nagykanizsa Hungary 61 C1
Naha Japan 87 A2
Nahāvand Iran 76 D5
Nahuel Huapí, Lago *lake* Argentina 29 B4
Nain Canada 7 D2
Nā'īn Iran 76 E5
Nairobi Kenya 37 B2
Najafābād Iran 76 E5
Najd *f.* Saudi Arabia 77 C3
Najin North Korea 86 B5
Najrān Saudi Arabia 77 C2
Nakhodka Rus. Fed. 73 L1
Nakhon Ratchasima Thailand 89 B2
Nakhon Sawan Thailand 89 B2
Nakhon Si Thammarat Thailand 89 A1
Nakonde Zambia 43 C4
Nakskov Denmark 47 B1
Nakuru Kenya 37 B2
Nālūt Libya 35 D2
Namak, Kavīr-e *salt flat* Iran 76 F5
Namakzar-e Shadad *salt flat* Iran 76 F5
Namangan Uzbek. 79 D3
Namatanai P.N.G. 96 C3
Nam Co *lake* China 82 D2
Nam Định Vietnam 88 B3
Namib Desert Namibia 42 A2
Namibe Angola 42 A3
Namibia Africa 42 A2
Namlea Indon. 91 D2
Namp'o North Korea 86 A4
Nampula Mozambique 43 C3
Namsos Norway 46 B4
Namtu Myanmar 88 A3
Namur Belgium 51 C2
Namur *admin div.* Belgium 51 C2
Nan Thailand 88 B2
Nan, Mae Nam *r.* Thailand 88 B2
Nanao Japan 87 C4
Nanchang China 85 E3
Nanchong China 85 C4
Nancy France 52 G5
Nanjing China 84 E4
Nan Ling *mts* China 85 D2
Nanning China 85 C2
Nanping China 85 E3
Nantes France 52 C4
Nantes à Brest, Canal de France 52 B4
Nantong China 84 F4
Nantucket Island U.S.A. 15 D2
Nanumea *atoll* Tuvalu 97 E3
Nanyang China 84 D4
Nao, Cabo de la *cape* Spain 57 F3
Napaimiut U.S.A. 4 C3
Napier New Zealand 100 F5
Naples Italy 59 E4
Napo *r.* Ecuador/Peru 26 C5
Narbonne France 53 E2
Nares Strait Canada 5 K4
Narmada *r.* India 80 C4
Närpes Finland 47 E3
Narrabri Australia 99 D2
Narva Estonia 68 C3
Narva Bay Estonia 68 B3
Narvik Norway 46 D5
Nar'yan-Mar Rus. Fed. 72 D3
Naryn Kyrg. 79 D3
Nashik India 80 C4
Nashua U.S.A. 15 C2
Nashville U.S.A. 16 B4
Näsijärvi *lake* Finland 47 E3
Nassau *i.* Cook Is 97 G2
Nassau The Bahamas 22 C4
Nasser, Lake *reservoir* Egypt 36 B5
Nässjö Sweden 47 C2
Nata Botswana 42 B2
Natal Brazil 27 J4
Natchitoches U.S.A. 11 D2
Natron, Lake Tanzania 37 B2
Natuna, Kepulauan *is* Indon. 90 B3
Natuna Besar *i.* Indon. 90 B3
Nauru Pacific Ocean 96 D3
Nauta Peru 26 C5
Nautla Mexico 19 E3
Navalmoral de la Mata Spain 56 C3
Navan Ireland 49 C3
Navapolatsk Belarus 69 C2
Navarino, Isla *i.* Chile 29 C1
Navoiy Uzbek. 78 C3

Navojoa Mexico 18 C4
Nawabshah Pakistan 80 B5
Naxçıvan Azer. 75 F2
Naxos *i.* Greece 65 D2
Nay Pyi Taw Myanmar 88 A2
Nazareth Israel 76 B5
Nazas *r.* Mexico 18 D4
Nazca Peru 26 C3
Nazilli Turkey 74 B2
Nazrēt Ethiopia 37 B3
Nazwá Oman 77 F3
N'dalatando Angola 42 A4
Ndélé C.A.R. 40 C3
Ndjamena Chad 40 B4
Ndola Zambia 42 B3
Nea Liosia Greece 65 C3
Neapoli Greece 65 C2
Neath U.K. 49 E2
Neblina, Pico da *mt.* Brazil 26 D6
Nebraska *admin div.* U.S.A. 12 A2
Nebrodi, Monti *mts* Italy 59 E2
Necker *r.* Germany 55 B3
Necochea Argentina 29 E5
Negev *desert* Israel 76 A5
Negotin Serbia 62 F4
Negra, Punta *pt* Peru 26 A4
Negro *r.* Argentina 29 D4
Negro *r.* Brazil 28 E9
Negro *r.* Uruguay 28 E6
Negros *i.* Phil. 91 D3
Neijiang China 85 C3
Nei Mongol Zizhiqu *admin div.* China 83 G4
Neiße *r.* Germany/Poland 60 B4
Nek'emtē Ethiopia 37 B3
Nellore India 81 D2
Nelson Canada 4 G1
Nelson *r.* Canada 5 I2
Nelson New Zealand 101 D4
Nelson, Estrecho *strait* Chile 29 B2
Nelspruit South Africa 43 C2
Neman Rus. Fed. 69 A2
Nemuro Japan 86 E5
Nemyriv Ukraine 66 C3
Nenagh Ireland 49 B3
Nene *r.* U.K. 49 G3
Nenjiang China 83 K5
Neosho U.S.A. 12 C1
Nepal Asia 81 E5
Nephi U.S.A. 9 C2
Ness, Loch *lake* U.K. 48 D5
Nestos *r.* Greece 64 D4
Netherlands Europe 50 E4
Nettilling Lake Canada 5 K3
Neubrandenburg Germany 54 D5
Neuchâtel Switz. 58 A7
Neuchâtel, Lac de *lake* Switz. 58 A7
Neufchâteau Belgium 51 D1
Neumünster Germany 54 B6
Neuquén Argentina 29 C5
Neuquén *r.* Argentina 29 C5
Neuruppin Germany 54 D5
Neusiedler See *lake* Austria 55 F2
Neustrelitz Germany 54 D5
Neuwied Germany 54 A4
Nevada *admin div.* U.S.A. 9 B2
Nevada, Sierra *mts* Spain 56 D2
Nevada, Sierra *mts* U.S.A. 9 A2
Nevado, Sierra del *mts* Argentina 28 C5
Nevers France 52 E4
Nevşehir Turkey 74 C2
New Amsterdam Guyana 27 F7
Newark U.S.A. 14 C2
New Bedford U.S.A. 15 C2
New Bern U.S.A. 16 D4
Newberry U.S.A. 16 C3
New Boston U.S.A. 11 D2
New Braunfels U.S.A. 11 C1
New Britain *i.* P.N.G. 96 B3
New Brunswick *admin div.* Canada 7 D1
New Caledonia *territory* S. Pacific Ocean 96 D1
Newcastle Australia 99 D2
Newcastle U.S.A. 8 E3
Newcastle upon Tyne U.K. 48 F4
New Delhi India 80 D5
New Georgia Islands Solomon Is 96 C3

New Georgia Sound *strait* Solomon Is 96 C3
New Guinea *i.* Asia 91 F2
New Hampshire *admin div.* U.S.A. 15 C2
Newhaven U.K. 49 G2
New Haven U.S.A. 15 C2
New Iberia U.S.A. 11 D2
New Ireland *i.* P.N.G. 96 C3
New Jersey *admin div.* U.S.A. 14 C2
Newman Australia 98 A3
New Mexico *admin div.* U.S.A. 9 D1
New Orleans U.S.A. 11 D1
New Plymouth New Zealand 100 E5
Newport *England* U.K. 49 F2
Newport *Wales* U.K. 49 C4
Newport *Arkansas* U.S.A. 11 D3
Newport *Oregon* U.S.A. 8 A3
Newport *Vermont* U.S.A. 15 C2
Newport News U.S.A. 16 D4
New Providence *i.* The Bahamas 22 C3
Newquay U.K. 49 D2
New Ross Ireland 49 C3
Newry U.K. 49 C4
New Siberia Islands Rus. Fed. 73 M4
New South Wales *admin div.* Australia 99 D2
Newton U.S.A. 12 B1
Newton Stewart U.K. 48 D4
Newtownabbey U.K. 49 D4
New York U.S.A. 14 C2
New York *admin div.* U.S.A. 14 B2
New Zealand Pacific Ocean 100
Neyrīz Iran 76 E4
Neyshābūr Iran 76 F6
Nezahualcóyotl, Presa *reservoir* Mexico 19 F2
Ngaoundéré Cameroon 40 B3
Ngaruawahia New Zealand 100 E6
Ngaruroro *r.* New Zealand 100 F5
Nguigmi Niger 39 E2
Nha Trang Vietnam 89 B2
Nhill Australia 99 D2
Nhulunbuy Australia 99 C4
Niagara Falls *town* Canada 6 C1
Niagara Falls *town* U.S.A. 14 B2
Niamey Niger 39 D2
Niangara Dem. Rep. Congo 41 C3
Nias *i.* Indon. 90 A3
Nicaragua N. America 21 C2
Nicaragua, Lake Nicaragua 21 B2
Nice France 53 G2
Nicobar Islands India 92 G5
Nicobar Islands India 81 G1
Nicosia Cyprus 74 C1
Nicoya, Golfo de *bay* Costa Rica 21 C1
Nicoya, Península de Costa Rica 21 B1
Nida Lithuania 69 A2
Nidd *r.* U.K. 49 F4
Nidzica Poland 60 E4
Niedere Tauern *mts* Austria 55 D2
Nienburg Germany 54 B5
Nieuw Amsterdam Suriname 27 F7
Nieuw Nickerie Suriname 27 F7
Nieuwpoort Belgium 51 A3
Niğde Turkey 74 C2
Niger Africa 39 D2
Niger *r.* Africa 38 C2
Nigeria Africa 39 D1
Niigata Japan 87 C4
Nijmegen Netherlands 50 D3
Nikopol' Ukraine 67 D2
Niksar Turkey 74 D3
Nikšić Montenegro 63 D3
Nikumaroro *atoll* Kiribati 96 F3
Nile *r.* Africa 36 B5
Nile Delta Egypt 36 B6
Nilgiri Hills India 80 D2
Nîmes France 53 F2
Ninety Mile Beach New Zealand 100 D7
Ningbo China 85 F3
Ningxia Huizu Zizhiqu *admin div.* China 83 G3
Ninove Belgium 51 B3
Niobrara *r.* U.S.A. 12 B2
Nioro Mali 38 C2
Niort France 53 C4
Nipigon Canada 6 B1
Nipigon, Lake Canada 6 B1
Niquelândia Brazil 27 H3
Niš Serbia 63 E3
Nitra Slovakia 61 D2
Niuatoputopu *i.* Tonga 96 F2

Niue *territory* Pacific Ocean 97 G2
Nivelles Belgium 51 C2
Nizamabad India 81 D3
Nizhneudinsk Rus. Fed. 73 H2
Nizhnevartovsk Rus. Fed. 72 F3
Nizhniy Novgorod Rus. Fed. 72 C2
Nizhnyaya Tunguska *r.* Rus. Fed. 72 G3
Nizhyn Ukraine 67 C3
Nizip Turkey 74 D2
Nkongsamba Cameroon 41 A3
Nobeoka Japan 87 B3
Nogales Mexico 18 B5
Nogent-le-Rotrou France 52 D5
Noirmoutier, Île de *i.* France 52 B4
Nome U.S.A. 4 B3
Noord-Brabant *admin div.* Netherlands 51 D3
Noord-Holland *admin div.* Netherlands 50 C4
Norak Tajik. 79 C2
Norderstedt Germany 54 C5
Nordhausen Germany 54 C4
Nordvik Rus. Fed. 73 J4
Nore *r.* Ireland 49 C3
Norfolk Broads *f.* U.K. 49 G3
Noril'sk Rus. Fed. 72 G3
Norman U.S.A. 11 C3
Normandy *f.* France 52 C5
Normanton Australia 99 D4
Ñorquinco Argentina 29 B4
Norra Storfjället *mts* Sweden 46 C4
Norrköping Sweden 47 D2
Norrtälje Sweden 47 D2
Norseman Australia 98 B2
Norsup Vanuatu 97 D2
Norte, Punta *pt Buenos Aires* Argentina 29 E5
Norte, Punta *pt Chubut* Argentina 29 D4
Northallerton U.K. 49 F4
Northampton U.K. 49 F3
North America 2
North Battleford Canada 5 H2
North Bay *town* Canada 6 C1
North Cape New Zealand 100 D7
North Cape Norway 46 F5
North Carolina *admin div.* U.S.A. 16 C4
North Channel U.K. 48 C4
North Dakota *admin div.* U.S.A. 12 A3
North Dorset Downs *hills* U.K. 49 E2
Northern Dvina *r.* Rus. Fed. 72 C3
Northern Ireland *admin div.* U.K. 49 C4
Northern Territory *admin div.* Australia 98 C4
North Esk *r.* U.K. 48 E5
North Frisian Islands Germany 54 B6
North Geomagnetic Pole Arctic Ocean 105 T1
North Head *cape* New Zealand 100 E6
North Island New Zealand 100 E5
North Korea Asia 86 A4
North Magnetic Pole Arctic Ocean 105 P1
North Mariana Islands Pacific Ocean 96 B5
North Platte U.S.A. 12 A2
North Platte *r.* U.S.A. 12 A2
North Pole Arctic Ocean 105 A1
North Ronaldsay *i.* U.K. 48 E6
North Saskatchewan *r.* Canada 5 H2
North Sea Europe 48 G5
North Siberian Lowland *f.* Rus. Fed. 73 I4
North Taranaki Bight *bay* New Zealand 100 E5
North Uist *i.* U.K. 48 C5
North West Cape Australia 98 A3
North West Highlands *f.* U.K. 48 D5
North York Moors *f.* U.K. 49 F4
Northwest Territories *admin div.* Canada 4 F3
Norton Sound *strait* U.S.A. 4 B3
Norway Europe 47 B3
Norway House Canada 5 I2
Norwegian Sea Norway 46 B4
Norwich U.K. 49 G3
Noshiro Japan 86 D5
Nottingham U.K. 49 F3
Nouâdhibou Mauritania 38 B3
Nouâdhibou, Râs *cape* Mauritania 38 B3
Nouakchott Mauritania 38 B2
Nouméa New Caledonia 97 D1

Nova Gradiška Croatia 62 C4
Nova Iguaçu Brazil 27 I1
Nova Kakhovka Ukraine 67 D2
Nova Odesa Ukraine 67 C2
Novara Italy 58 B6
Nova Scotia *admin div.* Canada 7 D1
Novaya Sibir', Ostrov *i.* Rus. Fed. 73 M4
Novaya Zemlya *is* Rus. Fed. 72 D4
Nové Zámky Slovakia 61 D1
Novi Pazar Serbia 63 E3
Novi Sad Serbia 62 D4
Novo Aripuanã Brazil 26 E4
Novodvinsk Rus. Fed. 72 C3
Novo Hamburgo Brazil 28 F7
Novohrad-Volyns'kyy Ukraine 66 B3
Novokuznetsk Rus. Fed. 72 G2
Novo Mesto Slovenia 55 E1
Novomoskovsk Rus. Fed. 72 B2
Novomoskovs'k Ukraine 67 D3
Novooleksiyivka Ukraine 67 D2
Novorossiysk Rus. Fed. 72 B1
Novosibirsk Rus. Fed. 72 G2
Novoukrayinka Ukraine 67 C2
Novovolyns'k Ukraine 66 B3
Novyy Port Rus. Fed. 72 F3
Nowy Sącz Poland 61 E2
Noyabr'sk Rus. Fed. 72 F3
Nu'aym *f.* Oman 77 F3
Nubian Desert Sudan 36 B5
Nueces *r.* U.S.A. 10 C1
Nueva Rosita Mexico 18 D4
Nuevitas Cuba 22 C3
Nuevo Casas Grandes Mexico 18 C5
Nuevo Laredo Mexico 19 E4
Nugget Point New Zealand 101 B1
Nui *atoll* Tuvalu 97 E3
Nuku'alofa Tonga 96 F1
Nukufetau *atoll* Tuvalu 97 E3
Nukulaelae *atoll* Tuvalu 97 E3
Nukunonu *atoll* Tokelau 96 F3
Nukus Uzbek. 78 B3
Nullarbor Plain Australia 98 B2
Numazu Japan 87 C4
Numfoor *i.* Indon. 91 E2
Nunavut *admin div.* Canada 5 J3
Nunivak Island U.S.A. 4 B3
Nuoro Italy 59 B4
Nuqrah Saudi Arabia 77 C4
Nura *r.* Kazakh. 79 C4
Nuremberg Germany 55 C3
Nurmes Finland 46 G3
Nusaybin Turkey 75 E2
Nyala Sudan 36 A4
Nyasa, Lake Africa 37 B1
Nyborg Denmark 47 B1
Nybro Sweden 47 C2
Nyíregyháza Hungary 61 E1
Nykarleby Finland 46 E3
Nykøbing Denmark 47 B1
Nyköping Sweden 47 D2
Nynäshamn Sweden 47 D2
Nyurba Rus. Fed. 73 J3
Nyzhn'ohirs'kyy Ukraine 67 D2

O

Oahe, Lake U.S.A. 12 A2
Oakland U.S.A. 9 A2
Oakover *r.* Australia 98 B3
Oamaru New Zealand 101 C2
Oates Land *f.* Antarctica 104 L2
Oaxaca Mexico 19 E2
Ob' *r.* Rus. Fed. 72 E3
Oban U.K. 48 D5
Obelisk *mt.* New Zealand 101 B2
Obi *i.* Indon. 91 D2
Obihiro Japan 86 D5
Obskaya Guba *strait* Rus. Fed. 72 F3
Ocala U.S.A. 17 C2
Occidental, Cordillera *mts* Colombia 26 B6
Occidental, Cordillera *mts* Peru 26 B3
Ocean Falls *town* Canada 4 F2
Oceania 94
Oceanside U.S.A. 9 B1
Ochakiv Ukraine 67 C2
Ochil Hills U.K. 48 E5
Ocolaşul Mare, Vârful *mt.* Romania 66 B2
Oconee *r.* U.S.A. 17 C3
Oda, Jebel *mt.* Sudan 36 B5
Ōdate Japan 86 D5
Ödemiş Turkey 74 A2

Odense Denmark 47 B1
Oder *r.* Germany 54 E4
Odessa Ukraine 67 C2
Odessa U.S.A. 10 B2
Odisha *admin div.* India 81 E4
Odra *r.* Germany/Poland 61 B4
Oeiras Brazil 27 I4
Ofanto *r.* Italy 59 F4
Offenbach am Main Germany 54 B4
Offenburg Germany 55 A3
Ogadēn *f.* Ethiopia 37 C3
Ōgaki Japan 87 C4
Ogallala U.S.A. 12 A2
Ogbomosho Nigeria 39 D1
Ogden U.S.A. 9 C3
Ogilvie *r.* Canada 4 E3
Oglio *r.* Italy 58 C6
Ogulin Croatia 62 B4
Ohakune New Zealand 100 E5
Ohau, Lake New Zealand 101 B2
Ohio *admin div.* U.S.A. 13 E2
Ohio *r.* U.S.A. 13 E1
Ohrid Macedonia 63 E2
Ohrid, Lake Albania/Macedonia 63 E2
Oiapoque Brazil 27 G6
Oise *r.* France 52 E5
Ōita Japan 87 B3
Oiti *mt.* Greece 65 C3
Ojinaga Mexico 18 D4
Ojos del Salado, Nevado *mt.* Argentina 28 C7
Okahukura New Zealand 100 E5
Okanogan *r.* U.S.A. 8 B4
Okavango Delta *f.* Botswana 42 B3
Okaya Japan 87 C4
Okayama Japan 87 B3
Okeechobee, Lake U.S.A. 17 C2
Okha India 80 B4
Okha Rus. Fed. 73 M2
Okhotsk Rus. Fed. 73 M2
Okhotsk, Sea of Japan/Rus. Fed. 73 M2
Okhtyrka Ukraine 67 D3
Okinawa *i.* Japan 87 A2
Okinawa-shotō *is* Japan 87 A2
Oki-shotō *is* Japan 87 B4
Oklahoma *admin div.* U.S.A. 10 C3
Oklahoma City U.S.A. 11 C3
Okmulgee U.S.A. 11 C3
Oksskolten *mt.* Norway 46 C4
Oktyabr'skoy Revolyutsii, Ostrov *i.* Rus. Fed. 73 H4
Öland *i.* Sweden 47 D2
Olavarría Argentina 29 D5
Olbia Italy 59 B4
Old Crow Canada 4 E3
Oldenburg Germany 54 B5
Oldenzaal Netherlands 50 E4
Oldham U.K. 49 E3
Old Head of Kinsale Ireland 49 B2
Olean U.S.A. 14 B2
Olekma *r.* Rus. Fed. 73 K3
Olekminsk Rus. Fed. 73 K3
Oleksandriya Ukraine 67 D3
Olenek Rus. Fed. 73 J3
Olenek *r.* Rus. Fed. 73 J4
Olenekskiy Zaliv *bay* Rus. Fed. 73 K4
Oléron, Île d' *i.* France 53 C3
Olevs'k Ukraine 66 B3
Oliva, Cordillera de *mts* Argentina/Chile 28 C7
Ollagüe Chile 28 C8
Olmaliq Uzbek. 79 D3
Olomouc Czech Rep. 61 C2
Oloron-Ste-Marie France 53 C2
Olsztyn Poland 60 E4
Olteniţa Romania 66 B2
Olympia U.S.A. 8 A4
Olympus, Mount Greece 64 C4
Olympus, Mount U.S.A. 8 A4
Olyutorskiy Zaliv *bay* Rus. Fed. 73 O2
Omagh U.K. 49 C4
Omaha U.S.A. 12 B2
Oman Asia 77 G2
Oman, Gulf of Asia 77 F3
Ombrone *r.* Italy 58 C5
Omdurman Sudan 36 B4
Ommen Netherlands 50 E4
Omolon *r.* Rus. Fed. 73 N3
Omono *r.* Japan 86 D4
Omsk Rus. Fed. 72 F2
Omsukchan Rus. Fed. 73 N3
Omulew *r.* Poland 60 E4
Ōmuta Japan 87 B3
Ondjiva Angola 42 A3

Onega, Lake Rus. Fed. 72 B3
Oneida Lake U.S.A. 14 B2
Oneonta U.S.A. 14 B2
Oneşti Romania 66 B2
Ongole India 81 E3
Onitsha Nigeria 39 D1
Ono-i-Lau *i.* Fiji 96 F1
Onslow Bay U.S.A. 16 D3
Ontario *admin div.* Canada 6 B2
Ontario, Lake Canada/U.S.A. 14 B2
Oostende New Zealand 100 E4
Oosterschelde *estuary* Netherlands 50 B3
Oost-Vlaanderen *admin div.* Belgium 51 B2
Opala Dem. Rep. Congo 41 C2
Opava Czech Rep. 61 C2
Opelika U.S.A. 17 B3
Opelousas U.S.A. 11 D2
Opihi *r.* New Zealand 101 C2
Opole Poland 60 C3
Oporto Portugal 56 A4
Opotiki New Zealand 100 F5
Opunake New Zealand 100 D5
Oradea Romania 66 A2
Oran Algeria 34 B2
Orange Australia 99 D2
Orange France 53 E4
Orange *r.* Namibia/South Africa 42 A2
Orange U.S.A. 11 D2
Orange, Cabo *cape* Brazil 27 G6
Orange Walk Belize 20 B3
Oranjestad Aruba 23 C4
Orăştie Romania 66 A2
Ord, Mount Australia 98 B4
Ordu Turkey 75 D3
Oregon *admin div.* U.S.A. 8 A3
Oregon City U.S.A. 8 A4
Orel Rus. Fed. 72 B2
Orenburg Rus. Fed. 72 D2
Oreti *r.* New Zealand 101 B1
Orewa New Zealand 100 E6
Orhei Moldova 66 C2
Oriental, Cordillera *mts* Bolivia 26 D2
Oriental, Cordillera *mts* Colombia 26 C7
Oriental, Cordillera *mts* Peru 26 C3
Orinoco *r.* Colombia/Venezuela 26 E7
Orinoco, Delta del Venez. 26 E7
Orissaare Estonia 68 A3
Oristano Italy 59 B3
Oristano, Golfo di *bay* Italy 59 B3
Orivesi *lake* Finland 46 G3
Oriximiná Brazil 27 F5
Orizaba Mexico 19 E2
Orizaba, Pico de *volcano* Mexico 19 E2
Orkney Islands U.K. 48 E6
Orlando U.S.A. 17 C2
Orléans France 52 D4
Orne *r.* France 52 C5
Örnsköldsvik Sweden 46 D3
Orocué Colombia 26 C6
Orona *atoll* Kiribati 96 F3
Oroquieta Phil. 91 D3
Orós, Açude *reservoir* Brazil 27 J4
Orosei Italy 59 B4
Orosei, Golfo di *bay* Italy 59 B4
Orsha Belarus 69 C2
Orsk Rus. Fed. 72 D2
Ortonville U.S.A. 12 B3
Oruro Bolivia 28 C8
Osa, Península de Costa Rica 21 C1
Ōsaka Japan 87 C3
Osakarovka Kazakh. 79 D4
Osh Kyrg. 79 D3
Oshakati Namibia 42 A3
Oshawa Canada 6 C1
O-shima *i.* Japan 87 C3
Osijek Croatia 62 D4
Ösjön *lake* Sweden 46 C3
Oskarshamn Sweden 47 D2
Oslo Norway 47 B3
Osmancık Turkey 74 C3
Osmaniye Turkey 74 D2
Osnabrück Germany 54 B5
Osorno Chile 29 B4
Osorno Spain 56 C5
Oss Netherlands 50 D3
Ossa Greece 65 C3
Ossa, Mount Australia 99 D1
Ostend Belgium 51 A3
Österdalälven *lake* Sweden 47 C3
Østerdalen *f.* Norway 47 B3
Östersund Sweden 46 C3
Ostrava Czech Rep. 61 D2
Ostróda Poland 60 D4

Ostrov Rus. Fed. 72 A2
Ostrowiec Świętokrzyski Poland 60 E3
Ostrów Mazowiecka Poland 60 E4
Ostrów Wielkopolski Poland 60 C3
Ostrzeszów Poland 60 C3
Osŭm *r.* Bulgaria 64 D5
Ōsumi-kaikyo *strait* Japan 87 B3
Ōsumi-shotō *is* Japan 87 B3
Osuna Spain 56 C2
Oswego U.S.A. 14 B2
Otago Peninsula New Zealand 101 C2
Otaki New Zealand 100 E4
Otar Kazakh. 79 D3
Otaru Japan 86 D5
Otatara New Zealand 101 B1
Otjiwarongo Namibia 42 A2
Otorohanga New Zealand 100 E5
Otranto Italy 59 G4
Otranto, Strait of Albania/Italy 59 G4
Otta Norway 47 B3
Ottawa Canada 6 C1
Ottawa *r.* Canada 6 C1
Ottawa U.S.A. 13 D2
Ottawa Islands Canada 5 J2
Ottignies Belgium 51 C2
Ottumwa U.S.A. 13 C2
Otukpo Nigeria 39 D1
Ouachita *r.* U.S.A. 11 D2
Ouachita, Lake U.S.A. 11 D2
Ouachita Mountains U.S.A. 11 C2
Ouaddi *f.* Chad 40 C4
Ouagadougou Burkina Faso 38 C2
Ouarâne *f.* Mauritania 38 C3
Ouargla Algeria 35 C2
Ouarzazate Morocco 34 B2
Oudenaarde Belgium 51 B2
Ouessant, Î d' *i.* France 52 A5
Ouesso Congo 41 B3
Ouistreham France 52 C5
Oujda Morocco 34 B2
Oulainen Finland 46 F4
Oulu Finland 46 F4
Oulujärvi *lake* Finland 46 F4
Oupeye Belgium 51 D2
Ourense Spain 56 B5
Ouricuri Brazil 27 I4
Ouse *r.* U.K. 49 F3
Outer Hebrides *is* U.K. 48 C5
Outokumpu Finland 46 G3
Ovalle Chile 28 B6
Ovamboland *f.* Namibia 42 A3
Overijssel *admin div.* Netherlands 50 E4
Övertorneå Sweden 46 E4
Oviedo Spain 56 C5
Ovruch Ukraine 66 C3
Owando Congo 41 B2
Owen Stanley Range *mts* P.N.G. 96 B3
Owyhee *r.* U.S.A. 8 B3
Oxelösund Sweden 47 D2
Oxford New Zealand 101 D3
Oxford U.K. 49 F2
Oxnard U.S.A. 9 B1
Oyama Japan 87 C4
Oyapock *r.* Brazil/French Guiana 27 G6
Oyoqquduq Uzbek. 78 C3
Özalp Turkey 75 E2
Ozark Plateau U.S.A. 13 C1
Ozarks, Lake of the U.S.A. 13 C1
Ózd Hungary 61 E2
Ozernovskiy Rus. Fed. 73 N2

P

Pabianice Poland 60 D3
Pachuca Mexico 19 E3
Pacific Ocean 102 H6
Pacoval Brazil 27 G5
Padang Indon. 90 B2
Paderborn Germany 54 B4
Padeşu, Vârful *mt.* Romania 66 A2
Padre Island U.S.A. 11 C1
Padua Italy 58 C6
Paducah *Kentucky* U.S.A. 16 B4
Paducah *Texas* U.S.A. 10 B2
Paeroa New Zealand 100 E6
Pag *i.* Croatia 62 B4
Pagadian Phil. 91 D3
Pagai Selatan *i.* Indon. 90 B2
Pagai Utara *i.* Indon. 90 B2
Paget, Mount Atlantic Ocean 29 I2
Paide Estonia 68 B3
Päijänne *lake* Finland 47 F3

Paisley U.K. 48 D4
Pakaraima Mountains Brazil 26 E6
Pakistan Asia 80 A5
Pakxé Laos 89 B2
Palana Rus. Fed. 73 N2
Palatka Rus. Fed. 73 N3
Palau Pacific Ocean 91 E3
Palaw Myanmar 89 A2
Palawan *i.* Phil. 90 C3
Palembang Indon. 90 B2
Palena Chile 29 B4
Palencia Spain 56 C5
Palermo Italy 59 E3
Palestine U.S.A. 11 C2
Pali India 80 C5
Palikir Micronesia 96 C4
Palk Strait India/Sri Lanka 81 D1
Palliser, Cape New Zealand 101 E4
Palliser Bay New Zealand 101 E4
Palma de Mallorca Spain 57 G3
Palmas Brazil 27 H3
Palmas, Cape Liberia 38 C1
Palmeirais Brazil 27 I4
Palmerston Island Cook Is 97 G2
Palmerston North New Zealand 100 E4
Palmi Italy 59 E3
Palmira Colombia 26 B6
Palopo Indon. 91 D2
Palos, Cabo de *cape* Spain 57 E2
Palu Indon. 91 C2
Pamiers France 53 D2
Pamir *mts* Asia 79 D2
Pamlico Sound *strait* U.S.A. 16 D4
Pampas *plain* Argentina 28 D5
Pamplona Spain 57 E5
Pamukkale Turkey 74 B1
Panaji India 80 C3
Panama N. America 21 C1
Panama, Gulf of Panama 21 D1
Panama, Isthmus of N. America 21 C1
Panama Canal Panama 21 D1
Panama City Panama 21 D1
Panama City U.S.A. 17 B3
Panay *i.* Phil. 91 D4
Pančevo Serbia 62 E4
Panevėžys Lithuania 69 B2
Pangkalanbuun *volcano* Indon. 90 C2
Pangkalansusu Indon. 90 A3
Pangkalpinang Indon. 90 B2
Pangnirtung Canada 5 L3
Pantelleria, Isola di *i.* Italy 59 D2
Panzhihua China 85 B3
Paola Italy 59 F3
Papakura New Zealand 100 E6
Paparoa Range *mts* New Zealand 101 C3
Papatoetoe New Zealand 100 E6
Paphos Cyprus 74 B1
Papua, Gulf of P.N.G. 96 B3
Papua New Guinea Oceania 96 B3
Pará, Rio do *r.* Brazil 27 H5
Paraburdoo Australia 98 A3
Paracatu Brazil 27 H2
Paragould U.S.A. 11 D3
Paraguai *r.* Brazil 27 F2
Paraguay *r.* Argentina/Paraguay 28 E7
Paraguay S. America 28 E8
Parakou Benin 39 D1
Paramaribo Suriname 27 F7
Paraná Argentina 28 D6
Paraná *r.* Argentina 28 E6
Paraná Brazil 27 H3
Paraná *r.* Brazil 27 H3
Paranaguá Brazil 28 G7
Paranaíba Brazil 27 G2
Paranaíba *r.* Brazil 27 G2
Paranapanema *r.* Brazil 28 F8
Paranavaí Brazil 28 F8
Paraúna Brazil 27 G2
Pardo *r.* Mato Grosso do Sul Brazil 28 F8
Pardo *r.* São Paulo Brazil 28 G8
Pardubice Czech Rep. 61 B3
Parecis, Serra dos *hills* Brazil 26 E3
Parengarenga Harbour New Zealand 100 D7
Parepare Indon. 91 C2
Parima, Serra *mts* Brazil 26 E6
Parintins Brazil 27 F5
Paris France 52 E5
Paris U.S.A. 11 C2
Parker U.S.A. 9 C1
Parkersburg U.S.A. 16 C4

127

Parkes Australia 99 D2
Parma Italy 58 C6
Parnaíba Brazil 27 I5
Parnaíba r. Brazil 27 I5
Parnassos mt. Greece 65 C3
Parnassus New Zealand 101 D3
Pärnu Estonia 68 B3
Paropamisus mts Afgh. 78 C2
Paros i. Greece 65 D2
Parry, Cape Canada 4 F4
Parry Islands Canada 5 G4
Parsęta r. Poland 60 B5
Parthenay France 52 C4
Paru r. Brazil 27 G5
Pasadena U.S.A. 9 B1
Pasado, Cabo cape Ecuador 26 A5
Pascagoula U.S.A. 17 B3
Paşcani Romania 66 B2
Pasir Putih Malaysia 90 B3
Paso Río Mayo Argentina 29 B3
Passau Germany 55 D3
Passero, Capo cape Italy 58 E2
Passo Fundo Brazil 28 F7
Pastavy Belarus 69 B2
Pastaza r. Peru 26 B5
Pasto Colombia 26 B6
Pasvalys Lithuania 68 B3
Patagonia f. Argentina 29 B3
Patea New Zealand 100 E5
Patea r. New Zealand 100 E5
Paterson U.S.A. 14 C2
Patna India 81 F5
Patos Albania 63 D2
Patos, Lagoa dos lake Brazil 28 F6
Patos de Minas Brazil 27 H2
Patquía Argentina 28 C6
Patraïkos Kolpos bay Greece 65 B3
Patras Greece 65 B3
Pau France 53 C2
Paulistana Brazil 27 I4
Paulo Afonso Brazil 27 J4
Pauls Valley town U.S.A. 11 C2
Pavia Italy 58 B6
Pavlodar Kazakh. 79 D4
Pavlohrad Ukraine 67 D3
Payakumbuh Indon. 90 B2
Payette U.S.A. 8 B3
Paysandú Uruguay 28 E6
Pazardzhik Bulgaria 64 D5
Peace r. Canada 4 G2
Peace River town Canada 4 G2
Peale, Mount U.S.A. 9 D2
Pearl r. U.S.A. 17 B3
Peć Kosovo 63 E3
Pechora r. Rus. Fed. 72 D3
Pechory Estonia 68 B3
Pecos U.S.A. 10 B2
Pecos r. U.S.A. 10 B2
Pécs Hungary 61 D1
Pedro Juan Caballero Para. 28 E8
Peebles U.K. 48 E4
Pee Dee r. U.S.A. 17 D3
Peel r. Canada 4 E3
Pegasus Bay New Zealand 101 D3
Pegu Myanmar 88 A2
Pehuajó Argentina 28 D5
Peipus, Lake Estonia/Rus.Fed. 68 B3
Peixe Brazil 27 H3
Pekanburu Indon. 90 B3
Pelat, Mont mt. France 53 C3
Peleng i. Indon. 91 D2
Pello Finland 46 E4
Pelotas Brazil 28 F6
Pelotas, Rio das r. Brazil 28 F7
Pemangkat Indon. 90 B3
Pemba Mozambique 43 D3
Pemba Zambia 42 B3
Pemba Island Tanzania 37 B2
Pembroke U.K. 49 D2
Peñalara mt. Spain 56 D4
Peña Nevada, Cerro mt. Mexico 19 E3
Peñaranda de Bracamonte Spain 56 C4
Penas, Golfo de gulf Chile 29 A3
Pencoso, Alto de hills Argentina 28 C6
Pendleton U.S.A. 8 B4
Peninsular Malaysia Malaysia 90 B3
Pennines hills U.K. 49 E4
Pennsylvania admin div. U.S.A. 14 B2
Penny Icecap Canada 5 L3
Penobscot r. U.S.A. 15 D3
Penrith U.K. 49 E4
Pensacola U.S.A. 17 B3
Pentland Firth strait U.K. 48 E6
Penza Rus. Fed. 72 C2

Penzance U.K. 49 D2
Penzhinskaya Guba bay Rus. Fed. 73 O3
Peoria U.S.A. 13 D2
Pergamino Argentina 28 D6
Perico Argentina 28 C8
Périgueux France 53 D3
Perito Moreno Argentina 29 B3
Perlas, Archipiélago de las is Panama 21 D1
Perlas, Punta de pt Nicaragua 21 C2
Perm' Rus. Fed. 72 D2
Pernik Bulgaria 64 C5
Perpignan France 53 E2
Perryton U.S.A. 10 B3
Perth Australia 98 A2
Perth U.K. 48 E5
Peru S. America 26 C4
Perugia Italy 58 D5
Pervomays'k Ukraine 67 C3
Pesaro Italy 58 D5
Pescara Italy 58 E5
Pescara r. Italy 58 E5
Peshawar Pakistan 80 C6
Peshkopi Albania 63 E2
Petatlán Mexico 18 D2
Peterborough Canada 6 C1
Peterborough U.K. 49 F3
Peterhead U.K. 48 F5
Petersburg U.S.A. 16 D4
Petersville U.S.A. 4 C3
Petit Mécatina r. Canada 7 E2
Petoskey U.S.A. 13 E3
Petrich Bulgaria 64 C4
Petrolina Brazil 27 I4
Petropavlovsk-Kamchatskiy Rus. Fed. 73 N2
Petropavlovskoye Kazakh. 79 C4
Petroşani Romania 66 A2
Petrozavodsk Rus. Fed. 72 B3
Pforzheim Germany 55 B3
Phangnga Thailand 89 A1
Phanom Dong Rak, Thiu Kaeo mts Cambodia/Thailand 88 B2
Phan Rang-Thap Cham Vietnam 89 B2
Phan Thiêt Vietnam 89 B2
Phatthalung Thailand 89 B1
Phayao Thailand 88 A2
Phet Buri Thailand 89 A2
Philadelphia U.S.A. 14 B1
Philippeville Belgium 51 C2
Philippines Asia 91 D4
Philippine Sea Asia 91 D4
Phitsanulok Thailand 88 B2
Phnom Penh Cambodia 89 B2
Phoenix U.S.A. 9 C1
Phoenix Islands Pacific Ocean 96 F3
Phôngsali Laos 88 B3
Phônsavan Laos 88 B2
Phrae Thailand 88 B2
Phuket Thailand 89 A1
Piacenza Italy 58 B6
Pianosa, Isola i. Italy 58 C5
Piatra Neamţ Romania 66 B2
Piauí r. Brazil 27 I4
Piave r. Italy 58 D6
Picardy f. France 52 D5
Pichanal Argentina 28 D8
Pichilemu Chile 28 B6
Picos Brazil 27 I4
Piedras, Punta pt Argentina 28 E5
Piedras, Río de las r. Peru 26 C3
Piedras Negras Mexico 19 D4
Pieksämäki Finland 47 F3
Pielinen lake Finland 46 G3
Pierre U.S.A. 12 A2
Pietermaritzburg South Africa 43 C2
Pietrosa mt. Romania 66 B2
Pihlajavesi lake Finland 47 G3
Pikes Peak U.S.A. 9 E2
Piła Poland 60 C4
Pilcomayo r. Bolivia/Paraguay 28 E8
Pilica r. Poland 60 E3
Pimenta Bueno Brazil 26 E3
Pinamar Argentina 29 E5
Pinang i. Malaysia 90 B3
Pınarbaşı Turkey 74 D2
Pinar del Río Cuba 22 B3
Pinatubo, Mount volcano Phil. 91 D4
Pindus Mountains Greece 65 B3
Pine Bluff U.S.A. 11 D3
Pinedale U.S.A. 8 D3
Pinega Rus. Fed. 72 C3
Pineios r. Greece 65 C3
Pine Island Bay bay Antarctica 104 G2

Pinerolo Italy 58 A6
Pingdingshan China 84 D4
Pingxiang Guangxi China 85 C2
Pingxiang Jiangxi China 85 D3
Pinotepa Nacional Mexico 19 E2
Pinsk Belarus 69 B2
Pioche U.S.A. 9 C2
Piorini, Lago lake Brazil 26 E5
Piotrków Trybunalski Poland 60 D3
Piquiri r. Brazil 28 F8
Piracicaba Brazil 28 G8
Piraeus Greece 65 C2
Piripiri Brazil 27 I5
Pirot Serbia 63 F3
Piru Indon. 91 D2
Pisa Italy 58 C5
Pisa, Mount New Zealand 101 B2
Písek Czech Rep. 61 B2
Pisidia f. Turkey 74 B2
Pissis, Cerro mt. Argentina 28 C7
Pisuerga r. Spain 56 C4
Pisz Poland 60 E4
Pit r. U.S.A. 9 A3
Piteå Sweden 46 E4
Piteşti Romania 66 B2
Pitlochry U.K. 48 E5
Pittsburgh U.S.A. 14 B2
Pittsfield U.S.A. 15 C2
Piura Peru 26 A4
Piz Bernina mt. Italy/Switz. 58 B7
Plainview U.S.A. 10 B2
Plaquemine U.S.A. 11 D2
Plasencia Spain 56 B4
Platinum U.S.A. 4 B2
Platte r. U.S.A. 12 B2
Plattsburgh U.S.A. 14 C2
Plauen Germany 55 D4
Plaza Huincul Argentina 29 C5
Pleasanton U.S.A. 10 C1
Pleasant Point town New Zealand 101 C2
Plenty, Bay of New Zealand 100 F6
Pleven Bulgaria 64 D5
Płock Poland 60 D4
Pločno mt. Bos. Herz. 62 C3
Ploieşti Romania 66 B2
Plomb du Cantal mt. France 53 E3
Plovdiv Bulgaria 64 D5
Plymouth U.K. 49 D2
Plzeň Czech Rep. 61 A2
Pô Burkina Faso 38 C2
Po r. Italy 58 C6
Pobeda, Gora mt. Rus. Fed. 73 M3
Pocahontas U.S.A. 11 D3
Pocatello U.S.A. 8 C3
Poços de Caldas Brazil 27 H1
Podgorica Montenegro 63 D3
Podkamennaya Tunguska r. Rus. Fed. 73 H3
P'ohang South Korea 87 A4
Pohnpei is Micronesia 96 C4
Pointe-à-Pitre Guadeloupe 23 F2
Pointe-Noire Congo 41 B2
Poitiers France 52 D4
Pokaran India 80 C5
Pokhara Nepal 81 E5
Poland Europe 60 C3
Polatlı Turkey 74 C2
Polatsk Belarus 69 C2
Polessk Rus. Fed. 69 A2
Policastro, Golfo di bay Italy 59 E3
Polillo Islands Phil. 91 D4
Pollino, Monte mt. Italy 59 F3
Polohy Ukraine 67 E3
Polokwane South Africa 42 B2
Poltava Ukraine 67 D3
Polygyros Greece 64 C4
Polykastro Greece 64 C4
Polynesia is Pacific Ocean 102 G5
Pombal Portugal 56 A3
Pomio P.N.G. 96 B3
Ponca City U.S.A. 11 C3
Ponce Puerto Rico 23 F2
Ponferrada Spain 56 B5
Ponta Grossa Brazil 28 F7
Pontchartrain, Lake reservoir U.S.A. 11 D2
Pontes e Lacerda Brazil 27 F2
Pontevedra Spain 56 A5
PontiAnak Indon. 90 B2
Pontine Islands Italy 59 D4
Pontoise France 52 E5
Pontypool U.K. 49 E2
Poole U.K. 49 F2
Poopó, Lago de lake Bolivia 26 D2

Poor Knights Islands New Zealand 100 E7
Popayán Colombia 26 B6
Popigay r. Rus. Fed. 73 I4
Poplar Bluff U.S.A. 13 C1
Popocatépetl, Volcán volcano Mexico 19 E2
Poprad Slovakia 61 E2
Porangatu Brazil 27 H3
Porbandar India 80 B4
Pori Finland 47 E3
Porirua New Zealand 101 E4
Poronaysk Rus. Fed. 73 M1
Porsangerfjorden strait Norway 46 F5
Porsangerhalvøya peninsula Norway 46 F5
Porsgrunn Norway 47 B2
Portage U.S.A. 13 D2
Portage la Prairie Canada 5 I1
Portalegre Portugal 56 B3
Port Angeles U.S.A. 8 A4
Port Arthur U.S.A. 11 D1
Port Askaig U.K. 48 C4
Port Augusta Australia 99 C2
Port-au-Prince Haiti 23 D2
Port Blair India 81 G2
Port Chalmers New Zealand 101 C2
Port-de-Paix Haiti 23 D2
Portel Brazil 27 G5
Port Elizabeth South Africa 42 B1
Port Ellen U.K. 48 C4
Port-Gentil Gabon 41 A2
Port Harcourt Nigeria 39 D1
Port Hedland Australia 98 A3
Port Hope Simpson Canada 7 E2
Port Huron U.S.A. 13 E2
Portimão Portugal 56 A2
Port Kaituma Guyana 27 F7
Portland Australia 99 C2
Portland Maine U.S.A. 15 C2
Portland Oregon U.S.A. 8 A4
Portlaoise Ireland 49 C3
Port Lavaca U.S.A. 11 C1
Port Lincoln Australia 99 C2
Port Louis Mauritius 43 E2
Port Macquarie Australia 99 E2
Port Moresby P.N.G. 96 B3
Porto Alegre Brazil 28 F6
Porto dos Gaúchos Óbidos Brazil 27 F3
Porto Esperidião Brazil 27 F2
Porto Murtinho Brazil 28 E8
Porto-Novo Benin 39 D1
Porto Primavera, Represa reservoir Brazil 27 G1
Porto Seguro Brazil 27 J2
Porto Torres Italy 59 B4
Porto-Vecchio France 53 H1
Porto Velho Brazil 26 E4
Portoviejo Ecuador 26 A5
Port Pirie Australia 99 C2
Portree U.K. 48 C5
Portrush U.K. 48 C4
Port Said Egypt 36 B6
Portsmouth U.K. 49 F2
Portsmouth Kentucky U.S.A. 16 C4
Portsmouth New Hampshire U.S.A. 15 C2
Port Sudan Sudan 36 B4
Port Talbot U.K. 49 E2
Portugal Europe 56 A3
Port Vila Vanuatu 97 D2
Posadas Argentina 28 E7
Poso Indon. 91 D2
Posse Brazil 27 H3
Post U.S.A. 10 B2
Poteau U.S.A. 11 D3
Potenza Italy 59 E4
Poti Georgia 75 E3
Potiskum Nigeria 39 E2
Potosí Bolivia 26 D2
Potsdam Germany 54 D5
Poughkeepsie U.S.A. 14 C2
Pouthĭsăt Cambodia 89 B2
Poverty Bay New Zealand 100 F5
Powell, Lake reservoir U.S.A. 9 C2
Poyang Hu lake China 85 E3
Pozantı Turkey 74 C2
Požarevac Serbia 62 E4
Poza Rica Mexico 19 E3
Poznań Poland 60 C4
Pozoblanco Spain 56 C3
Prachuap Khiri Khan Thailand 89 A2

Prague Czech Rep. 61 B3
Praia Cape Verde 38 A2
Prairie Dog Town Fork r. U.S.A. 10 B2
Prairie du Chien U.S.A. 13 C2
Prapat Indon. 90 A3
Prato Italy 58 C5
Pregolya r. Rus. Fed. 69 A2
Přerov Czech Rep. 61 C2
Prescott U.S.A. 9 C1
Presidencia Roque Sáenz Peña Argentina 28 D7
Presidente Dutra Brazil 27 I4
Presidente Epitácio Brazil 28 F8
Presidente Manuel A Roxas Phil. 91 D4
Presidente Prudente Brazil 28 F8
Presidio U.S.A. 10 B1
Prešov Slovakia 61 E2
Prespa, Lake Europe 63 E2
Presque Isle town U.S.A. 15 D3
Preston U.K. 49 E3
Preto r. Brazil 27 H3
Pretoria South Africa 42 B2
Preveza Greece 65 B3
Prey Vêng Cambodia 89 B2
Pribilof Islands U.S.A. 4 B3
Price U.S.A. 9 C2
Prievidza Slovakia 61 D2
Prijedor Bos. Herz. 62 C4
Prijepolje Serbia 62 D3
Prilep Macedonia 63 E2
Prince Albert Canada 5 H2
Prince Alfred, Cape Canada 4 F4
Prince Charles Island Canada 5 K3
Prince Edward Island admin div. Canada 7 D1
Prince Edward Islands Indian Ocean 93 C1
Prince George Canada 4 F2
Prince of Wales Island Australia 99 D4
Prince of Wales Island Canada 5 I4
Prince of Wales Island U.S.A. 4 E2
Prince Patrick Island Canada 4 G4
Prince Rupert Canada 4 E2
Princess Elizabeth Land f. Antarctica 104 O2
Príncipe i. São Tomé and Príncipe 41 A3
Pripet r. Belarus 69 C2
Priština Kosovo 63 E3
Privas France 53 F3
Prizren Kosovo 63 E3
Probolinggo Indon. 90 C2
Professor van Blommestein Meer reservoir Suriname 27 F6
Providence U.S.A. 15 C2
Providence, Cape New Zealand 101 A1
Provins France 52 E5
Provo U.S.A. 9 C3
Prudhoe Bay town U.S.A. 4 D4
Pruszków Poland 60 E4
Prut r. Moldova/Romania 66 C2
Pryluky Ukraine 67 D3
Przemyśl Poland 61 F2
Psara i. Greece 65 D3
Pskov, Lake Estonia/Rus.Fed. 68 B3
Pucallpa Peru 26 C4
Puch'on South Korea 87 A4
Puducherry India 81 D2
Puebla Mexico 19 E2
Pueblo U.S.A. 9 E2
Puelches Argentina 29 C5
Puelén Argentina 29 C5
Puente-Genil Spain 56 C2
Puerto Aisén Chile 29 B3
Puerto Alegre Bolivia 26 E3
Puerto Ángel Mexico 19 E2
Puerto Armuelles Panama 21 C1
Puerto Asís Colombia 26 B6
Puerto Ayacucho Venez. 26 D7
Puerto Barrios Guat. 20 B3
Puerto Carreño Colombia 26 D7
Puerto Cabezas Nicaragua 21 C2
Puerto Cisnes Chile 29 B4
Puerto Escondido Mexico 19 E2
Puerto Heath Bolivia 26 D3
Puerto Inírida Colombia 26 D6
Puerto Isabel Bolivia 27 F2
Puerto Leguizamo Colombia 26 C5
Puerto Limón Costa Rica 21 C2
Puertollano Spain 56 C3
Puerto Madryn Argentina 29 C4
Puerto Máncora Peru 26 A5

Puerto Montt Chile 29 B4
Puerto Natales Chile 29 B2
Puerto Peñasco Mexico 18 B5
Puerto Plata Dom. Rep. 23 D2
Puerto Portillo Peru 26 C4
Puerto Princesa Phil. 90 C3
Puerto Rico *territory* Caribbean Sea
  23 E2
Puerto Santa Cruz Argentina 29 C2
Puerto Sastre Para. 28 E8
Puerto Vallarta Mexico 18 C3
Pukaki, Lake New Zealand 101 C2
Pukapuka *i.* Cook Is 97 G2
Pukch'ŏng North Korea 86 A5
Pukekohe New Zealand 100 E6
Puketeraki Range *mts* New Zealand
  101 D3
Puketoi Range *hills* New Zealand
  100 F4
Puksubaek-san *mt.* North Korea 86 A5
Pula Croatia 62 A5
Pul-e Khumrī Afgh. 79 C2
Puŀtusk Poland 60 E4
Puná, Isla *i.* Ecuador 26 A5
Pune India 80 C3
Puning China 85 E2
Punjab *admin div.* India 80 D6
Punta, Cerro de *mt.* Puerto Rico 23 E2
Punta Arenas Chile 29 B2
Punta Delgada Argentina 29 D4
Punta Gorda Belize 20 B3
Puntarenas Costa Rica 21 C2
Puntland *f.* Somalia 37 C3
Punto Fijo Venez. 26 C8
Pur *r.* Rus. Fed. 72 F3
Puri India 81 F3
Purmerend Netherlands 50 C4
Purus *r.* Brazil 26 E5
Pusan South Korea 87 A4
Putao Myanmar 88 A3
Putian China 85 E3
Putrajaya Indon. 90 B3
Puttalam Sri Lanka 81 D1
Putumayo *r.* Colombia 26 C5
Puvurnituq Canada 6 C2
Puy de Dôme *mt.* France 53 E3
Puy de Sancy *mt.* France 53 E3
Puysegur Point New Zealand 101 A1
Pyasina *r.* Rus. Fed. 72 G4
P''yatykhatky Ukraine 67 D3
Pyè Myanmar 88 A2
Pye, Mount New Zealand 101 B1
Pyhäjoki *r.* Finland 46 F4
Pyhäselkä *lake* Finland 47 G3
Pylos Greece 65 B2
P'yŏngyang North Korea 86 A4
Pyramid Lake U.S.A. 9 B3
Pyrenees *mts* Europe 53 C2
Pyrgos Greece 65 B2
Pyryatyn Ukraine 67 D3

Q

Qal'ah-ye Now Afgh. 78 C2
Qalāt Afgh. 79 C2
Qamanittuaq Canada 5 I3
Qamdo China 82 E2
Qarshi Uzbek. 78 C2
Qatar Asia 77 E4
Qattara Depression Egypt 36 A5
Qax Azer. 75 F3
Qāyen Iran 76 F5
Qazangödağ *mt.* Armenia/Azer. 75 F2
Qazımämmäd Azer. 75 G3
Qazvīn Iran 76 D6
Qeshm Iran 77 F4
Qiemo China 82 C3
Qijiaojing China 82 D4
Qilian Shan *mts* China 82 E3
Qinā Egypt 36 B5
Qingdao China 84 F5
Qinghai *admin div.* China 82 E3
Qinghai Hu *f.* China 82 E3
Qinhuangdao China 84 E5
Qinzhou China 85 C2
Qionghai China 85 D1
Qiqihar China 83 J5
Qom Iran 76 E5
Qo'ng'irot Uzbek. 78 B3
Qo'qon Uzbek. 79 D2
Qoraqalpog'iston Uzbek. 78 B3
Quang Ngai Vietnam 89 B2
Quanzhou China 85 E2
Quba Azer. 75 G3

Quchan Iran 76 F6
Québec Canada 7 C1
Québec *admin div.* Canada 6 C2
Queen Charlotte Islands Canada *see*
  Haida Gwaii
Queen Charlotte Sound *strait* Canada
  4 F2
Queen Elizabeth Islands Canada 5 I4
Queen Mary Land *f.* Antarctica
  104 O2
Queen Maud Gulf Canada 5 H3
Queen Maud Land *f.* Antarctica
  104 A2
Queensland *admin div.* Australia
  99 D3
Queenstown Australia 99 D1
Queenstown New Zealand 101 B2
Queimada, Ilha *i.* Brazil 27 G5
Quelimane Mozambique 43 C3
Quellón Chile 29 B4
Querétaro Mexico 19 D3
Quetta Pakistan 80 B6
Quetzaltenango Guat. 20 A2
Quezon City Phil. 91 D4
Quibala Angola 42 A3
Quibdó Colombia 26 B7
Quilmes Argentina 28 E6
Quilon India 80 D1
Quimilí Argentina 28 D7
Quimper France 52 A4
Quince Mil Peru 26 C3
Quincy U.S.A. 15 C2
Quito Ecuador 26 B5
Qŭrghonteppa Tajik. 79 C2
Quy Nhơn Vietnam 89 B2
Quzhou China 85 E3

R

Raahe Finland 46 F4
Raalte Netherlands 50 E4
Raba Indon. 90 C2
Rabat Morocco 34 B2
Rabaul P.N.G. 96 C3
Rābigh Saudi Arabia 77 B3
Race, Cape Canada 7 E1
Radom Poland 60 E3
Radomsko Poland 60 D3
Raetihi New Zealand 100 E5
Rafaela Argentina 28 D6
Rafḩā' Saudi Arabia 76 C4
Rafsanjān Iran 76 F5
Ragusa Italy 59 E2
Rahachow Belarus 69 C2
Rahimyar Khan Pakistan 80 C5
Raichur India 80 D3
Rainier, Mount *volcano* U.S.A. 8 A4
Raipur India 81 E4
Rajahmundry India 81 E3
Rajasthan *admin div.* India 80 C5
Rajkot India 80 C4
Rajshahi Bangladesh 81 F4
Rakaia *r.* New Zealand 101 C3
Rakhiv Ukraine 66 B3
Rakvere Estonia 68 B3
Ralik Chain *is* Marshall Is 96 C5
Rāmhormoz Iran 76 D5
Râmnicu Vâlcea Romania 66 B2
Ramsgate U.K. 49 F2
Rancagua Chile 28 B6
Ranchi India 81 F4
Ranco, Lago *lake* Chile 29 B4
Randers Denmark 47 B2
Rangiora New Zealand 101 D3
Rangitaiki *r.* New Zealand 100 F5
Rangitata *r.* New Zealand 101 C3
Rangitikei *r.* New Zealand 100 E4
Rangpur Bangladesh 81 F5
Rankin Inlet Canada 5 I3
Ranong Thailand 89 A1
Ransiki Indon. 91 E2
Rapallo Italy 58 B6
Rapid City U.S.A. 12 A2
Rarotonga *i.* Cook Is 97 H1
Rasa, Punta *pt* Argentina 29 D4
Ras Dejen *mt.* Ethiopia 36 B4
Ra's Fartak *pt* Yemen 77 E2
Rasht Iran 76 D6
Raso, Cabo *cape* Argentina 29 C4
Ras Tannūrah Saudi Arabia 77 E4
Ratak Chain *is* Marshall Is 97 D5
Rat Buri Thailand 89 A2
Rathenow Germany 54 D5
Rathlin Island U.K. 48 C4

Rattray Head U.K. 48 F5
Rättvik Sweden 47 C3
Raukumara Range *mts* New Zealand
  100 F5
Rauma Finland 47 E3
Ravenna Italy 58 D6
Rawaki *i.* Kiribati 97 F3
Rawalpindi Pakistan 80 C6
Rawicz Poland 60 C3
Rawlins U.S.A. 9 D3
Rawson Argentina 29 C4
Raymondville U.S.A. 11 C1
Razgrad Bulgaria 64 E5
Razim, Lacul *lagoon* Romania 66 C2
Ré, Île de *i.* France 53 C4
Reading U.K. 49 F2
Reading U.S.A. 14 B2
Realicó Argentina 28 D5
Rechytsa Belarus 69 C2
Recife Brazil 27 K4
Recreo Argentina 28 C7
Red *r.* U.S.A. 11 D2
Red Bluff U.S.A. 9 A3
Red Deer Canada 5 G2
Redding U.S.A. 9 A3
Red Lake *town* Canada 6 A2
Red Lakes U.S.A. 12 C3
Red River Vietnam 88 B3
Ree, Lough *lake* Ireland 49 C3
Reefton New Zealand 101 C3
Regensburg Germany 55 D3
Reggane Algeria 34 C1
Reggio di Calabria Italy 59 E3
Reggio nell'Emilia Italy 58 C6
Regina Canada 5 H2
Reigate U.K. 49 F2
Reims France 52 F5
Reina Adelaida, Archipiélago de la *is*
  Chile 29 B2
Reindeer Lake Canada 5 H2
Reinosa Spain 56 C5
Reliance Canada 5 H3
Rena Norway 47 B3
Reni Ukraine 66 C2
Rennes France 52 C5
Reno *r.* Italy 58 D6
Reno U.S.A. 9 B2
Renwick New Zealand 101 D4
Reo Indon. 91 D2
Republican *r.* U.S.A. 12 A1
Repulse Bay *town* Canada 5 J3
Resistencia Argentina 28 E7
Resolute Canada 5 I4
Resolution Island Canada 5 L3
Resolution Island New Zealand
  101 A2
Rethymno Greece 65 D1
Réunion *i.* Mauritius 43 E2
Reus Spain 57 D1
Reutlingen Germany 55 B3
Revillagigedo, Islas *is* Mexico 18 B2
Rewa India 81 E4
Reykjavik Iceland 44
Reynosa Mexico 19 E4
Rēzekne Latvia 68 B3
Rhine *r.* Germany 54 A4
Rhinelander U.S.A. 13 D3
Rhode Island *admin div.* U.S.A. 15 C2
Rhodes Greece 65 F2
Rhodes *i.* Greece 65 F2
Rhodope Mountains Bulgaria/Greece
  64 D4
Rhône *r.* France/Switz. 53 F2
Riau, Kepulauan *is* Indon. 90 B3
Ribble *r.* U.K. 49 E3
Ribe Denmark 47 B1
Ribeira Brazil 28 G8
Ribeirão Preto Brazil 27 H1
Riberalta Bolivia 26 D3
Ribniţa Moldova 66 C2
Richardson Mountains New Zealand
  101 B2
Richfield U.S.A. 9 C2
Richmond New Zealand 101 D4
Richmond *Kentucky* U.S.A. 16 C4
Richmond *Virginia* U.S.A. 16 D4
Ridder Kazakh. 79 E4
Riesa Germany 54 D4
Riesco, Isla *i.* Chile 29 B2
Rīga Latvia 68 B3
Riga, Gulf of Estonia/Latvia 68 A3
Riihimäki Finland 47 F3
Rijeka Croatia 62 B4
Rimini Italy 58 D6
Rimouski Canada 7 D1

Ringkøbing Denmark 47 B2
Ringvassøya *i.* Norway 46 D5
Rio Branco Brazil 26 D3
Río Colorado Argentina 29 D5
Río Cuarto Argentina 28 D6
Rio de Janeiro Brazil 27 I1
Río Gallegos Argentina 29 C2
Rio Grande Brazil 27 G2
Rio Grande *town* Brazil 28 F6
Río Grande Mexico 18 D3
Rio Grande   *r.* U.S.A. 9 D2
Rio Grande City U.S.A. 10 C1
Ríohacha Colombia 26 C8
Rioja Peru 26 B4
Río Mulatos Bolivia 26 D2
Río Negro, Embalse del *reservoir*
  Uruguay 28 E6
Rioni *r.* Georgia 75 E3
Río Tigre Ecuador 26 B5
Rio Verde Brazil 27 G2
Rio Verde de Mato Grosso Brazil
  27 G2
Ripon U.K. 49 F4
Ritzville U.S.A. 8 B4
Riva del Garda Italy 58 C6
Rivas Nicaragua 20 B2
Rivera Argentina 29 D5
Rivera Uruguay 28 E6
Riverside U.S.A. 9 B1
Riverton New Zealand 101 B1
Rivière-du-Loup Canada 7 D1
Rivne Ukraine 66 B3
Riwaka New Zealand 101 D4
Riyadh Saudi Arabia 77 D3
Rize Turkey 75 E3
Rizhao China 84 E5
Rjuvbrokkene *mt.* Norway 47 A2
Road Town Virgin Is (U.K.) 23 F2
Roanne France 53 F4
Roanoke *r.* U.S.A. 16 D4
Robertsfors Sweden 46 E4
Roberval Canada 7 C1
Robinson Ranges *hills* Australia
  98 A3
Robson, Mount Canada 4 G2
Roca, Cabo da *cape* Portugal 56 A3
Rocca Busambra *mt.* Italy 59 D2
Rocha Uruguay 28 F6
Rochefort Belgium 51 D2
Rochefort France 53 C3
Rochester *Minnesota* U.S.A. 13 C2
Rochester *New York* U.S.A. 14 B2
Rockford U.S.A. 13 D2
Rockhampton Australia 99 E3
Rodez France 53 E3
Roebourne Australia 98 A3
Roebuck Bay Australia 98 B4
Roermond Netherlands 51 D3
Roeselare Belgium 51 B2
Roja Latvia 68 A3
Rokiškis Lithuania 68 B2
Roma Australia 99 D3
Roma Romania 66 B2
Romain, Cape U.S.A. 17 D3
Roman Romania 66 B2
Romang, Pulau *i.* Indon. 91 D2
Romania Europe 66 B2
Romanzof, Cape U.S.A. 4 B3
Romblon Phil. 91 D4
Rome Italy 59 D4
Rome U.S.A. 14 B2
Romny Ukraine 67 D3
Roncador, Serra do *hills* Brazil 27 G3
Ronda Spain 56 C2
Rondón Colombia 26 C7
Rondonópolis Brazil 27 G2
Rønne Denmark 47 C1
Ronne Entrance *bay* Antarctica 104 E2
Ronne Ice Shelf Antarctica 104 E2
Ronse Belgium 51 B2
Roosendaal Netherlands 51 C3
Roquefort France 53 C3
Roraima, Mount Guyana 26 E7
Røros Norway 46 B3
Rosario Argentina 28 D6
Rosario Mexico 18 A5
Rosário Oeste Brazil 27 F3
Roscommon Ireland 49 B3
Roscrea Ireland 49 C3
Roseau Dominica 23 F2
Roseburg U.S.A. 8 A3
Rose Island American Samoa 97 G2
Rosenberg U.S.A. 11 C1
Rosenheim Germany 55 D2
Roşiori de Vede Romania 66 B2
Ross, Mount New Zealand 101 E4

Rossan Point Ireland 48 B4
Rosslare Ireland 49 C3
Rosso Mauritania 38 B2
Ross Sea Antarctica 104 J2
Røssvatnet *lake* Norway 46 C4
Rostock Germany 54 D6
Rostov-na-Donu Rus. Fed. 72 B1
Roswell U.S.A. 9 E1
Rota *i.* N. Mariana Is 96 B5
Rote *i.* Indon. 91 D1
Rotherham U.K. 49 F3
Rothesay U.K. 48 D4
Rotorua New Zealand 100 F5
Rotorua, Lake New Zealand 100 F5
Rotterdam Netherlands 50 C3
Roubaix France 52 E6
Rouen France 52 D5
Rough Ridge *mts* New Zealand
  101 B2
Rovaniemi Finland 46 F4
Rovigo Italy 58 C6
Rovinj Croatia 62 A5
Royale, Isle U.S.A. 13 D3
Royan France 53 C3
Ruahine Range *mts* New Zealand
  100 F5
Ruapehu, Mount *volcano*
  New Zealand 100 E5
Ruapuke Island New Zealand 101 B1
Rub' al Khālī *desert* Saudi Arabia
  77 D2
Rubtsovsk Rus. Fed. 72 G2
Rūdbār Afgh. 78 C2
Rudnyy Kazakh. 78 C4
Rufiji *r.* Tanzania 37 B2
Rufino Argentina 28 D6
Rugby U.K. 49 F3
Rugby U.S.A. 12 A3
Rügen *i.* Germany 54 D6
Ruhnu *i.* Estonia 68 A3
Ruhr *r.* Germany 54 A4
Ruidoso U.S.A. 9 D1
Rukwa, Lake Tanzania 37 B2
Rum *i.* U.K. 48 C5
Ruma Serbia 62 B4
Runanga New Zealand 101 C3
Runaway, Cape New Zealand 100 F6
Rundu Namibia 42 A3
Ruoqiang China 82 C3
Ruse Bulgaria 64 D5
Rushon Tajik. 79 D2
Russell New Zealand 100 E7
Russellville U.S.A. 11 D3
Russian Federation Asia/Europe 72 E3
Rustavi Georgia 75 F3
Ruston U.S.A. 11 D2
Ruteng Indon. 91 D2
Rutland U.S.A. 15 C2
Rutland Water *reservoir* U.K. 49 F3
Ruzayevka Kazakh. 79 C4
Ružomberok Slovakia 61 D2
Rwanda Africa 37 A2
Ryazan' Rus. Fed. 72 B2
Rybinsk Rus. Fed. 72 B2
Rybinskoye Vodokhranilishche
  reservoir Rus. Fed. 72 B2
Rybnik Poland 61 D3
Ryōtsu Japan 87 C4
Rzeszów Poland 61 F3

S

Saale *r.* Germany 54 C4
Saarbrücken Germany 55 A3
Saaremaa *i.* Estonia 68 A3
Šabac Serbia 62 D4
Sabadell Spain 57 G4
Sabah *admin div.* Malaysia 90 C3
Sabana, Archipiélago de *is* Cuba
  22 B3
Sabhā Libya 35 D1
Sabinas Mexico 19 D4
Sabinas Hidalgo Mexico 19 D4
Sabirabad Azer. 75 G3
Sable, Cape Canada 7 D1
Sable, Cape U.S.A. 17 C2
Sable Island Canada 7 E1
Şabyā Saudi Arabia 77 C2
Sabzevār Iran 76 F6
Sacramento U.S.A. 9 A2
Sacramento Mountains U.S.A. 9 D1
Sado *r.* Portugal 56 A3

Sadoga-shima i. Japan 87 C4
Säffle Sweden 47 C2
Safford U.S.A. 9 D1
Safi Morocco 34 B2
Sagar India 81 D4
Sagres Portugal 56 A2
Sagua la Grande Cuba 22 B3
Sagyndyk, Mys pt Kazakh. 78 B3
Sahand, Küh-e mt. Iran 76 D6
Sahara desert Africa 34 C1
Sahel f. Africa 38 C2
Saidpur Bangladesh 81 F5
Saimaa lake Finland 47 G3
St Abb's Head U.K. 48 E4
St-Amand-Montrond France 52 E4
St Andrews U.K. 48 E5
St Ann's Bay town Jamaica 22 C2
St Anthony Canada 7 E2
St Arnaud Range mts New Zealand 101 D3
St Augustine U.S.A. 17 C2
St Austell U.K. 49 D2
St-Barthélemy territory Caribbean Sea 23 F2
St-Brieuc France 52 B5
St Charles U.S.A. 13 C1
St Cloud U.S.A. 12 C3
St Croix r. Canada/U.S.A. 15 D3
St Croix i. Virgin Is (U.S.A.) 23 F2
St David's U.K. 49 D2
St David's Head U.K. 49 D2
St-Denis Mauritius 43 E2
St-Dié France 52 G5
St-Dizier France 52 F5
Saintes France 53 C3
St-Étienne France 53 F3
St Gallen Switz. 58 B7
St-Gaudens France 53 D2
St George Australia 99 D3
St George U.S.A. 9 C2
St George, Cape P.N.G. 96 C3
St George's Grenada 23 F1
St George's Channel Ireland/U.K. 49 C2
St Helena i. S. Atlantic Ocean 31 G4
St Helena Bay South Africa 42 A1
St Helens U.K. 49 E3
St Helens, Mount volcano U.S.A. 8 A4
St Helier Channel Is 49 E1
St Joe r. U.S.A. 8 B4
Saint John Canada 7 D1
St John r. U.S.A. 15 D3
St John's Antigua and Barbuda 23 F2
St John's Canada 7 E1
St Johns U.S.A. 9 D1
St Johnsbury U.S.A. 15 C2
St Joseph U.S.A. 12 C1
St Kilda i. U.K. 48 B5
St Kitts and Nevis Caribbean Sea 23 F2
St-Laurent-du-Maroni French Guiana 27 G7
St Lawrence inlet Canada 7 D1
St Lawrence, Gulf of Canada 7 D1
St Lawrence Island U.S.A. 4 B3
St-Lô France 52 C5
St-Louis Senegal 38 B2
St Louis U.S.A. 13 C1
St Lucia Caribbean Sea 23 F1
St-Malo France 52 B5
St-Malo, Golfe de gulf France 52 B5
St-Martin territory Caribbean Sea 23 F2
St Matthew Island U.S.A. 4 A3
St Matthias Group is P.N.G. 96 B3
St Moritz Switz. 58 B7
St-Nazaire France 52 B4
St-Niklaas Belgium 51 C3
St Paul U.S.A. 13 C2
St Peter Port Channel Is 49 E1
St Petersburg Rus. Fed. 72 B2
St Petersburg U.S.A. 17 C2
St Pierre and Miquelon is France 7 E1
St Pölten Austria 55 E3
St-Quentin France 52 E5
St Vincent and the Grenadines Caribbean Sea 23 F1
St-Vith Belgium 51 E2
Saitama Japan 87 C4
Saittanulkki hill Finland 46 F4
Sajama, Nevado mt. Bolivia 26 D2
Sakai Japan 87 C4
Sakākah Saudi Arabia 76 C4
Sakakawea, Lake U.S.A. 12 A3
Sakarya r. Turkey 74 B3
Sakata Japan 86 C4

Sakhalin i. Rus. Fed. 73 M1
Sakishima-shotō is Japan 87 A2
Sakon Nakhon Thailand 88 B2
Sakura Japan 87 D4
Sal i. Cape Verde 38 A2
Sala Sweden 47 D2
Saladillo r. Argentina 28 D6
Salado r. Buenos Aires Argentina 28 E5
Salado r. Santa Fe Argentina 28 D6
Salado r. Mexico 19 E4
Salado, Quebrada de r. Chile 28 B7
Şalālah Oman 77 E2
Salamanca Mexico 18 D3
Salamanca Spain 56 C4
Salavan Laos 89 B1
Salawati i. Indon. 91 E2
Šalčininkai Lithuania 69 B2
Saldus Latvia 68 A3
Sale Australia 99 D2
Salekhard Rus. Fed. 72 E3
Salem India 81 D2
Salem U.S.A. 8 A3
Salerno Italy 59 E4
Salerno, Golfo di gulf Italy 59 E4
Salgado r. Brazil 27 J4
Salgueiro Brazil 27 J4
Salihli Turkey 74 B2
Salihorsk Belarus 69 B2
Salina U.S.A. 12 B1
Salina Cruz Mexico 19 E2
Salinas U.S.A. 9 A2
Salinosó Lachay, Punta pt Peru 26 B3
Salisbury r. U.K. 49 F2
Salisbury U.S.A. 16 D4
Salisbury Plain U.K. 49 E2
Salluit Canada 6 C3
Salmon r. U.S.A. 8 B4
Salmon River Mountains U.S.A. 8 B3
Salo Finland 47 E3
Salt r. U.S.A. 9 C1
Salta Argentina 28 C8
Saltillo Mexico 19 D4
Salt Lake City town U.S.A. 9 C3
Salto Uruguay 28 E6
Salto Grande, Embalse de reservoir Uruguay 28 E6
Salton Sea lake U.S.A. 9 B1
Salvador Brazil 27 J3
Salween r. China/Myanmar 88 A2
Salyan Azer. 75 G2
Salzburg Austria 55 D2
Salzgitter Germany 54 C5
Samaipata Bolivia 26 E2
Samandağı Turkey 74 C2
Samani Japan 86 D5
Samar i. Phil. 91 D4
Samara Rus. Fed. 72 D2
Samarinda Indon. 90 C2
Samarqand Uzbek. 79 C2
Sāmarrā' Iraq 76 C5
Şamaxı Azer. 75 G3
Samba Dem. Rep. Congo 41 C2
Sambalpur India 81 E4
Sambas Indon. 90 B3
Sambir Ukraine 66 A3
Samborombón, Bahía bay Argentina 29 E5
Sambre r. Belgium/France 51 C2
Şämkir Azer. 75 F3
Samoa Pacific Ocean 97 F2
Samos i. Greece 65 E2
Samosir i. Indon. 90 A3
Samothraki i. Greece 64 D4
Sampit Indon. 90 C2
Sam Rayburn Reservoir U.S.A. 11 D2
Samsun Turkey 74 D3
San Mali 38 C2
Şan'ā' Yemen 77 C2
Sanandaj Iran 76 D6
San Angelo U.S.A. 10 B2
San Antonio U.S.A. 10 C1
San Antonio, Cabo cape Cuba 22 B3
San Antonio de los Cobres Argentina 28 C8
San Antonio Oeste Argentina 29 D4
San Benedicto, Isla i. Mexico 18 B2
San Bernardino U.S.A. 9 B1
San Bernardo Chile 28 B6
San Blas, Cape U.S.A. 17 B2
San Borja Bolivia 26 D3
San Carlos Venez. 26 D7
San Carlos de Bariloche Argentina 29 B4
San Cristobal i. Solomon Is 96 D2
San Cristóbal Venez. 26 C7

Sancti Spíritus Cuba 22 C3
Sandakan Malaysia 90 C3
Sandane Norway 47 A3
Sandanski Bulgaria 64 C4
Sanday i. U.K. 48 E6
Sanderson U.S.A. 10 B2
San Diego U.S.A. 9 B1
Sandıklı Turkey 74 B2
Sandnes Norway 47 A2
Sandnessjøen Norway 46 C4
Sandpoint U.S.A. 8 B4
Sandviken Sweden 47 D3
Sandwich U.K. 49 G2
Sandy Cape Australia 99 E3
Sandy Lake town Canada 6 A2
San Felipe Mexico 18 B5
San Fernando Mexico 19 E3
San Fernando Phil. 91 D4
San Fernando Spain 56 B2
San Fernando Trinidad and Tobago 23 F1
San Fernando de Apure Venez. 26 D7
San Francisco Argentina 28 D6
San Francisco U.S.A. 9 A2
San Francisco de Macorís Dom. Rep. 23 D2
San Francisco de Paula, Cabo cape Argentina 29 C3
Sangir, Kepulauan is Indon. 91 D3
Sangkulirang Indon. 90 C3
Sangli India 80 C3
Sangre de Cristo Range mts U.S.A. 9 D2
Sangue r. Brazil 27 F3
San Hipólito, Punta pt Mexico 18 B4
San Ignacio Bolivia 26 D3
San Jorge, Golfo de gulf Argentina 29 C3
San José Costa Rica 21 C1
San Jose Phil. 91 D4
San Jose U.S.A. 9 A2
San José, Isla i. Mexico 18 B3
San José de Jáchal Argentina 28 C6
San José del Cabo Mexico 18 C3
San José del Guaviare Colombia 26 C6
San José de Mayo Uruguay 28 E6
San Juan Argentina 28 C6
San Juan r. Costa Rica/Nicaragua 21 C2
San Juan Puerto Rico 23 E2
San Juan r. U.S.A. 9 C2
San Juan Bautista Para. 28 E7
San Juan Bautista Tuxtepec Mexico 19 E2
San Juan Mountains U.S.A. 9 D2
San Julián Argentina 29 C3
San Lorenzo Ecuador 26 B6
San Lorenzo mt. Spain 57 D5
San Lorenzo, Monte mt. Argentina/ Chile 29 B3
Sanlúcar de Barrameda Spain 56 B2
San Luis Argentina 28 C6
San Luis Obispo U.S.A. 9 A2
San Luis Potosí Mexico 18 D3
San Marcos U.S.A. 10 C1
San Marino Europe 58 D6
San Marino town San Marino 58 D5
San Martín r. Bolivia 26 E3
San Martín, Lago lake Argentina/ Chile 29 B3
San Martín de los Andes Argentina 29 B4
San Matías, Golfo gulf Argentina 29 D4
San Miguel El Salvador 20 B2
San Miguel de Tucumán Argentina 28 C7
Sanming China 85 E3
San Nicolás de los Arroyos Argentina 28 D6
San Pablo Phil. 91 D4
San Pedro Bolivia 26 E2
San Pedro, Sierra de mts Spain 56 B3
San Pedro de las Colonias Mexico 18 D4
San Pedro de Ycuamandyyú Para. 28 E8
San Pedro Sula Honduras 20 B3
San Pietro, Isola di i. Italy 59 B3
Sanquhar U.K. 48 E4
San Quintín, Cabo cape Mexico 18 A5
San Rafael Argentina 28 C6
San Remo Italy 58 A5

San Salvador El Salvador 20 B2
San Salvador i. The Bahamas 22 D3
San Salvador de Jujuy Argentina 28 C8
San Severo Italy 59 E4
Santa Ana Bolivia 26 D2
Santa Ana El Salvador 20 B2
Santa Ana U.S.A. 9 B1
Santa Bárbara Mexico 18 C4
Santa Barbara U.S.A. 9 B1
Santa Clara Colombia 26 D5
Santa Clara Cuba 22 C3
Santa Clarita U.S.A. 9 B1
Santa Cruz r. Argentina 29 C2
Santa Cruz Bolivia 26 E2
Santa Cruz U.S.A. 9 A2
Santa Cruz de Tenerife Canary Islands 34 A1
Santa Cruz do Sul Brazil 28 F7
Santa Cruz Islands Solomon Is 97 D2
Santa Elena, Cabo cape Costa Rica 20 B2
Santa Fe Argentina 28 D6
Santa Fe U.S.A. 9 D2
Santa Isabel Argentina 28 C5
Santa Isabel i. Solomon Is 96 C3
Santa Margarita, Isla i. Mexico 18 B3
Santa Maria Brazil 28 F7
Santa Maria U.S.A. 9 A1
Santa Maria di Leuca, Capo cape Italy 59 G3
Santa Marta Colombia 26 C8
Santana Brazil 27 I3
Santander Spain 56 D5
Santarém Brazil 27 G5
Santarém Portugal 56 A3
Santa Rosa Argentina 29 D5
Santa Rosa Brazil 28 F7
Santa Rosa California U.S.A. 9 A2
Santa Rosa New Mexico U.S.A. 9 E1
Santa Rosa de Copán Honduras 20 B2
Santa Rosa do Purus Brazil 26 C4
Santa Rosalía Mexico 18 B4
Santiago Brazil 28 F7
Santiago i. Cape Verde 38 A2
Santiago Chile 28 B6
Santiago Dom. Rep. 23 D2
Santiago Panama 21 C1
Santiago de Compostela Spain 56 A5
Santiago de Cuba Cuba 22 C3
Santiago del Estero Argentina 28 D7
Sant Jordi, Golf de gulf Spain 57 F4
Santo André Brazil 28 G8
Santo Antão i. Cape Verde 38 A2
Santo Antônio, Cabo cape Brazil 27 J3
Santo Domingo Dom. Rep. 23 E2
Santoña Spain 56 D5
Santorini i. Greece 65 D2
Santos Brazil 28 G8
Santo Tomé Argentina 28 E7
San Valentín, Cerro mt. Chile 29 B3
San Vicente El Salvador 20 B2
San Vicente de Cañete Peru 26 B3
San Vincenzo Italy 58 C5
São Borja Brazil 28 E7
São Carlos Brazil 27 H1
São Félix Mato Grosso Brazil 27 G3
São Félix Pará Brazil 27 G4
São Francisco r. Brazil 27 J4
São José do Rio Preto Brazil 27 H1
São Luís Brazil 27 I5
São Marcos, Baía de bay Brazil 27 I5
São Mateus Brazil 27 J2
Saône r. France 52 F4
São Paulo Brazil 28 G8
São Roque, Cabo de cape Brazil 27 J4
Sao-Siu Indon. 91 D3
São Tomé São Tomé and Príncipe 41 A3
São Tomé i. São Tomé and Príncipe 41 A3
São Tomé, Cabo de cape Brazil 27 I1
São Tomé and Príncipe Africa 41 A3
São Vicente, Cabo de cape Portugal 56 A2
Sapporo Japan 86 D5
Sapri Italy 59 E4
Saqqez Iran 76 D6
Sarāb Iran 76 D6
Sara Buri Thailand 89 B2
Sarajevo Bos. Herz. 62 D3
Sarandë Albania 63 E1
Saransk Rus. Fed. 72 C2
Sarasota U.S.A. 17 C2
Saratoga Springs town U.S.A. 14 C2

Saratov Rus. Fed. 72 C2
Saravan Iran 76 G4
Sarawak admin div. Malaysia 90 C3
Saray Turkey 74 A3
Sardinia i. Italy 59 B4
Sarektjåkkå mt. Sweden 46 D4
Sar-e Pul Afgh. 78 C2
Sargodha Pakistan 80 C6
Sarh Chad 40 B3
Sārī Iran 76 E6
Sariwŏn North Korea 86 A4
Sarıyer Turkey 74 B3
Sark i. Channel Is 49 E1
Sarkand Kazakh. 79 D3
Şarkışla Turkey 74 D2
Şarköy Turkey 74 A3
Sarmi Indon. 91 E2
Särna Sweden 47 C3
Sarny Ukraine 66 B3
Saros Körfezi bay Turkey 74 A3
Sarpsborg Norway 47 B2
Sarrebourg France 52 G5
Sarria Spain 56 B5
Sarthe r. France 52 C4
Saryarka plain Kazakh. 79 C3
Sarykamyshskoye Ozero lake Turkm./ Uzbek. 78 B3
Saryozek Kazakh. 79 D3
Saryshagan Kazakh. 79 D3
Sarysu r. Kazakh. 79 C3
Sary-Tash Kyrg. 79 D2
Sasebo Japan 87 A3
Saskatchewan admin div. Canada 5 H2
Saskatchewan r. Canada 5 H2
Saskatoon Canada 5 H2
Sassandra Côte d'Ivoire 38 C1
Sassari Italy 59 B4
Sassnitz Germany 54 D6
Satpayev Kazakh. 79 C3
Satpura Range mts India 80 C4
Satu Mare Romania 66 A2
Saudi Arabia Asia 77 C3
Sault Sainte Marie Canada 6 B1
Sault Sainte Marie U.S.A. 13 E3
Saumalkol' Kazakh. 79 C4
Saumlakki Indon. 91 E2
Saurimo Angola 42 B4
Sava r. Europe 62 D4
Savai'i i. Samoa 96 F2
Savannah U.S.A. 17 C3
Savannah r. U.S.A. 17 C3
Savannakhét Laos 88 B2
Save r. Mozambique/Zimbabwe 43 C2
Savona Italy 58 B6
Savu Sea Indon. 91 D2
Sawel Mountain U.K. 48 C4
Saýat Turkm. 78 C2
Sayhūt Yemen 77 E2
Saylac Somalia 36 C4
Saynshand Mongolia 83 H4
Sayre U.S.A. 14 B2
Scafell Pike hill U.K. 49 E4
Scarborough Trinidad and Tobago 23 F1
Scarborough U.K. 49 F4
Schaffhausen Switz. 58 B7
Schagen Netherlands 50 C4
Schefferville Canada 7 D2
Scheldt r. Belgium 51 C3
Schenectady U.S.A. 14 C2
Schiermonnikoog i. Netherlands 50 E5
Schleswig Germany 54 B6
Schwäbische Alb mts Germany 55 B2
Schwedt an der Oder Germany 54 E5
Schweinfurt Germany 55 C4
Schwerin Germany 54 C5
Scilly, Isles of U.K. 49 C1
Scioto r. U.S.A. 13 E1
Scotia Sea S. Atlantic Ocean 104 D3
Scotland admin div. U.K. 48 E5
Scranton U.S.A. 14 B2
Scunthorpe U.K. 49 F3
Scuol Switz. 58 C7
Scutari, Lake Albania/Montenegro 63 D3
Sealy U.S.A. 11 C1
Searcy U.S.A. 11 D3
Seattle U.S.A. 8 A4
Sebastián Vizcaíno, Bahía bay Mexico 18 A4
Şebinkarahisar Turkey 75 D3
Sechura, Bahía de bay Peru 26 A4
Secretary Island New Zealand 101 A2
Secunderabad India 81 D3

Stephenville U.S.A. 10 C2
Sterling U.S.A. 9 E3
Sterlitamak Rus. Fed. 72 D2
Steubenville U.S.A. 13 E2
Stewart Canada 4 F2
Stewart r. Canada 4 E3
Stewart Island New Zealand 101 A1
Steyr Austria 55 E3
Stikine r. Canada 4 E2
Stillwater U.S.A. 11 C3
Stirling U.K. 48 E5
Stjørdalshalsen Norway 46 B3
Stockholm Sweden 47 D2
Stockport U.K. 49 E3
Stockton U.S.A. 9 A2
Stockton-on-Tees U.K. 49 F4
Stœng Trêng Cambodia 89 B2
Stoke-on-Trent U.K. 49 E3
Stolin Belarus 69 B1
Stonehaven U.K. 48 E5
Stony Rapids town Canada 5 H2
Stora Lulevatten lake Sweden 46 D4
Storavan lake Sweden 46 D4
Støren Norway 46 B3
Stornoway U.K. 48 C6
Storsjön lake Sweden 46 C3
Storskrymten mt. Norway 46 B3
Storuman Sweden 46 D4
Storuman lake Sweden 46 D4
Stour r. U.K. 49 G2
Stowbtsy Belarus 69 B2
Strabane U.K. 48 C4
Stralsund Germany 54 D6
Stranda Norway 46 A3
Stranraer U.K. 48 D4
Strasbourg France 52 G5
Stratford New Zealand 100 E5
Stratford U.S.A. 10 B3
Stratford-upon-Avon U.K. 49 F3
Strathy Point U.K. 48 D6
Straubing Germany 55 D3
Strelka Rus. Fed. 73 N3
Strimonas r. Greece 64 C4
Stroeder Argentina 29 D4
Stromboli, Isola i. Italy 59 E3
Strömsund Sweden 46 C3
Stronsay i. U.K. 48 E6
Struer Denmark 47 B2
Struma r. Bulgaria 64 C4
Strumica Macedonia 63 F2
Stryy Ukraine 67 A3
Sturt Stony Desert Australia 99 D3
Stuttgart Germany 55 B3
Stuttgart U.S.A. 11 D2
Suaçuí Grande r. Brazil 27 I2
Suakin Sudan 36 B4
Subotica Serbia 62 D5
Suceava Romania 66 B2
Suck r. Ireland 49 B3
Sucre Bolivia 26 D2
Sucuriú r. Brazil 28 F8
Sudak Ukraine 67 D2
Sudan Africa 36 A4
Sudbury Canada 6 B1
Sudd swamp South Sudan 37 A3
Sudety mts Czech Rep./Poland 60 B3
Suez Egypt 36 B5
Suez, Gulf of Egypt 36 B5
Suffolk U.S.A. 16 D4
Şuḩār Oman 77 F3
Suhl Germany 54 C4
Suining China 85 C4
Suir r. Ireland 49 C3
Suizhou China 85 D4
Sukadana i. Indon. 90 B2
Sukkur Pakistan 80 B5
Sula i. Norway 47 A3
Sula, Kepulauan is Indon. 91 D2
Sullana Peru 26 A5
Sulmona Italy 59 D5
Sulphur Springs town U.S.A. 11 C2
Sulu Archipelago is Phil. 91 D3
Sulu Sea Phil. 91 C3
Sumampa Argentina 28 D7
Sumatra i. Indon. 90 A3
Sumba i. Indon. 91 D2
Sumbawa i. Indon. 90 C2
Sumburgh Head U.K. 48 F6
Sumner New Zealand 101 D3
Sumqayıt Azer. 75 G3
Sumy Ukraine 67 D3
Sunbury U.S.A. 14 B2
Sunda, Selat strait Indon. 90 B2
Sunderland U.K. 48 F4
Sundsvall Sweden 47 D3
Sungailiat Indon. 90 B2

Sungai Petani Malaysia 90 B3
Sungurlu Turkey 74 C3
Suolijärvet lake Finland 46 G4
Suonenjoki Finland 46 F3
Superior U.S.A. 13 C3
Superior, Lake Canada/U.S.A. 13 D3
Süphan Dağı mt. Turkey 75 E2
Sūq ash Shuyūkh Iraq 76 D5
Suqian China 84 E4
Sur, Punta pt Argentina 29 E5
Surabaya Indon. 90 C2
Surakarta Indon. 90 C2
Surat India 80 C4
Surat Thani Thailand 89 A1
Surendranagar India 80 C4
Surgut Rus. Fed. 72 F3
Surigao Phil. 91 D3
Surin Thailand 89 B2
Suriname S. America 27 F6
Süsangerd Iran 76 D5
Suşehri Turkey 75 D3
Susquehanna r. U.S.A. 14 B2
Susuman Rus. Fed. 73 M3
Susurluk Turkey 74 B2
Sutak India 80 D6
Sutlej r. India/Pakistan 80 C5
Suva Fiji 97 E2
Suwałki Poland 60 F5
Suwarrow i. Cook Is 97 G2
Suwŏn South Korea 87 A4
Suzhou Anhui China 85 E4
Suzhou Jiangsu China 85 F4
Suzu Japan 87 C4
Suzuka Japan 87 C3
Svalbard territory Arctic Ocean 105 B1
Svatove Ukraine 67 E3
Sveg Sweden 47 C3
Svendborg Denmark 47 B1
Svinecea Mare, Vârful mt. Romania 66 A2
Svir Belarus 69 B2
Svitavy Czech Rep. 61 C2
Svitlovods'k Ukraine 67 D3
Svobodnyy Rus. Fed. 73 K2
Svyetlahorsk Belarus 69 C2
Swakopmund Namibia 42 A2
Swale r. U.K. 49 F4
Swan Hill town Australia 99 D2
Swan Islands Honduras see
   Cisne, Islas del
Swansea U.K. 49 E2
Swaziland Africa 43 C2
Sweden Europe 47 C3
Sweetwater U.S.A. 10 B2
Sweetwater r. U.S.A. 8 D3
Swift Current Canada 5 H2
Swindon U.K. 49 F2
Świnoujście Poland 60 B4
Switzerland Europe 58 A7
Sydney Australia 99 E2
Sydney Canada 7 D1
Syeverodonets'k Ukraine 67 E3
Syktyvkar Rus. Fed. 72 D3
Sylarna mt. Norway/Sweden 46 C3
Syracuse Italy 59 E2
Syracuse U.S.A. 14 B2
Syrdar'ya r. Asia 79 C3
Syria Asia 76 B5
Syrian Desert Asia 76 B5
Syros i. Greece 65 D2
Syzran' Rus. Fed. 72 C2
Szczecin Poland 60 B4
Szczecinek Poland 60 C4
Szczytno Poland 60 E4
Szeged Hungary 61 E1
Székesfehérvár Hungary 61 D1
Szekszárd Hungary 61 D1
Szolnok Hungary 61 E1
Szombathely Hungary 61 C1

T

Ṭabas Iran 76 F5
Tabatinga Colombia 26 D5
Table Cape New Zealand 100 F5
Tábor Czech Rep. 61 B2
Tabora Tanzania 37 B2
Tabrīz Iran 76 D6
Tabūk Saudi Arabia 76 B4
Tabwémasana Vanuatu 96 D2
Täby Sweden 47 D2

Tacheng China 82 B5
Tacloban Phil. 91 D4
Tacna Peru 26 C2
Tacoma U.S.A. 8 A4
Tacuarembó Uruguay 28 E6
Tadin New Caledonia 97 D1
Tadmur Syria 76 B5
Taegu South Korea 87 A4
Taejŏn South Korea 87 A4
Tafahi i. Tonga 96 F2
Taganrog, Gulf of Rus. Fed./Ukraine 67 E2
Tagbilaran Phil. 91 D3
Tagus r. Portugal 56 A3
Tahat, Mont mt. Algeria 35 C1
Tahoe, Lake U.S.A. 9 A2
Taibei Taiwan see T'aipei
Taidong Taiwan 85 F2
Taieri r. New Zealand 101 C2
Taihape New Zealand 100 E5
Tainan Taiwan 85 F2
Tainaro, Akra pt Greece 65 C2
T'aipei Taiwan 85 F3
Taiping Malaysia 90 B3
Taitao, Península de Chile 29 B3
Taivalkoski Finland 46 G4
Taivaskero hill Finland 46 F5
Taiwan Asia 85 F2
Taiwan Strait China/Taiwan 85 E2
Taiynsha Kazakh. 79 C4
Taiyuan China 84 D5
Taizhong Taiwan 85 F2
Taizhou China 85 F4
Ta'izz Yemen 77 C1
Tajikistan Asia 79 D2
Tajumulco, Volcán de volcano Guat. 20 A3
Tak Thailand 88 A2
Takaka New Zealand 100 D4
Takamatsu Japan 87 B3
Takaoka Japan 87 C4
Takapuna New Zealand 100 E6
Takêv Cambodia 89 B2
Takitimu Mountains New Zealand 101 A2
Taklimakan Desert China 82 B3
Takua Pa Thailand 89 A1
Talachyn Belarus 69 C2
Talaud, Kepulauan is Indon. 91 D3
Talavera de la Reina Spain 56 C3
Talca Chile 28 B5
Talcahuano Chile 29 B5
Taldykorgan Kazakh. 79 D3
Taliabu i. Indon. 91 D2
Tallahassee U.S.A. 17 C3
Tallinn Estonia 68 B3
Tallulah U.S.A. 11 D2
Taloyoak Canada 5 I3
Taltal Chile 28 B7
Taltson r. Canada 5 H3
Tamale Ghana 38 C1
Tamanrasset Algeria 35 C1
Tamar r. U.K. 49 D2
Tamazunchale Mexico 19 E3
Tambacounda Senegal 38 B2
Tambelan, Kepulauan is Indon. 90 B3
Tambora, Gunung volcano Indon. 90 C2
Tambov Rus. Fed. 72 C2
Tambre r. Spain 56 A5
Tâmega r. Portugal 56 A4
Tamiahua, Laguna de lagoon Mexico 19 E3
Tamil Nadu admin. div. India 81 D2
Tamiš r. Serbia 62 E4
Tampa U.S.A. 17 C2
Tampere Finland 47 E3
Tampico Mexico 19 E3
Tamsweg Austria 55 D2
Tamworth Australia 99 E2
Tana r. Kenya 37 C2
Tana, Lake Ethiopia 36 B4
Tanafjorden inlet Norway 46 G5
Tanami Desert Australia 98 C4
Tanana U.S.A. 4 C3
Tanaro r. Italy 58 B6
Ţăndărei Romania 66 B2
Tandil Argentina 29 E5
Tando Adam Pakistan 80 B5
Tanega-shima i. Japan 87 B3
Tanga Tanzania 37 C2
Tanganyika, Lake Africa 37 B2
Tangier Morocco 34 B2
Tangshan China 84 E5
Tanimbar, Kepulauan is Indon. 91 E2
Tanjang d'Urville pt Indon. 91 E2

Tanjay Phil. 91 D3
Tanjungpandan Indon. 90 B2
Tanjungredeb Indon. 90 C3
Tanjungselor Indon. 90 C3
Tanna i. Vanuatu 97 D2
Tanout Niger 39 D3
Tanta Egypt 36 B6
Tantoyuca Mexico 19 E3
Tanzania Africa 37 B2
Taonan China 83 J5
Tapachula Mexico 19 F1
Tapajós r. Brazil 27 F5
Tapauá Brazil 26 E4
Tapauá r. Brazil 26 D4
Tapi r. India 80 C4
Tapuaenuku mt. New Zealand 101 D4
Tapurucuara Brazil 26 D5
Taquarí r. Brazil 27 F2
Tara r. Bos. Herz./Montenegro 63 D3
Tarakan Indon. 90 C3
Tarancón Spain 57 D4
Taranto Italy 59 F4
Taranto, Gulf of Italy 59 F4
Tarapoto Peru 26 B4
Tararua Range mts New Zealand 100 E4
Tarauacá Brazil 26 C4
Taraz Kazakh. 79 D3
Tarbagatay, Khrebet mts Kazakh. 79 E3
Tarbes France 53 D2
Taree Australia 99 E2
Târgovişte Romania 66 B2
Târgu Jiu Romania 66 A2
Târgu Mureş Romania 66 B2
Târgu Secuiesc Romania 66 B2
Tariku r. Indon. 91 E2
Tarīm Yemen 77 D2
Tarim Basin China 82 B3
Tarīn Kōt Afgh. 78 C2
Tarlac Phil. 91 D4
Tarn r. France 53 D3
Tarnak Röd r. Afgh. 79 C2
Tarnica mt. Poland 61 F2
Tarnobrzeg Poland 60 E3
Tarnów Poland 61 E3
Tarragona Spain 57 F4
Tarsus Turkey 74 C2
Tartu Estonia 68 B3
Tashir Armenia 75 F3
Tashk, Daryācheh-ye lake Iran 76 E5
Tashkent Uzbek. 79 C3
Taskala Kazakh. 78 B4
Taskesken Kazakh. 79 E3
Tasman Bay New Zealand 100 D4
Tasmania admin. div. Australia 99 D1
Tasman Mountains New Zealand 101 D4
Tasman Sea Pacific Ocean 99 E2
Tatabánya Hungary 61 D1
Tatamailau, Foho mt. East Timor 91 D2
Tatarbunary Ukraine 66 C2
Tatarsk Rus. Fed. 72 F2
Tatarskiy Proliv strait Rus. Fed. 73 M2
Tatra Mountains Poland/ Slovakia 61 D2
Tatvan Turkey 75 E2
Taungdwyi Myanmar 88 A3
Taung-ngu Myanmar 88 A2
Taunton U.K. 49 E2
Taunus hills Germany 54 B4
Taupo New Zealand 100 F5
Taupo, Lake New Zealand 100 E5
Taurag Lithuania 69 A2
Tauranga New Zealand 100 F6
Tauroa Point New Zealand 100 D7
Taurus Mountains Turkey 74 C2
Tavira Portugal 56 B2
Tavoy Myanmar 89 A2
Tavşanlı Turkey 74 B2
Taw r. U.K. 49 D2
Tawau Malaysia 90 C3
Tawi-Tawi i. Phil. 91 C3
Taxiatosh Uzbek. 78 B3
Tay r. U.K. 48 E5
Tay, Firth of estuary U.K. 48 E5
Tay, Loch lake U.K. 48 D5
Taylor U.S.A. 11 C2
Tayma' Saudi Arabia 76 B4
Taymura r. Rus. Fed. 73 H3
Taymyr, Ozero lake Rus. Fed. 73 I4
Taymyr Peninsula Rus. Fed. 73 H4

Tây Ninh Vietnam 89 B2
Taytay Phil. 91 C4
Taz r. Rus. Fed. 72 F3
T'bilisi Georgia 75 F3
Tczew Poland 60 D5
Te Anau New Zealand 101 A2
Te Anau, Lake New Zealand 101 A2
Te Araroa New Zealand 100 G6
Te Awamutu New Zealand 100 E5
Tebicuary r. Para. 28 E7
Tebingtinggi Indon. 90 A3
Tebulos Mt'a Georgia/Rus. Fed. 75 F3
Tecka Argentina 29 B4
Tecomán Mexico 18 D2
Tecuci Romania 66 B2
Tees r. U.K. 49 F4
Tefé r. Brazil 26 D5
Tegucigalpa Honduras 20 B2
Tehrān Iran 76 E6
Tehuantepec, Gulf of Mexico 19 F2
Tehuantepec, Istmo de isthmus Mexico 19 F2
Teifi r. U.K. 49 D3
Tejen Turkm. 78 C2
Tejen r. Turkm. 78 C2
Tekapo, Lake New Zealand 101 C3
Tekirdağ Turkey 74 A3
Te Kuiti New Zealand 100 E5
Tel Aviv-Yafo Israel 76 A5
Teles Pires r. Brazil 27 F4
Telford U.K. 49 E3
Tembenchi r. Rus. Fed. 73 H3
Teme r. U.K. 49 E3
Temerluh Malaysia 90 B3
Temirtau Kazakh. 79 D4
Temple U.S.A. 11 C2
Temuco Chile 29 B5
Temuka New Zealand 101 C2
Tenasserim Myanmar 89 A2
Ten Degree Channel India 81 G1
Tennant Creek town Australia 99 C4
Tennessee admin. div. U.S.A. 16 B4
Tennessee r. U.S.A. 16 B4
Tenosique Mexico 19 F2
Tentudia mt. Spain 56 B3
Teófilo Otoni Brazil 27 I2
Te Paki New Zealand 100 D7
Tepatitlán Mexico 18 D3
Tepehuanes Mexico 18 C4
Tepic Mexico 18 D3
Teplice Czech Rep. 60 A3
Te Puke New Zealand 100 F6
Teramo Italy 58 D5
Tercan Turkey 75 E2
Teresina Brazil 27 I4
Terminillo, Monte mt. Italy 58 D5
Términos, Laguna de lagoon Mexico 19 F2
Termiz Uzbek. 79 C2
Termoli Italy 59 E4
Ternate Indon. 91 D3
Terneuzen Netherlands 51 B3
Terni Italy 58 D5
Ternopil' Ukraine 66 B3
Terrace Canada 4 F2
Terrassa Spain 57 G4
Terre Haute U.S.A. 13 D1
Terschelling i. Netherlands 50 D5
Teslin Canada 4 E3
Test r. U.K. 49 F2
Tetas, Punta pt Chile 28 B8
Tete Mozambique 43 C3
Tétouan Morocco 34 B2
Tetovo Macedonia 63 E3
Teuco r. Argentina 28 D8
Teviot r. U.K. 48 E4
Te Waewae Bay New Zealand 101 A1
Tewantin Australia 99 E3
Te Wharau New Zealand 101 E4
Texarkana U.S.A. 11 D2
Texas admin. div. U.S.A. 10 C2
Texas City U.S.A. 11 D1
Texel i. Netherlands 50 C5
Texoma, Lake U.S.A. 11 C2
Tezpur India 81 G5
Thabana-Ntlenyana mt. Lesotho 42 B2
Thai Binh Vietnam 88 B3
Thailand, Gulf of Asia 89 B2
Thai Nguyên Vietnam 88 B3
Thakhèk Laos 88 B2
Thames New Zealand 100 E6
Thames r. U.K. 49 G2
Thandwè Myanmar 88 A2

Usborne, Mount Falkland Is 29 E2
Usharal Kazakh. 79 E3
Ushtobe Kazakh. 79 D3
Ushuaia Argentina 29 C2
Usol'ye-Sibirskoye Rus. Fed. 73 I2
Ussuriysk Rus. Fed. 73 L1
Ustica, Isola di i. Italy 59 D3
Ust'-Ilimsk Rus. Fed. 73 I2
Ústí nad Labem Czech Rep. 60 B3
Ust'-Kamchatsk Rus. Fed. 73 O2
Ust'-Kamenogorsk Kazakh. 79 E3
Ust'-Kut Rus. Fed. 73 I2
Ust'-Maya Rus. Fed. 73 L3
Ust'-Olenek Rus. Fed. 73 J4
Ustyurt Plateau Kazakh./Uzbek. 78 B3
Utah admin div. U.S.A. 9 C2
Utena Lithuania 69 B2
Utica U.S.A. 14 B2
Utiel Spain 57 E3
Utrecht Netherlands 50 D4
Utrecht admin div. Netherlands 50 D4
Utrera Spain 56 C2
Utsunomiya Japan 87 C4
Uttaradit Thailand 88 B2
Uttarakhand admin div. India 81 D6
Uttar Pradesh admin div. India 81 D5
Uusikaupunki Finland 47 E3
Uvalde U.S.A. 10 C1
Uvs Nuur f. Mongolia 82 D6
Uwajima Japan 87 B3
Uyuni Bolivia 26 D1
Uyuni, Salar de salt flat Bolivia 26 D1
Uzbekistan Asia 78 C3
Uzhhorod Ukraine 66 A3
Užice Serbia 62 D3
Uzunköprü Turkey 74 A3

V

Vaal r. South Africa 42 B2
Vaasa Finland 46 E3
Vác Hungary 61 D1
Vacaria Brazil 28 F7
Vadodara India 80 C4
Vadsø Norway 46 G5
Vaduz Liechtenstein 55 B2
Værøy i. Norway 46 C4
Vaganski Vrh mt. Croatia 62 B4
Váh r. Slovakia 61 C2
Vaiaku Tuvalu 96 E3
Vaitupu i. Tuvalu 97 E3
Vakhsh Tajik. 79 C2
Valdepeñas Spain 56 D3
Valdés, Península Argentina 29 D4
Valdez U.S.A. 4 D3
Valdivia Chile 29 B5
Val-d'Or Canada 6 C1
Valdosta U.S.A. 17 C3
Valdres f. Norway 47 B3
Valença Brazil 27 J3
Valence France 53 F3
Valencia Spain 57 E3
Valencia Venez. 26 D8
Valencia, Golfo de gulf Spain 57 F3
Valencia de Alcántara Spain 56 B3
Valenciennes France 52 E6
Valera Venez. 26 C7
Valier, Mont mt. France 53 D2
Valinco, Gulf of France 52 H1
Valjevo Serbia 62 D4
Valka Latvia 68 B3
Valkeakoski Finland 47 F3
Valkenswaard Netherlands 51 D3
Valkyrie Dome mt. Antarctica 104 R2
Valladolid Mexico 19 G3
Valladolid Spain 56 C4
Valle de la Pascua Venez. 26 D7
Valledupar Colombia 26 C8
Vallejo U.S.A. 9 A4
Valletta Malta 59 E1
Valley City U.S.A. 12 B3
Valmiera Latvia 68 B3
Valozhyn Belarus 69 B2
Valparaíso Chile 28 B6
Vals, Tanjung cape Indon. 91 E2
Vammala Finland 47 E3
Van Turkey 75 E2
Van, Lake Turkey 75 E2
Vanadzor Armenia 75 F3
Vancouver Canada 4 F1
Vancouver U.S.A. 8 A4
Vancouver Island Canada 4 F1
Vandalia U.S.A. 13 D1
Vänern lake Sweden 47 C2

Vänersborg Sweden 47 C2
Vangaindrano Madagascar 43 D2
Van Horn U.S.A. 10 B2
Vanimo P.N.G. 96 B3
Vännäs Sweden 46 D3
Vannes France 52 B4
Vantaa Finland 47 F3
Vanua Levu i. Fiji 97 E2
Vanuatu Pacific Ocean 97 D2
Varanasi India 81 E5
Varangerfjorden strait Norway 46 G5
Varaždin Croatia 62 C5
Varberg Sweden 47 C2
Vardar r. Macedonia 63 F2
Varkaus Finland 46 F3
Varna Lithuania 69 B2
Varese Italy 58 B6
Varna Bulgaria 64 E5
Värnamo Sweden 47 C2
Várpalota Hungary 61 D1
Vaslui Romania 66 B2
Västerås Sweden 47 D2
Västerdalälven r. Sweden 47 C3
Västervik Sweden 47 D2
Vasyl'kiv Ukraine 67 C3
Vatican City Europe 59 D4
Vatra Dornei Romania 66 B2
Vättern lake Sweden 47 C2
Vaughn U.S.A. 9 D1
Vava'u Group is Tonga 96 F2
Vawkavysk Belarus 69 B2
Växjö Sweden 47 C2
Veendam Netherlands 50 E5
Veenendaal Netherlands 50 D4
Vega i. Norway 46 B4
Vejle Denmark 47 B1
Veles Macedonia 63 E2
Vélez-Málaga Spain 56 C2
Velhas r. Brazil 27 I2
Velika Morava canal Serbia 62 E4
Velikaya r. Rus. Fed. 73 P3
Velikiye Luki Rus. Fed. 72 B2
Velikiy Novgorod Rus. Fed. 72 B2
Veliko Tŭrnovo Bulgaria 64 D5
Velino, Monte mt. Italy 59 D5
Vel'sk Rus. Fed. 72 C3
Vellore India 81 D2
Vel'sk Rus. Fed. 72 C3
Venado Tuerto Argentina 28 D6
Vendôme France 52 D4
Venezuela S. America 26 D7
Venezuela, Golfo de gulf Venez. 26 C8
Venice Italy 58 D6
Venice, Gulf of Europe 58 D6
Venray Netherlands 51 D3
Ventspils Latvia 68 A3
Vera Argentina 28 D7
Vera Spain 57 E2
Veracruz Mexico 19 E2
Vercelli Italy 58 B6
Verde r. Para. 28 E8
Verde r. U.S.A. 9 C1
Verdun France 52 F5
Verín Spain 56 B4
Verkhnevilyuysk Rus. Fed. 73 K3
Verkhoyansk Rus. Fed. 73 L3
Verkhoyanskiy Khrebet mts Rus. Fed. 73 K4
Vermont admin div. U.S.A. 15 C2
Vernon U.S.A. 10 C2
Veroia Greece 64 C4
Verona Italy 58 C6
Versailles France 52 E5
Vert, Cap cape Senegal 38 B2
Verviers Belgium 51 D2
Vesele Ukraine 67 D2
Vesoul France 52 G4
Vesterålen is Norway 46 C5
Vestfjorden strait Norway 46 C4
Vesuvius volcano Italy 59 E4
Veszprém Hungary 61 C1
Vettore, Monte mt. Italy 58 D5
Veurne Belgium 51 A3
Vézère r. France 53 D3
Vezirköprü Turkey 74 C3
Viana do Castelo Portugal 56 A4
Vianópolis Brazil 28 G9
Viborg Denmark 47 B2
Vibo Valentia Italy 59 F3
Vic Spain 57 G4
Vicenza Italy 58 C6
Vichada r. Colombia 26 C6
Vichy France 53 E4
Victoria Argentina 28 D6
Victoria admin div. Australia 99 D2
Victoria r. Australia 98 C4
Victoria Canada 4 F1

Victoria Chile 29 B5
Victoria U.S.A. 11 C1
Victoria, Lake Africa 37 B2
Victoria, Mount P.N.G. 96 B3
Victoria Falls Zambia/Zimbabwe 42 B3
Victoria Island Canada 5 G4
Victoria Land f. Antarctica 104 K2
Victoria Range mts New Zealand 101 D3
Victorica Argentina 28 C5
Viedma Argentina 29 D4
Viedma, Lago lake Argentina 29 B3
Vienna Austria 55 F3
Vienne France 53 F3
Vienne r. France 52 D4
Vientiane Laos 88 B2
Vieques i. Puerto Rico 23 E2
Vierzon France 52 E4
Vieste Italy 59 F4
Vietnam Asia 88 B2
Vigan Phil. 91 D4
Vignemale mt. France 53 C2
Vigo Spain 56 A5
Vijayawada India 81 E3
Vikna i. Norway 46 B4
Vilagarcía de Arousa Spain 56 A5
Vilaine r. France 52 B4
Vila Real Portugal 56 B4
Vilhelmina Sweden 46 D4
Viljandi Estonia 68 B3
Vil'kitskogo, Proliv strait Rus. Fed. 73 H4
Villa Bella Bolivia 26 D3
Villach Austria 55 D2
Villahermosa Mexico 19 F2
Villa Insurgentes Mexico 18 B4
Villa María Argentina 28 D6
Villa Montes Bolivia 26 E1
Villa Ocampo Argentina 28 E7
Villaputzu Italy 59 B3
Villarrobledo Spain 57 D3
Villa Unión Argentina 28 C7
Villavicencio Colombia 26 C6
Villazon Bolivia 26 D1
Villefranche-sur-Saône France 53 F3
Villena Spain 57 E3
Villeneuve-sur-Lot France 53 D3
Villeurbanne France 53 F3
Vilnius Lithuania 69 B2
Vil'nyans'k Ukraine 67 D2
Vilvoorde Belgium 51 C2
Vilyuy r. Rus. Fed. 73 K3
Viña del Mar Chile 28 B6
Vindelälven r. Sweden 46 D3
Vineland U.S.A. 14 B1
Vinh Vietnam 88 B2
Vinita U.S.A. 11 C3
Vinkovci Croatia 62 D4
Vinnytsya Ukraine 66 C3
Vinson Massif mt. Antarctica 104 F2
Viranşehir Turkey 75 D2
Vire France 52 C5
Virginia admin div. U.S.A. 16 D4
Virginia Beach town U.S.A. 16 D4
Virgin Islands (U.K.) territory Caribbean Sea 23 F2
Virgin Islands (U.S.A.) territory Caribbean Sea 23 F2
Virovitica Croatia 62 C4
Virton Belgium 51 D1
Vis i. Croatia 63 C3
Visaginas Lithuania 69 B2
Visby Sweden 47 D2
Viscount Melville Sound strait Canada 5 G4
Viseu Brazil 27 H5
Viseu Portugal 56 B4
Vishakhapatnam India 81 E3
Viso, Monte mt. Italy 58 A6
Vistula r. Poland 60 D4
Viterbo Italy 58 D5
Viti Levu i. Fiji 97 E2
Vitim r. Rus. Fed. 73 J2
Vitória Brazil 27 I1
Vitória da Conquista Brazil 27 I3
Vitoria-Gasteiz Spain 57 D5
Vitsyebsk Belarus 69 C2
Vittel France 52 F5
Vizcaíno, Sierra mts Mexico 18 B4
Vizianagaram India 81 E3
Vlaams-Brabant admin div. Belgium 51 C2
Vlaardingen Netherlands 50 C3
Vladimir Rus. Fed. 72 C2
Vladivostok Rus. Fed. 73 L1

Vlieland i. Netherlands 50 C5
Vlissingen Netherlands 51 B3
Vlorë Albania 63 D2
Vltava r. Czech Rep. 61 B2
Vohimena, Tanjona cape Madagascar 43 D2
Volda Norway 46 A3
Volga r. Rus. Fed. 72 C1
Volgograd Rus. Fed. 72 C1
Volnovakha Ukraine 67 E2
Volochys'k Ukraine 66 B3
Volodymyr-Volyns'kyy Ukraine 66 B3
Vologda Rus. Fed. 72 B2
Volos Greece 65 C3
Volta, Lake reservoir Ghana 39 D1
Voreioi Sporades is Greece 65 C3
Vorkuta Rus. Fed. 72 E3
Vormsi i. Estonia 68 A3
Voronezh Rus. Fed. 72 B2
Vorskla r. Ukraine 67 D3
Võrtsjärv l. Estonia 68 B3
Võru Estonia 68 B3
Vosges mts France 52 G4
Voss Norway 47 A3
Vostochnyy Sayan mts Rus. Fed. 73 H2
Voznesens'k Ukraine 67 C2
Vranje Serbia 63 E3
Vratsa Bulgaria 64 C5
Vrbas r. Bos. Herz. 62 C4
Vršac Serbia 62 E4
Vuollerim Sweden 46 E4
Vyatka Rus. Fed. 72 C2
Vyerkhnyadzvinsk Belarus 68 B2
Vylkove Ukraine 66 C2
Vyshhorod Ukraine 67 C3

W

Wa Ghana 38 C2
Wabasca r. Canada 4 G2
Wabash r. U.S.A. 13 D1
Wabush Canada 7 D2
Waco U.S.A. 11 C2
Wad Pakistan 80 B5
Waddān Libya 35 D1
Waddenzee strait Netherlands 50 C4
Waddington, Mount Canada 4 F2
Wadi Halfa Sudan 36 B5
Wad Medani Sudan 36 B4
Wagga Wagga Australia 99 D2
Wahpeton U.S.A. 12 B3
Waiau r. New Zealand 101 D3
Waigeo i. Indon. 91 E2
Waiheke Island New Zealand 100 E6
Waihi New Zealand 100 E6
Waihou r. New Zealand 100 E6
Waikabubak Indon. 91 C2
Waikaia r. New Zealand 101 B2
Waikato r. New Zealand 100 E6
Waikawa Point New Zealand 100 F6
Waimakariri r. New Zealand 101 D3
Waimate New Zealand 101 C2
Waingapu Indon. 91 D2
Wainwright U.S.A. 4 C4
Waiouru New Zealand 100 E5
Waipaoa r. New Zealand 100 F5
Waipawa New Zealand 100 F5
Waipukurau New Zealand 100 F5
Wairarapa, Lake New Zealand 101 E4
Wairau r. New Zealand 101 D4
Wairoa New Zealand 100 E6
Wairoa r. Hawke's Bay New Zealand 100 F5
Wairoa r. Northland New Zealand 100 E7
Waitaki r. New Zealand 101 C2
Waitara New Zealand 100 E5
Waiuku New Zealand 100 E6
Wajir Kenya 37 C3
Wakasa-wan bay Japan 87 C4
Wakatipu, Lake New Zealand 101 B2
Wakayama Japan 87 C3
Wakefield New Zealand 101 D4
Wakkanai Japan 86 D6
Wałbrzych Poland 60 C3
Wałcz Poland 60 C4
Wales admin div. U.K. 49 E3
Walgett Australia 99 D2
Walla Walla U.S.A. 8 B4
Wallis and Futuna Islands territory Pacific Ocean 96 F2
Walsall U.K. 49 F3
Walsenburg U.S.A. 9 E2

Walvis Bay town Namibia 42 A2
Wanaka New Zealand 101 B2
Wanaka, Lake New Zealand 101 B2
Wanganui New Zealand 100 E5
Wanganui r. New Zealand 100 E5
Wanzhou China 85 C4
Warangal India 81 D3
Warburton r. Australia 99 C3
Ward, Mount Southland New Zealand 101 A2
Ward, Mount West Coast New Zealand 101 B3
Waremme Belgium 51 D2
Warkworth New Zealand 100 E6
Warrego r. Australia 99 D3
Warren Australia 99 D2
Warren U.S.A. 14 B2
Warri Nigeria 39 D1
Warrington U.K. 49 E3
Warrnambool Australia 99 D2
Warsaw Poland 60 E4
Warta r. Poland 60 B4
Warwick Australia 99 E3
Washington D.C. U.S.A. 14 A2
Washington admin div. U.S.A. 8 A4
Washington, Mount U.S.A. 15 C2
Waskaganish Canada 6 C2
Watampone Indon. 91 D2
Waterbury U.S.A. 15 C2
Waterford Ireland 49 C3
Watertown New York U.S.A. 14 B2
Watertown South Dakota U.S.A. 12 B2
Waterville U.S.A. 15 D2
Watford U.K. 49 F2
Watson Lake town Canada 4 F3
Wau P.N.G. 96 B3
Wau South Sudan 37 A3
Wausau U.S.A. 13 D2
Wear r. U.K. 49 F4
Weatherford U.S.A. 11 C2
Webi Shabeelle r. Somalia 37 C3
Weddell Sea Antarctica 104 D3
Weert Netherlands 51 D3
Weifang China 84 E5
Weihai China 84 F5
Weinan China 84 C4
Weipa Australia 99 D4
Weldiya Ethiopia 36 B4
Welkom South Africa 42 B2
Welland r. U.K. 49 F3
Wellesley Islands Australia 99 C4
Wellington New Zealand 100 E4
Wellington, Isla i. Chile 29 A3
Wellsford New Zealand 100 E6
Wels Austria 55 E3
Welshpool U.K. 49 E3
Wenchi Ghana 38 C1
Wendo Ethiopia 37 B3
Wensleydale f. U.K. 49 E4
Wenzhou China 85 F3
Weser r. Germany 54 B5
Wessel, Cape Australia 99 C4
Wessel Islands Australia 99 C4
West Bank territory Asia 76 A5
West Bengal admin div. India 81 F4
Western Australia admin div. Australia 98 B3
Western Ghats mts India 80 C2
Western Sahara territory Africa 34 A1
Westerschelde estuary Netherlands 51 B3
West Falkland i. Falkland Is 29 D2
West Frisian Islands Netherlands 50 C5
Weston-super-Mare U.K. 49 E2
West Palm Beach town U.S.A. 17 C2
Westport Ireland 49 B3
Westport New Zealand 101 C4
Westray i. U.K. 48 E6
West Siberian Plain Rus. Fed. 72 F3
West-Terschelling Netherlands 50 D5
West Virginia admin div. U.S.A. 16 C4
West-Vlaanderen admin div. Belgium 51 A2
Wetar i. Indon. 91 D2
Wewak P.N.G. 96 B3
Wexford Ireland 49 C3
Weymouth U.K. 49 E2
Whakaari i. New Zealand 100 F6
Whakatane New Zealand 100 F6
Whangamomona New Zealand 100 E5
Whalsay i. U.K. 48 F7
Whangarei New Zealand 100 E7
Wharfe r. U.K. 49 F3
Wheatland U.S.A. 8 E3
Wheeler Peak Nevada U.S.A. 9 C2

Acknowledgements

Photo Credits

Cover: Globe, AridOcean/Shutterstock; Giza pyramids, sculpies/Shutterstock; Maori carving, Ruth Black/Shutterstock; Amazon parrot, Marina Jay/Shutterstock; Taj Mahal, Scott Norsworthy/Shutterstock; Aeroplane, Oleksiy Mark/Shutterstock; Barn owl, Eric Isselee/Shutterstock; Jet stream, lvcandy/Shutterstock; Rome Colosseum, pisaphotography/Shutterstock; Hot air ballons, Vividz Foto/Shutterstock; Pileated Gibbon, Eric Isselee/Shutterstock

i: Jet stream, lvcandy/Shutterstock; Amazon parrot, Marina Jay/Shutterstock; Maori carving, Ruth Black/Shutterstock; Aeroplane, Oleksiy Mark/Shutterstock

iii: Hot air ballons, Vividz Foto/Shutterstock; Amazon parrot, Marina Jay/Shutterstock

v: Stromboli, Vulkanette/Shutterstock

viii: Nile, Frank11/Shutterstock

1: Mount Everest, Aleksandr Sadkov/Shutterstock

3: Grand Canyon, Diana Beato/Shutterstock

4: Totem pole, trappy76/Shutterstock; Inuit carving, Pitseolak Qimirpik/www.inuitsculpures.com; Pipline, Sam Chadwick/Shutterstock

5: Grizzly bear, Scott E Read/Shutterstock; Polar bear, Teresa/CC by SA 2.0; Mount McKinley, Gail Johnson/Shutterstock

6: Maple syrup, Zaneta Baranowska/Shutterstock; Snowmobile, glen gaffney/Shuttertock; Lake Superior, Elena Elisseeva/Shutterstock

7: Québec, Songquan Deng/Shutterstock.com; Bay of Fundy, Daniel Zuckerkandel/Shutterstock; Lobster, Eric Isselee/Shutterstock; Labrador dog, Lenkadan/Shutterstock; Niagara Falls, Sbittante/CC by SA 3.0

8: Iced lolly, Elena Schweitzer/Shutterstock; Bald eagle, Eric Isselee/Shutterstock

9: Old Faithful, Lee Prince/Shutterstock; Bison, Nagel Photography/Shutterstock

10: Steer, Mike Flippo/Shutterstock; Lizard, Matt Jeppson/Shutterstock; Jazz player, Jose Gil/Shutterstock.com; oil wells, Jim Parkin/Shutterstock; NASA, NASA

11: Flooding, AdStock R/Shutterstock.com; Delta, NASA; Balloon, Alekcey/Shutterstock; Helium, concept w/Shutterstock; Parking meter, cabania/Shutterstock

12: Football, Jun Ji/Shutterstock.com; Stone marker, Sue Smith/Shutterstock; Iced tea, Nitr/Shutterstock

13: Trampoline, Piotr Wawrzyniuk/Shutterstock; Tornado, Minerva Studio/Shutterstock

14: Basketball, Aspen Photo/Shutterstock.com; Liberty Bell, David W. Leindecker/Shutterstock; Autumn, cappi thompson/Shutterstock; Liberty Island, rorem/Shutterstock

15: Fortune cookie, Lucie Lang/Shutterstock; Pumpkin, Alexey Losevich/Shutterstock; Chicken, marilyn barbone/Shutterstock; Stock Exchange, Carol M. Highsmith/LOC

16: Alligator, Raffaella Calzoni/Shutterstock; Pentagon, Frontpage/Shutterstock; Cotton, Alaettin YILDIRIM/Shutterstock; Wright Flyer, David Ross/Shutterstock

17: Steamboat, Bailey Visual Life/CC by SA 2.0; Beale Street, Natalia Bratslavsky/Shutterstock; Disney castle, ShajiA

18: Boundary, Sgt 1st Class Gordon Hyde; Tomatoes, Scott Hales/Shutterstock; Tortilla, ampFotoStudio/Shutterstock

19: Silver, Pablo H Caridad/Shutterstock; Mayan temple, rui vale sousa/Shutterstock.com; Mariachi, Matt Apps/Shutterstock.com; Agave, csp/Shutterstock; Pinñta, modd/Shutterstock

20: Quetzal, worldswildlifewonders/Shutterstock; Girl, Petur Asgeirsson/Shutterstock.com; Cardamom, Didier Descouens/CC by SA 3.0

21: Worry dolls, Clara/Shutterstock; Great Blue Hole, USGS; Great Blue Hole Reef, NASA; Jaguar, Krzysztof Wiktor/Shutterstock; Banana, Asia Glab/Shutterstock; Sloth, Ivan Kuzmin/Shutterstock; Panama Canal, Chris Jenner/Shutterstock.com

22: Cigar-roller, dotshock/Shutterstock; Maracas, Alleksander/Shutterstock; Skateboarder, biletskiy/Shutterstock; Cricket, MAT/Shutterstock.com; Junkanoo, jo Crebbin/Shutterstock.com

23: Tarantula, Ryan M. Bolton/Shutterstock; Earthquake, arindambanerjee/Shutterstock.com; Film locations, Mana Photo/Shutterstock.com

25: Machu Pichu, tr3gin/Shutterstock

26: Bird, Steven Blandin/Shutterstock; Machu Picchu, Kelsey Green/Shutterstock

27: Amazon, NASA; Emeralds, Mmlynczak/CC by SA 3.0; Soybean, Le Do/Shutterstock; Frog, Dirk Ercken/Shutterstock

28: Atacama Desert, BMJ/Shutterstock

29: Guacho, Eduardo Rivero/Shutterstock.com; Waterfall, Rafael Martin-Gaitero/Shutterstock

30: Whale, NOAA; RMS Queen Mary 2, Luboslav Tiles/Shutteerstock

31: RMS Titanic, Willy Stöwer

33: Giza pyramids, sculpies/Shutterstock

34: Tagine, picturepartners/Shutterstock; Atlas Mountains, Vladimir Melnik/Shutterstock; Ksar, StephanScherhag/Shutterstock.com; Football, cdrin/Shutterstock.com; Tourism, Gray wall studio/Shuterstock

35: Oil Well, Cipiota/CC by 3.0; Locust, Steve Smith Photography/Shutterstock; Shoes, John Copland/Shutterstock; Leptis Magna, John Copland/Shutterstock

36: Nubian pyramids, urosr/Shutterstock; Nile, WitR/Shutterstock; Cairo, Brian Kinney/Shutterstock; Lake Assal, Endless Traveller/Shutterstock

37: Mosquito, Henrik Larsson/Shutterstock; Chichlid fish, Andreas Gradin/Shutterstock; Zebra, Eric Isselee/Shutterstock; Flamingo, Anna Omelchenko/Shutterstock; Wildebeest, Mogens Trolle/Shutterstock

38: Nouakchott, William Darcy Hall/CC by SA 3.0; Fort Elmina, trevor kittelty/Shutterstock; Cocoa beans, Danny Smythe/Shutterstock

39: Great Mosque, Attila JANDI/Shutterstock; Children, Hector Consea/Shutterstock.com; Drummers, Criben/shutterstock.com; Drum, ermess/Shutterstock; Market, James Michael Dorsey/Shutterstock; Akosombo Dam, ZSM/CC by SA 3.0

40: Cassava, Tristan tan/Shutterstock; Lake Chad, With kind permission of UNEP; Viper, Eric Isselee/Shutterstock; Malachite, Rob Lavinsky, iRocks.com/CC by SA 3.0; Refugees, Sam DCruz/Shutterstock.com

41: Chimpanzee, Sergey Uryadnikov/Shutterstock; Boats, Julien Harneis/CC by SA 2.0; Beetle, alslutsky/Shutterstock

42: Victoria Falls, InnaFelker/Shutterstock; Children, Nathan Holand/Shutterstock.com; Football fans, Luke Scmidt/Shutterstock.com; Protea, Jason Beck/CC by SA 2.5; Sand dunes, orxy/Shutterstock

43: Hippopotamus, Doroty/Shutterstock; Vanila pods, Goncharuk/Shutterstock; Boy, Pai Teravagimov/Shutterstock.com; Cape Town, michaeljung/Shutterstock

45: Acropolis, Athens, Greece, stefanel/Shutterstock

46: Liquorice, Bishonen; Ice Cream, Christopher Elwell/Shutterstock

47: Lego, Volodymyr Krasyuk/Shutterstock; Sauna, posztos/Shutterstock; Aurora Borelis, Jamen Percy/Shutterstock

48: St David's, Lian Deng/Shutterstock; Sandwich, Sergey Peterman/Shutterstock; Cheese, Paul Cowan/Shutterstock

49: Caernarfon, Oliver Hoffmann/Shutterstock; Underground, Tupungato/Shutterstock.com

50: Flags, jorisvo/Shutterstock

51: Chocolates, courtyardpix/Shutterstock; Port, Jelle vd Wolf/Shutterstock; Family, Pressmaster/Shutterstock

52: Denim, Julia Zakharova/Shutterstock; Monaco, Michael Stokes/Shutterstock.com; Cycling, Josh Hallett/CC by SA 2.0; Louvre, William Perugini/Shutterstock.com

53: Eiffel Tower, majeczka/Shutterstock; Andorra, Gurgen Bakhshetsyan/Shutterstock; Mont Blanc, ovidiu iordache/Shutterstock

54: Liechtenstein, avner/Shutterstock; Horses, Dr Ajay Kumar Singh/Shutterstock; Berlin Wall, andersphoto/Shutterstock.com

55: Castle, Boris Stroujko/Shutterstock; Dancers, Kateryna Larina/Shutterstock

56: Fishing, Miguel Azevedo e Castro/Shutterstock; Olives, Madlen/Shutterstock

57: Flamenco, Jack.Q/Shutterstock.com; Football, Natursports/Shutterstock.com; Alhambra, S.Borisov/Shutterstock

58: Glass, elen_studio/Shutterstock; Fondue, bonchan/Shutterstock; Railway, Dan Breckwoldt/Shutterstock; Vineyard, Samot/Shutterstock

59: Car, EvrenKalinbacak/Shutterstock.com; Colosseum, Viacheslav Lopatin/Shutterstock; Pasta, Andrii Gorulko/Shutterstock

60: Children, Angyalosi Beata/Shutterstock.com; Bread, Paul Cowan/Shutterstock; Auschwitz, Sami Kallioniemi/Shutterstock; Mountain, PHB.cz (Richard Semik)/Shuttertock

61: Prague, Estea/Shutterstock; Puppets, PerseoMedusa/Shutterstock

62: Dalmatian, Eric Isselee/Shutterstock; Bridge, Mikael Damkier/Shutterstock; Raspberries, Pakhnyushcha/Shutterstock

63: Limestone, LianeM/Shutterstock; Islands, OPIS Zagreb/Shutterstock; Dancers, Stanislaw Tokarski/Shutterstock.com; Dubrovnik, cesc_assawin/Shutterstock

64: Yo-yo, Renewer/Shutterstock; Plate, Bibi Saint-Pol; Bread, Monika/CC by SA 2.0; Amphora, Ann Wuyts/CC by SA 2.0

65: Santorini, leoks/Shutterstock; Cheese, Apostolos Mastoris/Shutterstock; Acropolis, ivan bastien/Shutterstock

66: Chicken Kiev, Wallenrock/Shutterstock; Painted Monastery, Ardelean Dan/Shutterstock; Castle, Olimpiu Pop/Shutterstock;

67: Wine cellar, Limpopo/Shutterstock; Birds, iliuta goean/Shutterstock; War monument, Sergey Kamshylin/Shutterstock

68: Amber, Irena Misevic/Shutterstock; Crater, Mannobult/CC by SA 3.0; Bison, Vasiliy Koval/Shutterstock; Mushroom, Andrey Starostin/Shutterstock; Minsk, Dontsov Evgeny Victorovich/Shutterstock

69: Family, Goodluz/Shutterstock; Memorial, jasrim/Shutterstock

71: Great Wall of China, fotohunter/Shutterstock

72: Matryoshka Dolls, Tatiana Popova/Shutterstock; St Basil's Cathedral, Vladitto/Shutterstock

73: Siberian tiger, Dennis Donohue/Shutterstock; Seals, withGod/Shutterstock; Ballet dancers, Sergey Petrov/Shutterstock.com

74: Bosporus, Faraways/Shutterstock; Grand Bazaar, Luciano Mortula/Shutterstock.com

75: Coffee, Ekim Caglar/CC by SA 3.0; Grapes, 0258603967/Shutterstock; Mud volcano, Tonis Valing/Shutterstock; Oil well, Northfoto/Shutterstock; Mount Ararat, Henri Nissen/CC by SA 3.0; Turkish delight, Africa Studio/Shutterstock

76: Cedar tree, diak/Shutterstock; Mud, Arkady Mazor/Shutterstock

77: Mecca, Zurijeta/Shutterstock; Palm Island, Marat Dupri/Shutterstock; Kebab, saragosa69/Shutterstock; Date palm, imagesef/Shutterstock

78: Mosque, Zufar/Shutterstock; Space flight, vicspacewalker/Shutterstock.com; Ysyk-K<04o>l, Novoselov/Shutterstock

79: Manti, Sterilgutassistentin/CC by SA 3.0; Children, Lizette Potgieter/Shutterstock.com; Aral Sea, Gilad Rom/Shutterstock; Caviar, Smit/shutterstock

80: Zip wire, ©HighGround Adventures/www.highgroundnepal.com; Bengal tiger, Denise Allison Coyle/Shutterstock; Python, Matthew Cole/Shutterstock

81: Prayer flags, PENGYOU91/Shutterstock; Bollywood, testing/Shutterstock.com; Maldives, Paolo Gianti/Shutterstock

82: Great Wall, Hung Chung Chih/Shutterstock

83: Yak, nutsiam/Shutterstock; Ice sculpture, Lukas Hlavac/Shutterstock.com; Camel, Iakov/Shutterstock; Yurts, Tan Kian Khoon/Shutterstock

84: Terracotta army, Mario Savoia/Shutterstock; Shanghai, claudio zaccherini/Shutterstock; Shoes, Alexander Kalina/Shutterstock; Bhuddha, Zgpdszz/CC by SA 3.0; Giant panda, Hung Chung Chih/Shutterstock

85: Fireworks, Deymos/Shutterstock; Terraced rice paddies, PENGYOU91/Shutyerstock

86: Tsunami, U.S. Navy photo by Mass Communication Specialist 1st Class Matthew M. Bradley; Taekwon-do, zhu difeng/Shutterstock; Ocean dome, Megapixie (Max Smith); Ginseng, Irina1977/Shutterstock

87: Scramble crossing, SeanPavonePhoto/Shutterstock.com; Bullet train, John Leung/Shutterstock; Mout Fuji, Hiroshi Ichikawa/Shutterstock

88: Floating market, itsmejust/Shutterstock.com; Ruby, Rob Lavinsky, iRocks.com/CC by SA 3.0; Rubber, SOMKKU/Shutterstock

89: Welcome, szefei/Shutterstock; Angkor Wat, Alexey Stiop/Shutterstock; Rice, Worakit Sirijinda/Shutterstock; Water buffalo, kongsky/Shutterstock.com

90: Shadow puppets, Worldpics/Shutterstock; Fruit market, Daniel Zuckerkandel/Shutterstock.com; Railway, Cmglee/CC by SA 3.0; Children, NeilsPhotography/CC by SA 2.0

91: Java, Jan S./Shutterstock.com; Komodo dragon, Sergey Uryadnikov/Shutterstock

92: Tsunami, David Rydevik

93: Pirates, U.S. Navy photo; Wedding, Elena Yakusheva/Shutterstock

95: Ayers Rock, Stanislav Fosenbauer/Shutterstock

96: Festival, isaxar/Shutterstock.com; Lorikeet, Sergey Uryadnikov/Shutterstock; butterfly, Mark Pellegrini (Raul654)/CC by SA 2.5; Palm, fritz16/Shutterstock; Boat, Guido Amrein, Switzerland/Shutterstock.com

97: Stick chart, brewbooks/CC by SA 2.0; Polynesians, Plenz/CC by SA 2.0

98: Surf, Markus Gebauer/Shutterstock.com; Kangaroo, Anan Kaewkhammul/Shutterstock; Bushfire, Neale Cousland/Shutterstock; Crocodile, worldswildlifewonders/Shutterstock; Ayers Rock, Stanislav Fosenbauer/Shutterstock

99: Coral reef, Pete Niesen/Shutterstock; Aborigine, Steve Evans/CC by SA 2.0; Sydney, oblong1/Shutterstock.com

100: Kiwi bird, Eric Isselee/Shutterstock; Kiwi fruit, Nattika/Shutterstock; Geyser, Pichugin Dmitry/Shutterstock; Maori, ChameleonsEye/Shutterstock.com; Sheep, Pichugin Dmitry/Shutterstock

101: Moa, rook76/Shutterstock.com; Honey, srekap/Shutterstock; Mount Cook, Jonathan Keelty/CC by SA 2.0; Kakapo, Mnolf/CC by SA 3.0

102: Whitsunday Islands, Mark Schwettmann/Shutterstock; Vanuatu volcano, Vulkanette/Shutterstock; Green turtle, Isabelle Kuehn/Shutterstock

103: Alaska fishermen, MaxFX/Shutterstock; Pacific Ocean, idiz/Shutterstock

104: Ice, hecke61/Shutterstock; Penguins, Leksele/Shutterstock

105: Polar bears, Tom linster/Shuttertock; Iceberg, Dmytro Pylypenko/Shuttertock; Geothermal power, naten/Shutterstock

All other illustrations ©HarperCollins Publishers

CC by SA 2.0, CC by SA 2.5 and CC by SA 3.0, these works are all licenced under the Creative Commons Attributions Licences.
For more information see creativecommons.org

Caption text: Jenny Slater